INDIA

ITS ADMINISTRATION & PROGRESS

INDIA

ITS ADMINISTRATION & PROGRESS

JOHN STRACHEY

GYAN

Published by

Gyan Publishing House
5, Ansari Road
Daryaganj, New Delhi-110002
Phone: 011-47034999, 9811692060
E-mail: books@gyanbooks.com

Distribution Network
gyanbooks.com
India, USA, Canada, UK, Australia

ISBN: 978-93-6780-556-5 (HB)

First Published, 1903

2nd Impression 2024

Printed at: Gyan Press, Delhi.

INDIA ITS ADMINISTRATION & PROGRESS
Author: JOHN STRACHEY

INDIA

ITS ADMINISTRATION & PROGRESS

BY

SIR JOHN STRACHEY, G.C.S.I.

THIRD EDITION. REVISED AND ENLARGED

London
MACMILLAN AND CO., LIMITED
NEW YORK : THE MACMILLAN COMPANY
1903

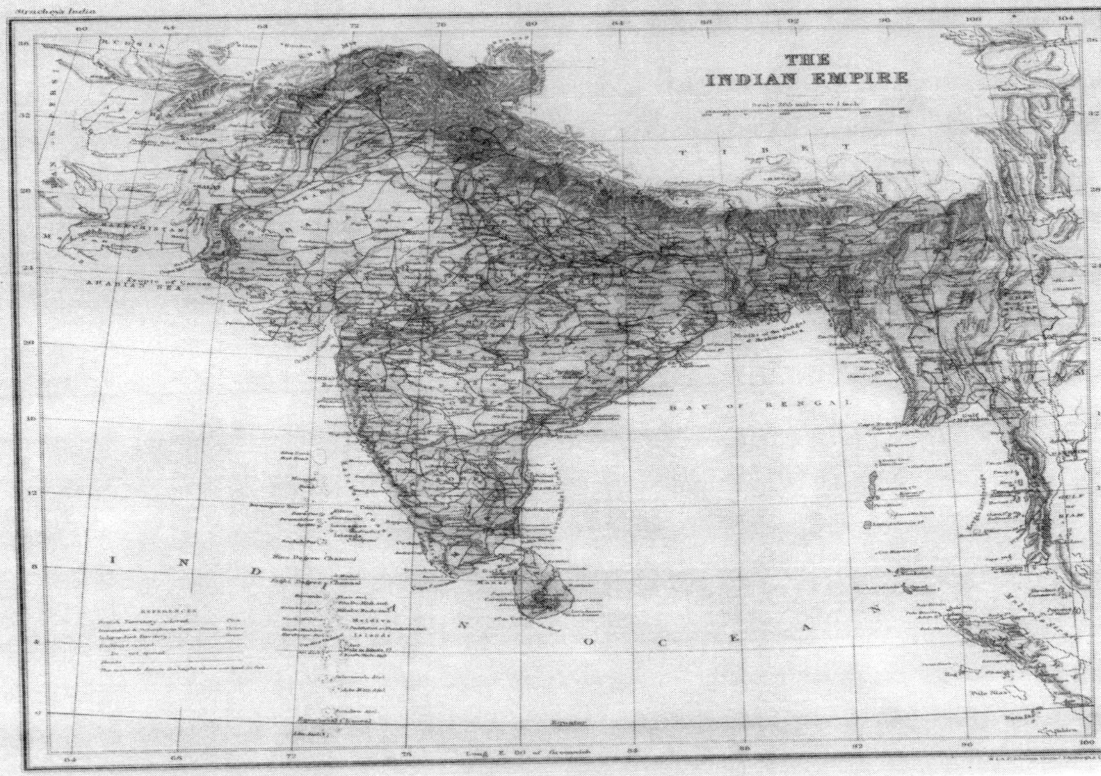
Strachey's India
THE INDIAN EMPIRE
TIBET
BAY OF BENGAL
ARABIAN SEA
INDIAN OCEAN
RUSSIA
Maldive Islands
REFERENCES
Equator
Long. E. of Greenwich

DEDICATION TO THE FIRST EDITION

TO

SIR JAMES FITZJAMES STEPHEN, K.C.S.I.

&c. &c. &c.

My dear Stephen,

Fifteen years ago you dedicated one of your books to me, and in now offering to you this less worthy gift, the fittest words that I can find are almost those which you addressed to me. I dedicate this book to you as an expression of strong personal regard and of gratitude for great kindness, and in recollection of that time in India when we served together and which neither of us can forget.

I am, my dear Stephen,

Your sincere friend and late colleague,

JOHN STRACHEY.

October 1888.

PREFACE TO THE THIRD EDITION

In 1884 I gave a course of lectures on subjects connected with India before the University of Cambridge. They formed the basis of the first edition of this work, published in 1888. Since that time great changes have been made in the constitution of the Indian Legislatures, in the organisation of the Civil Services and Army, and in other branches of the administration, while the progress of the country in wealth and material prosperity has been immense. A second and revised edition of the book was published in 1894, and so many alterations were then made that the work assumed a new shape, and no division into imaginary lectures remained. In the present edition the changes and additions necessary to make it give, as far as possible, an accurate description of existing facts, have been still greater, it has been much enlarged, parts of the work have been entirely re-written, and its title has been slightly altered. The changes thus made in the original form of the book have one drawback. While it was merely a course of lectures, it was obvious that it professed to be nothing more than a series of papers, not necessarily connected with each other, on various Indian topics; that many subjects of importance necessarily and designedly remained untouched; and that I did not pretend to attempt the impossible task of describing in a single volume the great continent of India. In that respect the purpose of the book remains as it was, but, instead of being a collection of lectures on certain Indian subjects, it has become a collection of chapters.

Mr. Baines, in his *Report on the Indian Census of 1891*, a work which I have often quoted, and to which it would be difficult to give more praise than it deserves, has applied to himself the words of Molière, "Je prends mon bien ou je le trouve," and every one who writes, with any just pretence to knowledge, on such a subject as India must say the same. There is no man living competent to give, from his own knowledge alone, an accurate description of a continent as large as civilised Europe, and one that in all its physical characteristics is far more various. Valuable works and official reports have been published in recent years, dealing with Indian subjects, or with special branches of the administration, and to these I have, in the body of the work, acknowledged my obligations. Among them I must here especially mention the contributions to our knowledge made by Sir Henry Maine, Sir James Stephen, Sir Alfred Lyall, Mr. Baines, Sir Denzil Ibbetson, Mr. Risley, and the Reports of the three Famine Commissions of 1880, 1898, and 1901. I am under many obligations of a more personal kind. Mr. A. N. Wollaston, Sir Steuart Bayley, Sir John Edge, Sir Charles Lyall, and Mr. Lionel Abrahams have given to me, in the preparation of this edition, both from their personal knowledge and from the records of the India Office, help for which I cannot sufficiently thank them. Mr. Bourdillon, now acting as Lieutenant-Governor of Bengal, and who possesses a knowledge and experience of the subject which few can equal, has been good enough to revise my account of that great province; and Sir Antony MacDonnell has not been prevented by his present arduous duties from going through the proofs of the chapters which treat of the United Provinces of Agra and Oudh, the government of which, a short time ago, he was administering with conspicuous ability. My special thanks are also due to Mr. Morison, the accomplished Principal of the Mohammedan College at Aligarh; to Sir Charles Elliott; to Sir Hugh Barnes, the Lieutenant-Governor of Burma; to my son, Major J. Strachey; and to Mr. G. H. M. Batten, who, in addition to much other assistance, has contributed to the book the most complete account which, in my opinion, has been written of all the facts connected with the opium revenue of India. Thus, if I may apply to such a subject as the improvement of this book the famous words of the poet, it has at least had the advantage of the help of "the masters of those who know."

When a man has been for many years writing and speaking on matters to which his life has been mainly devoted, there must be much about which he can say nothing new. As Mr. John Morley has written in somewhat similar circumstances, "These borrowings from my former self the reader will perhaps be willing to excuse on the old Greek principle that a man may say a thing once as he would have it said—*δὶς δὲ οὐκ ἐνδέχεται*—he may not say it twice." But it is not from myself alone that I have borrowed without acknowledgment in the present edition. In 1882 a book, now long out of print, was published by my brother, General Sir Richard Strachey, and myself on the Finances and Public Works of India. It was our joint production; our opinions were so much in unison, and were so constantly formed in close personal communication, that while I know that I owe far more to him than he has owed to me, it is impossible for me to say to which of us some parts of that book are to be attributed. In the present edition I have borrowed from it freely. And, having named my brother, I must add, because this is the last opportunity that I shall ever have of saying it, that there are, in my belief, few men living who have done so much, often in ways unknown to the outside world, for the improvement of Indian administration. It is to him that India owes the initiation of that great policy of the systematic extension of railways and canals which has been crowned with such extraordinary success, which has increased to an incalculable extent the wealth of the country, and has profoundly altered its condition. To him is due the conception of those measures of financial and administrative decentralisation which have had the most far-reaching consequences, and which were pronounced by Sir Henry Maine to be by far the greatest and most successful reforms carried out in India in his time. To his active support is largely due the initiation of the measures, which have proved of the highest value, for preventing the destruction of the Indian Forests, and for their scientific protection and management. He it was who first organised the great department of Public Works, and laid the foundations of the scientific study of Indian Meteorology. He was the first, many years ago, to advise that reform of the Currency which has now been carried out, and the delay of which has involved India in incalculable loss. If the Weights and Measures of India are still in a condition of mischievous chaos, it is because, through the powerful influence of ignorant prejudice, the Act which he introduced and carried through the Legislature, and which is still on the Statute Book, has remained a dead letter. He presided over the first of the Commissions which have taught us the true principles upon which Indian famines can be combated.

I suppose that no two men had greater opportunities, through a long course of years, than my brother and myself of obtaining knowledge regarding India. For many years we took part, often in close association, in its government, and it would be an affectation of humility to profess that this part was not an important one. There is hardly a great office of the State, from that of Acting-Viceroy, Lieutenant-Governor, or Member of Council downwards, which one or other of us has not held, and hardly a department of the administration with which one or other of us has not been intimately connected. The book of which my brother and myself were the joint authors was dedicated by us to the public servants of all classes, the results of whose labours for India we had endeavoured, in some measure, to record. Whatever may have been done by viceroys, and governors, and great commanders, the soldiers and civilians whose names have hardly been heard in England have done much more in building up the splendid fabric of our Indian Empire. It is by the everyday work of administration that the real foundations of our power have been maintained and strengthened, and the steady progress of the country has been secured. It is, indeed, to that part of their lives that Indian officials like my brother and myself, actively concerned although we have been in the work of the Central Government, look back with perhaps the greatest interest. We may be forgiven if we take pride in remembering that during the last century and a half four generations of our family have given to India the best portion of their lives.

A distinguished Frenchman, M. Harmand, did me the honour of translating into French the first edition of this book, and he prefaced his work with an Introduction which, if it had been less flattering to myself, I should have been glad to reproduce in English, showing as it did, the opinions of a most competent and intelligent foreign observer on the government of our Indian Empire. M. Harmand, during a long residence in the Asiatic possessions of France and in British India, in both of which he held important official posts, had rare opportunities of forming an accurate judgment on the problems which have to be solved by the Western rulers of Oriental peoples. He has discussed the principles on which the government of a great Eastern possession can alone be wisely conducted, and, taking India as his object-lesson, has endeavoured to show to his countrymen why the efforts of the English to establish a solid and self-supporting dominion in the East have been crowned with such extraordinary success. Another interesting book, written with aims similar to those of M. Harmand, has been published by M. Chailley-Bert, the worthy possessor of an illustrious name.[1] I

[1] *La Colonisation de l'Indo-Chine, l'Expérience anglaise.*

commend to Englishmen who feel an honourable pride in the work of the men who have built up and who are maintaining the wonderful structure of their Indian Empire, the calm and impartial testimony of M. Harmand and M. Chailley-Bert.

JOHN STRACHEY.

April 1903.

CONTENTS

CHAPTER I

INTRODUCTORY

CHAPTER II

THE GEOGRAPHY OF INDIA

CHAPTER III

THE HIMÁLAYA

CHAPTER IV

THE CONSTITUTION OF THE GOVERNMENT IN INDIA

CHAPTER V

THE HOME GOVERNMENT

CHAPTER VI

THE CIVIL SERVICES

CHAPTER VII

THE LAWS AND THE ADMINISTRATION OF JUSTICE

CHAPTER VIII

THE FINANCES AND PUBLIC REVENUES

CHAPTER IX

REVENUES OTHER THAN THOSE DERIVED FROM TAXATION

CHAPTER X

REVENUES OTHER THAN THOSE DERIVED FROM TAXATION (*continued*)

CHAPTER XI

REVENUES DERIVED FROM TAXATION

CHAPTER XII

REVENUES DERIVED FROM TAXATION (*continued*)

CHAPTER XIII

FOREIGN TRADE—HOME CHARGES—CURRENCY—WEIGHTS AND MEASURES

CHAPTER XIV

PUBLIC WORKS—FAMINE

CHAPTER XV

THE PUBLIC DEBT—FAMINE INSURANCE

CHAPTER XVI

EDUCATION IN INDIA

CHAPTER XVII

RACES—LANGUAGES—CASTES—RELIGIONS AND SUPERSTITIONS

CHAPTER XVIII

AN INDIAN PROVINCE

CHAPTER XIX

AN INDIAN PROVINCE (*continued*)

CHAPTER XX

AN INDIAN PROVINCE (*continued*)

CHAPTER XXI

AN INDIAN PROVINCE (*continued*)

CHAPTER XXII

BENGAL

CHAPTER XXIII

THE ARMY IN INDIA

CHAPTER XXIV

THE NATIVE STATES

CHAPTER XXV

CONCLUSION

CHAPTER I

INTRODUCTORY

English ignorance regarding India—India not a country but a continent—The name Hindustan—The great differences between the countries of India—Bengal and Northern India—No countries or nations of the European type—The English in India—The British Government—The growth of a single Indian nationality impossible—Danger of generalisations—The great changes in India—Progress of the country in wealth and good government.

SIR HENRY MAINE, referring to the ignorance regarding India which prevails even among educated men in England, declared his conviction that for one who desires to unveil the stores of interest which India contains, the first necessity is that he should not shrink from speaking on matters which appear to him too elementary to deserve discussion, that he should sympathise with an ignorance which few felicitous efforts have yet been made to dispel, and that he should remember that the language of administration and government in India has become so highly specialised and technical that it forms an imperfect medium for the communication of ideas to Englishmen. Believing this, I make no apology for beginning this book with some very elementary matters, and I ask at starting this elementary question, What is India? What does this name India really signify? The answer that I have sometimes given sounds paradoxical, but it is true. There is no such country, and this is the first and most essential fact about India that can be learned.

India is a name which we give to a great region including a multitude of different countries. There is no general Indian term that corresponds to it. The name Hindustan is never applied in India, as we apply it, to the whole of the Indian continent; it signifies the country north of the Narbada river, and especially the northern portion of the basins of the Ganges and Jumna.

I have been told by intelligent Natives of India who have visited Europe that they could see little difference between the European countries through which they had travelled; the languages being equally unintelligible offered to them no marks of distinction; the cities, the costumes, the habits of life, the manners and customs of the people, so far as a passing oriental traveller could judge, seemed much the same in England, in France, and in Italy. The differences between the countries of India—between, for instance, Bengal and the Punjab, or between Madras and Rajputána—seemed to them, on the other hand, immense, and beyond comparison greater than those existing between the countries of Europe. Englishmen have often similar impressions in visiting India; they cannot see the great diversities that exist. As to persons who know nothing of geology or botany or agriculture, rocks and trees and crops present comparatively few distinctive features, so it is with those who look with uninformed minds on conditions of life and society to which they have not been accustomed.

The differences between the countries of Europe are undoubtedly smaller than those between the countries of India. Scotland is more like Spain than Bengal is like the Punjab. European civilisation has grown up under conditions which have produced a larger measure of uniformity than has been reached in the countries of the Indian continent, often separated from each other by greater distances, by greater obstacles to communication, and by greater differences of climate. It is probable that not less than fifty languages, which may rightly be called separate, are spoken in India. The diversities of religion and race are as wide in India as in Europe, and political catastrophes have been as frequent and as violent. There are no countries in civilised Europe in which the people differ so much as the man of Madras differs from the Sikh, and the languages of Southern India are as unintelligible in Lahore as they would be in London. A native of Calcutta or Bombay is as much a foreigner in Delhi or Peshawar as an Englishman is a foreigner in Rome or Paris.

People sometimes complain that Indian authorities differ so greatly among themselves that it is hardly possible to learn the truth. These apparent contradictions have frequently no real existence, but arise from false generalisations.

To one, for instance, who has gained his knowledge of India in Lower Bengal, India is a country of almost constant heat and damp, luxuriant vegetation, rivers, tanks, rice-fields and cocoa-nuts, with few cities and no monuments of art, densely inhabited by a mild and timid population. To such an India as this, a vivid imagination could hardly conceive a completer contrast than the India of Agra or Lahore. Instead of one of the dampest and greenest countries of the earth, we find in the early summer one of the brownest and most arid, a country scorched with winds like the blast of a furnace, but in the winter it has the climate of an Italian spring, cold, frosty, and invigorating. In the latter season, instead of the tropical vegetation of Bengal, we find thousands of square miles covered with wheat and barley and the products of the temperate zone. It is a country with famous cities and splendid monuments, and its population is not inferior to that of many parts of Europe in manliness and vigour.

I have spoken of the different countries of India, but they are not countries in the ordinary European sense. A European country is usually a separate entity, occupied by a nation more or less socially and politically distinct. But in India, as Sir Alfred Lyall has explained in his *Asiatic Studies*, a work that is a mine of knowledge on Indian matters, there are no nations of the modern European type. The same fact has been clearly brought out by Professor Seeley in his lectures on *The Expansion of England*.

"Geographical boundaries," says Sir Alfred Lyall, "have no correspondence at all with distinctive institutions or groupings of the people, and have comparatively little political significance. Little is gained toward knowing who and what a man is by ascertaining the State he obeys, or the territory he dwells in; these being things which of themselves denote no difference of race, institutions, or manners. Even from the point of political allegiance, the Government under which a man may be living is an accidental arrangement, which the British Viceroy or some other inevitable power decided upon yesterday and may alter to-morrow. Nor would such a change be grievous unless it divorced from him a ruler of his own tribe or his own faith. . . . The European observer—accustomed to the massing of people in great territorial groups, and to the ideas (now immemorial in the West) contained in such expressions as fatherland, mother-country, patriotism, domicile, and the like—has here to realise the novelty of finding himself in a strange part of the world, where political citizenship is as yet quite unknown, and territorial sovereignty or even feudalism only just appearing. For a parallel in the history of

Western Europe we must go back as far as the Merovingian period, when chiefs of barbaric tribes or bands were converting themselves into kings or counts; or, perhaps, he should carry his retrospect much further, and conceive himself to be looking at some country of Asia Minor lying within the influence of Rome at its zenith, but just outside its jurisdiction. He gradually discovers the population of Central India to be distributed, not into great governments, or nationalities, or religious denominations, not even into widespread races, such as those which are still contending for political supremacy in Eastern Europe, but into various and manifold denominations of tribes, clans, septs, castes, and sub-castes, religious orders, and devotional brotherhoods."[1]

This is the first and most essential thing to learn about India—that there is not, and never was an India, or even any country of India, possessing, according to European ideas, any sort of unity, physical, political, social, or religious; no Indian nation, no "people of India," of which we hear so much.

Until we rightly appreciate the significance of such facts we shall, among other things, never understand how our Indian Empire has come into existence, and how this vast dominion is maintained by a handful of Englishmen. There was never, as Professor Seeley has said, any conquest of India by the English, according to the ordinary sense of the word "conquest." The conquest was rather, to borrow his expression, "in the nature of an internal revolution," directed by Englishmen, but carried out for the most part through the Natives of India themselves. No superiority of the Englishman would have enabled England to conquer by her own military power the continent of India with its 300 millions of people, nor could she hold it in subjection if it had been occupied by distinct nations. In

[1] *Asiatic Studies*, p. 152. Sir Alfred Lyall was specially referring to Central India in this passage, but it is equally true of India generally.

the words of Professor Seeley, "the fundamental fact is that India had no jealousy of the foreigner, because there was no India, and therefore, properly speaking, no foreigner."[1]

It is a consequence of all this, that in every great Indian province the political sympathies of large sections of the population towards men who, geographically speaking, are their own countrymen, are often as imperfect as they are towards their English masters. We have never destroyed in India a national government, no national sentiment has been wounded, no national pride has been humiliated; and this not through any design or merit of our own, but because no Indian nationalities have existed. They no more exist in the so-called Native States than in our own territories, and the most important of those States are ruled by princes who are almost as much foreigners to their subjects as we are ourselves.

The diversities between the countries of India and the people inhabiting them extend, more or less, to their administration by the British Government. The ordinary English notion is that the Secretary of State for India and the Viceroy and his Council carry on, somehow or other, the government of India. Few Englishmen understand how comparatively little these high authorities have to do with the actual administration, or appreciate the fact that the seven or eight chief provinces of British India, which may be compared, in area and population, to the chief countries of Europe, have all their separate and, in a great measure, their independent governments. Under circumstances of such extreme diversity as those which exist in India, no single system of administration could be appropriate.

[1] *The Expansion of England*, p. 206.

Instead of introducing unsuitable novelties from other countries, Indian or European, we have taken, in each province, with some unfortunate exceptions, the old local institutions as the basis of our own arrangements. Good or bad administration in India depends to a far greater extent on the Government of the province than on the distant authorities in Calcutta or London. The vast majority of the population is hardly conscious of the existence of the Viceroy and his Government. From time to time a glimpse is caught of the great Lord Sáhib. He passes perhaps along the streets of some famous city with a train of elephants recalling the traditions of Aurangzib, or at some immense gathering, far more picturesque and magnificent than any of the ceremonial shows of Europe, he receives in Darbár the homage of chiefs and princes. From the splendour of his surroundings people derive some vague notions of an authority above the powers by which they know that they are governed.

Although in the management of the greater portion of the public business immediately affecting the everyday interests of the 294 millions of people inhabiting India the part of the so-called Government of India is comparatively small, this central power, administered by the Governor-General in Council, under the supreme authority of the British Government at home, has, of course, from another point of view the highest importance. It regulates and harmonises the Governments of the British provinces, controls the Native States and our relations with foreign powers, provides for military defence, makes war and peace, and manages those branches of the administration which directly concern the general interests of the empire.

It must not be supposed that such bonds of union

can in any way lead towards the growth of a single Indian nationality. However long may be the duration of our dominion, however powerful may be the centralising attraction of our Government, or the influence of the common interests which grow up, no such issue can follow. It is conceivable that national sympathies may arise in particular Indian countries; but that they should ever extend to India generally, that men of Bombay, the Punjab, Bengal, and Madras should ever feel that they belong to one great Indian nation, is impossible. We might with as much reason and probability look forward to a time when a single nation will have taken the place of the various nations of Europe.

I wish especially to insist on the fact that we can never hope to arrive at any accurate knowledge of India until we properly appreciate the immense diversities of the countries included under that name, and understand that there is no part of the world in which it is more easy to be misled by generalisations.

The changes through which India has passed during the last half-century have been so great, that it is often very difficult to deduce useful inferences from the comparison of its present and past condition. The changes in the condition of the country, in its available resources, and in its requirements for necessary administrative and material progress have been numerous and profound.

The territorial extension of the British Empire in India since the middle of the nineteenth century has been immense. Great provinces have been added to it, with an area about equal to that of France and the German Empire put together, with a population of more than sixty millions. This fact is alone sufficient to show how easily we may be misled by general comparisons; but other changes not less important have occurred, and they have been hardly less remarkable in the older provinces than in the new.

There was formerly in British India, comparatively speaking, little of what we now think the first necessities of a civilised administration. When, in 1844, I first went from Calcutta to the North-Western Provinces, I was carried about a thousand miles in a palanquin on men's shoulders, and it took some three weeks to toil through a journey which is now accomplished in twenty-four hours; there were no other means of travelling through the richest and most civilised parts of India. Speaking generally, roads and bridges had only begun to appear; railways were not thought of; the value of irrigation as a means of affording protection to the people against famine had hardly been recognised; there were few barracks in which English soldiers could live with tolerable health and comfort; there were few jails in which a sentence of imprisonment did not carry with it a serious probability that it would prove a sentence of death.

British India, however, even at that time was entering on a phase of rapid change. The energies of the Government and its officers, which had at first been unable to do more than secure the bare existence of British power in India, by degrees rendered that power paramount. Then they were applied to its consolidation, and to the evolution of an organised system of administration out of the chaos bequeathed to us by the old rulers of the country. The firm establishment of order was followed by improvements in all directions. A vigorous impulse was given to material progress, and among the most active causes of the great changes which were beginning must be ranked the introduction of new and rapid means of communication. These not only directly developed the resources of the country, increased the wealth of the people, and profoundly altered the conditions of life, but they stimulated the vitality of every branch of the administration ; they brought the various provinces of the Empire closer together, and England closer to India ; English influence became stronger and stronger, and all classes, as they were more frequently and immediately brought into contact with European habits and civilisation, had set before them new and higher standards.

Even before the mutinies of 1857 this process of change had made great progress. After that revolution, which for a time nearly swept away our government through a large part of India, the change went on with accelerated speed. Thousands of Englishmen, not only soldiers, but Englishmen of almost every class, poured into India. Ten thousand things were demanded which India had not got, but which it was felt must be provided. The country must be covered with railways and telegraphs, and roads and bridges. Irrigation canals must be made to preserve the people from starvation. Barracks must be built for a great European army, and every sort of sanitary arrangement which could benefit the troops must be carried out. The whole paraphernalia of a great civilised administration, according to the modern notions of what that means, had to be provided.

This was true not only in regard to matters of imperial concern. Demands for improvement, similar to those which fell upon the Central Government, cropped up in every city and in every district of the country.

Compare, for instance, what Calcutta was when Lord Lawrence became Viceroy in 1864, and what it is now. This city, the capital of British India, supplies an excellent type of what has been everywhere going on. The filth of the city used to rot away in the midst of the population in pestilential ditches, or was thrown into the Hugli, there to float backwards and forwards with every change of tide. To nine-tenths of the inhabitants clean water was unknown. They drank either the filthy water of the river, polluted with every conceivable abomination, or the still filthier contents of the shallow tanks. The river, which was the main source of supply to thousands of people, was not only the receptacle for ordinary filth; it was the great graveyard of the city. I forget how many thousand corpses were thrown into it every year. I forget how many hundred corpses were thrown into it from the Government hospitals and jails, for these practices were not confined to the poor and ignorant; they were followed or allowed, as a matter of course, by the officers of the Government and of the municipality. I remember the sights which were seen in Calcutta in those days, in the hospitals, and jails, and markets, and slaughter-houses, and public streets. The place was declared, in official reports, written by myself in language which was not, and could not be, stronger than the truth required, to be hardly fit for civilised men to live in. There are now few cities in Europe with which many parts of Calcutta need fear comparison, and, although in the poorer quarters there is still much room for improvement, there is hardly a city in the world which has made greater progress.

I do not mean to say that Indian cities generally were as bad as Calcutta. This was far from being the case, but Calcutta affords, not the less, a good example of what has been and is still going on in India. Illustrations of the same sort might easily be multiplied. In 1865, for instance, in the city of Rangoon, containing, at that time, more than 100,000 people, with half a million tons of shipping, there was not a single public lamp, no supply of wholesome water, not a single drain except the surface drains at the sides of the streets, and no means of removing the filth out of the town. About the same time, the Royal Commission for inquiring into the sanitary state of the army in India declared that thousands of the lives of our soldiers had been and were still being sacrificed in consequence of bad and insufficient barrack accommodation, and neglect of every sanitary precaution. So again, the Government was told, and in many parts of India it was certainly true, that, in consequence of the insufficiency of jail accommodation, the prisoners were dying at a rate frightful to think of, and that the necessary proceedings of the courts of justice involved consequences repugnant to humanity.

Thus arose demands for the requirements of civilised life and of modern administration, which had to be provided, and to a great extent for the first time, within the space of a few years. This was true not only of material appliances, of roads, and railways, and canals, and barracks, and city improvements, and so forth; for the demand for improved administration became so strong that it is not too much to say that the whole of the public services were reorganised. Thus, for example, the police, which was in a most unsatisfactory condition throughout India, was, although even now it cannot be said to be good, placed on a completely new footing. The changes in the judicial service, and in the laws which it administers, have been great. Lord Lawrence, when he was Viceroy, declared that the inadequacy of the pay given to the Native judges, and to the chief ministerial officers of the courts, was a public scandal, many of these officers receiving salaries less than the wages earned in many parts of India by the better class of bricklayers and carpenters. No honest or satisfactory administration of justice was, under such conditions, possible.

The demands for every sort of public improvement, moral and material, which thus sprang up, could not be resisted. Whatever might be the cost, remedies had to be provided in the most complete way, and in the shortest time possible.

A greater or more admirable work was never conceived in any country than that which was undertaken, and which in a great degree has been accomplished by Englishmen in India, and which is still going on. That mistakes should have been made in dealing with a country larger and more populous than the whole of civilised Europe was inevitable. Nevertheless, the work has been excellently done, and with this further merit, that there has been little talk about it. For all this the credit is not due to the initiative of the Government alone. India has been fortunate in her Viceroys, but still more fortunate in the possession of a most admirable and hard-working body of public servants, to whose intelligence, devotion to their duties, and self-sacrifice, the results actually obtained are mainly due.

The vast majority of the population of India remains, in many respects, as it has remained from time immemorial, almost unchanged and unchangeable. It is still, in the words of Sir Henry Maine, "an energetic expression of the Past, hardly affected by its contact with the Western world." But, while this is true, it is not the less true that in material progress and in the improvement of the public administration the magnitude of the work that has been accomplished in India is extraordinary. In these respects the England of Queen Anne was hardly more different from the England of to-day, than the India of Lord Ellenborough from the India of Lord Curzon. The country has been covered with roads and railways; her almost impassable rivers have been bridged; the most magnificent canals and works of irrigation existing in the world have been constructed for the protection of the people against famine; our soldiers live in barracks that can hardly be equalled in Europe: quarters which once had a reputation little better than that of pest-houses are now among the healthiest in the British Empire, and the rate of mortality among the troops is not one-half what it was; the improvement in the jails and in the health of the prisoners has been equally remarkable; the cities and towns are totally different places from what they were.

Simultaneously with the progress of all these and a thousand other material improvements, with the increase of trade, the creation of new industries, and a vast development of wealth, there has gone on an equally remarkable change in every branch of the public administration. The laws have been codified, and improved, and simplified, and India has obtained, to a degree unthought of before, protection for life and property, and an honest administration of justice. All over India we have been building schools, and hospitals, and dispensaries. The Natives of India have been admitted to a far larger share in the government of their own country; municipal institutions, the first practical step in political education, have been established in every considerable town throughout British India. It is needless to continue this catalogue of the changes that have taken place; but it is not the least remarkable part of the story that the accomplishment of all this work, and the immense expenditure incurred, which have increased to an incalculable extent the wealth and comfort of the people, have added nothing to the actual burden of their taxation.

This is a subject to which I shall return; but a few other facts may here be given to illustrate the changes that have occurred in India.

In 1840 the total value of the imports and exports of British India was about £19,000,000; in 1901 it exceeded £150,000,000. The trade of India is more than twice as great now as that of the United Kingdom was in the beginning of the nineteenth century. In 1854, the first year for which any figures are forthcoming, the number of letters passing through the Post Office was 19,000,000, while in 1901 it was 545,000,000. It might be stated how many millions of tons of goods are now carried on the railways, and how many telegraphic messages are despatched; but as fifty years ago railways and telegraphs in India had only begun to exist, there would be no comparison to make.

All this implies no disparagement of the work of our predecessors. On the contrary, great as, with the aid of modern science and capital, our later progress has been, it is certain that ever since our countrymen first established themselves as the dominant power in Southern Asia, each successive period, when viewed in relation to the circumstances of the time, has yielded, in one direction or another, not less important results. No language of admiration can be too strong for the noble work accomplished in India by the soldiers and civilians of former days. The greatness of their work, and of the work of which they laid the foundations, may best be seen by a comparison of the neighbouring

Asiatic countries with British India. Not only has it been rescued from the incessant sequence of foreign conquest, plunder, and anarchy which had marked its past history, but in little more than a century it has acquired a position of peace, good government, and wealth, in which it will compare favourably with that of many of the States of Europe.

There have always been, and perhaps always will be, people who, according to the unfortunate English fashion of decrying the great achievements of their countrymen, endeavour persistently to show that, in consequence of the wickedness or folly of our Government, India is in a state bordering upon bankruptcy; that its people are becoming poorer and poorer, more and more miserable, more and more exposed to ruin and death by famine; that crushing taxation goes on constantly increasing; that an enormous and ruinous tribute is exacted in India to be spent in England, and I know not what else. I have no inclination to reply to statements of this sort. "I know," said the wisest of English statesmen, "the obstinacy of unbelief in those perverted minds which have no delight but in contemplating the supposed distress, and predicting the immediate ruin of their country. These birds of evil presage at all times have grated our ears with their melancholy song; and, by some strange fatality or other, it has generally happened that they have poured forth their loudest and deepest lamentations at the periods of our most abundant prosperity." [1]

It is not pretended that the social, material, and [illegible]ical conditions of India do not leave ample room [illegible]mprovement. Defects of many sorts can readily be [illegible]ted out. But it is through the progress made that

[1] Burke's *Third Letter on a Regicide Peace.*

these become known. In the arts of administration, as in all other applications of knowledge, our views widen with each successive step we take, and the emphatic recognition that much yet remains to be done for India neither dims the lustre of what has been accomplished nor should cool the ardour of those who there continue the strife with human misfortune, weakness, and ignorance.

That India has gone on, with a speed hardly surpassed in any country, steadily increasing in knowledge, in wealth, and in all the elements of progress; that every branch of the public administration has constantly improved in honesty and efficiency, and that of all the things for which England deserves honour in the world, there has been none greater or better than her government of India—these are to me facts not requiring to be argued about.

There are other critics of our Indian government who deserve to be spoken of with more respect than those "birds of evil presage" to whom I have referred. We often hear expressions of regret that the days of strong personal government have passed away. We are told that the men who, with much smaller personal authority than that of their predecessors, now carry on the everyday work of administration have neither the vigour nor the intimate knowledge of the country for which our officers were formerly so distinguished, and that they have less sympathy with the ideas and feelings of the people. While it may be admitted that there is in this an element of truth, I am satisfied, for my part, that we have gained far more than we have lost. Now that the distance between India and England is measured in days and not in months, the Englishman in India has become less Indian and more English in all his habits and in all his feelings. He may know less of some aspects of Indian life, but he is no longer cut off, as he once was, from the invigorating and most wholesome influence of his own country. Methods of administration which were once the only ones that were appropriate, have become unsuitable and impracticable, and I entirely disbelieve that the men of the present generation are one whit less capable than those who went before them; they know more and not less of all that it is most necessary for them to know, and the results of their work are more and not less excellent. There can hardly be a more striking proof that there has been no falling off in the qualities necessary for the wise and vigorous government of a great dependency than the manner in which, within recent years, new provinces have been transformed from a condition in which there was no tolerable government, and no safety for life or property, into peaceful and prosperous countries. No more remarkable story than that of the pacification and progress of Burma can be told of any portion of the Empire.

CHAPTER II

THE GEOGRAPHY OF INDIA

The Indian Empire: area and population—The main features of Indian geography—The Indo-Gangetic plain—Presidencies and Provinces—The table-land of Central and Southern India—Physical causes of the great differences between the countries of India—The monsoons.

THE Indian Empire has an area of more than 1,700,000 square miles, and a population of nearly 300 millions. In area and population it is greater than Europe without Russia. A line drawn from its northern boundary beyond the mountains of Kashmir to Cape Comorin, the southern extremity of its vast peninsula, exceeds 2000 miles in length, a distance almost as great as that from Gibraltar to St. Petersburg. It is nearly equally far from the borders of Baluchistán on the west to the point where the eastern frontier of Assam approaches the frontier of China.

Excluding Burma and the mountain countries of the north, India proper may be roughly divided into two regions.

The first of these is a vast alluvial plain, lying immediately below the Himálaya, and stretching with an unbroken surface for some 1700 miles across Northern India. Its eastern and central portions are watered by the Ganges and Bráhmaputra and their tributaries, the northern and western portions by the river-system of the

Indus. At its highest point, on the watershed between the feeders of the Indus and Ganges, it is not more than 1000 feet above the sea. At its eastern end, it extends over the delta of the Ganges and Bráhmaputra, and includes the greater part of the province of Bengal. At its northern and western extremities, it spreads down the Indus to the Arabian Sea, over the Punjab, the western states of Rajputána, and Sind. The central portion of the plain comprises the United Provinces of Agra and Oudh. The alluvial deposits of which this vast tract is composed are, as Sir Richard Strachey says, "so finely comminuted that it is no exaggeration to say that it is possible to go from the Bay of Bengal up the Ganges, through the Punjab, and down the Indus again to the sea, over a distance of 2000 miles and more, without finding a pebble, however small."[1] The Indo-Gangetic plain comprises the richest, the most fertile, the most populous, and historically the most famous countries of India. Its south-western extension includes the desert tracts of Western Rajputána and the almost rainless districts of Sind. It covers more than 500,000 square miles, an area almost as large as that of France, with the German and Austrian Empires, and it contains more than 160 millions of people.

The greater part of the northern plain, excluding the countries on the extreme west, was formerly included, for certain purposes, in the so-called Presidency of Bengal. I shall have to explain how the name Bengal has had, at different periods, different meanings, and how the term "Presidency," although still sometimes used in official papers, has almost ceased to have any special signification. British India is now divided not into the three presidencies of Bengal,

[1] *Encyclopædia Britannica*, Art. "Asia."

Madras, and Bombay, but into provinces, nine of which are extensive countries under separate Governments.

The second region of India lies to the south of the Indo-Gangetic plain, and includes the great triangular peninsula which projects into the Indian Ocean. It has an area of about 700,000 square miles, with a population of more than 120 millions.

The greater part of this tract consists of a hilly table-land,[1] having an average elevation above the sea of about 1500 feet, but rising in the south, in Mysore, to 3000 feet. It may be said, in general terms, to include the whole of that part of India which lies to the south of the Tropic of Cancer, with a relatively small extension to the north, where it gradually merges into the southern borders of the Gangetic plain. On the western and eastern sides of the peninsula, the table-land terminates in the ranges known as the Western and Eastern Gháts. Roughly speaking, they run parallel to the coast on the two sides of Southern India, leaving between them and the sea a more or less broad strip of low-lying land. The Eastern Gháts are an ill-defined range of no great height. The Western Gháts rise steeply from the sea to about 4000 feet, and near their southern extremity reach 8700 feet in the Nilgiri mountains. Farther north, nearly in the same line with the Western Gháts, the Aravali range, in which Mount Abu rises to 5600 feet, forms the western border of the table-land. The northern border cannot be sharply defined; it is broken up into hills which pass

[1] I take the following note from Sir Henry Yule: "A friend objects to this application of 'table-land' to so rugged a region of inequalities. But it is a technical expression in geography, applicable to a considerable area, of which the lowest levels are at a considerable height above the sea."—*Glossary of Anglo-Indian Words*, Art. "Tibet."

more or less gradually into the plains of the United Provinces.

The Vindhia and Satpura ranges, the highest points of which have an elevation of more than 4000 feet, run from west to east across the northern parts of the table-land of Central India. "Now pierced by road and railway (says Sir William Hunter), they stood as a barrier of mountain and jungle between Northern and Southern India, and formed one of the main difficulties in welding the whole into an empire. They consist of vast masses of forests, ridges, and peaks, broken by cultivated tracts of the rich cotton-bearing black soil, exquisite river valleys, and high-lying grassy plains."[1]

Through two deep and almost parallel depressions in this tract, the waters of the Narbada and Tapti flow westward to the Arabian Sea. With these exceptions, all the chief rivers of the peninsula, the Són, the Máhánadi, the Godáveri, the Kistna, and Kávari, flow eastward, and excepting the Són, which joins the Ganges, they all fall into the Bay of Bengal. The high ranges of the Gháts, on the western edge of the peninsula, throw off nearly the whole of its drainage to the eastward.

This table-land, with the low-lying tracts on its borders, comprises the British provinces of Madras and Bombay, the Central Provinces, and many of the chief Native States of India. Among the latter are the Marátha States of Gwalior and Indore, and those of Haidarabad and Mysore.

There are other extensive countries that I have not named, lying outside the two great regions into which India Proper may be roughly divided. On the north-eastern border of Bengal the British province of Assam,

[1] *The Indian Empire*, 3rd edit., p. 68.

with an area of nearly 50,000 square miles, and a population of more than 6,000,000, lies immediately below the Himálaya, and comprises the great and fertile valley of the Bráhmaputra after it issues from the mountains. On the opposite side of India, the North-West Frontier Province, formed in 1901 from districts transferred from the Punjab, and British Baluchistán farther south, are the outposts of our empire towards Afghánistán.

The French and Portuguese retain some small possessions, now little more than nominal signs of former greatness. The French possessions, of which the most important is Pondicherry, on the eastern coast, contain about 273,000 people; the Portuguese territory of Goa, on the western coast, has a population of nearly 500,000.

Lying on the east side of the Bay of Bengal is the great province of Burma, the latest addition to our Indian Empire. It is completely cut off by the sea or by mountains from India Proper, and differs essentially in every respect from every Indian country. Including the protected Shán States, it has an area of more than 236,000 square miles, with a population of 10,500,000. Its frontiers, on the east, march with those of China, French Indo-China, and Siam.

Politically, Aden, at the entrance to the Red Sea, belongs also to the Indian Empire.

The provinces of British India, including Burma, cover more than 1,000,000 square miles, and contain 232,000,000 people. The Native States cover nearly 700,000 square miles, with a population of 62,500,000.

Although the main natural features of India are comparatively simple, the differences between the climates and many of the physical conditions of its various countries are, as I have already said, often far greater than any that exist between the various countries of Europe. The explanation of this fact is not difficult.

Excepting in temperature, and in a rainfall the amount of which varies within no very wide limits, the general climatic conditions of the countries of Europe, excluding those in the extreme north, are not very different. On the other hand, it is hardly possible to imagine greater contrasts than those which often exist between the climates of various parts of India.

Take, for example, the two extremities of the great Indo-Gangetic plain—Sind on the western, and Lower Bengal on the eastern side of India. These countries are almost in the same latitude; each of them is an unbroken alluvial plain, slightly elevated above the sea. In Sind, so little rain falls that the country may be said to be rainless. It is the Egypt of India, and without artificial irrigation would be an uninhabitable desert. Bengal, on the other hand, is a country of tropically heavy rain and luxuriant vegetation. The rainfall on the mountains along its eastern borders is heavier than any that has been observed in any other part of the world. At Cherra Punji, on the Khasiya hills, on the frontiers of Eastern Bengal, the average yearly rainfall is between 500 and 600 inches, and 40 inches have been measured in a single day. The average annual rainfall of London is about 25 inches, a quantity less than that which not infrequently falls in twenty-four hours in many parts of India.

It is not difficult to imagine from this illustration, taken from two Indian provinces, how great must be the differences in physical conditions between countries presenting such extraordinary contrasts of climate.

The one characteristic, common at certain seasons

to the whole of India, except at great elevations, is excessive heat. The southern half of India, including nearly the whole of the Madras and Bombay Presidencies, lies within the tropic. The northern half, including nearly the whole of the Indo-Gangetic plain, lies north of the tropic. Although in the southern or tropical region the mean temperature of the year is higher, the variations of temperature between summer and winter are comparatively small; and it is in the second region, in the plains north of the tropic, where the days are longer and the power of the sun more continuous, that Indian heat reaches in the summer months its greatest intensity. In parts of the Punjab and of the United Provinces of Agra and Oudh, and in the desert on the borders of Sind, the temperature in May and June is probably exceeded in no part of the world; but this extreme heat brings by its own action the relief without which all life would perish.

"The dominant feature of Indian meteorology (I am quoting from the late Mr. Blanford, formerly the head of the Meteorological Department in India) is the alternation of the monsoons, the annual reversal of the prevailing wind-currents. This alternation is consequent on the fact that, in the early summer, the broad plains and table-lands of India are heated to a far higher temperature than the seas which bathe their shores; whereas, in the winter, the seas retain much of their warmth, while the land radiates away and throws off into stellar space much more heat than it receives from the oblique rays of the sun during the shorter winter days, and, especially as regards Northern India, speedily cools down to a temperature much below that of the surrounding seas."[1] Observations of these phenomena

[1] *Statistical Atlas of India*, chap. iii.

and their consequences, especially in regard to the winds and the rainfall, show us, as Mr. Blanford says, "how each season in succession affects in diverse modes the different portions of the country; why one province may sometimes be devastated by flood while another is parched with drought, and why, with special adaptation to the peculiarities of its own seasons and resources, each of them has its own agricultural system, its own staples, its own rotation of crops."

After March the heat in Northern India rapidly increases. As the air above the heated earth becomes hotter, the pressure becomes less. At the same time an increase of pressure is going on over the ocean south of the equator, which has then its winter. Thus, a current of air laden with moisture is gradually established towards the continent of India from the sea. This is the so-called south-west monsoon, which brings the periodical rains every year to India, when the heat of the summer has reached its greatest intensity. Towards the end of May the monsoon has usually become established in the south-western extremity of India, and before the end of June it has extended to the greater part of the northern provinces.

The quantity of rain that falls in any part of India depends mainly on the configuration of the surface of the land, and on its situation with reference to the vapour-bearing winds. As the amount of watery vapour which air can hold in suspension varies with the temperature of the air, and increases with the temperature, any cause which cools the current from the sea leads to condensation of the vapour and to the fall of rain.

One of the chief of such causes is the existence of mountains which stand in the path of the winds, and force the vapour-bearing currents to rise over them. Thus, the range of the Western Gháts, which form an almost continuous barrier along the western coasts of Southern India, meet first the whole force of the monsoon as it comes saturated with moisture from the sea. A great condensation of rain is the immediate result of the fall in the temperature of the hot moist air as it is forced to rise in passing across the mountains. On the face of the Gháts, not far from Bombay, the annual rainfall in some places exceeds 250 inches; but a very large part of the moisture which the current of air contains is drained away by the excessive precipitation near the coast, and, as the current flows on over the land, the quantity of rain is greatly reduced. At Poona, only 60 miles from the sea, the annual rainfall is not more than 26 inches.

Similar phenomena are observed in a still more remarkable form on the Himálaya. The line of maximum elevation is not far from the southern edge of the great mountain mass. When the monsoon winds strike the outer ranges of the Himálaya, a large amount of rain immediately results; the quantity diminishes as the wind passes over the mountains, and when it reaches the regions of perpetual snow, about 100 miles from the plains of India, almost the whole of its remaining moisture is condensed. Thus, the periodical rains are completely stopped by the ranges of the southern face of the Himálaya; they can find no entrance to the mountains beyond, or to the table-land of Tibet, one of the driest and most arid regions of the world.

Similar causes shut off the rain-bearing south-westerly winds from the Madras provinces, on the south-eastern coast of India. These winds cannot carry much moisture over the obstacle to their course formed by the Western Gháts, and little rain falls in the eastern districts of Madras during the summer months. But, as I shall presently notice, the remedy for this deficiency is not wanting.

Where, on the other hand, the configuration of the land is such that no obstacles are offered to the passage of the monsoon current from the sea, there may be no condensation of its moisture. Thus, when the wind strikes upon the coast of Sind, very slightly elevated above the sea, it finds a hotter and not a cooler surface than that which it has left, and it passes on with all its watery vapour for 1000 miles across the rainless plains to the Punjab, where at last the Himálaya converts the vapour into rain. If, as Sir Richard Strachey has observed, there had been a range of mountains connecting the high land of the Indian peninsula with that of Baluchistán, hardly a drop of rain would have reached the Punjab and the North of India.

It would be easy to multiply illustrations of the manner in which geographical position and configuration determine the fall of rain in the various provinces of India, and even local conditions of a kind which might have seemed of little importance produce remarkable results. Thus, for instance, a deep depression in a range of mountains may afford an opening for the entrance of the vapour-bearing currents of air, and give an ample supply of rain to a tract of country which would have been almost rainless if the mountains had been continuous. In this manner, the valleys of the Tapti and Narbada rivers, which enter the sea north of Bombay, are gates through which the monsoon finds access to the provinces of Central India, and makes them fertile and prosperous.

As the sun travels southward after midsummer,

the south-west monsoon passes gradually away, and towards the end of September it ceases to blow over Northern India. Causes acting in the converse direction, but similar to those which brought it with its rain-bearing currents, lead to its cessation. The temperature falls as the sun goes south, and the vast dry tracts of the Asiatic continent become rapidly colder; the barometric pressure over the land increases, and winds begin to blow from the north towards the south. These winds are the north-east monsoon.

This monsoon, although far less important than its predecessor to the greater part of India, is essentially necessary to Madras and the south-eastern provinces of the peninsula, which, as already explained, are cut off by their geographical position from the benefits of the monsoon from the south-west. When the wind from the north-east is established, these are the only parts of India which it reaches after passing across the sea, and, while everywhere else the current of air is dry, it takes up in its passage across the Bay of Bengal a supply of moisture. Under the operation of the same laws which give their rainy season in the summer to the other provinces, the moisture brought by the north-east wind from the sea is precipitated in rain on the eastern districts of Madras and Southern India from October to December.

This slight sketch of some of the main facts of Indian meteorology may serve to illustrate the causes which render the physical conditions of various parts of India so extremely different. As Mr. Blanford has observed, we may speak of the climates, but not of the climate of India. "The world itself (he says) affords no greater contrast than is to be met with, at one and the same time, within its limits." When these facts are understood, it will no longer seem surprising that India and its inhabitants, its natural productions, and all the conditions of life, should present such contrasts and diversities.

The following Table, taken from the "Statistical Abstract relating to British India," presented to Parliament 1902, gives the area and population of the British Provinces and Native States of India, according to the Census of 1901.

PROVINCE OR STATE.	Area in square miles.	Population.
PROVINCES.		
1. Ajmer-Merwara	2,711	476,912
2. Andamans and Nicobars	3,188	24,649
3. Assam	56,243	6,126,343
4. Baluchistán (*Districts and Administered Territories*)	45,804	308,246
5. Bengal	151,185	74,744,866
6. Berar	17,710	2,754,016
7. Bombay (*Presidency*)	123,064	18,559,561
Bombay	75,918	15,301,677
Sind	47,066	3,210,910
Aden	80	43,974
8. Burma	236,738	10,489,924
9. Central Provinces	86,614	9,876,646
10. Coorg	1,582	180,607
11. Madras	141,726	38,209,436
12. North-West Frontier Province	16,466	2,125,480
13. Punjab	97,209	20,330,339
14. United Provinces of Agra and Oudh	107,164	47,691,782
Agra	83,198	34,858,705
Oudh	23,966	12,833,077
Total, British Territory	1,087,404	231,898,807
NATIVE STATES.		
15. Baluchistán	86,511	502,500
16. Baroda State	8,099	1,952,692
17. Bengal States	38,652	3,748,544
18. Bombay States	65,761	6,908,648
19. Central India States	78,772	8,628,781
20. Central Provinces States	29,435	1,996,383
21. Hyderabad State	82,698	11,141,142
22. Kashmir State	80,900	2,905,578
23. Madras States	9,969	4,188,086
24. Mysore State	29,444	5,539,399
25. Punjab States	36,532	4,424,398
26. Rajputána States	127,541	9,723,301
27. United Provinces States	5,079	802,097
Total, Native States	679,393	62,461,549
Grand Total, India	1,766,797	294,360,356

CHAPTER III

THE HIMÁLAYA

The Himálaya—Its influence on India—Its geography—The great rivers of India—The story of the sources of the Ganges—British and Native Himálayan provinces—The Kumáon Himálaya—Scenery of the Himálaya.

I HAVE referred in some detail to the regions into which India is divided, but there is a third region which has been barely mentioned, on and outside its borders, the influence of which over a great part of the Indian continent is so important that some knowledge of it is essential to a proper comprehension of Indian geography. I refer to the Himálaya. Without these mountains some of the richest tracts of India would be deserts; they give to India her principal rivers, and, through the effect that they produce on the monsoons and the rainfall, they affect all the conditions of life in the plains above which they rise. This is a subject on which books on India have usually not much to say.

It is unfortunate that we are taught to call these mountains the Himālāya, instead of giving them their more euphonious old Sanskrit name Himālaya, "the abode of snow." There are excellent general accounts of the Himálaya in the ninth edition of the *Encyclopædia Britannica*, and in the fifth supplementary volume of that work, by Sir Richard Strachey and by Sir T. H.

Holdich respectively. As Sir Richard Strachey has shown, the Himálaya is not a mountain chain in the ordinary acceptation of the term. There stretches across a large part of Asia, immediately to the north of India, "a great protuberance above the general level of the earth's surface." We usually call the whole of its southern border by the name Himálaya, and its northern border, in a much less definite way, Kuenlun, and between them lies the mountainous table-land of Tibet, with an average elevation above the sea of 15,000 feet or more. Neither the Himálaya, nor Kuenlun, nor the Tibetan table-land, have any special or separate existence, the whole constituting one huge agglomeration of mountains.

A range of mountains like those to which we are accustomed in Europe gives no notion of the Himálaya. It extends from east to west for some 2000 miles, and the average distance from its southern to its northern edge exceeds 500 miles. The Himálaya, thus defined, would stretch from England to the Caspian, and it covers 1,000,000 square miles, an area as large as that of Great Britain, and the German and Austrian Empires, France, Spain, and Italy all together. Mountains like those of Europe have never been obstacles very difficult to pass, but except for a comparatively short distance on the north-western frontiers of India, where the mountains of Afghánistán and Baluchistán run southwards from the ranges of perpetual snow, the Himálaya and its offshoots form a barrier between India and the rest of Asia which for all practical purposes may be called impassable. Except in the quarter that I have named, the Himálaya has in all ages given protection to India along a frontier 2000 miles in length. But the exception has been a serious one.

From this vulnerable side, in the course of the last eight hundred years, a swarm of invaders has five times come down upon India, sometimes to conquer, sometimes only to destroy.

As might be supposed from its vast proportions, the Himálaya comprises many countries, differing from each other in almost everything except in this, that they consist entirely of mountains. We find in them every possible variety of climate, of vegetation, and of all natural products, and they are peopled by tribes of various character in most different stages of civilisation. The Himálaya offers a good illustration of the misleading generalisations which are common in regard to almost everything Indian. Some authorities tell us that the mountains between the plains of India and the regions of perpetual snow are bleak and bare and arid, and that their scenery, in spite of its stupendous scale, is uninteresting; others tell us that they are covered with forest and rich vegetation, and present, in the higher regions, scenes more beautiful and sublime than anything to be found in Europe. Both stories are true; but considering, as I have just said, that these mountains would stretch from England to the Caspian, we might as reasonably expect to find the same conditions in the Grampians, the Alps, and the Caucasus, as to find them everywhere in the Himálaya.

It is only with that portion of the Himálaya which rises immediately above the plains of Northern India that I am now concerned. The highest peaks hitherto measured in the Himálaya or in the world are, for the most part, found on the southern side of the watershed between India and Tibet, at a distance of about 100 miles from the Indian plains. Mount Everest, in the Eastern Himálaya, reaches more than 29,000 feet; many of the peaks exceed 25,000, and still higher points may possibly remain to be discovered. On the north and north-west of Kashmir some of the peaks are hardly inferior to Mount Everest and the highest summits of the eastern portions of the chain. The elevation of the passes from India into Tibet is seldom less than 16,000 feet, and the average elevation of the watershed probably exceeds 18,000 feet. The table-land of Tibet is usually 15,000 or 16,000 feet above the sea.

I have already referred to the manner in which the lofty mountains that rise along the southern margin of the Himálaya form an impassable obstacle to the periodical rains of the south-west monsoon. The moisture-bearing currents cannot pass such a barrier, and all their vapour is condensed on the southern or Indian side of the chain. It is now well known that this furnishes the simple explanation of the fact formerly discussed by Humboldt and others, and long misunderstood, that the line of perpetual snow is lower on the southern than on the northern slopes of the Himálaya. Although on the latter, in Tibet, the winter cold is almost arctic in its intensity, very little snow will be found there in the summer even at 20,000 feet, because the air is so dry that snow can hardly form, while on the southern slopes of the chain the snow-line is found at an elevation of 15,000 or 16,000 feet.

The greatest rivers of India all come from the Himálaya. It is remarkable that, although their courses through India to the sea are so widely divergent, their chief sources are not far apart from each other, and are all on the northern or Tibetan side of the Indian watershed. They are in the high Tibetan plateau, near the lake of Mánasarowar and the peak of Kailás, names among the most sacred of Hindu mythology. This is strictly true of the Indus, the Sutlej, and the Bráhmaputra, and, although the Ganges seems to be an exception, it can hardly be said to be one.

The true story of the sources of the Ganges is curious. We all know how, in the eighteenth century, Bruce was supposed to have discovered the sources of the Nile, and how it afterwards appeared that he had been to the head, not of the great river, but of one of its tributaries. Something of the same sort may be said of the Ganges.

Almost every work on the geography of India still tells us that the Ganges has its origin in the glacier, or, as it is often and inaccurately called, the snow-bed of Gangotri, where it issues from the ice-cave, the "cow's mouth" of the sacred books of the Hindus. The truth is that, apart from mythology and religion and common belief, and judging as we judge less holy streams, Gangotri has no claim to be called the source of the Ganges, designating by that name the river that issues from the mountains at Hardwár. The river which comes from Gangotri is the Bhágirathi, one of the numerous Himálayan feeders of the true Ganges. The main stream is that of the Alaknanda, which has a much longer course and, at all seasons of the year, a much larger body of water than the Bhágirathi; its most distant sources are on the southern side of the watershed, near the Niti and Mána passes into Tibet, and it collects the drainage of the peaks and glaciers of the Kumáon and Garhwál Himálaya, from Nanda Devi to the sacred shrines of Badrináth and Kedárnáth. These two streams unite about 40 miles above Hardwár. But the Ganges, applying that name, according to universal custom, to the combined river that flows through Bengal past Patna and Rájmahál, and thence on to the sea, has also, like the Indus, the Sutlej, and the Bráhmaputra, its trans-

Himálayan sources. The Gogra, or more correctly the Ghágra, which joins the Ganges above Patna, about 500 miles from the sea, is hardly known to European fame, but in the upper portion of its course it is a much larger river than the Ganges. It rises on the north of the Indian Himálaya, not far from the sources of the other great rivers, near the lake of Mánasarowar, finds its way through the mountains of Nepál, under the name of Kauriáli, and flows on through Oudh until it joins the Ganges. The Kauriáli, near the borders of Nepál, after it has entered the plains, is said to have a minimum discharge of 11,000 cubic feet per second, whereas that of the Ganges at Hardwár is only 6300 feet. Whether at the junction between the Ganges and the Gogra, the former, after its longer course through the plains of India, has become the larger stream, is a question to which no certain answer has hitherto been given. It may seem curious that it should still be possible to doubt whether the Gogra can properly be called an affluent of the Ganges, or whether it ought not rather to be held that the Ganges, in its passage from the mountains to the sea, falls into a river greater than itself, the very name of which is hardly known in Europe. The question has no material importance, and the truth is that no standard has hitherto been clearly recognised by which to determine the characters that justify us in speaking of any particular affluent of a river as its source. It remains undecided whether that term should be applied to the affluent which has the longest course, which has the greatest catchment area, or which has the superior volume; and, if volume be the test, whether this is to be measured where the stream is at its highest, its lowest, or its average level.

Like the rivers that I have named, the Irawadi and

the Salwin, the great rivers of Burma, have also their main sources on the northern or Tibetan side of the Himálaya.

Between Assam, the British province on the extreme north-east of India, and the western frontiers of Kashmir, a distance of 1500 miles, the countries of the Indian Himálaya and its offshoots cover more than 150,000 square miles, and contain some 6,500,000 people. They are mostly under Native rule, and among them the most important is Nepál, the one State in India, or on its borders, which has remained entirely independent of our power. In 1815 and 1816 the Nepalese measured their strength against ours, and lost in consequence Kumáon and Garhwál, their richest districts. Since that time they have preserved an unvarying policy of absolute but thoroughly friendly isolation. The British representative at Kátmándu, their capital, is treated almost as a highly honoured prisoner, and Central Africa is more accessible to European travellers than the greater part of Nepál. However unenlightened from our point of view this policy, which the geographical position and configuration of the country alone rendered possible, may have been, it has had the result of shutting out all causes and opportunities of dispute, and of preserving the independence of Nepál. The other Native Hill States are all under British control. The most important of them is Kashmir, with its dependencies in Western Tibet. I have spoken of the great differences between the various countries and peoples of these mountains. A remarkable illustration is seen in the contrast between the States on the Eastern and Western extremities of the Indian Himálaya. There are no braver soldiers than the little Gurkhas of Nepál, and few greater cowards than the stalwart Mohammedans of Kashmir.

In the Western Himálaya, in the Punjab Lieutenant-Governorship, several districts, of which Kángra is the most important, are under British administration, and in one of them, a small patch surrounded by Native States, is Simla, the summer headquarters of the Government of India. But the most considerable tract of British territory in the Himálaya is the province of Kumáon and Garhwál, bordering on the plains of Rohilkhand, in the Agra Province.

It would be foreign to my purpose to speak at length regarding this or any other portion of the chain, and, as I have just said, in treating of so vast a subject as the Himálaya it is easy to be misled by generalisations. I will, however, say something about Kumáon, because in its main features it affords instructive illustrations of many of the chief and most widely prevailing characteristics of these mountains, and because it is a country with which I have had unusual opportunities of making myself acquainted.

The province of Kumáon has an area of more than 12,000 square miles, and its population exceeds a million. Its whole surface is covered by mountains. They rise with strange suddenness from the plains of India. We pass almost in a moment into the mountains, and when we have once entered them, we hardly find level ground again until we have gone 400 or 500 miles across the Himálaya, Tibet, and the Kuenlun. The Gágar range, described with enthusiastic admiration by Bishop Heber, rises immediately above the plains to more than 8000 feet, and in one of its valleys lie the little lake and station of Naini Tál, the summer headquarters of the Lieutenant-Governor of the United Provinces of Agra and Oudh.

After travelling through Kumáon for more than

100 miles, through a constant succession of high ranges and deep gorges, we pass the great peaks of the Indian Himálaya, and cross over into Tibet, but, looking northward from the watershed, we see again fresh snowy ranges and mountains that look as endless and as vast as those that we have left behind.

In the earlier part of my Indian life I had the good fortune to be employed for about ten years in various offices in Kumáon and Garhwál, and I spent many summers in the higher regions of the Himálaya, sometimes among the almost countless glaciers at the sources of the Ganges and its tributaries, or visiting the passes into Tibet, one of them more than 18,000 feet above the sea, or on the forest-covered ranges immediately under the snowy peaks. I have seen much of European mountains, but in stupendous sublimity, combined with a magnificent and luxuriant beauty, I have seen nothing that can be compared with the Himálaya.

Although none of the Kumáon summits reach an elevation equal to that attained by a few of the peaks in other parts of the chain, for only two of them exceed 25,000 feet, it is probable that the average elevation of the snowy range of Kumáon is nowhere surpassed. For a continuous distance of some 200 miles the peaks constantly reach a height of from 22,000 to more than 25,000 feet.

The Alpine vegetation of the Kumáon Himálaya, while far more various, closely resembles in its generic forms that of the Alpine regions of Europe; but after we have left the plains for 100 miles and have almost reached the foot of the great peaks, the valleys are still, in many cases, only 2000 or 3000 feet above the sea, conveying, as Sir Richard Strachey says, "the heat and vegetation of the tropics among ranges covered with perpetual snow." Thus, he adds, the traveller may obtain at a glance a range of vision extending from 2000 to 25,000 feet, "and see spread before him a compendium of the entire vegetation of the globe from the tropics to the poles." Something similar may be said of the animal world. Tigers, for instance, are common in the valleys; and it is not very unusual to see their footprints in the snow among oaks and pines and rhododendrons 8000 or 10,000 feet above the sea.

If I wished to give to any one, acquainted only with European mountains, some notion of the scenery of the Kumáon Himálaya, at elevations of about 6000 to 10,000 feet, I should advise him to travel in the Italian valleys of the Alps, to which, on a far greater scale, the gorges of the Himálaya have often a stronger resemblance than those of Switzerland. The Val Anzasca, as we go up towards Macugnaga through the chestnut woods, with Monte Rosa always before us, is not unlike in miniature a valley in the Himálaya, and I hardly like to say that it is less beautiful. But the Indian mountains are grander, their forests are nobler, their whole vegetation is more rich and varied, and nowhere in Europe can we find the splendour of the atmospheric effects and colouring of the Himálaya.

Still less is comparison possible in the higher regions of the mountains. To the traveller who remembers the wild magnificence of the peaks and glaciers of the Himálaya, and the general sublimity of its aspect, Zermatt and Chamouny seem insignificant. The mere fact that the ranges of the Himálaya are often twice as high as those of the Alps gives no idea of their relative magnitude. The whole of the Bernese Alps might, it has been said, be cast into a single Himálayan valley. We might almost as reasonably, when the Scottish or

Welsh hills are white with snow, compare them with Mont Blanc and Monte Rosa, as compare anything in the Alps with Nanda Devi and Trisúl. If, preserving the form of its great obelisk, we could pile the Matterhorn on the Jungfrau, we should not reach the highest summits of the Himálaya, and should have a mountain less wonderful than the astonishing peak of Dunagiri.

Among earthly spectacles, it is hardly possible that any can surpass the Himálaya, as I have often seen it at sunset on an evening in October from the ranges thirty or forty miles from the great peaks. "For the picturesque beauty of its natural setting" (Sir Thomas Holdich writes), "in the midst of tropical mountain scenery, no less than for grandeur of outline and profound impression of majestic predominance, there is probably no rival in the world to Kanchinjunga as seen from Darjiling." One other such view, that from Binsar in Kumáon, stands out vividly in my own remembrance. This mountain is 8000 feet high, covered with oak and rhododendron. Towards the north we look down over pine-clad slopes into a deep valley, where, 6000 feet below, the Sarju runs through a tropical forest. Beyond the river it seems to the eye as if the peaks of perpetual snow rose straight up and almost close to us into the sky. From the bottom of the valley to the top of Nanda Devi we see at a glance almost 24,000 feet of mountain. The stupendous golden or rose-coloured masses and pinnacles of the snowy range extend before us in unbroken succession for more than 250 miles, filling up a third part of the visible horizon, while on all other sides, as far as the eye can reach, stretch away the red and purple ranges of the lower mountains. "In a hundred ages of the gods," writes one of the old Sanskrit poets, "I could not tell you of the glories of Himáchal."

I must add that few of those who spend the summer in the hill stations of Northern India have the opportunity of witnessing such scenes as these. If they suppose, at a place like Simla, that they have seen the Himálaya, they greatly deceive themselves.

CHAPTER IV

THE CONSTITUTION OF THE GOVERNMENT IN INDIA

Presidencies and provinces—The Presidency of Bengal—First constitution of the Government—Hastings and his Council—Changes between 1773 and 1833—The Governor-General of India in Council—Separation of the North-Western Provinces from Bengal—Renewal of the Charter in 1853—A Lieutenant-Governor appointed for Bengal—The mutiny of the Native army—Transfer of the government to the Crown—The existing constitution of the Supreme and Provincial Governments—The Indian legislatures—The Provincial Governments—Former cumbrous mode of transacting business—Changes made by Lord Canning—Reforms completed by Lord Lawrence—The Council converted into a Cabinet—Manner of transacting business—Power of Governor-General to overrule the Council—Migration of the Government to Simla—Relations between Supreme and Provincial Governments—Mr. Bright on the government of India—Decentralisation.

In the earlier times of the East India Company, the affairs of the three principal settlements in Bengal, Madras, and Bombay were, in each case, administered by a President and a Council composed of servants of the Company, and the term "Presidency" was applied to the whole tract over which their authority extended. The term has lasted to the present day, and is still used in official papers, but it has almost ceased to have any special meaning. British India is not divided into presidencies, but into provinces, nine of which are extensive countries under separate Governments. The presidencies of Madras and Bombay are now the provinces of the same names.

The term "Presidency of Bengal" requires some explanation.

The name Bengal has had, at different periods since the country came into our possession, very different meanings. It was originally applied, as it still is by the Natives of India, to the tract sometimes called Lower Bengal, including the deltas of the Ganges and Bráhmaputra, and inhabited by the people who speak Bengáli. The earliest factories and settlements on that side of India were established in Bengal, and, as British authority went on extending, the name Bengal was applied to all the territories administered from Fort William, the official headquarters in Calcutta. Thus, the Presidency of Bengal, or, according to its proper official designation, Fort William in Bengal, came to include not only Bengal and the neighbouring provinces of Behár and Orissa, but the whole of the British conquests in Northern India. Some remnants of the old system have lasted into our own times. There was, until 1894, a single army for the provinces of Bengal, the North-Western Provinces and Oudh, and the Punjab, and although, as I shall have again to notice, it had not a single native of Bengal in its ranks, it retained the name of the Bengal Army. This name still survives, for although the Army in the Punjab is now a separate body, the other provinces remain included in the so-called Bengal Command. Another survival from old times is seen in the Bengal Civil Service. The members of the Indian Civil Service, recruited under the system of open competition, are appointed, before they leave England, to the provinces to which under ordinary circumstances they remain permanently attached. The

Civil Services of the United Provinces of Agra and Oudh, and of the Punjab are, for all administrative purposes, as distinct from that of Bengal as from those of Madras and Bombay; but, in regard to some matters connected with annuities to widows and children, they are still treated as a single body and included in the so-called Bengal Civil Service.

The first Act of Parliament which prescribed a definite system of government for the affairs of India was that of 1773.[1] It provided for the appointment of a Governor-General and a Council of four members for the Presidency of Bengal. The administration was to be carried on in accordance with the votes of the majority of the Council, and the Governor-General had no power to set aside their decisions. Certain powers of control, vaguely defined, were given to the Government of Bengal over the presidencies of Madras and Bombay. Warren Hastings was the first Governor-General of Bengal. The scandalous dissensions in his Council, under the malignant influence of Francis, have become a well-known matter of history. They showed that government by the constantly shifting majority of a Council was impossible; but although similar facts repeatedly occurred to illustrate the folly of such a system, it was not until 1786 that a partial remedy was applied, after Lord Cornwallis had made it a condition of his acceptance of the office of Governor-General that the power of overruling his Council should be given to him. On the renewal of the Company's Charter in 1793,[2] the powers of the Governor-General were further extended; authority to overrule their Councils was given to the Governors of Madras and Bombay; the power of the Governments of those presidencies to make laws and

[1] Regulating Act, 13 Geo. III. c. 63.

[2] 33 Geo. III. c. 52.

regulations for their own territories was recognised; and the supreme authority of the Governor-General in Council over the whole of India was distinctly declared. No very important changes in the constitution of the Government were made after this until the renewal of the Charter in 1833,[1] when the trading powers of the Company ceased. The Governor-General in Council of Bengal then became the Governor-General of India in Council. Bengal was to be divided into two presidencies, Fort William in Bengal and Agra. The Governor-General was to be Governor of the former, and a Governor was to be appointed for the latter. The Agra presidency was not constituted, but by an amending Act passed in 1835[2] the territories which were to have been included in it were placed, under the name of the North-Western Provinces, under a Lieutenant-Governor without a Council. Madras and Bombay retained their Councils, but no Council was appointed for Bengal.

The Punjab became a Lieutenant-Governorship in 1859, and Burma in 1897. In 1901 a new province, the North-West Frontier Province, was formed, and, to avoid confusion from the similarity of names, the North-Western Provinces, with which Oudh had been included, became the United Provinces of Agra and Oudh.

In 1853 the Charter of the Company was again renewed,[3] and an important change in the Government was made. It had long been obvious that it was impossible for a single person to discharge the double duty of Governor-General of India and Governor of Bengal, and the administration of Bengal had notoriously become less efficient than that of any other province

[1] 3 and 4 Will. IV. c. 85. [2] 5 and 6 Will. IV. c. 52.
[3] 16 and 17 Vict. c. 95.

in India. The Governor-General was relieved from this charge, and a Lieutenant-Governor, without a Council, was appointed.

In 1857 came the mutiny of the Bengal Native army.

In the following year, by the "Act for the better government of India,"[1] the government was transferred from the East India Company to the Crown, and it was provided that all the powers of the Company and of the Board of Control should be exercised by a Secretary of State, in concert, in certain cases, with a Council. This Act, of which I shall again have to speak, applied almost solely to the Government in England, and the Government in India was carried on as before.

In 1861 important changes were made in the constitution both of the Supreme and Provincial Governments in India. The "Indian Councils Act"[2] then passed still regulates, for the most part, the Governments in India. I shall describe its principal provisions.

The Governor-General and the Ordinary members of his Council are appointed by the Crown. No limit of time is specified for their tenure of office, but custom, not often disregarded, has fixed it at five years. The term "Viceroy" has been commonly applied to the Governor-General since the transfer of the government to the Crown, but it is not recognised by law. There are five Ordinary members of Council, and, by an Act passed in 1874,[3] a sixth member may, at the discretion of the Crown, be appointed for public works. Three of the members must have served in India for at least ten years; two of them are members of the Covenanted Civil Service, and the third is a military officer; but

[1] 21 and 22 Vict. c. 106.
[2] 24 and 25 Vict. c. 67.
[3] 37 and 38 Vict. c. 91.

this distribution is a matter of custom, not of law. One of the two remaining members must be a Barrister, or a member of the Faculty of Advocates in Scotland, of not less than five years' standing; he has charge of the legislative department. The fifth member has charge of the finances. The Commander-in-Chief in India may also be, and in practice always is, an Extraordinary member of the Council. The Governors of Madras and Bombay become Extraordinary members if the Council meets within their presidencies. Whenever it is declared by the Governor-General in Council to be expedient that the Governor-General should visit any part of India without his Council, he may nominate one of the members of his Council to be President of the Council. The President, during the absence of the Governor-General, exercises the powers which the Governor-General may exercise at meetings of the Council, except that of assenting to or withholding assent to laws; and the Governor-General, when so absent, may himself exercise all or any of the powers which he might exercise as Governor-General in Council, except the power of making laws. The Council may assemble at any place in India which the Governor-General in Council appoints.

For the purposes of legislation, Additional members are nominated to the Council. The Legislative Council is often spoken of as if it had a separate existence, but this is a mistake; only one Council is known to the law. The Additional members are nominated by the Governor-General, and they join the Council when it meets for legislative purposes. Not less than one-half of their number must be persons not holding offices under the Government; some of them are always Natives of India. The Lieutenant-Governor of any province in which the

Council may meet acts as an Additional member. When the Council meets for legislative purposes, and the Ordinary members are present, the Government can usually command a majority of votes.

Under the Indian Councils Act of 1861 the maximum number of Additional members was twelve, all of whom were nominated at the discretion of the Governor-General. The Council, when it met for legislation only, could occupy itself with no matters except those directly connected with the legislative business before it. It had no concern whatever with any of the functions of the executive government. The Provincial Legislatures, of which I shall have again to speak, were similarly constituted, and their powers were similarly limited.

In 1892 an important change was made in the constitution of all the Indian Councils. It had long been felt that the time had come when the administration might gain much advantage if public opinion could be brought more largely to bear upon it. This was especially true of the Provincial Governments, the ordinary business of which is of a kind in which local knowledge is necessary, and on which the expression of intelligent independent criticism may often be very valuable. By an Act of Parliament, passed in 1892,[1] it was provided that the number of Additional members in the Council of the Governor-General should not be less than ten nor more than sixteen. The exact number is left to the discretion of the Governor-General for the time being. The Governor-General in Council, with the approval of the Secretary of State in Council, makes rules defining the manner in which the nominations of Additional members are to be made, under

[1] 55 and 56 Vict. c. 14.

which the annual Financial Statement of the Government may be discussed, and under which questions may be asked. It was obviously impossible to obtain, by any system of popular election or otherwise, any direct representation on the Governor-General's Council of the multifarious interests of the vast populations of the numerous countries of the Indian Empire, and the following procedure was adopted in the rules passed under the Act. There are sixteen Additional members, of whom six are officials appointed by the Governor-General, and ten are non-official. Four of the latter are appointed by the Governor-General on the recommendation of a majority of the non-official Additional members of the Provincial Legislatures, each of these bodies recommending one member. A fifth member is recommended by the Calcutta Chamber of Commerce. The Governor-General can, if he thinks fit, decline to accept a recommendation thus made, and in that case a fresh recommendation is submitted to him. The remaining five non-official members are nominated at the discretion of the Governor-General, "in such manner as shall appear to him most suitable with reference to the legislative business to be brought before the Council, and the due representation of the different classes of the community." In the words of a despatch from the Government of India, "measures may at one time be before the Council, relating to interests which ought to be specially represented in their discussion; at another time the legislative work may be of a different description, calling for the selection of representatives from particular local divisions of the empire, or of persons chosen to represent the most skilled opinion upon large measures affecting British India as a whole. It is desired also to reserve to the Governor-General the liberty of inviting representatives from Native States."

Under the law as it stood, before the passing of the Act of 1892, there was no opportunity of criticising the financial policy of the Government except on those occasions when financial legislation was necessary. Under the rules now in force, the annual Financial Statement must be made publicly in the Council; every member is at liberty to make any observations that he thinks fit, and the Financial member of Council and the President have the right of reply.

Rules have also been made defining the conditions under which questions may be asked in the Council. The questions, of which due notice has to be given, must be requests for information only, and must not be put in argumentative, or hypothetical, or defamatory language, nor is discussion permitted in respect of an answer given to a question on behalf of the Government. These two restrictions are substantially identical with those in force in the British House of Commons. The President may disallow any question which, in his opinion, cannot be answered consistently with the public interests.

Certain Acts of Parliament under which the Government of India is constituted cannot be touched, and no law can be made affecting the authority of Parliament or allegiance to the Crown, but with these exceptions the legislative powers of the Governor-General in Council over the whole of British India are unrestricted. Measures affecting the public debt or revenues of India, the religion of any of His Majesty's subjects, the discipline or maintenance of the military or naval forces, and the relations of the Government with Foreign States, cannot be introduced by any member without the previous sanction of the Governor-General. Every Act requires the Governor-General's assent. The assent of the Crown is not necessary to the validity of an Act, but the Crown can disallow any Act that has been passed.

Apart from these ordinary legislative powers, the Governor-General in Council was authorised in 1870[1] to make, without calling in the Additional members, "Regulations" having the force of law for the less advanced parts of the country, where a system of administration simpler than that in force elsewhere is desirable. The effect of this was to put on a legal basis the administration of the so-called "Non-Regulation Provinces."

Further, in cases of urgent necessity, the Governor-General can, on his own authority and without reference to his Council, make Ordinances which have the force of law for six months. This power was given by the Act of 1861 for the first time. It has seldom been exercised, and only for reasons of temporary convenience.

The constitution of the Executive Governments in Madras and Bombay was not altered by the Act of 1861, and they still retain some signs of their former dignity and partial independence. On certain matters they correspond directly with the Secretary of State, a privilege not possessed by other Provincial Governments. The Governor and the Ordinary members of Council are appointed by the Crown. The Governor is usually an English statesman sent from England. Two members of the Civil Service constitute the Council. Until 1893 there was, in each of the two Presidencies, a Commander-in-Chief, who was also a member of the Council, but, as I shall have to notice in describing the constitution of

[1] 33 Vict. c. 3, sec. 1.

the Army in India, the offices of Provincial Commander-in-Chief were, in that year, abolished. The power of legislation, which had been taken away in Madras and Bombay by the Act of 1833, was restored in 1861.

Under the Act of 1892, to which I have already referred, changes similar to those made in the Council of the Governor-General were also made in the Councils of the Governments of Madras and Bombay. Additional members are nominated by the Governor, and they join the Council when it meets for legislative purposes. Their number, both in Madras and Bombay, is twenty, of whom, under the rules laid down, not more than nine can be officials. The system under which the non-official Additional members are chosen is so nearly identical in the two provinces, that it will be sufficient to describe that adopted in one of them. I take the Bombay Council as the example. There are eleven non-official members. Nominations to eight of these seats are made by the Governor on the recommendation of various bodies and associations. The Corporation of Bombay and the Senate of the University each recommend one member. Six members are recommended by groups of Municipal Corporations, groups of District Local Boards, classes of large landholders, and by such Associations of merchants, manufacturers, or tradesmen as the Governor in Council may prescribe. The remaining non-official members are nominated by the Governor "in such manner as shall in his opinion secure a fair representation of the different classes of the community."

The rules for the discussion of the annual Financial Statements in the Provincial Councils are the same as those applicable to the Council of the Governor-General, except that the discussion must be limited to those branches of revenue and expenditure which are under the control of the Provincial Government. The rules regarding questions are also the same, with two restrictions. Questions cannot be asked or answered as to any matters other than those under the control of the Provincial Government; and in matters which are or have been the subject of controversy between the Provincial Government and the Government of India or the Secretary of State, no question can be asked or answer given except on matters of fact.

All laws passed by the Provincial Legislatures require the sanction of the Governor-General, and may be disallowed by the Crown. The powers of the Governor-General in Council to legislate for all matters throughout India are not affected by the establishment of the Provincial Legislatures, but, as a general rule, the latter are left to deal with subjects of provincial and local interest. They cannot repeal or amend any Act of Parliament, or any law passed in India before the time when the Indian Councils Act of 1861 came into operation, nor, except with the previous sanction of the Governor-General, can they take into consideration any measure affecting the public debt, customs, imperial taxation, currency, the post office and telegraph, the penal code, religion, the military and naval forces, patents, copyright, or relations with Foreign States.

In the other great provinces of India the Executive Governments are differently constituted from those of Madras and Bombay. Bengal, the United Provinces of Agra and Oudh, the Punjab, and Burma are administered by Lieutenant-Governors; they must be chosen from officers in the service of the Crown who have served in India for at least ten years; they are appointed by the Governor-General with the approval of the Crown; and, with one exception, they have always been members of the Covenanted Civil Service.[1] The Lieutenant-Governors have no Councils for executive business, but the Governor-General in Council may establish in each province a Council for legislative purposes only. This power has been exercised in each of the Lieutenant-Governorships; I shall have occasion to refer again to their Legislative Councils; they are similar in their constitution to those in Madras and Bombay, the Lieutenant-Governor taking the place of the Governor; but in the Punjab and in Burma, the Councils having been formed under the Statute of 1861 and not under that of 1892, the members are all nominated. The Governments of the Central Provinces and Assam are administered by Chief Commissioners. Excepting in name and dignity and in amount of salary and patronage, there is no great difference between them and Lieutenant-Governors. For provinces which have no legislatures of their own, laws are passed by the Governor-General in Council.

I must now speak of the manner in which the executive business of the Governor-General in Council is transacted. The system is very different from that in force under the Government of the East India Company. Although after the Act of 1793 the power of the Governor-General to over-rule his Council was not open to question, the fundamental idea, on which previous legislation had been based, still remained, that the Government was to be carried on by the Governor-General in concert with the whole Council. All public business of every kind, however trivial, was supposed to come before all the members of the Government. Questions were ordinarily decided by the majority, the Governor-General having a casting vote if the votes

[1] 5 and 6 Will. IV. c. 52, sec. 2, and 16 and 17 Vict. c. 95, sec. 16.

were equal. If the Governor-General determined to over-rule the majority, it was provided that he and the members of Council should "mutually exchange with and communicate in writing to each other the grounds and reasons of their respective opinions." They were then to meet a second time, and if both parties retained their first opinions, their minutes were to be entered on the consultations, and the orders of the Governor-General were to be carried out.

In his *Essay on Representative Government*, published in 1861, when the procedure which I have described was still legally in force, Mr. J. S. Mill described the manner in which he considered that Ministers in charge of the great departments of an Executive Government ought to be assisted by Councils:—

"The Councils should be consultative merely, in this sense that the ultimate decision should rest undividedly with the Minister himself: but neither ought they to be looked upon, or to look upon themselves as ciphers, or as capable of being reduced to such at his pleasure. The advisers attached to a powerful and perhaps self-willed man ought to be placed under conditions which make it impossible for them, without discredit, not to express an opinion, and impossible for him not to listen to and consider their recommendations, whether he adopts them or not. The relation which ought to exist between a chief and this description of advisers is very accurately hit by the constitution of the Governor-General and those of the different presidencies in India. These Councils are composed of persons who have professional knowledge of Indian affairs, which the Governor-General and Governors usually lack, and which it would not be desirable to require of them. As a rule, every member of Council is expected to give an opinion, which is, of course, very often a simple acquiescence; but if there is a difference of sentiment, it is at the option of every member, and is the invariable practice, to record the reasons of his opinion; the Governor-General or Governor doing the same. In ordinary cases the decision is according to the sense of the majority; the Council, therefore, has a substantial part in the Government, but if the Governor-General or Governor thinks fit, he may set aside even their unanimous opinion, recording his reasons. The result is that the chief is, individually and effectually, responsible for every act of the Government. The members of Council have only the responsibility of advisers; but it is always known, from documents capable of being produced, and which, if called for by Parliament or public opinion, always are produced, what each has advised, and what reasons he gave for his advice; while from their dignified position and ostensible participation in all acts of government, they have nearly as strong motives to apply themselves to the public business, and to form and express a well-considered opinion on every part of it, as if the whole responsibility rested with themselves."

I must continue my quotation, for Mr. Mill's commentary on the system thus described is remarkable:—

"This mode of conducting the highest class of administrative business is one of the most successful instances of the adaptation of means to ends which political history, not hitherto very prolific in works of skill and contrivance, has yet to show. It is one of the acquisitions with which the art of politics has been enriched by the experience of the East India Company's rule; and like most of the other wise contrivances by which India has been preserved to this country, and an amount of good government produced which is truly wonderful considering the circumstances and the materials, it is probably destined to perish in the general holocaust which the traditions of Indian government seem fated to undergo, since they have been placed at the mercy of public ignorance and the presumptuous vanity of political men."

Mr. Mill's anticipations have been to some extent verified. The manner of transacting business which existed under the East India Company has perished, but, I venture to say, not for the reasons which he predicted, but because it was not the wise contrivance which he supposed. The principle which he laid down was undoubtedly true, that while a man in the position of Governor-General of India ought to possess, in the last resort, power to act upon his own judgment, he ought also to be obliged to hear the opinions of experienced councillors, and that those councillors should have the right of making their opinions known, whether they were followed or not. This principle has not been infringed. If Mr. Mill had himself seen in operation the system which he described, he would, I am sure, have given it a different character. The truth is that a more cumbrous, I might say a more impossible, system of administration for a great empire could hardly have been invented than that which prevailed under the Government of the East India Company, when every case was supposed to be laid before the Governor-General and the whole Council, and to be decided by them collectively. The only reason that enabled such a system to last so long was that in matters requiring prompt and vigorous action it was not really acted upon.

In the latter years of the East India Company, and for a few years after the transfer of the government to the Crown, the Governor-General was frequently separated from his Council. His presence was often required in Northern India by reasons of political necessity. He was authorised to exercise, while absent from the Council, all the powers of the Governor-General in Council, except the power of legislation. The Council remained in Calcutta under the presidency of the senior member, who exercised, during the Governor-General's absence, all the powers of the Governor-General in Council, except the power of giving assent to laws. There was a double Government, with a division of authority and responsibility fatal to good administration. Sir Henry Maine has described, from his own observation as a member of Council, the manner in which the system actually worked :—

"A division of business was made between the Governor-General in the Upper provinces and the President in Council at Calcutta. Everything which was of importance was referred directly to the Governor-General, and there was either a rule or an understanding that if any matter which came before the President in Council assumed, contrary to expectation, the least importance, it should be sent on to the Governor-General. . . . Except in regard to matters belonging to the Foreign department, of which it was usual for the Governor-General himself to undertake the primary management, the severance of the Governor-General from the Council dislocated the whole machinery of Government. I was myself in Calcutta, as a member of Council during the absence of Lord Elgin in the Upper provinces, in the summer of 1863. I believe it to be impossible for any human arrangement to have worked more perversely. Lord Elgin was distinguished by remarkable caution —though I doubt whether his caution was practically greater than that which any man comparatively fresh from England would display under similarly vast responsibilities—and all or most important matters were transferred by him over a distance of 1500 miles for the opinions of his Council. The result was that a great deal of work was done twice over, and a great deal not done at all."[1]

In earlier times, when there were no railways or telegraphs, and hardly any roads, the duties of the Government were very different from what they are now. Kingdoms were annexed and conquered, and stirring events were constantly going on, but the ordinary business of administration was comparatively small. But in the years immediately preceding the mutinies of 1857 rapid changes were in progress in all branches of the Government, and when the great reign of Lord Dalhousie was over he declared it to be morally and physically impossible that the Governor-General should efficiently discharge all the duties imposed upon him.

The events of 1857 made the burden still heavier.

[1] Memorandum on the Administration of Bengal, December 2, 1867.

The insertion by Parliament of a few words in the Indian Councils Act of 1861 gave to Lord Canning and his successors the means of reforming a system of government which had become intolerable. It empowered the Governor-General to make from time to time rules and orders for the more convenient transaction of business in his Council, and provided that any order made or act done in accordance with such rules and orders should be deemed to be the order or act of the Governor-General in Council. These provisions made it possible to bring legally to an end the system under which the whole Council was supposed to take part collectively in the disposal of all the business of the Government.

Rules were made by Lord Canning, assigning to each member of the Council the charge of a separate department of the administration, and the Council was virtually converted into a Cabinet, of which the Governor-General was the head. When this change was made it became obvious that the separation, for long periods of time, of the Governor-General from his Council was incompatible with efficient administration. The reform of procedure was completed by Lord Lawrence. Since his time the old plan of double government, under which the Governor-General was frequently absent from the Council, with a President in Council in Calcutta, has been abandoned. It is now never adopted except as an occasional measure of merely temporary convenience.

Although the separation of departments in India is less complete than in England, and the authority of a member of Council much less extensive and exclusive than that of an English Secretary of State, the members of Council are now virtually Cabinet ministers, each of whom has charge of one of the great departments of the

Government. Their ordinary duties are rather those of administrators than of councillors. The Governor-General regulates the manner in which the public business shall be distributed among them. He usually keeps the Foreign department in his own hands; the other departments are—Home, Revenue and Agriculture, Finance and Commerce, Military, Public Works, and Legislative. While the member of Council takes the place of the English Secretary of State, there is in each department a Secretary holding a position analogous to that of a permanent Under-secretary in England. It is the duty of this secretary to place every case before the Governor-General or member in charge of his department, in a form in which it is ready for decision. He submits with it a statement of his own opinion. In minor cases the member of Council passes orders which are final. If the matter be one of greater importance, he sends on the papers, with his own orders, to the Governor-General for his approval. If the Governor-General concurs, and thinks further discussion unnecessary, the orders are issued. If he does not concur, he directs that the case shall be brought before the Council, as in England an important case might come before the Cabinet. The duty rests upon the secretary, apart from his responsibility towards the member of Council in charge of the department, of bringing personally to the knowledge of the Governor-General every matter of special importance. All orders of the Government are issued in the name of the Governor-General in Council.

Although, when a question comes before the whole Council, it is usually decided in accordance with the opinion of the majority, power is reserved by law to the Governor-General to act on his own opinion alone, whenever the safety, tranquillity, or interests of the British possessions in India may, in his judgment, be essentially affected.[1] Recourse to this power is very seldom necessary. The only occasion in recent times on which it has been exercised in a matter of importance occurred in March 1879, when Lord Lytton, in opposition to the opinion of a majority of his Council, partially abolished the Indian import duty on English cotton goods. The occasion will be remembered in the economic history of India, because this measure rendered inevitable the application for a time to India of the policy of freedom of trade.

Another consequence has followed from the changes that I have described. The abandonment by Lord Lawrence of the system of double government, and the establishment of the departmental responsibility of the members of Council, rendered it necessary that when the Governor-General left Calcutta for Northern India he should be accompanied by the Council. Lord Lawrence made Simla the ordinary summer headquarters of the Government. There was formerly much criticism of these annual migrations, but no one who has had personal knowledge of the Government of India doubts the increased efficiency of its administration since it has passed a portion of every year in a climate less enervating than that to which it was exposed in the tropical heat of Calcutta, and in which Englishmen can work as vigorously as at home. The Government does not go to Simla for a holiday, but for the hardest and most continuous portion of its work. The evil influence of the climate is not the only reason why the Government of India should not remain permanently in Bengal. It has no local duties. Its business is one of general control,

[1] 33 Vict. c. 3, sec. 5.

and the countries of Northern and Western India will always be those which demand the largest share of its attention and anxiety.

I shall give in another chapter some account of the manner in which the administration of a great British province is carried on. There has been since 1870 a great and beneficial change in the relations between the Supreme and Provincial Governments.

In the speeches on India made by Mr. Bright, about the time when the Government of India was transferred to the Crown, one of the principles on which he insisted was the necessity of decentralising the Government. There is much in those speeches with which I am unable to agree, and much that was once true has ceased to be applicable, but I wish to quote some passages which seem to me to indicate the principles on which government in India can alone be successfully conducted. Mr. Bright's speeches are accessible to every one, and I need not be accused of misrepresenting his views if I quote only those passages with which I myself agree, and which serve my present purpose:—

"The point which I wish to bring before the Committee and the Government is this, because it is on this that I rely mainly—I think I may say, almost entirely—for any improvement in the future of India. I believe a great improvement may be made, and by a gradual process that will dislocate nothing. What you want is to decentralise your Government. . . . You will not make a single step towards the improvement of India unless you change your whole system of government—unless you give to each presidency a Government with more independent powers than are now possessed. What would be thought if the whole of Europe were under one Governor who knew only the language of the Feejee Islands, and that his subordinates were like himself, only more intelligent than the inhabitants of the Feejee Islands are supposed to be? . . . How long does England propose to govern India? Nobody answers that question, and nobody can answer it. Be it

50, or 100, or 500 years, does any man with the smallest glimmering of common-sense believe that so great a country, with its twenty different nations and its twenty languages, can ever be bound up and consolidated into one compact and enduring empire? I believe such a thing to be utterly impossible. We must fail in the attempt if ever we make it, and we are bound to look into the future with reference to that point."

Mr. Bright, seeing that the union of the various countries of India into a single state was impossible, went on to propose that each of the five great provinces should have a separate and almost independent Government of its own, directly subject to the British Crown, and that the Central Government of India under the Governor-General in Council should be abolished. It is with no want of respect for Mr. Bright that I say that the latter suggestion was one which could not possibly be adopted. There is clearly nothing more essential to the maintenance of our empire in India than a strong central authority; but Mr. Bright's belief was undoubtedly true that there can be no successful government in India unless the fundamental fact of the immense diversities of Indian countries and peoples be recognised, and each great province be administered by its own separate Government with a minimum of interference from outside.

There was a time when the tendency in India was towards greater centralisation; but since the Viceroyalty of Lord Mayo the current has happily turned in the other direction, and the Provincial Governments are now far more independent than they were. This change has been mainly the result of the measures of financial decentralisation initiated in 1870, and which were pronounced by Sir Henry Maine to be "much the most successful administrative reform which had taken place in India in his time."[1] I shall speak of this in another chapter.

The Government of India now interferes very little with the details of provincial administration. The fact is recognised that the Provincial Governments necessarily possess far more knowledge of local requirements and conditions than any to which the distant authorities of the Central Government can pretend.

Although the Governor-General in Council exercises only a general supervision over the internal administration of the empire, there are some branches of the public business which concern the whole of India, and which obviously can be efficiently managed by the central authority alone. The military defence of India, and the conduct of our relations with Foreign Powers and with the Native States of India, rest with the Supreme Government. While the duty of administering the laws rests with the Provincial Governments, and with the local courts and authorities, the Government of India is mainly responsible for the excellence or imperfection of the laws themselves. Subject to the control of the Secretary of State, it makes provision for the construction of the railways and canals, without which there can be no proper development of the public wealth, or protection against drought and famine. It administers the post office and telegraph. It is mainly responsible for the management of the finances, and it lays down the principles by which the fiscal policy of the empire is to be guided.

[1] *The Reign of Queen Victoria*—"India," vol. i. p. 516.

CHAPTER V

THE HOME GOVERNMENT

The Home Government—The Secretary of State and Council of India—Mode of transacting business—Nature of control over the Government of India—Parliamentary interference—Its dangers.

I MUST now refer to the Act of 1858, by which the Government of India was transferred to the Crown. It provided that all the powers of the East India Company and Board of Control should be exercised by a Secretary of State, in concert, in certain cases, with a Council, and, although various changes have been made in it by subsequent legislation, it remains in essential respects still in force.[1]

The Council, styled the Council of India, consisted, as it was first constituted, of fifteen members appointed by the Secretary of State. In 1889 power was given to him to reduce the number of the Council to ten, by abstaining from filling vacancies whenever he thought fit to do so. Three of the members "having professional or other peculiar qualifications" may be appointed for life; the others hold office for ten years, and this term may, for special reasons of public advantage, which must be laid before Parliament, be extended for five years

[1] The principal Acts referring to this subject are the following:—Act 21 and 22 Vict. c. 106; Act 22 and 23 Vict. c. 41; Act 23 and 24 Vict. c. 100; Act 32 and 33 Vict. c. 97; Act 39 Vict. c. 7; Act 52 and 53 Vict. c. 65.

more. The majority of the Council must be persons who have served or resided in India for at least ten years, and who have not left India more than ten years before their appointment. Most of the members are always men who have held high office in India. Several of them have usually belonged to the Indian Civil Service, and have been Lieutenant-Governors of provinces or members of the Viceroy's Council; others are soldiers, engineers, bankers, or men of diplomatic, official, or mercantile experience. The object aimed at by the law is to give to the Secretary of State, who must ordinarily have little personal knowledge of the details of Indian administration, the help of a body of experts.

The position of the Council differs essentially from that formerly held by the Court of Directors of the East India Company, for, unlike that body, which possessed and exercised large independent powers, it has no initiative authority. Questions of the greatest importance, notorious to all the world, may be pending, but the Council can give no opinion on them until they are laid before it by the Secretary of State.

Every order proposed to be made by the Secretary of State must, before it is issued, either be submitted to a meeting of the Council, or be placed in the Council-room for seven days for the perusal of the members, unless the Secretary of State considers the matter urgent, in which case, recording his reasons, he may make the order. If there is a difference of opinion between him and the Council his decision prevails, but there is one limitation on the powers thus given to him. He cannot order expenditure without the consent of a majority of the Council. The Act of 1858 provides that "the expenditure of the revenues of India, both in India and elsewhere, shall be subject to the control of the

Secretary of State in Council, and no grant or appropriation of any part of such revenues, or of any other property coming into the possession of the Secretary of State in Council by virtue of this Act, shall be made without the concurrence of a majority of votes at a meeting of the Council."

The powers thus given to the Council in controlling expenditure are, however, far from being as great as at first sight they seem to be, for they can only be exercised in regard to the ordinary business of the administration. Orders involving large expenditure may be given by the Secretary of State without either the consent or the knowledge of the Council. In dealing with questions affecting the relations of the Government with Foreign Powers, making war or peace, prescribing the policy to be followed towards Native States, and generally in matters in which secrecy is necessary, the Secretary of State acts on his own authority alone. Before the transfer of the Government to the Crown, the Board of Control was empowered to send to India any orders on these subjects through the Secret Committee, which consisted of not more than three members of the Court of Directors, and those powers were transferred to the Secretary of State. Despatches from India on similar matters may be marked "Secret" in India, and they are not communicated to the members of the Council unless the Secretary of State so directs. Such questions as an Afghan war, negotiations with Russia and the Amir of Kabul regarding the affairs of Afghanistan, or the annexation of Burma, do not come before the Council. Its members have not only no power of interference, but they have no recognised means of obtaining information in regard to such subjects other than those of the general public.

Apart from questions of this character, most of the ordinary business passes through the Council, and, consisting as it does of men possessing special experience of Indian affairs, its advice is naturally, in the great majority of cases, followed by the Secretary of State.

The business is distributed among the various departments, each of which is in charge of a permanent secretary, and the Secretary of State appoints, for consideration of the questions coming before each department, a committee consisting of four or five members of the Council. They are chosen according to their presumed knowledge of the subjects likely to be referred to them. The recommendations of the committees are laid before the Secretary of State, and, if he so directs, before the Council.

It has often been said that one result of the transfer of the Government of India to the Crown has been to increase very greatly the interference of the Home Government, and to weaken the authority of the Government in India itself. Having myself been a member of the Government of India for nearly nine years, under five Viceroys, from Lord Lawrence to Lord Ripon, and afterwards a member for ten years of the Council of the Secretary of State, this is a point on which I feel that I have authority to speak. The increased facilities of communication, the establishment of telegraphs, the greater interest in India taken by the British public and by Parliament, the growth of the business of the Home Government in consequence of the large investments of British capital in India, and other causes, have made the relations between the two countries far more intimate than was formerly necessary or possible, and have made more frequent the cases in which final orders cannot be passed in India;

but it is an error to suppose that the Secretary of State is constantly interfering in the ordinary work of Indian administration. The description of the Home Government given by Mr. J. S. Mill in the time of the East India Company is as applicable now as when he wrote :—

> "It is not," he said, "so much an executive as a deliberative body. The Executive Government of India is, and must be, seated in India itself. The principal function of the Home Government is not to direct the details of administration, but to scrutinise and revise the past acts of the Indian Governments; to lay down principles and issue general instructions for their future guidance, and to give or refuse sanction to great political measures which are referred home for approval."

The action of the Secretary of State is mainly confined to answering references made to him by the Government in India, and, apart from great political or financial questions, the number and nature of those references mainly depend on the character of the Governor-General for the time being. Some men in that position like to minimise personal responsibilities, and to ask for the orders of the Home Government before taking action. Others prefer to act on their own judgment and on that of their councillors. The Secretary of State initiates almost nothing.

So long as the Government of India is content to carry on the administration without largely increasing the cost of existing establishments, and without incurring new and heavy charges, it is practically almost independent, so far as its action in the internal affairs of India is concerned. Even in matters connected with the public expenditure, in regard to which, as I have said, special responsibilities which cannot be avoided have been placed by Parliament on the Secretary of

State in Council, the financial powers of the Governor-General in Council and of the local Governments have been largely extended since the transfer of the government to the Crown.

So far as the Secretary of State is a free agent, the foregoing observations require no qualification. He has no disposition to interfere needlessly in the details of administration in India. Pressure, however, not easy to resist, is sometimes brought to bear upon him.

The growth of interest in the good government of India among the people of this country, and among their representatives in Parliament, is earnestly to be desired, but if such interest is to be practically useful it must be intelligent and prudent, and be kept apart from the slippery domain of party politics. It cannot be said that these conditions have always been fulfilled. More than one instance could be quoted in which serious injury to India has been caused or threatened by the interference of the House of Commons in matters in regard to which the great majority of its members are profoundly ignorant, but out of which some temporary political advantage was apparently to be gained, or which possessed some special interest for the always numerous body of doctrinaires and fanatics. "Nothing," says Goethe, "is more dangerous than ignorance in action," and it may be feared that among the difficulties and perils of the future that are in store for our Indian dominion, not the least serious may be those that spring from the ignorant action of the British House of Commons.[1]

[1] The following passage deserves quotation as an illustration of political foresight. It was written in 1857 by Mr. J. S. Mill, shortly before the transfer of the Government of India from the Company to the Crown:—

"In the exceptional cases in which Parliament and the Nation interfere in Indian affairs, the interference will not be founded on knowledge of the sub-

Although by far the greater part of the administrative improvement of the last thirty years has been due to the Governments in India, credit for some of it must be given to the Government at home. A body constituted like the Home Government of India is slow to move and sometimes obstructive, and its general policy has been conservative and cautious. The more ardent among Indian reformers have sometimes chafed under the restrictions placed upon them, but in their anxiety for improvement they are sometimes more aggressive than is politically prudent. The most important part of our administration in India has the advantage of being carried on by comparatively young men. This is an advantage of inestimable value, and one to which no small part of the general vigour and excellence of Indian administration is due. After thirty-five years' service retirement is compulsory, and this salutary rule, not often broken through, has this for its result, that every one of the highest offices of the State is held by a man in the prime of life. One of the weakest points in our government is the incessant process of change in the *personnel* of the administration, and the constant waste of mature experience. Neither the Viceroy nor any member of his Council, nor any Governor or Lieutenant-Governor, usually holds his office for more than five years, nor is there much greater permanency in the tenure of other offices held by Englishmen. The climate, and the peculiar conditions under which the government

ject and will probably be for the most part confined to cases where an Indian question is taken up from party motives as the means of injuring a Minister, or when some Indian malcontent, generally with objects opposed to good government, succeeds in interesting the sympathies of the public in his favour. For it is not the people of India but rich individuals and societies representing class interests who have the means of engaging the ear of the public through the press and through agents in Parliament."

has to be carried on in a foreign country by a small body of men, make constant changes unavoidable. This renders it difficult to maintain at all times a wise continuity of policy, and in this respect the India Office sometimes exercises a useful influence. The advisers of the Secretary of State, although their knowledge is apt to get rusty, often know more about India than most of the officers of the Government in India itself; they preserve the traditions of administration and the lessons of experience.

CHAPTER VI

THE CIVIL SERVICES

Principles on which first appointments are made—The Covenanted Service—System of nomination before 1853—System of open competition—Natives of India in the Covenanted Service—The Statute of 1833—The Queen's Proclamation of 1858—The Statute of 1870—Admission of Natives to posts of importance—Lord Lytton's rules—Public Service Commission—Imperial and Provincial Services—Small number of Englishmen in the Civil Service—The greater part of the administration in Native hands—High character of Native officers—Their salaries—Necessity for maintaining English principles of government—Question of holding competitive examinations in India—Transfer of important offices to the Provincial Services—The Public Works, Telegraph, Police, Forest, and Educational Services.

IT was long ago laid down as a maxim in regard to the employment of European officers in the more important branches of the public service in India, that the first selection of young men shall not be made in that country, but shall rest with the authorities in England, while, after the first selection, those authorities shall exercise no interference. The distribution of offices, and all questions of appointment and promotion, are left absolutely to the Governments in India itself. "It is a historical fact" (I am quoting from an official paper) "that the observance of this wholesome rule has more than anything else conduced to the purity of Indian patronage, and to its general freedom from party and political bias." I doubt whether there is any other country where appointments to the highest offices are made with so strong a desire that the men who are the most competent shall be chosen, and where jobbery is so rare.

The Statute of 1793,[1] modified by that of 1861,[2] reserved to members of the so-called Covenanted Service, appointed in England, the right to hold, in ordinary circumstances, the principal civil offices in India under the rank of Member of Council.[3] These offices are enumerated in a Schedule of the latter Act. It includes the offices of the Secretaries to Government, the Head of the Account Department, the Civil and Session Judges, Magistrates and Collectors of Districts in the Regulation Provinces, Joint and Assistant Magistrates and Collectors, Members and Secretaries of the Board of Revenue, Commissioners of Revenue, and others. Persons not belonging to the Covenanted Service can only be appointed, under special circumstances, with the approval of the Secretary of State, and a majority of his Council. These Statutes are still in force, but, as I shall presently show, they have been modified, in one important respect, by other legislation.

Until 1853, the first appointments to the Covenanted Service were made by the Directors of the East India Company by nomination. In that year the nomination system was abolished by Parliament,[4] and the service

[1] 33 Geo. III. c. 52. [2] 24 and 25 Vict. c. 54.

[3] The meaning of the term "Covenanted" is as follows:—The superior servants of the East India Company were obliged to enter into covenants, under which they bound themselves not to engage in trade, not to receive presents, to subscribe for pensions for themselves and their families, and other matters. This custom has been maintained. Successful candidates, after passing their final examinations, enter into covenants with the Secretary of State before receiving their appointments.

[4] 16 and 17 Vict. c. 95.

was thrown open to public competition of all British subjects, without distinction of race. In 1854 regulations for the competitive examinations to be held in accordance with the Act were prepared by a Committee under the presidency of Lord Macaulay, and these, although altered from time to time, have for the most part remained in force ever since. The main object of the competition was declared to be this,—to secure for the Indian Civil Service young men who had received the best, the most liberal, the most finished education that this country affords. The scheme of examination was accordingly made to embrace most of the subjects of the Honour School of the Universities of Great Britain and Ireland. The limits of age for candidates have varied. Since 1892 they have been from 21 to 23. Successful candidates remain for one year on probation, at the end of which time they have to pass a final examination in subjects specially connected with the duties they will have to perform in India. Candidates who are found to have a competent knowledge of these subjects then receive their appointments to the Civil Service of India. Candidates are encouraged by the grant of a special allowance of £100 to pass their year of probation at one of the Universities or Colleges approved by the Secretary of State.

No one now doubts that this competitive system has been successful in its results. It cannot be said that it has given us better officers than the old system of nomination which it superseded, but it has certainly led to no falling off in general efficiency. No country has ever possessed a more admirable body of public servants than the Civil Service of India, and in that term I here include not only its Covenanted members, but those of its other branches, and the numerous military officers who have contributed to its success.

Although the competitive examinations for the Covenanted Civil Service are open to all classes of British subjects, the number of Natives of India who have been successful in obtaining appointments in it has been small. In 1902 it comprised 1067 members, of whom 40 were Natives. Other means have, however, been provided by which they can rise to high office.

Parliament has from time to time enacted measures with the avowed object of giving to Natives of India a larger share in the administration. The Act of 1833[1] declared that "no Native of the said territories, nor any natural-born subject of His Majesty resident therein, shall by reason only of his religion, place of birth, descent, colour, or any of these, be disqualified from holding any place, office, or employment under the East India Company," but while the nomination system lasted, no Native of India received an appointment to the Covenanted Service. The Statute of 1858, which transferred the Government of India from the Company to the Crown, re-affirmed the system introduced in 1853, by which the Covenanted Service was thrown open to the public competition of Englishmen and Natives of India alike; and on the 1st November 1858, when the transfer of the Government was completed, a Proclamation was issued declaring it to be the will of Her Majesty, that "so far as may be, our subjects, of whatever race or creed, be freely and impartially admitted to offices in our Services, the duties of which they may be qualified by their education, ability, and integrity to discharge."

In 1870 another important measure was enacted.

[1] 3 and 4 Will. IV. c. 85.

The Statute of that year[1] declared it to be "expedient that additional facilities should be given for the employment of Natives of India of proved merit and ability in the Civil Service of Her Majesty in India," and that subject to rules to be made by the Governor-General in Council, with the sanction of the Secretary of State, such Natives might be appointed to any of the offices which had been reserved by law to the members of the Covenanted Service.

Thus two roads were opened, by which high office in India may be reached. The road through competition in England is open to Englishmen and Natives alike; that through "proved merit and ability" is open to Natives alone.

It will be understood, from what has been already said, that the system of holding competitive examinations in England was designed with the object of obtaining for the Indian Civil Service, in the best practicable manner, a sufficient number of officers to fill the posts which must ordinarily be held by Englishmen. The Statute of 1870, on the other hand, was designed with the object of giving to Natives of India another means of access to offices for which it was admitted that they might be fit, but from which they were practically, to a great extent, shut out. The declared intention of Parliament was to provide "additional facilities for the employment of Natives of India of proved merit and ability." It was obvious that this could not be done by any fresh system of competitive examination, for not only would such a system have been unsuitable to India, but it could not afford the necessary evidence of that "proved merit and ability" on which the right to employment was to depend. It was recognised by

[1] 33 Vict. c. 3.

Parliament, as the Duke of Argyll, who was then Secretary of State, wrote to the Government of India when announcing the passing of the Act, that "our duty towards the Natives of India in respect of giving them a larger share of employment in the administration of their own country is a duty which must mainly be discharged in India on the principle of careful and cautious selection." He pointed out that if this were wisely done we should gain the advantages of a competitive examination of the best kind, that we must proceed gradually, employing Natives in those offices and places which, in the actual condition of things, the Government of India might determine were really suited to them, and he gave this wise and statesmanlike warning, that "it should never be forgotten, and there should never be any hesitation in laying down the principle that it is one of our first duties to the people of India to guard the safety of our own dominion. . . . In the full belief of the beneficial character of our administration, and of the great probability that on its cessation anarchy and misrule would reappear, the maintenance and stability of our rule must ever be kept in view as the basis of our policy, and to this end a large proportion of British functionaries in the more important posts seems essential."

Nothing could be done towards carrying out the provisions of the Act of 1870 until rules had been made by the Governor-General, and the Act remained almost a dead letter until 1879, when rules were laid down by Lord Lytton with the approval of the Secretary of State. Under these rules, when they came into full operation, a sixth part of the whole number of offices reserved to the Covenanted Civil Service would have been held by Natives of India. In order to give gradual effect to this object the number of young men appointed in England was in 1880 reduced by one-sixth. Appointments were made by selection by the Provincial Governments, tests of qualification being supplied by special examinations, and in 1889, when the system was changed, about sixty Natives of India had obtained offices which had previously been reserved for men appointed in England. In 1902 there were forty Native gentlemen holding important judicial and other offices, who had been appointed under the rules of 1879. Those rules, however, were not found to work satisfactorily, and after much discussion it was decided by the Secretary of State, Lord Kimberley, in 1886, that a Commission should be appointed by the Government of India with instructions "to devise a scheme which might reasonably be hoped to possess the necessary elements of finality, and to do full justice to the claims of Natives of India to higher employment in the public service." In the previous year Lord Kimberley had pointed out in a despatch to the Government of India, that the Act of 1870 was intended by Parliament to be "the primary remedy for any defects that might show themselves in the competitive system established in 1853, and for any inconvenience or injustice which the Natives of India might be shown by experience to suffer through the necessary adaptation of the examination in London to the circumstances of home-born rather than of Indian competitors." The Act, he said, was "a measure of remarkable breadth and liberality, affording an unlimited field of experiment in methods of selection."

The Commission appointed by the Government of India was carefully constituted. Its president was Sir Charles Aitchison, Lieutenant-Governor of the Punjab;

its members, fifteen in number, were chosen from the principal provinces of India, and six of them were Native gentlemen. The Commission visited every province of India except Burma; it examined several hundred witnesses, members of the various branches of the administration, and representatives of the educated classes of the non-official Native and European community. The report of the Commission was unanimous, and this was the more satisfactory, because it expressed the opinion of men chosen from the most intelligent section of the Native public, both Hindu and Mohammedan, and its proposals afforded, in their judgment, a due measure of satisfaction to the reasonable expectations of their countrymen. The main principles of the scheme recommended by the Commission have been carried into effect.

Under the system that was thus established, the Civil Service for the management of the higher branches of the Executive and Judicial Administration is divided into two sections. The first of these consists of an Imperial Service, called the Civil Service of India, recruited by competition in England, under suitable conditions and standards of its own, open, without distinction of race, to all subjects of His Majesty, European or Native. Its numbers are to be no more than will enable it to fill the majority of the highest civil offices, with such number of less important offices as may be sufficient to provide a course of training for the younger men. The second of the two services is a Provincial Service, recruited in each of the chief provinces, under conditions suitable to local circumstances, and consisting almost entirely of Natives of the Province.

Until 1889 the Civil Service was usually, but not

quite accurately, said to consist of two great divisions, the Covenanted and the Uncovenanted Services. The former is now the Civil Service of India. The latter had no existence as a single and separate body. Every public servant, employed in the civil administration, who did not belong to the Covenanted Civil Service or to the Army was an Uncovenanted officer. The term "Uncovenanted Service" is no longer used, its members now forming part of the Provincial Services.

It is a common but complete mistake to suppose that the greater part of the Civil administration in India is retained in the hands of Englishmen, and that Natives of the country are excluded from important posts. Nothing could be farther from the truth. The number of Englishmen in the Civil Service is so small that it is not the least extraordinary fact connected with our Indian dominion that we should be able with such a handful of men to control the administration of so vast an empire.

In 1902, in the whole of British India, there were only 864 civil charges ordinarily, but by no means always, held by members of the Covenanted Service. This branch of the service comprised, as I have already said, 1067 members, but these numbers include officers on leave and others not actually employed. Including military officers in Civil employ and others, about 1200 Englishmen are employed in the civil government of 232 millions of people, and in the partial control of 62 millions more.

Although the highest offices of control, which are comparatively very few in number, are necessarily held by Englishmen, by far the greater and a most important part of the actual administration is in Native hands. Excluding the 864 offices to which I have already referred, and excluding also all posts of minor importance, nearly all of which are held by Natives, there are about 3700 persons holding offices in the superior branches of the executive and judicial services, and among them there are only about 100 Europeans. The number of Natives employed in the public service has gone on constantly increasing, and, with very rare exceptions, they now hold all offices other than those held by the comparatively small body of men appointed in England. Under orders passed in 1879 by the Government of Lord Lytton, which apply to all the offices to which I am now referring, and which are still in force, no person other than a Native of India can be appointed to any post in the executive or judicial services carrying a salary of 200 rupees a month and upwards without the previous sanction of the Governor-General in Council.

All these are facts which have usually been completely ignored in the numerous discussions that have taken place in Parliament and elsewhere regarding the employment of Natives of India in posts of importance.

The organisation of our great and highly efficient Native Civil Service is one of the most successful achievements of the British Government in India. Native officers manage by far the greater part of the business connected with all branches of the revenue, and with the multifarious interests in land. Natives dispose of the greater part of the magisterial work. The duties of the Civil Courts throughout India, excepting the Courts of Appeal, are almost entirely entrusted to Native judges. Native judges sit on the Bench in each of the High Courts. For many years past, Native judges have exercised jurisdiction, in all classes of civil cases, over Natives and Europeans alike. Forty years ago the Native Civil Service was badly paid, comparatively inefficient, and not always trustworthy. In these respects there has been a great change. Nothing in the recent history of India has been more remarkable than the improvement that has taken place in the standard of morality among the higher classes of Native officials. Much of this has certainly been due to the fact that their position and salaries are far better than they were, and that temptations to corruption have been removed, but it cannot be doubted that much has been due to their better education. Another powerful cause has been in silent and constant operation. The Native officials have had before them, through a long course of years, the example of the irreproachable integrity of the Englishmen employed in the higher ranks of the public service. Living in an atmosphere of official uprightness has made Native judges and magistrates upright also.

The salaries given to Natives in posts of importance are very liberal, and they certainly do not err on the side of being too small. With, possibly, the exception of England, there is no country in Europe in which judicial and executive officers receive salaries equal to those given in the Native Civil Service of India.[1]

[1] It is impossible to make any accurate comparison between salaries in countries where the value of money, the conditions of life, and the official duties to be performed are very different. Subject to this warning, which, however, tells strongly in favour of what I have said regarding the salaries paid to Natives of India, I give the following facts. In Bengal a High Court judge, whether English or Native, receives £3200 a year. The salaries of the Native subordinate judges range from £480 to £800, and those of the Munsifs (the lowest class of judges) from £160 to £320. The salaries attached to posts formerly reserved to officers of the Covenanted Civil Service, and now held by Natives in the Provincial Services, vary from £640 to £1600. The salaries of the higher grades in the executive service are not very dissimilar. In Algeria, the highest judicial officer, the First President of the Court of Appeal, who is always a Frenchman, receives £720, with a furnished house. No other judge has more than £400. The Juges de Paix, also Frenchmen, receive from £108 to £160 a year, with furnished houses. The salary of no Mohammedan judicial officer, a native of

Salaries depend on the service to which a man belongs, and are not affected by questions of nationality. Thus, in the Imperial Service, recruited in England, the rules regarding pay, leave, and pension are the same for all members, whether they are European or Native. In the Provincial Services, recruited in India, the conditions of service are fixed on independent grounds. They are regulated in both cases by consideration of the terms necessary to secure the desired qualifications.

I have shown how extremely small is the number of Englishmen in the Covenanted or Imperial Service, which may be said to represent the only permanent English official element in India. The Public Service Commission laid great stress upon this fact, and on the consequent necessity of recruiting that service in a manner which shall always secure the maintenance of English principles and methods of government. They therefore rejected as altogether inadmissible the proposal that competitive examinations for Native candidates should be held in India, as well as in England. That proposal was afterwards revived by a resolution, passed under circumstances on which I will not dilate, by the

Algeria, exceeds £60. The Préfet of Algiers receives £1000, and two other Préfets receive £800 ; each Préfet has also a travelling allowance of £200 a year and a furnished house. No Sous-Préfet has more than £360. In France itself the salaries of the higher judicial and executive officers are smaller than those given to Natives in India. For instance, the First President of the Cour de Cassation receives £1200. In the Cour d'Appel, the salaries of the First Presidents range from £600 to £1000, and of the other Presidents from £300 to £550. In the Tribunaux de Première Instance the salaries of the judges are from £144 to £800. The Juges d'Instruction receive from £115 to £384 ; the Juges de Paix from £72 to £320. In many cases these salaries are supplemented by the grant of furnished houses and by various allowances, usually of small amount. A comparison between the salaries given to officers of the executive service in India and in France would show similar results. The great majority of the Préfets in France, who hold offices second in importance to hardly any in the country, receive less than Native Deputy Magistrates of the higher grades in Bengal.

House of Commons, without any knowledge of the facts or consideration of the probable consequences. It was not, however, acted upon by the Government.[1] The principle on which the Commission insisted is "that the conditions of the open competitive examination in England should be framed with the object of securing candidates trained in the highest and best form of English education. If, under such conditions, Native candidates succeed, they will then, as Lord Macaulay said, enter the service in the best and most honourable way. . . . Natives of India who undergo English training and show the degree of enterprise, strength of character, and other qualities without which success can scarcely be expected in the English examination, are to be welcomed as suitable recruits for the Covenanted Civil Service." No assumption of the possession of such qualities can be made in the case of Natives whose education and training have been entirely Indian. They may be thoroughly competent for many important offices, but we cannot depend on their possessing the habits of thought, the sympathy with English principles of administration, the vigour and the energy which are necessary qualifications for employment in a comparatively small service constituting the *corps d'élite* entrusted with the highest functions of government. There are other considerations of importance. "To attract English youths of suitable education and intellectual promise to the Covenanted Service in India, it is necessary to offer greater inducements in salary, pension, and furlough than would be requisite were the duties to be performed in their own country or under less unfavourable conditions of climate. To compensate successful Native candidates for the incon-

[1] See Chapter V. p. 71.

venience of presenting themselves at the examination in England, and to avoid an invidious distinction, advantages similar to those given to Englishmen are allowed them. But it would impose an unnecessary, and therefore unjustifiable, burden on the revenues of India, to provide larger emoluments or furlough privileges than are sufficient to attract Natives of high education and ability to an examination for the public service in India. This consideration has constantly been kept in view by the Government of India. As education in that country has from time to time qualified, more extensively, Natives to take part in the administration, European agency has been curtailed, and the field for the employment of Natives has been extended. At the same time, the Statute of 1870 has put it in the power of the Government to secure the services of Natives who have given proof of eminent capacity for employment in any of the offices reserved by the Statute of 1861." [1]

The constitution of the Provincial Service involved a reduction and a transfer to Natives of India of one-sixth of the posts reserved by the Statute of 1861 to the Covenanted Civil Service, and there is now "a series of offices, rising from the subordinate classes of administrative business to a very high level of superior and responsible duties, judicial and executive, which throw open a sure and honourable prospect of employment to persons appointed in India, and of continuous promotion to officers of tried merit and ability." [2]

The number of appointments in the Provincial Service thus assigned exclusively to Natives of India is very considerable. Thus, for example, in Bengal, twenty of the offices formerly reserved to the Covenanted Civil

[1] Despatch from Secretary of State to Government of India, Sept. 12, 1889.

[2] Secretary of State to Government of India, Sept. 12, 1889.

Service may now be held by Natives; among them are six Judge-ships, and four appointments of Magistrate and Collector, the highest judicial and executive posts, as I shall hereafter explain, in an Indian district.

Rules have been laid down in each province prescribing the conditions under which the Provincial Government may appoint Natives of proved merit and ability to any of these offices. The first and paramount condition of appointment in every case is proved fitness for the post, and, apart from such fitness, seniority gives no claim. Barristers and pleaders, Natives of India, who have been enrolled for not less than ten years, may, in special cases, be appointed to judicial offices, although they do not belong to the Provincial Service.

The Statute of 1870, under which these rules were made, applied only to the appointment of Natives of India to offices formerly reserved by Statute to the Covenanted Civil Service. It did not allow the appointment of Europeans to such offices, other than members of that service, and in this respect it left untouched the restrictions imposed by the Act of 1861. Under that Act, in the so-called Regulation Provinces of Bengal, Madras, Bombay, and the Province of Agra, no Europeans other than members of the Covenanted Service can hold any of the offices reserved by law to that service unless they are appointed with the special sanction of the Secretary of State and a majority of his Council. The Act of 1861 does not apply to the Non-Regulation Provinces, the Punjab, Oudh, Central Provinces, Assam, and Burma. In those parts of India there has been no restriction on the discretion of the Government to exercise the power of appointment in any way that it thinks fit, and a considerable share in the higher branches of the civil administration has been entrusted to military officers belonging to the Staff Corps, and to others.

In addition to the two branches of the Civil Service that have been described, there is a very large subordinate service in each province, from which promotion to the Provincial Service may be made as a reward for conspicuous merit. This is essentially a Native service, in which practically no Europeans are employed. Some of the offices comprised in it, although inferior in dignity to those belonging to the superior services, are important and well paid.

I have hitherto referred only to the executive and judicial services. In other important branches of the administration there is a division similar to that between the Imperial and Provincial Services, the members being partly recruited in England, and consisting chiefly of Englishmen, and partly of members recruited in India, and mainly composed of Natives. A division of this sort into two branches is made in the departments of Public Works, Telegraph, Police, and Education.

The English branch of the Public Works Department is recruited from officers of the Royal Engineers, from properly qualified officers of the Indian army, and from students at the Royal Indian Civil Engineering College at Cooper's Hill maintained by the Secretary of State. There are four Engineering Colleges in India, and they furnish to Natives of India, and to them alone, access to the higher grades of the Public Works Department. For many of the more important posts, which require special scientific and technical knowledge, it is at present seldom possible to find Natives possessing the necessary qualifications. The superior branch of the Telegraph Department is chiefly recruited from Cooper's Hill College. In the superior branch of the Indian Police

Service a strong European element is necessary, and for first appointments officers are recruited partly through open competition in England and partly in India. The Superior Educational Service is divided into two sections: the Indian Service, to which the first appointments are made by selection by the Secretary of State, and the Provincial Services, which are recruited exclusively in India. For the first, or Indian Service, the Secretary of State usually selects graduates of the Universities of the United Kingdom who have had experience in teaching. For the Forest Service the superior officers are chosen from men who have been successful in a competitive examination in England; this examination is open to all classes without distinction of race.[1]

I shall return, in a subsequent chapter, to the subject of the employment of Natives of India in posts of high importance.[2]

[1] Full particulars regarding the admission to all the principal Indian services—Civil, Military, and Marine,—and tables showing the salaries given to all the chief officers of the administration will be found in the *India List, and India Office List*, published annually.

[2] Chapter XXV.

CHAPTER VII

THE LAWS AND THE ADMINISTRATION OF JUSTICE

The foundations of the existing Judicial System—Regulations and Acts—The Laws and the Courts before the transfer of the Government to the Crown—Regulation and Non-Regulation Provinces—The Indian Law Commission—Lord Macaulay and the Penal Code—The progress of codification—Sir Henry Maine on the Indian Codes—Sir James Stephen on the Indian Penal Code—The establishment of High Courts—The Code of Criminal Procedure—Constitution of the Criminal Courts—Criminal jurisdiction over European British subjects—Changes in the Law in 1884—The codification of the Civil Law—Hindu and Mohammedan Law—The Code of Civil Procedure—Constitution of the Civil Courts—Civil jurisdiction over Europeans—The "Black Act" of 1836—The Native Judges—Defects in the existing Judicial System.

ALTHOUGH much had been done by Warren Hastings to reform and organise all branches of the public service, the main foundations of the existing administration of justice in India were laid in the time of Lord Cornwallis. In 1793 the issue of formal and definite legislative enactments began in the series of laws known as the Bengal, Madras, and Bombay Regulations. Since 1833 the term "Regulation" has ceased to be used; the laws are called, as in England, "Acts." These Regulations and Acts, and such Acts of Parliament as apply to India, constitute, apart from Hindu and Mohammedan law, of which I must speak separately, the civil and criminal law of British India.

Before the transfer of the Government to the Crown, the administration of criminal justice was in an unsatisfactory condition. The police was often oppressive, inefficient, and corrupt. In the greater part of British India, the criminal law and procedure were a jumble based on the old Mohammedan law, eked out and rendered tolerable by the Regulations and Acts of our own Government, by fragments of English law, and by the decisions and instructions of the superior courts. Civil justice was in a worse condition. The law was only to be found in a wilderness of enactments and "circular orders" of the courts, and as the number of these increased they became in course of time, as Sir Henry Cunningham says, "hoplessly unwieldy, entangled, and confusing. Human diligence shrank from the task of searching amid the voluminous provisions of obsolete or repealed legislation for a germ of living law, and grave illegalities not unfrequently occurred, owing to the ignorance which the chaotic condition of the statute-book rendered almost inevitable."[1]

These difficulties were increased by the devotion of the superior Indian courts of that time to technicalities which survived long after they had ceased in England to be seriously mischievous. Even in the later years of the East India Company, the civil courts often seemed to be intended rather for the performance of certain forms and ceremonies than for the administration of justice.

While this was the condition of the law and procedure, the expansion of the empire was in more or less constant progress, and when new provinces were annexed the Government shrank from taking the judicial system of the older provinces as a model. Apart from such

[1] *India and its Rulers*, p. 203.

reasons, when the people had never been accustomed to anything but personal rule of the roughest sort, it was often necessary, on the first introduction of our government, to concentrate executive and judicial authority in the same hands. Government by regular course of law cannot be substituted in a moment for a government of irresponsible power. Moreover, the simpler forms of administration were much cheaper.

It thus came to pass that there were two systems in force—one in the older provinces, and the other in the territories which had more recently come into our possession. The former were called "Regulation," and the latter "Non-Regulation" provinces. A Non-Regulation province was one to which the old Regulations and Acts in force in the Regulation provinces had not been extended, in which fewer officers were employed, and in which executive and judicial functions were, to a great extent, exercised by the same persons. Bengal, the North-Western Provinces, Madras, and Bombay were Regulation Provinces; the Punjab, Oudh, the Central Provinces, and British Burma were Non-Regulation.

It is a mistake, though a common one, to suppose that in the more advanced of the Non-Regulation Provinces, as, for example, in the Punjab, when the Government was transferred to the Crown, the administration was conducted in a rough and ready way, in accordance with our officers' own notions of equity, unhampered by law. The Government of the Punjab, in 1860, really deserved better than the Government of the North-Western Provinces or of Bengal, so far as the judicial administration was concerned, to be called a Government by law. In the former the laws, though simple, were rational, intelligible, and certain; in the latter the system was so chaotic that there was virtually almost no law at all. When the admirable codes of law and procedure, of which I shall presently speak, were introduced, less change had to be made in the system of administering criminal and civil justice in the Non-Regulation than in the Regulation Provinces.

The superiority of the administration which was so marked in the Non-Regulation Provinces towards the close of the East India Company's Government ceased before many more years had passed. Improvement in the older provinces went on rapidly, and, although differences in the form of the administration still exist, the distinctions between Regulation and Non-Regulation Provinces have become much less important than they were. A few comparatively wild tracts alone remain outside the pale of the codes of law and procedure which apply to the whole of British India.

The first steps towards the simplification and improvement of the law were taken in the time of the East India Company, but they led to little practical result before the transfer of the Government to the Crown. In 1833 it was provided by the Act of Parliament which renewed the Company's charter that a fourth member of Council should be appointed, in concert with a Commission, for the purpose of preparing a body of law for British India. Lord Macaulay was appointed member of Council, and the first subject taken up was the preparation of a Penal Code. This work fell chiefly upon Lord Macaulay, and it was completed by him while he was in India, between 1834 and 1838. The code remained as a mere draft for twenty-two years, and it was not until 1860 that it became law. During this interval it was revised from time to time by Lord Macaulay's successors, and especially by Sir Barnes Peacock, the last Chief Justice of the Supreme

Court of Calcutta. In the words of Sir James Stephen, "The long delay in the enactment of the Penal Code had thus the singular but most beneficial result of reserving a work which had been drawn up by the most distinguished author of the day for a minutely careful revision by a professional lawyer, possessed of as great experience and as much technical knowledge as any man of his time. An ideal code ought to be drawn by a Bacon and settled by a Coke."[1]

Although many valuable recommendations for the improvement of the criminal and civil law were made by the Commission of which Lord Macaulay was a member, the Penal Code was the only important result of its labours. In 1853, when the Company's charter was again renewed,[2] a fresh Commission was appointed in England, and this was followed in 1861 by a third Commission, for the purpose of preparing a body of substantive law for India, "and also to consider and report on such other matters relating to the reform of the laws of India as might be referred to them by the Secretary of State." To these two Commissions, whose work continued until 1870, and to the eminent men who since the time of Lord Macaulay have held the office of legal member of Council, we owe the succession of excellent laws which have been passed by the Indian Legislature, and which form chapters in a system of codified law. This system is not yet complete, but there is no country where the work of codification has made greater progress. "British India," writes Sir Henry Maine, "is now in possession of a set of codes which approach the highest standard of excellence which this species of legislation has reached. . . . In form, intelligibility, and

[1] *History of the Criminal Law*, vol. iii. p. 300.

[2] 16 and 17 Vict. c. 95.

in comprehensiveness, the Indian codes stand against all competition."[1]

The Penal Code, which became law in 1860, was followed in 1861 by the Code of Criminal Procedure. Substantially, the whole criminal law of British India is contained in these two laws.

In regard to the merits of the Indian Penal Code no one could speak with higher authority than Sir James Stephen, and in forming his judgment he not only had the advantage of his English experience, but of personal knowledge gained by observation in India. He pronounced it to be "by far the best system of criminal law in the world," and I cannot doubt that he was right in his prediction that it will prove the most remarkable and lasting monument of Lord Macaulay, its author. The authority of his other writings is far from as indisputable as it was, but his Penal Code has (in Sir James Stephen's words) "triumphantly supported the test of experience for upwards of twenty-one years, during which time it has met with a degree of success which can hardly be ascribed to any other statute approaching the same dimensions."

I cannot do better than continue my quotation :—

"The Indian Penal Code may be described as the criminal law of England freed from all technicalities and superfluities, systematically arranged, and modified in some few particulars (they are surprisingly few) to suit the circumstances of British India. . . . It is practically impossible to misunderstand the Penal Code, and, though it has been in force for more than twenty years, and is in daily use in every part of India by all sorts of courts and amongst communities of every degree of civilisation, and has given rise to countless decisions, no obscurity or ambiguity worth speaking of has been discovered in it. . . . Since its enactment it has been substantially the only body of

[1] *The Reign of Queen Victoria*—"India," vol. i. p. 503.

criminal law in force in India, though a few other statutes contain penal provisions on various special subjects. I have already expressed my opinion that the Indian Penal Code has been triumphantly successful. The rigorous administration of justice of which it forms an essential part has beaten down crime throughout the whole of India to such an extent that the greater part of that vast country would compare favourably, as far as the absence of crime goes, with any part of the United Kingdom, except perhaps Ireland in quiet times and apart from political and agrarian offences. Apart from this, it has met with another kind of success. Till I had been in India I could not have believed it to be possible that so extensive a body of law could be made so generally known to all whom it concerned in its minutest details. I do not believe that any English lawyer or judge has anything like so accurate and comprehensive and distinct a knowledge of the criminal law of England as average Indian civilians have of the Penal Code. Nor has all the ingenuity of commentators been able to introduce any serious difficulty into the subject. After twenty years' use it is still true that any one who wants to know what the criminal law of India is has only to read the Penal Code with a common use of memory and attention." [1]

Until 1861 the Supreme Courts established by Royal Charter in Calcutta, Madras, and Bombay exercised original criminal and civil jurisdiction over all classes within the limits of the three Presidency towns. The principal criminal and civil courts established by the Company's Government in the Mofussil (as everything outside the Presidency towns was termed) were called respectively the Sudder Nizámat and Sudder Diwáni Adálat. They were the supreme courts of appeal, and capital sentences were referred to the Nizámat Adálat for confirmation.

In 1861 the Supreme and Sudder Courts were

[1] *History of the Criminal Law*, vol. iii. p. 332. The passages quoted were written by Sir James Stephen in 1881, and they were equally true more than twenty years later.

abolished by Act of Parliament,[1] and in substitution for them High Courts with both criminal and civil jurisdiction were established by Letters Patent, one for each of the provinces of Bengal, Madras, Bombay, and the North-Western Provinces. For parts of India not included in any of those provinces, High Courts were formed under other names by the legislative authority of the Government of India; in the Punjab and in Lower Burma there are Chief Courts with three or more judges; in the other provinces the chief appellate authority is an officer called the Judicial Commissioner. The judges of the High Courts are partly English barristers and partly members of the Indian Civil Service, and there are in each court one or more Native judges chosen from the Native judicial service or from the pleaders. The High Courts in each province are the Courts of Appeal from the District Courts, criminal and civil, and their decisions are final, except in certain cases in which an appeal lies to His Majesty in Council, and is heard by the Judicial Committee of the Privy Council in England.

The High Courts exercise constant supervision over all the subordinate courts. Elaborate returns are regularly sent to them at short intervals, showing in great detail the business disposed of, and, as the evidence in every case has to be recorded, the High Courts are able, by examining the returns, by sending for proceedings, and by calling for explanations, as well as from the cases that come before them in appeal, to keep themselves acquainted with the manner in which all the courts are discharging their duties.

The Code of Criminal Procedure, which became law in 1861, has been recast and amended from time to

[1] 24 and 25 Vict. c. 104.

time, but in essential respects it has not been much altered. It is in force throughout British India, although a few of its provisions have, in some parts of the country, been modified to meet special requirements. Among all the laws of India there is no one more important than this, which regulates the machinery by which peace and order are maintained, and by which crime is prevented and punished. It describes the constitution of all the criminal courts; it defines the powers which each court can exercise; it classifies the offences under the Penal Code or other laws which each judge or magistrate can try; it regulates the manner in which police investigations are to be carried on; the powers of the police to make arrest with or without the warrant of a magistrate; the proceedings to be taken for keeping the peace and for preventing unlawful assemblies; for the removal of public nuisances; the manner in which accused persons are to be brought before the magistrate, in which inquiries and trials are to be held, in which evidence is to be heard and recorded, in which commitments to the superior courts are to be made; it contains rules for the trial of cases with juries and assessors, for the admission of appeals, for the revision of sentences and orders by the superior courts, and for many other matters more or less directly connected with criminal procedure. As Sir James Stephen said in one of his speeches in India, this code is the principal means through which the practical everyday business of governing the empire is carried on. The system which it lays down is complete, efficient, and successful.

In every province there are a certain number of divisions, in each of which a Court of Session is established, presided over by a Sessions judge. Additional, joint, and assistant Sessions judges may be appointed.

Every Sessions division consists of a certain number of districts, to each of which a magistrate, called the District magistrate, is attached. Any number of subordinate magistrates that may be required are appointed in the district, subject to the general control of the District magistrate. In the cities of Calcutta, Madras, and Bombay there are magistrates called Presidency magistrates. To enable a magistrate or judge to exercise jurisdiction over European British subjects, he must be appointed a justice of the peace, and a justice of the peace must himself be a European British subject. There are certain exceptions to this rule. The judges of the High Courts, the Sessions judges, District magistrates, and Presidency magistrates are justices of the peace *ex officio*, and the law does not require that they shall be European British subjects.

A High Court may pass any sentence authorised by the Penal Code or other law. All trials before the High Court are by jury.

A Sessions judge may pass any sentence authorised by law, but sentences of death are subject to confirmation by the High Court. All trials before the Court of Session are either by jury or with assessors.

There are three classes of magistrates :—

(1) Courts of Presidency magistrates, and of magistrates of the first class, in which District magistrates are included; they can pass sentences of imprisonment not exceeding two years, and of fine not exceeding 1000 rupees. In cases in which they are not competent finally to decide, they commit for trial to the Court of Session or High Court.

(2) Courts of magistrates of the second class. They can pass sentence of imprisonment not exceeding six months, or of fine not exceeding 200 rupees.

(3) Courts of magistrates of the third class. They can pass sentences of imprisonment not exceeding one month, or of fine not exceeding 50 rupees.

In certain cases and under certain restrictions, magistrates of the first class, or, if specially so empowered, magistrates of the second class, can pass sentences of whipping.

Excepting the High Courts established by Letters Patent, the judges of which are appointed by the Crown, all the judges and magistrates are appointed by the Provincial Governments.

While the substantive criminal law is the same for all classes, certain distinctions of procedure have always been maintained in regard to criminal charges against European British subjects.[1] Until 1872, excepting in trivial cases, a European British subject could only be tried or punished by one of the High Courts. The result was often a complete denial of justice, for prosecutors and witnesses might have to travel for many hundred miles before a case could be heard. This state of things was remedied in 1872, when the Code of Criminal Procedure was re-enacted, in accordance with the proposals of Sir James Stephen, who was legal member of Council. It was then provided that European British subjects should be liable to be tried for any offences by magistrates of the highest class, who were also justices of the peace, and by judges of Sessions Courts; but it was necessary, in both cases, that the magistrate or

[1] The following definition of the term "European British subject" is given in the Code of Criminal Procedure:—"European British subject means—(1) any subject of Her Majesty born, naturalised, or domiciled in the United Kingdom of Great Britain and Ireland, or in any of the European, American, or Australian Colonies or Possessions of Her Majesty, or in the Colony of New Zealand, or in the Colony of the Cape of Good Hope or Natal; (2) any child or grand-child of any such person by legitimate descent."

judge should himself be a European British subject. A magistrate might pass sentence of imprisonment for three months and fine of 1000 rupees; a Sessions judge might imprison for one year, and fine. Cases requiring severer punishment were referred to the High Court. In the towns of Calcutta, Madras, and Bombay, the Presidency magistrates were justices of the peace by virtue of their offices, and, whether they were Europeans or Natives, they could try and punish European British subjects.

Matters remained in this position until 1883, when the Government of India considered that the law regarding jurisdiction over European British subjects required alteration. Some of the Native members of the Covenanted Civil Service had reached a stage when, in the ordinary course of promotion, they would become District magistrates and judges in the Courts of Session. Under the Code of Criminal Procedure no Native holding one of these offices could try any charge against a European British subject. The Government considered that the law in this respect ought to be altered. It was stated that "the Government of India had decided to settle the question of jurisdiction over European British subjects in such a way as to remove from the code, at once and completely, every judicial disqualification which is based merely on race distinctions."

This declaration, made in uncompromising terms, provoked a storm of indignation on the part of the European community throughout India. It was not confined to the non-official classes, but extended almost equally to the servants of the Government; it reached a point at which it threatened to become a cause of serious political anxiety, and nothing could be more lamentable than the animosities, the prejudices, and bad feeling between Europeans and Natives that were excited.

The controversy ended with the virtual though not avowed abandonment of the measure proposed by the Government. Act III. of 1884, by which the law previously in force was amended, cannot be said to have diminished the privileges of European British subjects charged with offences, and it left their position as exceptional as before. The general disqualification of Native judges and magistrates remains; but if a Native be appointed to the post of District magistrate or Sessions judge, his powers in regard to jurisdiction over European British subjects are the same as those of an Englishman holding a similar office. This provision, however, is subject to the condition that every European British subject brought for trial before the District Magistrate or Sessions judge has the right, however trivial be the charge, to claim to be tried by a jury of which not less than half the number shall be Europeans or Americans. No similar claim can be made by Natives charged with offences, and it is a claim which could not be made by an Englishman in any magistrate's court in his own country. The Legislature virtually declared that the summary powers of the European District magistrate over European offenders should be taken away, not because this was held to be in itself desirable, but because such powers could not be given to a District magistrate who is a Native. While this change was made in the powers of District magistrates, the law in regard to other magistrates remained unaltered. All English magistrates of the first class, outside the Presidency towns, other than the District magistrate, are appointed to be justices of the peace, and they exercise jurisdiction over European British subjects as they did before; but no Native magistrates in similar positions can be appointed to be justices of the peace or exercise such jurisdiction. It may happen, when a charge against a European British subject comes before a District magistrate, that a sufficient number of Europeans and Americans cannot be found in the district to constitute a jury; the case must then, under the orders of the High Court, be transferred for trial to another district where a jury can be formed. Thus a possibility is afforded for the occasional revival of the scandals and denials of justice and hardship which were common before 1872, when the trial of European British subjects could only take place before the High Courts, and complainants and witnesses were liable to be sent away to great distances from their homes. Fortunately this need hardly occur in practice, because the District magistrate, to whom alone these provisions apply, will usually take care to try in his own court no charge against a European British subject, but will transfer it, as he can always do, to one of his European subordinates, whose summary powers of dealing with such cases have not been touched. The law was certainly not changed for the better, but for practical purposes it remained much as it was before Act III. of 1884 was passed. The only other change was that District magistrates trying European British subjects with a jury were authorised to pass sentence of imprisonment, which may extend to six months, or fine, which may extend to 2000 rupees, or both.

It may be feared that the result of all this has been that we must leave to a distant future the hope that the Government of India will be able to place the law regarding jurisdiction over European British subjects on a satisfactory footing.

The codification of the criminal law of British India

is complete. The codification of the civil law is a far more difficult task. Both Hindus and Mohammedans are in possession of great bodies of law, parts of which are believed by them to be of more or less divine origin, containing elaborate instructions on every sort of subject affecting property, inheritance, and the relations of life, and, unless these laws have been modified by British legislation, they are recognised and administered by our courts. Except where Native customs and feelings and prejudices are repugnant to humanity and justice, we are bound to respect them, and the mere suspicion that we desired to interfere with them might be politically dangerous. No one is likely to attempt to codify the Mohammedan law, and there is no single body of Hindu law that is generally recognised; it differs in different provinces, and is constantly modified by local and personal custom. A large part of the substantive civil law is, therefore, and must remain, untouched by our legislation. Those branches, however, both of substantive and adjective law, where these difficulties do not apply, have been dealt with in a comprehensive manner. Codes relating to contracts, negotiable instruments, transfer of property, trusts, easements, and other subjects, evidence, limitation, and a complete Code of Civil Procedure, have already been enacted, and these, with certain exceptions, saving local and other usages and customary rights, are generally applicable throughout British India. Another important chapter of the Civil Code, the Succession Act of 1865, contains the law of intestate and testamentary succession; but the greater part of it applies only to Europeans, East Indians, and some other classes domiciled in British India, and has no application to Hindus or Mohammedans. Subject to the serious exceptions that I have noticed, there is hardly any country in which the laws are contained in so small a compass, in which they are so excellent both in substance and in form, and in which they are so easily intelligible.

The codification and simplification of the law has been one of the greatest reforms of modern times in India. There has been a prevalent but mistaken notion that India has suffered from over-legislation. Speaking generally, the result of recent legislation, apart from that which must always be required to meet current wants of the day, has been greatly to reduce the body of the law, to get rid of obsolete enactments, and to consolidate and simplify the laws in force. Many illustrations of what has been done in this direction might be given. Thus, the law under which the civil courts in Bengal were constituted had formerly to be searched for in thirteen Regulations and Acts scattered over seventy-seven years; now it is to be found in one short Act of thirty-eight sections. I remember Sir James Stephen giving to the Legislative Council in India ocular demonstration of the nature of the process that had been going on, by pointing to a series of huge volumes which contained the law as it used to be, and which the table before him could scarcely hold, and then showing us a few octavo volumes which contained all the existing Acts of the Legislature.

I have referred, for the most part, to those laws only which are in force throughout India, but local conditions vary so greatly that there are many other laws applicable to particular provinces only.

It cannot be said that the practical administration of justice has been as successful in the civil as in the criminal courts, but the improvement has been great since the transfer of the Government to the Crown.

Before 1859 the procedure was extremely complex and technical, the delays and opportunities for corruption and fraud were endless, the Native judges were often very imperfectly educated, and their integrity was sometimes open to grave suspicion. They were so miserably paid that no high standard of honesty or efficiency could be expected. In 1859 the Code of Civil Procedure was enacted, and it has from time to time been amended. It has rendered the procedure of the courts simple and reasonable; the position of the Native judges has been greatly improved; they are now a well-educated class, with a good knowledge of law, and highly paid, and an immense change has taken place in their character and competency.

The constitution of the civil courts, below the High Courts of which I have already spoken, varies somewhat in different provinces; but in Bengal, the Agra Province, Madras, and Bombay, it is substantially uniform. There are usually three classes of courts: those of District judges, Subordinate judges, and Munsifs or Subordinate judges of the second class. The judge exercises a general control over all the courts in his district, and hears certain classes of appeals. The Subordinate judge can try, subject to some restrictions, cases of any value. The jurisdiction of the Munsif varies. In some provinces he can hear suits not exceeding 5000 rupees, in others his powers are more limited. Appeals lie to the High Court from the decisions of the District judge. There are also Small Cause Courts, which decide cases of small amount without appeal. In the Punjab, the Central Provinces, Oudh, and Burma the system is somewhat different, but it need not now be described.

Until the year 1836, European British subjects were under the jurisdiction of the Supreme Courts alone. It was then decided, by Act XI. of 1836, that they should be made amenable to the civil courts of the Company, and that in this respect no distinctions should be maintained between them and the Natives of India. This measure, commonly known as the "Black Act," was received in Calcutta with the furious opposition described by Lord Macaulay, the history of which is familiar to the readers of his life. Lord Macaulay was then a member of the Governor-General's Council, and to him is mainly due the honour of having insisted upon passing this wise and necessary law. The opposition of the Europeans, although to the last degree violent, was virtually confined to Calcutta, and as the number of the English outside the Presidency towns was then comparatively small, the outcry against the Government was less formidable than that of 1883. I quote from a minute of Lord Macaulay the following description of the state of things that then prevailed :—

"Till the passing of Act XI. of 1836 an Englishman at Agra or Benares who owed a small debt to a native, who had beaten a native, who had come with a body of bludgeon-men and ploughed up a native's land, if sued by the injured party for damages, was able to drag that party before the Supreme Court of Calcutta (a distance perhaps of 1000 miles), a court which in one most important point—the character of the judges—stands as high as any court can stand, but which in every other respect I believe to be the worst in India, the most dilatory, and the most ruinously expensive. . . . The expenses of litigation in England are so heavy that people sit down quietly under wrongs and submit to losses rather than go to law, and yet the English are the richest people in the world. The people of India are poor, and the expenses of litigation in the Supreme Court are five times as great as the expenses of litigation at Westminster. An undefended cause which might be prosecuted successfully in the Court of King's Bench for about £8 cannot be prosecuted in the Supreme Court under £40. Officers of the court are enabled to accumulate in a few years, out of the substance of ruined suitors, fortunes larger than the oldest and most distinguished servant of the Company can expect to carry home after thirty or forty years of eminent service. I speak of Bengal, where the system is now in full operation. At Madras, the Supreme Court has, I believe, fulfilled its mission. It has done its work. It has beggared every rich native within its jurisdiction, and is inactive for want of somebody to ruin."

Since 1836 no distinctions of race have been recognised in the civil courts throughout India. At the present time, Native judges preside over the great majority of the courts; excepting the higher appellate tribunals, in which, however, they also have seats, almost the whole administration of civil justice is in their hands. They exercise jurisdiction in all classes of civil cases over Natives and Europeans alike. The Lord Chancellor said in the House of Lords in 1883, as the result of his experience of Indian cases appealed to the Privy Council, that "in respect of integrity, of learning, of knowledge, of the soundness and satisfactory character of the judgments arrived at, the judgments of the Native judges were quite as good as those of the English." In regard to the character and capacity of the Native judges of the High Courts, and of the great majority of those presiding over the subordinate civil courts, the truth of this opinion will not be questioned, and in disposing of business of this sort, superior knowledge of the language and habits of the people often gives to the Native many advantages over the Englishman.

Notwithstanding the great improvement that has taken place, the system under which civil justice is administered cannot be said to be altogether satisfactory. It is often difficult for an ignorant population to understand, and it is too mechanical and rigid in its operation. For the more difficult class of cases it is excellent, but for the mass of the judicial business in India the machinery is too elaborate for the work. In the vast majority of the suits annually brought before the courts, the value of the property or the amount in dispute is very small. I am afraid there is much truth in a remark of Sir Lepel Griffin, that our courts are often more mysterious to an Indian peasant than the maze at Hampton Court to an uninstructed visitor. They are also too expensive. Heavy stamp duties still exist; they were originally imposed partly as a means of obtaining revenue to meet the expenses of the courts, and partly under the unfortunate notion, not yet altogether exploded, that needless litigation is encouraged by making recourse to the courts cheap and easy.

CHAPTER VIII

THE FINANCES AND PUBLIC REVENUES

Responsibility for financial control—Reforms after the mutinies of 1857—Financial decentralisation—Existing system—Growth of the public revenues—Their present amount—Small proportion derived from taxation—The sources and amount of the public income.

I HAVE explained that the final responsibility for the control of the finances of India has been placed by Parliament on the Secretary of State in Council. He cannot divest himself of this duty, but the administration could not be carried on unless the authorities in India itself were invested with ample financial discretion. The Secretary of State has therefore delegated to the Government of India large but strictly defined powers, under which it can sanction fresh expenditure and create new offices of minor importance. This is for ordinary times, but in cases of emergency, when reference to England would cause delay injurious to the public interests, there is practically no limit to the financial powers which the Government of India exercises.

In the time of the East India Company a properly organised system of financial administration hardly existed. After the mutinies of 1857 an immense increase of expenditure took place; their suppression and the restoration of order involved an addition of more than £42,000,000 to the public debt; there was hardly a branch of the administration which was not more or less reorganised, and demands arose for every sort of improvement. The revenues were insufficient, and the financial difficulties of the Government were serious. No reforms were more urgent than the establishment of an efficient system of public accounts and of strict financial control throughout India. This work was begun most efficiently in 1860 by Mr. James Wilson, the well-known Secretary to the Treasury in England, and the first financial member of the Governor-General's Council under the Crown, and it was afterwards actively continued and completed.

In carrying out these reforms it was perhaps inevitable at the outset that the Central Government should retain in its own hands a larger measure of financial control than it would ultimately be expedient that it should exercise. In its anxiety to prevent extravagance it imposed rules of such stringency that no financial authority remained except its own. The whole of the revenues from all the provinces of British India were treated as belonging to a single fund, expenditure from which could be authorised by the Governor-General in Council alone. The Provincial Governments were allowed no discretion in sanctioning fresh charges. They could order, without the approval of the Supreme Government, and without its knowledge, the adoption of measures vitally affecting the interests of millions of people; they could make changes in the system of administration that might involve serious consequences to the State; they could, for instance (and this is a case which actually occurred), alter the basis on which the assessment of the land revenue had been made, but they could carry out no improvements, great or small, for which the actual expenditure of money was required. If it became necessary to spend £20 on a road between two local markets, to rebuild a stable that had tumbled down, or to entertain a menial servant on wages of 10s. a month, the matter had to be formally reported for the orders of the Government of India. No central authority could possibly possess the knowledge or find the time for the efficient performance of such functions throughout so vast a tract of country. The result was complete absence of real financial control, frequent wrangling between the Supreme and Provincial Governments, and interference by the former not only in financial but in administrative details with which the local authorities were alone competent to deal. Under these circumstances, as Sir Richard Strachey wrote at the time, "the distribution of the public income degenerated into something like a scramble, in which the most violent had the advantage, with very little attention to reason; as local economy brought no local advantage, the stimulus to avoid waste was reduced to a minimum, and as no local growth of the income led to local means of improvement, the interest in developing the public revenues was also brought down to the lowest level."

In 1867 definite proposals were made by Sir Richard Strachey for the reform of this system, and in 1871 they were adopted by Lord Mayo, who was then Viceroy. They were based on the principle that there was only one means by which local economy and efficient financial administration could be secured; that each Provincial Government must be made responsible for the management of its own local finances; a certain income capable of expansion by good administration was in each case to be assigned, and, subject to some general conditions, the manner in which that income might be expended on the various branches of the public service was to be left to the Provincial Government to determine.

The system of financial decentralisation inaugurated by Lord Mayo was largely developed during the viceroyalty of Lord Lytton, when I was myself Financial Member of the Council, and a similar policy has been followed by his successors. The effect has been felt throughout the whole system of Indian administration. While no useful powers of financial control have been surrendered by the Central Government, the Provincial Governments have been freed from vexatious interference which weakened their authority and efficiency, and their relations towards the Government of India have become more harmonious. They are entrusted with the management of those branches of the revenue which depend for their productiveness on good administration, and they have now a direct and, so to speak, a personal interest in rendering that management as efficient as possible, because they know that a large portion of any increase of income that may be obtained will be at their disposal for useful expenditure within their own provinces. There has been obtained, at the same time, a stronger and more real power of control by the Central Government than was before possible.

The financial arrangements between the Supreme and Provincial Governments vary in detail, but are in each case similar in principle. Some branches of the public administration are obviously imperial rather than provincial in their nature. The Government of India must, for instance, be responsible for the military defence of the Empire, for payment of the interest on the Public debt, and for the charges to be met by the Home Government. Some departments, such as the Post Office, Telegraphs, and Mint, must be managed throughout India on a uniform system, and are more conveniently controlled by the central authority. Receipts and charges under the following heads are treated wholly or chiefly as imperial—Opium, Salt, Customs, Tributes from Native States, Post Office, Telegraph, Mint, the Public Debt, Railways, and Army Services. The revenues from Land, Stamps, Excise, Assessed Taxes, and other sources, are shared in varying proportions between the Imperial and Provincial Governments. In 1900-01, out of a total gross revenue of £75,300,000, the Provincial Governments were entrusted with the expenditure of £18,600,000.[1] From this income they had to provide for the greater part of the expenditure incurred on the various departments of the civil administration entrusted to them; for the collection of the land revenue, for the courts of justice, jails, police, education, medical services, civil buildings and roads, and for a multitude of other charges.

An arrangement is made under which each Provincial Government receives for a specified term, usually for five years, certain revenues from which it has to meet certain charges. The amount in each case is

[1] Before 1873 the gold value of the rupee was usually not much less than 2s., or one-tenth of a pound sterling, and, until 1886, it was the custom, in the public accounts, to convert rupees into pounds at this conventional rate. Thus, for example, Rs.1000 was shown in the accounts as £100. In consequence of the great depreciation in the gold value of the rupee, to which reference will be made hereafter, it became impossible to maintain this system. The accounts were then shown in tens of rupees, and the symbol officially adopted to represent ten rupees was Rx. The rupee having now permanently obtained an approximate value of 1s. 4d., the public accounts are shown at that ratio in pounds sterling, and the English sovereign is received at the Government treasuries as the equivalent of fifteen rupees. The system of currency actually in force is explained in Chapter XIII. It will be understood that the great changes which have taken place from time to time in the gold value of the rupee, and in the unit adopted for the public accounts, make it almost impossible to draw comparisons, except approximately, between the figures of different periods.

regulated by the estimated requirements of the province. Subject to general rules and conditions, the detailed management of the assigned revenues and services is left to the Provincial Governments; they have the benefit of any economies that they can effect; and they receive either the whole or a share of any increase of revenue which may accrue during the period of the arrangements between them and the Government of India. There is under ordinary circumstances a steady growth in the productiveness of the revenues administered by the Provincial Governments. They have thus, if their management be good, an increasing income to meet increasing demands for material and administrative improvements. When the time for a new arrangement arrives, the Imperial Government takes such share as it thinks fit to claim in the increase of the revenue which has accrued.

I have already quoted the opinion of Sir Henry Maine on these measures of decentralisation. I believe with him that no more important and successful reforms have been made in Indian administration since the transfer of the government to the Crown. But they have not reached their final limits. I have repeatedly insisted that the primary fact lying at the root of all knowledge about India is the immense diversity of the countries and peoples which it comprises, but it is a fact which centralisation of the Government ignores. While our empire was being gradually built up, concentration and centralisation in the administration were often inevitable. Now that it has been constituted on a firm and peaceful basis, decentralisation is an essential condition of progress. The time will come when, in regard to many of the ordinary matters of internal administration, each great province of India will be virtually almost a separate state. Not only will this result be obtained without the sacrifice of any part of that supreme authority of the Central Government which it is essential to maintain, but we shall gain a largely increased measure of political security. No central Government, as Sir Henry Maine has observed, entrusted with the charge of such an unexampled undertaking as the rule of India, can escape serious occasional errors. "Under a centralised Government there is danger of generalising a local mistake. Localised, a mistake can be corrected with comparative ease; it becomes dangerous in proportion to the area of its diffusion."

It has been said with truth that India has become one of the great powers of the world, and so far as her public finances are concerned she has practically no dependence on Great Britain. Financially this country contributes nothing to the maintenance of her Indian Empire. For all the work that she undertakes for India, whether it be for the British army by which India is garrisoned, the charges for the India Office at home, or for any other services, great or small, she receives full payment. Although, in some matters, India has sometimes been treated with scant generosity, there can be no doubt that the general principle which England has laid down has been altogether wise. Great dependencies, if they are to be permanently maintained, must, as M. Harmand has observed, "be organised like true States, provided with all the organs essential to the existence and working of a State, and possessed of all the characteristics which go to form a State, excepting one—political independence. . . . An autonomous administration alone is in a position to develop local resources, to utilise them judiciously, and to administer them with prudence and foresight, to become acquainted with the needs of the subject populations, to legislate in conformity with their special conditions, and to lead them onward to prosperity; in short, to enable these communities to live their own life, to defend themselves with their own unaided resources from the attacks of external foes, and to keep them, when peace is concluded, still attached to the mother-country."[1]

A few figures will show what India has become financially, and they will illustrate the remarkable changes of the last half-century.

In 1840 the gross revenues of India were £21,000,000; in 1857, the year before the assumption of the Government by the Crown, they were £32,000,000; in 1901 they were £75,000,000. Equally remarkable figures might be given for the public expenditure. I will give one example only. In 1840 the gross expenditure on account of all classes of public works in India hardly exceeded £200,000; in 1857 it had risen to nearly £3,000,000; in 1901, including the cost of working the railways and canals, interest on the public works debt and capital outlay on construction, it exceeded £30,500,000.

It is true that few of these figures are really comparable, but I give them to illustrate the magnitude of the changes that have taken place in India. One fact, which I have already mentioned, is sufficient to show that it is only for this purpose that such comparisons can usefully be made. Since 1840, six great provinces, covering some 500,000 square miles, with a population of more than 60,000,000, have been added to the empire.

[1] *L'Inde.* Preface by M. Jules Harmand to the French translation of the first edition of this work.

The immense growth of the revenues has not been due to increased taxation. If, without going back to a time with which no comparisons are possible, we compare the present revenues of British India with those of thirty or forty years before, we shall find that there has been a diminution rather than an increase in the public burdens. The land revenue, measuring it by its incidence on the area assesssed, is everywhere lighter than it was. The salt duties were generally higher than they are now. Customs duties heavier than those now imposed were levied in the former period on almost every article of import and export.

I do not propose to speak of the present financial position of India, of surpluses, deficits, and so forth. It is sufficient to say that there is no great country in Europe, except our own, where that position is, on the whole, so satisfactory. The amount of the public income and expenditure is affected in all countries by circumstances which are constantly changing. But I shall describe the principal sources from which the revenues are derived, and give some of the more important facts connected with Indian taxation, trade, and economical interests.

The gross annual revenues of British India at the present time amount to more than £75,000,000, but it would be a mistake to suppose that this sum represents the amount taken from the people by taxation. The State in India has at all times reserved to itself resources which in other countries belong to individuals, and which render heavy taxation unnecessary. There is certainly no country in the world possessing a civilised Government in which the public burdens are so light. The taxation falling annually on the population of British India is about 1s. 9d. per head. If we were to include the land revenue it would be less than double that amount, but this would be no more reasonable than, in a similar calculation for our own country, to reckon as taxation a large proportion of the rent paid to private landholders.

In 1900-01, out of a gross income of £75,272,000, only £20,816,000 was raised by taxes properly so called; £54,456,000 was derived from other sources. If we compare these figures with the corresponding figures of the English revenues, we find that, in the latter case, in 1900-01, out of a total revenue of £130,385,000, more than £100,000,000 was derived from taxation. In England, taxation supplies five-sixths, and in India not much more than one-fourth of the public income. The difference is really greater, for the Indian figures include not only the receipts of the Imperial Government, but those derived from provincial and local sources of revenue throughout India, excepting taxes raised in municipalities for the service of the towns.

The following table shows the actual gross revenues of India for 1900-01 under each of the principal heads:—

Sources of Revenue.		Receipts, 1900-01.	
		£	£
Gross revenue derived from sources other than taxation	Land revenue . . .	17,503,000	
	Opium	5,102,000	
	Forests	1,298,000	
	Tributes from Native States	578,000	
	Interest	651,000	
	Post Office and Telegraph .	2,253,000	
	Mint	3,173,000	
	Receipts by civil departments and miscellaneous	1,773,000	
	Railways	18,294,000	
	Irrigation works . .	2,556,000	
	Other public works . .	458,000	
	Receipts by military departments	817,000	
			54,456,000
Gross revenue derived from taxation	Salt	5,967,000	
	Stamps	3,343,000	
	Excise	3,937,000	
	Provincial rates . .	2,563,000	
	Customs	3,372,000	
	Assessed taxes . . .	1,322,000	
	Registration . . .	313,000	
			20,816,000
Total gross revenue . .		. .	75,272,000

Many of these receipts do not represent sources of net revenue. In the Indian accounts the gross receipts in every branch of the administration are entered, whether net revenue is yielded or not. For example, the Government lends money to Native States and to various public bodies, and receives from them payments of interest; these are shown among the gross receipts; but on the other side of the account there is an entry for interest on the public debt. Until not long ago the income received from railways and irrigation works was exceeded by the expenditure on those classes of works. Under other heads, representing real sources of net revenue, the expenses of collection are shown on the other side of the account. Thus, for instance, while in 1900-01 £17,503,000 was entered as the gross amount of the land revenue, £2,816,000 appeared under expenditure as charges of collection. There are other receipts called "departmental," but with one or two exceptions I need not refer to them, or to receipts under heads which do not show a net income. Setting off against expenditure receipts of this kind, and deducting from the gross revenues charges of the kind that I have mentioned, the actual net revenue of British India in 1900-01 was £42,343,000.

I shall now explain what are the great sources of revenue.

CHAPTER IX

REVENUES OTHER THAN THOSE DERIVED FROM TAXATION

The land revenue—Its nature described—Its incidence under Native and British Governments—Moderation of assessments—Aurangzíb's revenues—Rates on land.

THE most important of all the sources of revenue in India is the Land revenue, which yields a gross amount of more than £17,000,000 a year, and this is not derived from taxation properly so called.

From time immemorial the ruling power throughout India has been entitled to a share of the produce of every acre of land, unless it has transferred or limited its right, and this share is the so-called land revenue. Regulation XIX. of 1793, by which the Permanent Settlement was created in Bengal, declared that right to be "the ancient law of the country," and it is a right that has never been disputed or doubted.

Mr. Fawcett has described the land revenue of India in a passage which I cannot do better than quote :—

"The Government in India exercises over a great portion of the soil the same rights of property as those which an English landlord exercises over his own estate. The Government in India takes the place of individual landlords, and the cultivators of the soil rent their land from the Government instead of from private landholders. . . . As far as the cultivators of the soil are concerned, it can be a matter of no consequence whatever to them whether they pay a land tax to the Government, or whether they pay rent to private landowners. Hence a land tax is no harder upon the cultivator; nor does this impost cause any loss to the rest of the community. It, therefore, follows that a land tax, so long as it does not exceed a rack-rent, cannot increase the price of products raised from the land, for those who grow products would not sell them cheaper if they paid rent to a private landlord instead of paying the same amount to the Government in the form of a land tax. A land tax consequently differs from all other taxes, for it possesses the excellent quality of providing a large revenue for the State without diminishing the wealth of any class of the community. Those, therefore, are completely in error who quote the aggregate amount of taxation which is raised in India in order to prove how heavily the people of that country are taxed. At least £20,000,000 per annum is obtained in India by the land tax, but it would be as unreasonable to consider this amount as a burden laid upon the people as it would be to consider that the whole rent which is paid to English landlords in this country is an impost levied on the cultivators of the soil."[1]

Instead of giving opinions of my own to the same effect, I will make another quotation from Mr. J. S. Mill :—

"A large portion of the revenue of India consists of the rent of land. So far as this resource extends in any country, the public necessities of the country may be said to be provided for at no expense to the people at large. Where the original right of the State to the land of the country has been reserved, and its natural—but no more than its natural—rents made available to meet the public expenditure, the people may be said to be so far untaxed; because the Government only takes from them as a tax what they would otherwise have paid as rent to a private landlord. . . . It is, of course, essential that the demand of revenue should be kept within the limits of a fair rent. Under the Native Governments, and in the earlier periods of our own, this limit was often exceeded. But, under the British rule, in every instance in which the fact of excessive assessment was proved by large outstanding balances and increased difficulty of

[1] *Manual of Political Economy*, 5th edit., p. 568.

realisation, the Government has, when the fact was ascertained, taken measures for reducing the assessment. The history of our government in India has been a continued series of reductions of taxation; and in all the improved systems of administration the object has been not merely to keep the Government demand within the limits of a fair rent, but to leave a large portion of the rent to the proprietors. . . . Thus, by far the largest item in the public revenue of India is obtained virtually without taxation, because obtained by the mere interception of a payment which, if not made to the State for public uses, would generally be made to individuals for their private use."[1]

Since the middle of the last century the land revenue of British India has more than doubled in amount, but it must not be supposed that the burden on the land has become heavier. The truth is that the process, described by Mr. Mill as "a continued series of reductions of taxation," has gone on during this period without intermission. The increase of land revenue has been mainly due to the extension of the empire. Since 1840 there has been, as I have already noticed, an addition of some 500,000 square miles of territory. In our older provinces the growth of the land revenue has been entirely the result of increase in the area of cultivation and in the value of agricultural produce, and in no instance has it been due to enhancement of the incidence of the Government demand. There has been, on the contrary, in the words of the Government of India, "a progressive reduction of assessments extending throughout the last century, and becoming more instead of less active during its second half."[2]

There has never, so far as our knowledge goes, been a Government in India that has taken so small a share

[1] *Memorandum of the Improvements in the Administration of India*, 1858.

[2] Papers regarding the Land revenue system of British India. Presented to Parliament 1902.

in the profits of the soil as that taken by ourselves. This is true of every province of British India. Under all preceding Governments, and under Native Governments to this day, there has been, in the words of Mr. Thomason, "no other limit to the demand upon the land than the power of the Government to enforce payment and the ability of the people to pay."

Under the system laid down by Akbar, and carried into effect in the year 1582 by the famous settlement of Todar Mal, the sovereign was held to be practising a wise moderation when he fixed his share of the gross produce of the land at 33 per cent, but this was much less than was ordinarily demanded. The Maráthas took at least one-half; and the same proportion was ordinarily assumed to be their proper share by the Governments that preceded us in Madras. The result of minute inquiries made towards the end of the last century showed that the Native rulers in Bengal usually took about 54 per cent. In the Punjab, when we first occupied the province, it was found that the share of the gross produce taken by the Sikh Government was from 40 to 50 per cent. Elphinstone, in his *History of India*, thus sums up the facts in regard to the land revenue under Native Governments: "The sovereign's full share is now reckoned at one-half. A country is reckoned moderately assessed if he only takes one-third"; and in one of his minutes, referring to the Deccan, he says that it seems to have been "the original principle in all settlements for the Government to take half and leave half to the cultivator."

Compare the foregoing facts with the following.

Instead of sweeping off the whole or the greater part of the surplus profit of the land, our Government never takes more than a fixed share, the rate of which necessarily varies, but which only in exceptional cases exceeds 7 or 8 per cent of the gross out-turn. Many of the Native States of Bombay have been surveyed and settled on the system adopted by our Government, and their rates are usually 10 to 15 per cent higher than in the British districts. In the Agra Province, where the basis of the assessment is the rental of the land, and not the gross produce, our Government, at the beginning of last century, took 90 per cent of the rent. We took the same proportion under the permanent settlement in Bengal. In the United Provinces of Agra and Oudh the share of the State is now less than 50 per cent of the rental, an amount estimated to be equivalent to 7·8 per cent of the gross produce.[1]

In Bengal the incidence is much less, but this has been the result of special causes, to which I shall again refer.

Although the demands made upon the land by the British Government are far lighter than those of the Governments that preceded it, it must be remembered that the principles on which our demands have been regulated are altogether different from theirs, and comparisons between the two are misleading. While our policy has been to encourage the growth of private property in land, and to take for the State only a moderate share of the rental or produce, former Governments hardly recognised the existence of such property, and frequently took from the cultivator an amount as large as the full rack-rent which might have been taken by a private landlord, or the whole of the

[1] In regard to the proportions of the gross and net produce now taken as revenue, see the Reports of the Indian Famine Commissioners of 1880 and 1901, and the Resolution of the Government of India, 16th January 1902, on the Land Revenue system of British India, presented to Parliament 1902. See also Chapter XIX. and note on p. 334.

surplus profit after the expenses of cultivation had been defrayed. The cultivator was entitled to subsistence; everything else belonged to the State.[1] This is often the assumption in Native States at the present time. In the words of Mr. J. S. Mill: "Except during the occasional accident of a humane and vigorous local administration, the exactions had no practical limit but the inability of the peasant to pay more." At the same time, when the peasant has no rights of property, and cultivates as a rack-rented tenant, it cannot be assumed that he pays less under our system than he paid before, when there was no private landlord between him and the State.

An interesting investigation was made by the late Mr. Edward Thomas, in his *Revenue Resources of the Moghul Empire*, into the question of the amount of the revenue derived from the land and other sources by the Moghal Emperors; but the materials which he was able to collect were very imperfect. The revenues doubtless reached their highest point under Aurangzíb. Mr. Thomas tells us that two manuscripts in the British Museum, copies apparently of official docu-

[1] "The following maxim is believed to express the ruling idea of the revenue system maintained under the Emperor Akbar:—'There shall be left for every man who cultivates his land as much as he requires for his own support till the next crop be reaped, and that of his family, and for seed. This much shall be left to him; what remains is land-tax, and shall go to the public treasury.'"—Sir E. Buck's *Statistical Atlas of India*, p. 22.

I quote also the following passage from the Report of the Indian Famine Commission of 1901. "We have in the *Ain-i-Akbari* an authoritative contemporary record of what the share and the method of assessing it were in the most highly organised and efficient native administration that India has had. Briefly stated, the land was classed according to its productiveness; . . . a general average out-turn for each kind of crop was struck, 'one third part of which is exacted as the royal dues.' . . . We know that this third part of the produce was constantly exceeded under the pressure of State necessity, or by farmers who contracted for the payment of the land revenue; but apart from such excesses it is manifest that in the Moghul *régime* the land revenue assessments were far more severe than any now enforced by the British Government."

ments, give the land revenue of the empire for 1664-65 at £26,743,000 and £24,056,000.[1] Bernier, about the same time, gave the amount as £22,593,000; his details for the various provinces differ greatly from those in the Museum manuscripts, and Bernier himself describes his list as "ce mémoire que je ne crois pas trop exact ni véritable." Towards the end of the seventeenth century a Venetian physician, Manucci, was employed at the Court of Aurangzíb, and an account of much that he learned there is to be found in Catrou's *Histoire générale de l'Empire du Mogol* (Paris, 1702). A list is given by Catrou, on Manucci's authority, of the amount of the land revenue in each province in 1697, when Aurangzíb's empire was much larger than it had been thirty years before. The total reaches the sum of £38,719,000. Whether these figures represent the demand or the collections is not stated, but no doubt the former is intended. Three manuscripts in the India Office Library give the amount of Aurangzíb's land revenue at sums varying between £34,187,000 and £34,641,000; the years to which they refer are not stated, and although the totals do not much differ, the discrepancies in the details are great.

Considering that the present land revenue of the British Government amounts only to £17,500,000, drawn from a more extensive empire than that of Aurangzíb, the sums said to have been received or demanded from the land by the latter seem at first sight to deserve little credit. It seems, however, by no means impossible that even the largest amount mentioned may be approximately correct, because, as I

[1] In these and the following figures taken from Mr. Thomas, the rupee is assumed to have been equivalent to 2s.

have just explained, no comparisons are really possible between the land revenue of former Governments and our own. The £38,000,000, or whatever may have been the actual amount of Aurangzíb's revenue from land, included not only all that we now take as land revenue, but the greater part of the profit that we leave to private proprietors. For example, the rental of the landholders of Bengal is now probably not less than £12,000,000, of which less than £3,000,000 is taken by the State. If a ruler like Aurangzíb were to take our place, nearly the whole sum would be claimed by him which is now intercepted by the zemindars.[1]

[1] After detailing the revenues of Aurangzíb, Manucci says:—"On est étonné sans doute d'une si prodigieuse opulence, mais il faut considérer que tant de richesses n'entre dans les trésors du Mogol que pour en sortir tous les ans, du moins en partie, et pour couler une autre fois sur ses terres. La moitié de l'empire subsiste par les libéralités du prince, ou du moins elle est à ses gages. Outre ce grand nombre d'officiers et de soldats qui ne vivent que de la paye, tous les paysans de la campagne, qui ne labourent que pour le souverain, sont nourris à ses frais, et presque tous les artisans des villes, qu'on fait travailler pour le Mogol, sont payés du trésor impérial. On conjecture assez quelle est la dépendance des sujets, et par conséquent, quelle est leur déférence pour leur maître."

Although I see nothing incredible in the amount which Aurangzíb's land revenue is said to have reached, the evidence given by Mr. Thomas to support the opinion that the total revenue of the empire was £77,438,000 seems to me altogether insufficient. It is arrived at by doubling the amount of the land revenue, and is based on the following passage from Catrou's work. After enumerating the miscellaneous sources of revenue, he says, on Manucci's authority: "Tout ce casuel de l'empire égale, à peu près, ou surpasse même, les immenses richesses que l'empereur perçoit des seuls fonds de terre de son domaine." Another Italian traveller, Careri, writing in 1695, says: "I was told that the Mogul receives from only his hereditary countries 80 crores of rupees (£80,000,000) a-year." There is apparently no other authority, excepting these general statements, for the conclusion that the total revenues of Aurangzíb approached £80,000,000, and I cannot think that they deserve credence. This question of the amount of the revenues of the Moghal Emperors has been reconsidered by Sir W. Hunter in his *Indian Empire* (3rd edition, 1893, pp. 357 and 547). His conclusion is that during the last century of the Moghal empire the average net land revenue demand was probably about £32,000,000. An elaborate discussion of the subject will also be found in Mr. Stanley Lane-Poole's *Aurangzíb* (Rulers of India Series). His conclusions are that in 1700 A.D. the Moghal land revenue was as much as

Although the land revenue of India is not derived from taxation properly so called, but is a portion of the rent or produce reserved by the State, in accordance with immemorial custom, the land is not entirely exempt from taxation. It is liable to certain rates which vary in the different provinces, but which are everywhere light. They are mainly applied to local purposes, such as the construction and maintenance of roads, schools, hospitals, and dispensaries.

The subject of the manner in which the land revenue is assessed and administered is one which I shall notice in a subsequent chapter.[1]

£43,000,000. I have left my own remarks on this subject unaltered, as they stood in the first edition of this work, because they seem to me to be as good an approximation to the truth as with our present information can be given. No confidence can, in my opinion, be placed in particular figures which purport to represent the amount of the Moghal revenues.

[1] See Chapter XIX.

CHAPTER X

REVENUES OTHER THAN THOSE DERIVED FROM TAXATION (*continued*)

The opium revenue—Its amount—Mr. Batten on the opium question—Introduction of opium into India—State monopoly under Moghal Government—Existing system—Value of Indian poppy crops—Alleged reasons for suppression of opium trade—Opium in China—Wars with China—Chefoo Convention—Effects of consuming opium—Consumption in China and India—Society for suppression of the opium trade—Its misrepresentations—Consumption by Sikhs and Rájputs—System of excise—Royal Commission of 1893—Forests—Tributes from Native States—Post office—Telegraphs.

NEXT to the Land revenue and Salt, the most productive source of the public income in India is Opium. The gross amount of the opium revenue in 1900-01 was £5,102,000. The average net annual revenue shown under that head for the five years ending with that year was £2,540,000, but to this must be added revenue obtained from opium consumed in India and credited under the head of Excise. It consists of duty and license fees for the sale of the drug, and an acreage tax on poppy grown in the Punjab. The average receipts from these sources for the same period were £668,000, making a total average net revenue from opium of £3,208,000. The seasons for the greater part of this quinquennial period were abnormally bad, and the actual net revenue for the year 1900-01 exceeded £4,000,000.

Questions connected with the system under which the Indian Government derives this great revenue have been the subject of so much discussion in this country, and of so much ignorant, although honest misrepresentation, that it is desirable to state somewhat fully what I believe to be the truth. I am fortunate in being able to do this with an authority and accuracy not dependent on my own knowledge and experience alone. No more complete account of the facts regarding opium in India has ever been made public than that contained in a paper read by Mr. G. H. M. Batten, formerly of the Indian Civil Service, before the Society of Arts in March 1892, and Mr. Batten has been good enough to make the following abridgment of his paper, and to allow me to insert it in this chapter of my work. When necessary, the figures have been corrected to bring them up to date:—

"Apart from moral considerations, the opium question, so far as India is concerned, is generally discussed as if it were one affecting only the public resources of the Indian Administration, but it is much more far-reaching. The amount of revenue realised is but a part and not the greater part of the actual pecuniary value of the poppy crop and its products, while the well-being and happiness of hundreds of thousands of the people of India would be greatly affected by its extinction.

"India is essentially an agricultural country, and nearly the whole of its exports consist of products of the soil. One of the most important and valuable of these products is the opium-yielding poppy. It is impossible to state with accuracy when this plant was first introduced into India. There is little record of its early history, but it is known that the Mohammedans had succeeded, in the fifteenth century, in introducing the cultivation of the poppy into Cambay and Malwa, and that when the Emperor Akbar, in the latter half of the next century, established the Moghal Empire over Central India, he found Malwa opium a characteristic product of that country. He and his successors regarded opium as of necessity a State monopoly. There is ample evidence to prove that a large trade had been going on in opium between India and surrounding countries long before the East India Company, in 1773, undertook the supervision of the manufacture of opium in Bengal, Behar, and Orissa.

"The Company, in fact, inherited from the Moghal Government this important and legitimate source of revenue on an article of luxury which India had shown itself capable of producing in high perfection, and for which there was a large demand both in and out of that country. At first they continued the system of farming the exclusive right of opium manufacture, but this was found to entail many abuses. Amongst them was the pressure brought by the contractors, in spite of the most stringent regulations to the contrary, on the cultivators, whom they forced to carry on the cultivation, and whom they cheated in various ways. It also led to the adulteration of the drug and its illicit sale. The consequences were so injurious to the revenue that, in 1797, the contract system was abandoned, and the Government assumed the monopoly of manufacture through its own agencies, a system which has remained in force until the present day. There was, indeed, at that time, no practicable alternative. The strongest opponent to the system of Government manufacture would hardly contend that the growth of the poppy and the manufacture of opium should have been left free and unrestricted, as that would infallibly have led to a great increase in the produce of the drug, and probably to its deterioration. On the other hand, if it ever entered into the conception of the Court of Directors to suppress, in the interests of morality, the cultivation of the poppy in the territories then in their possession, it is doubtful whether they would have had the power in those times to have done so, and it is certain that they could not have controlled the production of the vast poppy-growing tracts outside those territories in Malwa, Cambay, and elsewhere. The only result would have been that the opium consumers in India would have been supplied from sources outside British territory, and that the export trade would have been transferred to ports other than British. It would certainly have been impossible in those days to establish a Customs line to prevent the entry of opium into the Company's possessions. The Company would have sacrificed its revenue, and no one would have been benefited except the people of the territories outside the Company's possessions, at the expense of those within them.

"The State monopoly continues to be administered by the Bengal Government, although its operations now extend into the United Provinces of Agra and Oudh. Under it, no person may cultivate the poppy except with a license from the Government, and every cultivator is bound to sell the opium produced from his crop to the Government, in whose two factories, at Patna and Ghazipur, it is manufactured into the opium of commerce. A portion of the manufactured opium is retained for consumption in India through vendors licensed by the Excise Department, and the remainder is sold monthly, by auction, in Calcutta to merchants, who export it. The Government prescribes rules for the cultivation of the poppy, the manufacture, possession, transport, import or export, and sale of opium, and any contravention of such rules is subject to stringent penalties, which may extend to imprisonment for one year or fine of 1000 rupees, or both. Poppy illegally cultivated, and opium the subject of any offence against the law, is liable to confiscation, together with the vessels, packages, and coverings in which it is found, and their other contents, and the animals and conveyances used in carrying it.

"Like most crops, the poppy is subject to wide seasonal fluctuations, which formerly greatly affected the market prices of opium, led to speculation and gambling amongst the buyers for export, and caused corresponding uncertainty in the Government revenue. When, owing to the shortness of the supply, the price in Calcutta rose high, the direct effect was to stimulate the production of other opium competing in the foreign market with the Bengal drug, and amongst these the native production of China. Thus—and I would call particular attention to this fact, as having an important bearing on the question before us—the diminution of the supply of Indian opium to China was an incentive to the extension of poppy cultivation in China. To remedy the evils thus arising from the uncertainties of the seasons, the Government decided, thirty-five years ago, to limit the sales of opium in Calcutta to a quantity which would permit the formation of a reserve stock in plenteous years to meet deficiency in years of scarcity.

"Recognising the fact that the Chinese demand a large supply of opium, and that to whatever extent India was unable to satisfy that demand, it would be met, either by increase of the produce in China itself or by increased imports from other countries, the

Government of India has thought it right, in the interests of the people of India, to shape its measures so as not to lose the natural advantages India possesses in the superior quality of its produce. Any one familiar with the records of the Government of India relating to this subject, must admit this is a fair representation of its policy and motives, and that nowhere in those records can be found any indication of a desire to stimulate the consumption of opium by the Chinese.

"In pursuance of this policy, the Government yearly regulates the extent of the poppy cultivation, guided chiefly by the market prices and the stock of opium in hand. No one is forced to grow a crop of poppy against his will. The sole inducement is the price offered by the Government for the produce. Since 1895 this price has been 5 rupees a seer, which is exactly equivalent to 2½ lbs. troy. The Government makes advances, not bearing interest, before the crop is sown, and from time to time during its progress, thus saving the ryots from the exorbitant demands of the village money-lender. The crop, which is sown in the autumn and gathered in the spring, succeeds an autumn crop usually of Indian corn. The yield of opium per acre varies. For the five years ending 1900-01, the average produce per acre was 12·7 lbs. avoirdupois, which, at 6 rupees a seer, gave the cultivator a gross return of nearly 37 rupees per acre. In addition to this, he receives payment for the poppy flower petals and the stalks and leaves, which are used in the factory for packing the opium cakes. The total average annual payments by the Bengal Government to the poppy cultivators exceed £1,500,000.

"Besides the produce purchased by the Government, the seeds of the poppy are an important article of consumption and commerce. They are eaten parched, or employed as a condiment in the preparation of food; but perhaps their chief use is for the expression of oil, for which purpose they are not only largely used in India, but are exported in considerable quantities, chiefly to Belgium, France, and the United Kingdom. The average produce of seed per acre, after deducting what is required for sowing, is stated to be about 260 lbs., yielding by native processes from 80 to 100 lbs. of oil. This oil is edible, and is used largely in Europe, either as a substitute for, or adulteration of, salad oil. It is also used for illumination, mixing with paints, soap, and varnish-making. The oil-cake is eaten by the poorer classes and by cattle, being rich in nitrogen. The young seedlings, which are removed at the first weedings of the crop, are sold and eaten as a salad. These by-products of the poppy crop are perfectly free from opium.

"In spite, therefore, of the labour entailed in the culture of the poppy, which requires frequent watering, and in spite of the vicissitudes of the season, which greatly affect this crop, the cultivation is popular, and the refusal of licenses is looked upon as a grievance by the ryots, as well as the landowners to whom they pay their rent.

"As I have already stated, the cultivator is bound by law to deliver the whole of the opium produced to the Government agents. It is manufactured at the factories at Ghazipur and Patna into the opium of commerce, under the supervision of the scientific experts who are employed by the Government, and is then sent to Calcutta, where it is sold for export at auction by monthly instalments. The greatest care is taken to preserve the purity of the drug and the uniformity of its consistence. It is owing to this care, added to the natural advantages of soil and climate, that Indian opium has maintained its high reputation in the Chinese market, where it is admitted by the practical test of price to be far superior to the drug produced in China. Sir Robert Hart, the Inspector-General in China, in a report written in 1881, states that 'the native product sells for one-half of the price obtained for the foreign drug.' In determining the number of chests to be annually manufactured and sold, the Government is guided principally by the state of the reserve stock, the aim being to keep up a reserve equal to half a year's supply. It is also guided, as I have already stated, by the prices obtained at auction. If the prices rise much, production in China and Persia is stimulated, and it is necessary to increase the production in India to maintain its market; on the other hand, if the prices fall low, and opium becomes cheap, consumption is stimulated, and the production has to be restricted. The object of the Government, as I have explained, is to maintain, so far as possible, uniformity in the price, and thus to avoid fluctuations in the market and in the revenue.

"The average annual auction sale proceeds for the five years ending 1900-01 were £3,234,700; the annual average number of chests sold was 40,890, each chest containing 140 lbs. The price per chest was thus a little under £80. In the first four of these years the crops were abnormally bad, and the average gross annual revenue may be taken at £4,000,000. This is a considerable falling off from the revenue of former years, and is ascribed to the extension of cultivation in China and to the improvement in that country of the preparation of the drug.

"The Bengal Government supplies the Excise Department not only in Bengal, but also in all the other Provinces, except the Madras and Bombay Presidencies, with opium for consumption in India. The average receipts from this source amount to about £150,000 a year. The opium is sold to the consumers through licensed vendors, to whom it is supplied at an enhanced price, and who have to pay fees for the licenses to vend. The average receipts by the Local Governments from this source amount to about £650,000 a year.

"The declared value of the poppy seed exported from Bengal on the average of the five years ending 1900-01 was £163,400. In 1900-01 it amounted to £207,700.

"Summing up these figures, we obtain the following result for the Bengal poppy crop:—

Auction sale proceeds on opium for export .	£4,000,000
Excise opium credited to Opium Department .	150,000
Receipts of Provincial Governments from the vend of Excise opium	650,000
Value of poppy seed exported . . .	200,000
Total .	£5,000,000

"In order to arrive at the ultimate annual value of the Bengal poppy crop, we must add several items which cannot be precisely estimated. These are the profits to Indian merchants and shippers on the opium exported, the profits to the Indian vendors of Excise opium, the value of the poppy seed consumed in India as seed-oil or oil-cake, and of the young plants used as food, and finally, the value of the illicit opium, which, in spite of all precautions, the cultivators are able to pass into consumption. On a moderate estimate, the value of this large trade cannot be taken at less than £2,000,000, bringing up the annual total value of the Bengal poppy crop to over £7,000,000.

"The territory in which this crop is produced may be described as a belt of country between 500 and 600 miles in length, with an average breadth of 180 miles, running north-west and south-east, between the 78th and 85th parallels of longitude, and the 24th and 29th parallels of latitude. The total area may be taken at about 100,000 square miles, lying in the Province of Behar (Bengal), and in the United Provinces of Agra and Oudh. The average area cultivated with poppy for the five years ending 1900-01 was 586,400 acres, or less than one per cent of the whole tract referred to, and this for only half the year, as another crop is almost invariably obtained from the same land during the other half. In the year 1900-01 no fewer than 1,477,000 cultivators were employed on the crop.

"The only other province in British India where the poppy is allowed to be cultivated is the Punjab. It is there grown under license in nearly every district. The cultivator may dispose of his poppy crop standing to license-holders, who extract the opium; or he may extract the opium himself, and dispose of it, or of the produce, in the shape of poppy heads, to licensed vendors. The poppy heads are used as an infusion, forming a poppy tea, which is drunk by the Sikhs, who are forbidden by their religion to use tobacco in any form. The public revenue derived from the opium crop is included in the Excise receipts of Provincial Governments shown above. The profits to the cultivators and vendors are difficult to estimate. For the four years ending with 1900-01 the average area under poppy cultivation was 6258 acres, and the average production of opium was 106,300 lbs., besides poppy heads and other by-products.

"Outside of British India, the cultivation of the poppy is confined to certain native States in Central India and Rajputana, and the territory of the Gaikwar. The opium there produced is known by the generic name of Malwa opium. There are no trustworthy statistics showing the acreage under poppy, or the total quantity of opium produced. After providing for the home consumption within the native States, which must be a very large quantity, as the habit of consuming opium there has been long established and is widespread, the remainder is consumed in those parts of British India not supplied with Bengal opium, also in Hyderabad and Mysore, or is exported by sea to China, the Straits Settlements, etc.

"The importation of Malwa opium into British territory is

subject to very stringent regulations. Previous to the year 1831, by separate treaties with the Native States, the British Government reserved to itself a monopoly of Malwa opium, which was purchased by the British Resident at Indore, and sold by auction either at Bombay or Calcutta. But in that year it was deemed advisable, chiefly on account of the large quantity of opium smuggled to the Portuguese settlements on the coast, to relinquish the monopoly (which involved much unpalatable interference in the internal affairs of the Native States), to open the trade to the operations of private enterprise, and to substitute, as a source of revenue, the grant, at a specified rate of duty, of passes to cover the transit of Malwa opium through British territory. The present rate on opium for foreign export is Rs.500, or £33 : 6 : 8 a chest.

"All opium transported out of the Native States of Central India, Rajputana, and Baroda, has to be weighed and tested at scales established at convenient places in those States under the superintendence of officers of the British Government. The transport is permitted only under passes granted on payment of the duty and by certain specified railway routes. The average number of chests that passed the scales in the five years ending 1900-01 was 24,155, and the average number exported by sea from Bombay was 23,310, the average declared value of which was £1,926,270. The remainder of the Malwa opium leaving the Native States—about 875 chests—is consumed in India, chiefly in the Bombay Presidency; but the Madras Presidency, Hyderabad, and Mysore are also supplied from this source, and some goes to the Punjab. The value of these 875 chests may be taken at about £7000, making a total value, for 24,155 chests, of £2,096,000. To this must be added, as in the case of the Bengal opium, the profits of the merchants and shippers exporting the opium, and of the vendors in India, say nearly £1,000,000.

"The average annual exports of poppy seed from Bombay are valued at £250,000. Thus, the total annual value of the Malwa opium brought into British territory, and of the Malwa poppy seed exported from India, cannot be less than £3,250,000.

"There remains to be considered the value of the Malwa opium consumed in the Native States of Central India, Rajputana, and Baroda; also the value of the Malwa poppy seed not exported from India, and of the other by-products of the crop. As

I have already said, there are no data available for ascertaining or estimating the acreage under poppy cultivation in the Native States in question, much less for determining the quantity and value of the whole products of that crop. The population of those States is more than 20,000,000. We know that a considerable proportion of the people of these States has, for centuries, been in the habit of consuming opium, we know that the restrictions placed on the cultivation of the poppy, and on the vend of opium in British India, do not exist in these States, and we know that a vast quantity of opium is smuggled out of them. If we estimate the value of the crop, exclusive of the value of the product licitly exported, at £2,000,000, it will certainly be under the real value.

"The total annual value of the poppy crops in India may thus be estimated to be as follows :—

Bengal crop	£7,000,000
Malwa crop, licitly consumed in British India and exported by sea . . .	3,250,000
Malwa crop, consumed in Central India, Rajputana, and Baroda, and smuggled thence	2,000,000
Total .	£12,250,000

"This, less cost of production and transport, is divided between the producers and manufacturers, the landlords, the British and native administrations, the middlemen, merchants, shippers, vendors, etc., of India, and is paid by the ultimate consumers, principally Chinese.

"This is a very moderate estimate of the sum India is asked to sacrifice annually by suppressing her opium trade. The demand for this sacrifice is made not by the people of India, not by the people of China, not by the responsible administrators of those countries, but by an irresponsible party of philanthropists seeking to obtain their ends by the despotic action of the Parliament of the United Kingdom, in which India has no representatives.

"What are the reasons put forth for demanding the destruction by a foreign country of a valuable Indian industry which, besides satisfying an internal demand in India itself, provides one-tenth of the whole export trade of merchandise from India?

"The basis of this demand is the hypothesis that, except for medicinal purposes, the use of opium is wholly pernicious, that it demoralises and ruins, body and soul, the consumer, and that it produces no countervailing benefits which for a moment can be compared with the evils it causes.

"A second reason given is that the English people have created the demand for opium by the Chinese, that they have compelled the importation of Indian opium into China by force of arms, and that they are, therefore, morally responsible for the asserted degradation of the Chinese from the use of this drug.

"If there is one fact more certain than any other connected with this question, it is that the people of China had used opium for centuries before the people of England had any voice in the affairs of India. A valuable *Historical Note on Opium in China* has recently been drawn up by Dr. Edkins, of the Chinese Customs Service, and published by order of Sir Robert Hart, the Inspector-General of the Imperial Maritime Customs of China. From this Note it appears that opium was first brought to China by the Arabs early in the eighth century, and it is frequently mentioned by Chinese writers of that time.

"But, it is said, the English have forced Indian opium on the Chinese. The war with China, which terminated in 1842, has been called the Opium War, and its immediate cause was no doubt the seizure and destruction by the Chinese of a large number of chests of Indian opium belonging to English merchants. But contemporary history shows that the real objections of the Chinese were not to the import of opium, but to the necessity of paying for it in silver. Commander J. Eliot Bingham, who served in that war, and wrote its history, shows that the imports into China of opium, metals, cotton, etc., exceeded the exports of tea, silk, etc., by £2,500,000. The Chinese held the economic fallacy that this state of things was injurious to their country, as it drained away their silver. The Imperial edicts enlarged more on the abstraction of their sycee silver than on the injury from opium to the morals of the people.

"But to whatever extent the wars with China were connected with the smuggling of Indian opium, it is certain that since 1858, when the Treaty of Tientsin was signed, the Chinese Government has had a perfectly free hand in the matter of the importation of opium. By that treaty certain commercial concessions were arranged, which included the legitimatising of the import of opium, subject to a duty being levied thereon. But in the treaty itself there was no mention of, or allusion to, the opium trade. Lord Elgin wrote that he intentionally abstained from urging any treaty recognition of that trade. The preparation of the tariff devolved on Mr. Lay, the Chinese Secretary to Lord Elgin's special mission, at the desire of the Chinese no less than that of Lord Elgin. Mr. Lay, in a letter to the *Times* of the 22nd October 1880, wrote:—

"'When I came to "opium," I inquired what course they proposed to take in respect to it. The answer was, "We have resolved to put it into the tariff as foreign medicine." I urged a moderate duty in view of the cost of collection, which was agreed to. This represents, with strict accuracy, the amount of "extortion" resorted to. . . . The Chinese Government admitted opium as a legal article of import, not under constraint, but of their own free will deliberately.'

"In the *Times* of the 25th of same month, a letter appeared from Mr. Laurence Oliphant, who was secretary to Lord Elgin's Mission, in which he confirmed the statement made by Mr. Lay. He says he, with the Commissioner appointed by the Chinese Government, went through the tariff elaborated by Mr. Lay with the subordinate Chinese officials:—

"'When we came to the article "opium," I informed the Commissioner that I had received instructions from Lord Elgin not to insist on the insertion of the drug in the tariff, should the Chinese Government wish to omit it. This he declined to do. I then proposed that the duty should be increased beyond the figures suggested in the tariff; but to this he objected, on the ground that it would increase the inducements to smuggling. . . . I trust that the delusion that the opium trade now existing with China was "extorted" from that country by the British Ambassador may be finally dispelled.'

"In 1876, an Agreement, called the Chefoo Convention, was arrived at between the Governments of Great Britain and China, in which the British Minister, Sir Thomas Wade, promised to move his Government to make certain special arrangements as to the import of opium. These arrangements were finally carried out by an additional Article, signed at London in 1885. By this Article an addition to the import duty of 30 taels per chest was agreed to. It amounts to a further 80 taels per chest, and frees the opium from any further duty or tax whilst in transport in the interior, being, in fact, a composition of the *likin* tax. When the package is opened at the place of consumption, it is subject to any tax which may be levied on native opium.

"The receipts of the Chinese Government from the import of opium average 8⅔ millions of Haikwán taels a year. The great appreciation which has taken place in the value of gold has, of course, lowered the exchange value of the silver tael, and this, no doubt, affects China in the payment of debts to gold standard countries; but for internal purposes the value of the tael has been little affected. This large revenue, equal now to about £2,000,000, and forming more than one-third of the entire Customs revenue of China, is collected by the department presided over by Sir Robert Hart—a department admirably administered, and scrupulously accounting for its collections to the Imperial Government at Pekin. The *likin*, for which the payment of 80 taels per chest is a composition, was formerly collected as transit duties by the local Chinese authorities through whose provinces the opium passed. The Imperial Government received only such portion of the collections as they could manage to get out of the Provincial Governments, who, on the other hand, strove to retain as much as possible. The arrangements under the Chefoo Convention are, therefore, very advantageous to the Imperial Government at Pekin, which cannot afford to dispense with this large revenue derived from the import of opium.

"It is clear that Indian opium is now imported into China with the full approval and consent of the Chinese Government. It is equally certain that Great Britain would never fire a gun to force Indian opium on the Chinese.

"I have already referred to the early history of opium in China. Sir Robert Hart said, in 1881, that 'Native opium was known, produced, and used long before any European began the sale of the drug along the coast.' The production of opium in China has gone on steadily increasing, and has been encouraged by the restrictions and heavy taxation placed on Indian opium by the Government of India. All travellers and the Consular authorities testify to the vast areas under poppy cultivation. The produce of native opium has been estimated to be from three to ten times the quantity of the imported drug. Chinese opium is now much better prepared than it formerly was, and it has practically driven Indian opium out of the markets of Northern China, and, so far as we know, it supplies the bulk of the demand in the inland and western provinces. The local drug is much cheaper than imported opium. The Burma revenue officers are constantly striving to prevent importation of cheap Chinese opium into Burma.

"Of the numerous recent travellers in China, I will quote only Mr. Hosie, a Consular Agent, who, in 1883, travelled from February to June through the provinces of Sse-ch'uan, Yünnan, and Kueichon. His diary has almost daily references to the extensive poppy cultivation through which he passed. In many places it was the principal crop. With regard to the Government prohibition, he writes :—

"'I have noticed in several places west of the provincial capital a proclamation dated the 9th November 1882, by the Governor-General of Sse-ch'uan, prohibiting the cultivation of the poppy, and enjoining a more extended sowing of the cereals. It was always more or less mutilated, whether intentionally or not I cannot say. At all events, poppy was frequently growing on the side of the road opposite to that on which the proclamation was posted. It is one thing to issue instructions, another to see that they are carried out.'

"The prohibition is evidently in the nature of a pious opinion, meant for show and not for use.

"Mr. Hosie, writing on the 5th June 1883, says :—

"'It seems superfluous daily to mention poppy as a crop. To-day, however, it was exceedingly prominent, growing everywhere on the hill-sides and Bottom lands. Large rice bowls heaped with the drug were exposed at the door of almost every shop in every hamlet and village, not a bowl here and there, but several, eight being a very common number. In fact, the whole country reeks and stinks of opium.'

"With these facts before us, how can it be maintained that the consumption of opium in China can be affected by the imports of Indian opium, except in so far that these supply a purer and more expensive article, the suppression of which would lead to larger products of native opium of inferior quality?

"I could multiply to any extent the evidence of the extensive cultivation of poppy in China, but I think I have said enough to show that it is a fact which cannot be denied.

"I will now proceed to discuss the crucial question as to the effects of consuming opium, of which there are various forms. In China the usual form is by what is called smoking opium. In India it is eaten. In Europe it is drunk in the form of laudanum, or a tincture prepared in spirits of wine. We must consider what is the effect on the average consumer, and not confine our attention to the cases of those persons only who indulge in the habit to excess, cases which I shall show are exceptional.

"It may be safely said that all but a very small percentage of the people of this country are absolutely ignorant of the normal effects of the habit of using opium. The popular ideas on the subject which prevail are largely due to De Quincey, who, in 1822, published the confessions of an English opium-eater. Many have read this fascinating work, and many more have heard of it, and look upon De Quincey as the 'shocking example' of such a habit. But I venture to say that his confessions completely disprove the allegations put forward by the opponents of the use of the drug. He was a man of a naturally delicate and nervous constitution, whose early life was subject to great physical hardship and exposure. He was driven at the age of nineteen by excruciating rheumatic pains to the use of opium, in which he indulged during the rest of his life, for a long period in excessive quantities. He married, and had a large family of sons and daughters. He retained his mental qualities unimpaired, led an active literary life, was one of the most brilliant, accomplished, and intellectual writers England has produced, and lived to the good age of seventy-five years. De Quincey's experiences are quite consistent with the assertion that the moderate use of opium, by a person in good health, may be continued for years, not only without any harmful effects, but with absolute benefit.

"Let us now see what is the effect on the Chinese, who resort to the more innocuous habit of smoking opium. In February 1882, three lectures were given in St. James's Hall by the late Mr. William Brereton, and were subsequently published under the title, *The Truth About Opium*. Mr. Brereton lived and practised as a solicitor for nearly fifteen years in Hong Kong, where he had daily experience of the custom and effects of opium-smoking. He was in no way engaged in the opium trade, and had no pecuniary interest in it, but felt it his duty to endeavour to dispel what he called the unfounded delusions which have taken possession of the public mind on the subject. His book is a storehouse of facts and arguments. It is written in a bright and intelligent style, and I strongly recommend its perusal to any one interested in the question. The facts have never been denied, or the arguments answered by any one having a personal knowledge of the subject.

"Mr. Brereton states that, having had daily intercourse with the people from whom the best and most trustworthy information on the subject of opium and opium-smoking could be obtained, his experience is that opium-smoking as practised by the Chinese is perfectly innocuous, and that this is a fact so patent that it forces itself upon the attention of every intelligent resident in China who has given ordinary attention to the subject. He quotes numerous high authorities in support of this view. Amongst these I may mention Dr. Philip Ayres, for many years Inspector of Hospitals in Hong Kong; Mr. John Crawfurd, F.R.S., a *savant* of high reputation, who had been Governor of the Straits Settlements, and had travelled for many years in the East; Dr. Oxley, a physician and naturalist of eminence, and who has had a larger experience than any man in Singapore, where there is the highest rate of the consumption of the drug; Dr. Sinibaldo de Mas, who had been for many years the Envoy Extraordinary and Minister Plenipotentiary of the Court of Spain at Pekin: he had travelled much in China, India, Java, Borneo, and Malacca, and learned the Chinese language; Baron Richthofen, the most experienced traveller who ever visited Sse-ch'uan, where the habit of opium-smoking is extraordinarily prevalent; Mr. Colborne Baber, who knew more of that province and its people than any living Englishman; Mr. W. Donald Spence, Her Majesty's Consul at Tchang, who in 1881 visited the capital of Sse-ch'uan; Sir Henry Pottinger, Her Majesty's Governor-General and Minister Plenipotentiary in China, and others. The evidence of all these persons, given from their own personal knowledge and experience, confirms that of Dr. Eatwell, which was as follows:—

"'Having passed three years in China, I may be allowed to state, as the result of my observation, and I can affirm thus far, that the effects of the abuse of the drug do not come very frequently under observation, and that when cases do occur, the habit is frequently found to have been induced by the presence of some painful chronic disease, to escape from the suffering of which the patient has fled to this resource. . . . As regards the effects of the habitual use of the drug on the mass of the people, I must affirm that no injurious results are visible. The people are generally a muscular and well-formed race, the labouring portion being capable of great and prolonged exertion under a fierce sun, in an unhealthy climate.'

"The picture drawn by the opponents of opium is that those who are in the habit of using it are a set of degraded, depraved, miserable wretches, enfeebled in mind and body, unfit for the active duties of life—thieves, vagabonds, and beggars. They do not admit—or, at any rate, never refer to the possibility of—the existence of moderate consumers, who, although they take their daily dose, are not only none the worse for it, but are actually benefited. Yet we know from numerous unimpeachable witnesses that the abuse of opium by the Chinese is the exception and its moderate and beneficial use is the rule.

"Turning now to the evidence as to the effect of opium consumption by the people of India, we find that early in 1892 a Parliamentary Blue-book (c. 6562) was published on this subject. It contains the reply of the Government of India to a memorial of the Society for the Suppression of the Opium Trade, complaining of the increased consumption of the drug in India—a complaint which has been triumphantly disproved. This Blue-book contains the opinions of experienced officers engaged in the administration of the country, writing from their own personal knowledge, which it was a part of their duty to acquire, as to the effects of opium consumption on the people of India.

"The evidence of these officers from every part of India is singularly unanimous, and it completely establishes the contention that it is the abuse and not the use of opium which is harmful, that moderate use is the rule, and that excess is the exception.

"The most eminent medical officers in India have testified to the same effect. The only Province in which the local authorities have given a contrary opinion is Burma, and even there they declare that 'there are large numbers of the non-Burmese community (Chinese and Indians), constituting, perhaps, the most thriving and industrious section of the population, to whom the drug is a necessity of life and by whom it is rarely abused.'

"We have, then, a great *consensus* of opinion arrived at by a number of independent persons of high character and reputation; gentlemen of ability and integrity, who have attained to responsible positions, in which they have had the best opportunities of ascertaining the truth; whose duty it has been to state the truth, and who have had no personal interest in perverting it. They deliberately declare that the daily use of opium in moderation is not only harmless, but of positive benefit, and frequently even a necessity of life; that this moderate use is the rule, and that excess is the exception. On the other hand, we are told by a society, chiefly consisting of Englishmen who have no personal knowledge of the facts, that all this evidence goes for nothing, and that the use of opium, except for strictly medicinal purposes, is an unmitigated evil, and ruins every one who habitually has resort to it. If we accept this view, which differentiates opium from every other stimulant used by great masses of people, we must believe that all those experienced persons who have testified to the direct contrary are either grossly incapable or grossly dishonest. It is no use mincing words; a man must be one or the other who, having lived for years amongst an opium-consuming people, and having made a careful study of the effects of the habit, deliberately declares as the result of his inquiries that which is untrue.

"The Society for the Suppression of the Opium Trade proposes—

"1. That the Bengal system of licensing the growth of the poppy and of manufacturing opium be at once stopped, except so far as may be needful for legitimate medical use.

"2. That the necessary measures be at once taken, by raising the tax or otherwise, to prevent any extension of the cultivation of the poppy in Malwa, so as to compensate for the diminution of the supply from Bengal.

"What is meant by 'legitimate medical use'? When we find whole tribes of people, living in malarious and fever-stricken tracts, using the opium daily as a prophylactic, is that a legitimate medical use? Or is it intended that no one shall be permitted to purchase opium except under the written authority of a duly certificated member of the medical profession? How many of the opium consumers in India are within reach of an English doctor? Could you trust the native Baids, Hakíms, and Pansáris, the doctors and druggists of the country, with this power? Anybody with any knowledge of India would laugh at such an idea. How then are you to meet this great practical difficulty?

"It may be possible in British territory, by the exercise of despotic power, to prevent the poppy being grown, but what are 'the necessary measures' so vaguely suggested for preventing its extension in the native States? Every tyro in Excise or Customs administration knows that the power to raise duties on an article in large demand is limited by the means of preventing its illicit production and sale, and that if you increase the profits of smuggling, you will proportionately have to increase your preventive measures. Unless British officers and establishments were appointed to overrun the native States, and to interfere with the agricultural operations of the people, the cessation of the growth of the poppy in British territory would infallibly lead to an enormous extension of the cultivation in native States. The export thence of opium could only be prevented by Customs barriers, and patrols round Rajputana and Central India, involving a line between 2000 and 3000 miles in length, and heavy expenditure on the establishments. How would the native States concerned regard such measures? I have no hesitation in saying that the discontent occasioned not only in those States, but amongst our own people, including the Sikhs—from whom the flower of our native army is recruited—would constitute a very serious political danger.

"But how are you to conciliate the native States for interference in their poppy cultivation? Will the people of India, or the people of this country, submit to be taxed in order to compensate these native States, and to reconcile their rulers to an army of British preventive officers scattered over their territories? And if you reconcile the rulers by paying them, how are you to conciliate their people, who have been accustomed for centuries to the unrestricted use of opium? Without such preventive measures British India will be supplied with the Malwa drug, which, from its great value in a small bulk, is comparatively easy to smuggle. And these preventive measures must be of the strictest kind, involving the searching of the persons and goods of all travellers, and domiciliary visits, to detect the carriage, and prevent the storing of the drug.

"I now come to the third proposal of the Society for the Suppression of the Opium Trade. It is as follows:—

"3. That the Chinese Government be approached with proposals for diminishing the export of Malwa opium, simultaneously with the suppression of the growth of the poppy throughout China.

"I do not wish to use disrespectful language, but I can hardly speak of such a proposal with gravity. The Chinese Government, who have for centuries fulminated futile edicts, threatening the heaviest pains and penalties against the growth of the poppy and the use of opium, but whose officials have never had the will or the power to enforce them, and who are known to connive at the open and unconcealed infringement of the law, are to be 'approached' by the British Government, with this request:—'Now that we are doing our best to deprive you of Indian opium, which your people for centuries have demanded on account of its superior quality; now that we have, by our restrictive measures, encouraged the growth of the poppy in China, and the home production of an inferior article, to such an extent that whole provinces are covered with its cultivation; now that we are mulcting your import customs revenue of about £2,000,000 sterling a year: will you be good enough at once to stop the cultivation in China, and deprive your people of an article which we believe to be an unmitigated evil; although there is a large body of Englishmen who, from personal experience, have testified that it is harmless to the great mass, who are moderate consumers?' How would such a request be met? If the solemn and self-possessed Chinaman has any sense of humour, by inextinguishable laughter.

"I am aware that many of the opponents of opium would also prohibit the use of alcoholic drinks in the United Kingdom, but before 'approaching' China, let the people of this country set the example, and make the liquor traffic, except for purely medicinal purposes, illegal; let them forbid by law the cultivation of the hop plant, and the growth of barley for distillation or malting; let them forbid the import of wine and spirits from the Continent of Europe and elsewhere, and then they will be in a position to 'approach' China with a prayer for the destruction of the poppy cultivation and the trade in opium.

"It has been suggested that if the culture of poppy were prohibited other crops would take its place and thus supply a great part of the loss. But would the farmers of Kent be satisfied if the temperance party were to say to them, 'We will pass a law to prohibit your cultivating hops. You can, however, grow potatoes or gooseberries instead"?

"It is true that a more moderate party in this country does not go the length of prohibiting the cultivation of the poppy and the manufacture of opium in Bengal. They are shocked at the direct management by the Government of these industries. No question has been more fully discussed in India than this, there are volumes of correspondence relating to it, but the upshot of all these discussions has invariably been the recognition of the fact that, under any other system, the cultivation could not be so well restricted, that smuggling would be more rife, that the cultivators would be brought under influence of speculators, from which they are at present guarded, and that whatever evils now exist would be largely increased. The Society for the Suppression of the Opium Trade recognise this, and in the pamphlet I have quoted, declare that the proposal is entirely inadequate, and that their demand is nothing short of absolute prohibition.

"India has had the advantage of drawing from England, for more than one hundred years, a number of upright, honest, and able administrators. It is remarkable that there is not a single instance of an Englishman who has been directly responsible for the well-being of India, and who has had an important voice in its administration, who has ever suggested the prohibition of the cultivation of the poppy. That has been left for a party of irresponsible persons in this country, whose want of knowledge is patent to every one who has studied the question on the spot.

"In conclusion, I would say to the Society for the Suppression of the Opium Trade—You may make this a party question; you may win votes relying on the uninstructed philanthropy of your fellow-countrymen; you may, through Parliament, use the despotic power of the British Government to destroy one of the most valuable products of India, and subject the people to new taxation in order to supply the loss of revenue now paid chiefly by the Chinese; you may deprive hundreds of thousands of Her Majesty's Indian subjects of a prophylactic which enables them to resist fatigue, to sustain privation, and to save life; you may thereby increase suffering, sickness, and mortality; you may cover India with an army of preventive officers to watch another army of smugglers, created to satisfy a natural demand of which you have suppressed the legitimate supply; you may harass the people by personal searches and domiciliary visits; you may thus create discontent amongst our native subjects, and disaffection in the best forces of our native army; you may, by unwarranted and unprecedented interference in their internal administration, and, owing to the pecuniary losses both rulers and subjects will sustain, disgust and alienate the native States of Central India and Rajputana, our bravest and most loyal allies; you may drive the consumers of opium to alcohol and hemp; you may do all this, but you will never persuade the Chinese to follow in your footsteps, and abandon the ever-increasing culture of the poppy. In short, you may inflict on India a cruel injury, the extent and the consequences of which you are incapable of calculating; but you will fail in any way to benefit China, unless you count it a benefit greatly to extend the cultivation of the poppy, and the manufacture of opium within her borders."

I can add very little to the account which has thus been given by Mr. Batten. I passed thirty-eight years of my life in India, and during that time I held a great variety of offices, beginning with those of little importance, to the very highest posts in the civil service of the State. I was brought into personal communication with all classes, from the greatest princes to the humblest ryots. I endeavoured to learn the truth upon this subject, and I am entitled to say that I can speak with knowledge of the facts, both as regards the people of India and the policy of the Government. I can confirm, in every respect, Mr. Batten's conclusions. Taking India as a whole, the proportion of its vast population that is accustomed to the use of opium is extremely small. Certain classes, however, have long been in the habit of consuming it, and it is a remarkable fact that these classes include the races that are physically the finest in all India. Among them the Sikhs and Rájputs are especially conspicuous. The Sikhs are the flower of our Indian army, and one of the bulwarks of our Indian Empire; it would be difficult to find in any country of the world a more manly, handsome, and vigorous people, and their use of opium is almost universal. Statements that the consumption of opium in India has been fostered by our Government with the object of obtaining revenue are absolutely without foundation. There is little doubt that more opium was consumed in India under Native rule, one hundred and fifty years ago, than now, and the stringent system of excise established by our Government has so greatly increased the price of the drug that consumption is reduced to a minimum. The danger is that this policy may be carried too far, and that, by making opium too dear and too difficult to obtain, we may not only encourage smuggling, but may cause people who have been content with the moderate and beneficial use of opium to have recourse to alcohol, or to cheaper and more noxious stimulants, the consumption of which no Government can prevent.

As regards China, as Mr. Batten has shown, the population practically depends for the supply of opium not upon the imports from India but on that produced at home. If all that were said about the ruin of the Chinese by opium were true, instead of being, as it is, altogether false, the prohibition of the imports from India would afford no remedy. If the richer classes in China were deprived of Indian opium they would suffer as the richer classes in Europe would suffer if they were deprived of the choice vintages of Bordeaux and Burgundy, or as tobacco-smokers would suffer if no more cigars were to come from Cuba. In such a case, in our own country, the frequenters of public-houses would be conscious of no hardship, and the vast majority of the opium-smokers of China would be equally unconscious if they received no more opium from India. If, in deference to ignorant prejudice, India should be deprived of the revenue which she now obtains from opium, an act of folly and injustice would be perpetrated as gross as any that has ever been inflicted by a foreign Government on a subject country. India now possesses the rare fortune of obtaining from one of her most useful products a large revenue without the imposition of taxes on her own people, and we are asked to sacrifice the manifest and vital interests of these people, to whose good we are pledged by the highest duties, in hope of protecting others, against their will, from imaginary evils; in other words, to inflict certain injury where we have the power, in pursuit of a benevolent chimera which must elude us. Truly, to use the words of Condorcet, "*l'enthousiaste ignorant est la plus terrible des bêtes féroces.*"

Mr. Batten has brought out very clearly the essential fact, usually altogether ignored, that the revenue derived from opium exported to China constitutes a comparatively small part of the Indian interests involved. There has been much idle talk about the readiness of England to bear, in whole or in part, the loss that the suppression of the cultivation and sale of opium would cause. It would be waste of words to say much regarding a proposition which it is certain will never be carried into effect. England, which levied in 1900-01 a revenue of £32,700,000 from alcoholic liquors, and whose "drink-bill" is said to amount to more than £150,000,000 a year, would never be guilty of such extravagant and hypocritical folly as to think of paying for the suppression of opium cultivation in India. But it is well that English people should understand that no money payment, however large, could make good to India the loss of this great industry. If England were to make to her a free gift of £100,000,000, or indeed much more, it would be no compensation for the material injury that she would suffer, and still less could there be compensation for the ruinous political consequences that would inevitably follow.

In 1893, a year after Mr. Batten's paper, and the greater part of the present chapter were written, a Royal Commission under the presidency of Lord Brassey was appointed, in accordance with a Resolution of the House of Commons, to inquire into the whole subject of the cultivation of the poppy in India and the manufacture and sale of opium. The Commission met in Calcutta in November 1893; it spent several months in India; it visited many parts of the country, and examined more than 700 witnesses, of whom 466 were natives of India or China and 257 Europeans. The Commission submitted its Report in April 1895. Its work was mainly devoted to an inquiry into the facts connected with the consumption of opium in India. China was not directly included in the Order of Reference, nor was that country visited by the Commission. In regard to India, the Report of the Commission and the voluminous evidence taken by it so entirely confirmed the conclusions stated by Mr. Batten and by myself that reference to it in detail is needless, nor have I thought it necessary to make any changes in this chapter as it was originally written. No change whatever was recommended by the Commission in the principles on which the administration of the opium revenue is carried on in India, and no change has been made. In regard to China, comparatively little evidence was taken by the Commission, but its conclusions, so far as they were stated in its Report, were the same as those given in Mr. Batten's paper.

"On a review," it said, "of the whole evidence in regard to opium-smoking among the Chinese, we conclude that the habit is generally practised in moderation, and that when so practised injurious effects are not apparent, but that when the habit is carried to excess, disastrous consequences, both moral and physical, inevitably follow. Assuming this conclusion to be well founded, we may fairly compare the effects of opium-smoking among the Chinese to those of alcoholic liquors in the United Kingdom. . . . Upon the general question, the position which Great Britain may properly take up is clearly put by Mr. O'Conor, Her Majesty's representative at Peking, in his covering letter addressed to the Commission. He says: 'If the use of the drug in China depended on the supply received from India it might be a practical question what measures could or ought to be taken to discourage its importation. But this is not the issue. The quantity of opium grown in China is increasing enormously. Even the nominal prohibition of the cultivation of the poppy no longer exists throughout the whole empire, and were the importation of Indian opium to be stopped, China would in a few years so increase her production, as not only to supply her own wants, but probably to export opium to foreign countries.'"

I may leave this subject with the following quotation from one whose knowledge and authority no one can call in question:—

"In speaking of the occasional sources of friction between China and ourselves, I do not allude to the opium question, which, in the hands of enthusiastic or prejudiced ignorance in London, has been presented to English audiences in a guise that excites a smile in every Treaty Port in China. There, at least, everybody knows that the helpless Celestial is neither being forced nor befooled by an insidious and immoral Government at Calcutta; that if not an ounce of Indian opium ever again passed through a Chinese custom-house, Chinamen would go on smoking their own inferior drug as keenly as ever; and that the pretence that China is hostile to the British people or to Christian missions because we introduced to her the opium habit (which she had already practised for centuries), is about as rational as to say that the national soreness that sometimes arises between England and France is due to our resentment at having to cross the Channel for our best brandy."

"Indian opium," Lord Curzon adds, "is only smoked by about two in every thousand of the population."[1]

There remain to be briefly noticed a few other heads of revenue not derived from taxation.

In 1900-01, £1,298,000 was received under the head of Forests. This revenue was derived from the sale of timber and other produce from the Government forests; but more than half of it was spent on forest conservancy and other charges necessary for the preservation of the forests, and the net income in 1900-01 was only £568,000. Before the transfer of the Government to the Crown, practically nothing had been done towards the preservation of the forests of India, which are very extensive and valuable, and their destruction was rapidly going on. They cover altogether some 200,000 square miles. In 1861 a separate Forest department was created. Up to 1901 more than 87,000 square miles of forests had been demarcated, and strictly reserved for the benefit of the public under the management of officers who have received special scientific instruction in forestry in Germany or France or at Cooper's Hill. The creation and development of this department, for the protection of a valuable source of the public wealth, is one of the most important reforms of modern times in India.

[1] *Problems of the East*, by the Hon. George N. Curzon, M.P., 1894.

The Tributes and contributions from Native States are fixed by treaties, and yielded in 1900-01 £578,000. They are chiefly paid for the maintenance of troops locally required. The Government of India is responsible for the preservation of peace throughout the whole of India, and the contributions that it receives from the Native States are an insignificant return for the services that it renders.

The revenue yielded by the Post Office was almost equalled by the expenditure. The Government has not aimed at making a profit from the Post Office. The receipts increased from £177,000 in 1856-57 to £1,357,000 in 1900-01. They have been largely devoted to the improvement of the postal service, and the net revenue from this source was £135,000. There is no country where the rates of postage are so low, or where the Post Office is better managed. The number of letters, newspapers, and parcels passing through the post was 38,000,000 in 1856 and 532,000,000 in 1901 There could hardly be a more striking illustration of the progress of the country.

The construction of telegraph lines was commenced in 1850, and up to 1900-01 £4,728,000 had been expended on their construction. In 1901 there were 182,000 miles of wire in India, and more than 6,500,000 messages were delivered. The gross receipts from the telegraphs in 1900-01 amounted to £754,000, and gave a return of 6 per cent on the capital expended in their construction.

I shall refer in another chapter to the revenue derived from Railways and works of Irrigation.

CHAPTER XI

REVENUES DERIVED FROM TAXATION

The Salt Tax—Sources of salt supply—Former system of levying duties—The Inland Customs Line—Its abolition—The present system—Result of reforms—The stamp revenue—Excise on spirits and drugs—Misrepresentations—Principles of excise administration—Assessed taxes—Income Tax—Registration.

TAXES, properly so called, yielded altogether in India, in 1900-01, a gross revenue of £20,816,000. Among them the most important is the tax on salt. It gave in 1900-01 a gross income of £5,967,000.

The system under which the Salt duties are levied varies in different parts of India. Bengal and Assam, with 81 millions of people, obtained, until not many years ago, almost the whole of their salt from England. There are hardly any local sources of supply for these provinces except the sea, but on the greater part of the coasts of Bengal salt cannot be made cheaply by solar evaporation; the climate is damp, and the difficulty is increased by the vast quantity of fresh water brought to the Bay of Bengal by the Ganges and Bráhmaputra. The locally produced salt cannot compete with that imported by sea. Owing to the fact that the exports from India are largely in excess of the imports, freights to India are very low, and salt costs little to import. The tax in Bengal is levied as an import duty at the port of entry. Before 1888 nearly all the salt consumed in Bengal was brought from Cheshire; but in consequence principally of a great increase in the price of English salt caused by the action of the Salt Syndicate, a large supply is now furnished by Arabia and Germany. Increased facilities of inland communication have also encouraged the displacement of foreign salt by salt manufactured in other Indian provinces.

In Madras and Bombay, although the facilities for communication with other countries are equally great, foreign salt does not compete with that produced locally, for the manufacture of salt from the sea by solar evaporation is an easy process. The duty in Madras is collected partly under an excise system, and partly under a monopoly, by which all salt is manufactured for the Government and sold at a price which gives a profit equal to the duty. In Bombay the duty is levied as an excise.

The United Provinces of Agra and Oudh, and parts of the Central Provinces and of the Punjab, derive their chief supply of salt from lakes or springs impregnated with salt in the Native States of Rájputána. The salt is prepared by solar evaporation at works controlled by the Government. Farther north, the greater part of the Punjab is supplied from rock-salt, which is found in inexhaustible quantities. The salt is extracted and sold by the Government, the duty being included in the selling price. In Burma the greater part of the salt comes from England and Germany, and from Madras; there is also a considerable local manufacture.

Until 1882-83, the amount of duty varied in different provinces. It was higher in Bengal than in Madras and Bombay. So long as there were no railways and few roads, the inconvenience of these different rates was not much felt; but as communication improved, it became more and more impossible to prevent salt taxed at a lower rate from coming into provinces where the tax was higher, and a system gradually grew up in India to which, for extraordinary folly, it would be hard to find a parallel.

In 1843, with the object of shutting out the cheaper salt from provinces where it had been made artificially dear, and of keeping out from British territory the untaxed salt of Native States, the establishment of an Inland Customs Line was commenced, and by 1870 it had extended itself across the whole of British India from a point north of Attock, on the Indus, to the Máhánadi, on the borders of Madras, a distance of 2500 miles. Along the greater part of its length it was a huge material barrier, which Sir M. E. Grant Duff, speaking from personal observation, said could be compared to nothing else in the world except the Great Wall of China; it consisted chiefly of an immense impenetrable hedge of thorny trees and bushes, supplemented by stone walls and ditches, across which no human being or beast of burden or vehicle could pass without being subjected to detention and search. If this Customs Line had been put down in Europe, it would have stretched, in 1869, from Moscow to Gibraltar. It was guarded by an army of officers and men, some 12,000 in number, divided into beats which were constantly patrolled by night and day, and were watched from 1700 guard-posts. It may easily be imagined what obstruction to trade, what abuses and oppression, what annoyance and harassment to individuals, took place. The interference was not confined to traffic passing into the British provinces, or to salt alone, for an export duty was levied on sugar produced in our own territories when it passed from British territory into Native States, and sometimes when it passed from one part of British territory to another. This was a most objectionable and indeed irrational tax, levied as it was on one of the most important agricultural staples of our own provinces. Obstructions were thus offered to traffic from whichever direction it came.

It was impossible to get rid of this Inland Customs Line while the salt tax was levied at different rates in different provinces, and until we had the means of controlling the manufacture and taxation of salt produced in the great salt tracts of the Native States and brought into our own territories.

The first steps towards a better system were taken by the Government of Lord Mayo in 1869. An amicable arrangement was ably and successfully negotiated by Mr. A. O. Hume with the Native States of Jaipur and Jodhpur, under which we acquired the sole right of manufacturing salt at the Sámbhar salt lake, the chief of the salt sources of Rájputána, and from which a large proportion of the supply of Northern India is derived.

No further steps were taken until 1873, but in that year (I am quoting from a despatch of the Government of India), "Mr. G. H. M. Batten, the Commissioner of Inland Customs, first suggested to the Government that inquiries should be made and negotiations entered into with a view to the British Government being enabled to levy an excise duty on salt at the principal places of production in Rájputána, and to suppress or restrict all other salt manufacture in the Native States. He pointed out that by this measure, and this measure alone, would it become possible to remove the Inland Customs Line." The Government of Lord Northbrook then entered into an arrangement with Jodhpur, by which all the important salt sources of that State were transferred to British management. An important reduction was also made in the length of the Customs Line in its southern section, where it passed through British territory only.

In 1878, under the Government of Lord Lytton, by my own advice, the export duty on sugar was abolished, and in the following year the Inland Customs Line finally disappeared. It was still, at that time, 1500 miles long, a distance as great as that from London to Constantinople, and its existence was declared by Lord Lytton to be a great political and commercial scandal. There is nothing in my Indian life that I remember with more satisfaction than the fact that it was my good fortune, as Financial Member of the Government, to help Lord Lytton in carrying to completion the reform of a system which for many years I had denounced.

The abolition of the Customs Line was rendered possible by two measures. By the first the duties on salt throughout India, although for financial reasons they could not be at once completely equalised, were made to approximate so nearly that salt could not profitably be taken from one province to another. By the second measure agreements were entered into with the Native States of Rájputána and Central India, under which the British Government obtained leases and control of all the more important sources of salt manufacture. Liberal compensation was given to the chiefs of the Native States for loss of revenue. These measures led almost immediately to a large increase in the consumption of salt and to a large increase of revenue.[1]

[1] This account of a great reform would not be complete without some reference to the eminent services of Mr. A. O. Hume, Sir Alfred Lyall, and Sir Henry

The final completion of these reforms, by the equalisation of the salt duties throughout India at a reduced rate, was reserved for Sir Evelyn Baring, now Lord Cromer, as Financial Member of the Government of Lord Ripon. In 1882 the duty was fixed at two rupees per maund (82 lbs.).

The measures that have been described had as their ultimate object much more than the removal of the Inland Customs Line, and the equalisation of the duties upon salt. That object was explained by myself in 1877, in the Legislative Council, on behalf of the Government of India, to be that of giving to the people throughout India the means of obtaining an unlimited supply of salt at the cheapest possible cost; I said that the interests of the people and of the public revenue were identical, and that the only just and wise system was to levy a low rate of duty on an unrestricted consumption. That policy was not long maintained. In January 1888 the salt tax was raised to two and a half rupees per maund, and so it remained for the next fifteen years. Neither in the consumption of salt nor in the revenue was the progress satisfactory. In March 1903 the tax was reduced by the Government of Lord Curzon to its former rate of two rupees.

The temptation is great in times of financial pressure to have recourse to the expedient of increasing the duty on salt. The vast majority of the people on whom the tax falls are probably unaware of the existence of the tax. The masses remain unmoved and silent, while the small and wealthier minority, who

Daly, who conducted the negotiations with the Native States, and to those of Mr. G. H. M. Batten, who, at the headquarters of the Government of India, was, in regard to all the questions involved, its chief adviser.

alone can make their voices heard, give loud approval to measures which impose no appreciable obligation upon themselves. No efforts should be spared to reduce to the utmost the price of salt throughout India, and thereby to stimulate consumption. Nor is this policy desirable merely for the reason, essentially important as this is, that the cost to the poor of one of the necessaries of life should not needlessly be enhanced, but because it will certainly, from a purely financial point of view, be advantageous. Nor should it be forgotten that a time of extreme political emergency may come when a large and immediate addition to the revenues is necessary, and when fresh direct and unpopular taxation cannot possibly be imposed. In such circumstances, the tax on salt might, if it were very low, and the consumption of salt were unrestricted, be temporarily increased without serious objection, for the Government would thus be able to obtain, by a small increase of duty, large additional resources, almost without the knowledge of the people. Salt ought to be looked on as a financial reserve, which might be drawn upon in case of urgent necessity, but not otherwise. I do not assert, nor do I believe, that the tax at the rate which prevailed from 1888 to 1903 was felt as an actual hardship by the people, but its reduction has been one of the wisest measures of the Government of Lord Curzon.

The duty on salt is the only obligatory tax which falls upon the masses of the population, and although they are very poor it is not a serious burden. It is equivalent to an annual tax of about fourpence per head. The case was very different once, when high duties, unwise policy, and, above all, imperfect means of communication, made it impossible for the poorest classes in some parts of India to obtain a sufficient supply of salt.

In the existing conditions of India a moderate tax upon salt is open in principle to little objection. The reasons for this conclusion were summed up by the Duke of Argyll, when Secretary of State for India, in a passage which I cannot do better than quote:—

> "On all grounds of general principles, salt is a perfectly legitimate subject of taxation. It is impossible in any country to reach the masses of the population by direct taxes. If they are to contribute at all to the expenditure of the State, it must be through taxes levied upon some articles of universal consumption. If such taxes are fairly adjusted, a revenue can thus be raised, not only with less consciousness on the part of the people, but with less real hardship upon them than in any other way whatever. There is no other article in India answering this description upon which any tax is levied. It appears to be the only one which, at present, in that country can occupy the place which is held in our own financial system by the great articles of consumption from which a large part of the imperial revenue is derived. I am of opinion, therefore, that the salt tax in India must continue to be regarded as a legitimate and important branch of the public revenue. It is the duty, however, of the Government to see that such taxes are not so heavy as to bear unjustly on the poor by amounting to a very large percentage upon their necessary expenditure. The best test whether an indirect tax is open to this objection is to be found in its effect upon consumption." [1]

The Stamp revenue is derived partly from stamps on commercial papers, and partly from fees, levied by means of stamps, on proceedings in the judicial courts. It amounted in 1900-01 to £3,343,000, of which £998,000 was derived from commercial stamps, and the rest from court fees.

The revenue under the head of Excise is derived

[1] Despatch to Government of India, January 21, 1869.

from duties on spirits and intoxicating drugs. Tobacco, which is grown in almost every village and is consumed by nearly every man in India, and by very many women, is subject to no duty. The people of India generally are extremely abstemious; the consumption of spirits is for the most part confined to the lower classes, but even among them there is, in the words of the Government of India, "a condition of things which, if it existed in England, would be regarded almost as a millennium of temperance. Drunkenness in the English sense of the term hardly exists in India." Whereas in the United Kingdom there was one liquor shop to about 242 of the population, the proportion in India was one to more than 2400. There has been a large and steady increase in the excise revenue. In 1870 it was less than £1,250,000; in 1880 it was £2,840,000; and it was £3,937,000 in 1900-01. Benevolent people in England, carried away by the enthusiasm of ignorance, have found in such figures as these the opportunity for indignant protest against the wickedness of a Government which, with the object of obtaining revenue, affords, in defiance of native opinion, constantly increasing facilities for drinking. There is no foundation for such assertions. The sole cause of the increase of revenue has been improved administration and the suppression of illicit distillation and sale. I quote from a despatch of the Government of India the following summary of the facts :—

"Few subjects have of recent years obtained greater attention at the hands of the Government than questions relating to excise administration. In each of the three larger Governments the excise system has, within the last six or seven years, been completely examined in its operation and in its effects. These examinations have been made under the instructions of the Local

Governments, and in direct communication with us, and the principles on which they have been based, and which have been unanimously accepted by all the authorities concerned, have been these: that liquor should be taxed and consumption restricted, as far as it is possible to do so without imposing positive hardships upon the people and driving them to illicit manufacture. The facts now placed on record show that in this policy the Local Governments have been completely successful, and that the great increase of excise revenue in recent years, which has been taken as evidence of the spread of drinking habits, really represents a much smaller consumption of liquor, and an infinitely better regulated consumption, than the smaller revenue of former years. . . .

"There is not the slightest reason to imagine that in the days of native administration the Indian populations refrained from indulgence in a practice which it requires the constant watchfulness of the British administration to prevent. Under the Mohammedan administration, which immediately preceded the British rule, the facilities for drinking were very much greater than have ever since existed, and the prevalence of drinking habits was quite as much complained of. The reports of the Chief Commissioners of the Central Provinces and of Assam prove that it is precisely those tribes and races which have been the least accessible to the influences of British rule which are most addicted to intoxicating drinks and drugs. We have at the present day ample evidence on this very point in the conflict between the British and Native excise systems wherever British and Native territory meet. These are the only points where the British system breaks down, because the restrictions imposed upon manufacture and consumption on the British side of such frontiers are not met by equivalent restrictions on the other side. One of the main difficulties which the excise authorities have to meet is that of excluding from British territory the more lightly taxed and more easily obtained spirit available in Native States.

"It is only by strong preventive establishments that illicit distillation can be prevented. The great increase in the revenue does not mark the extension of drinking habits, but is the result of a great and general increase in the rate of tax, which it would have been entirely impossible to realise but for the great improvement in preventive measures which has accompanied it.

In fact, the ability of the Excise department to prevent illicit distillation is the only limit which is imposed in practice to increase in the rate of taxation."

Speaking generally, there has been almost everywhere since 1880 a decrease in the number of liquor shops and in the consumption of liquors. The real question now is not whether restriction has been carried far enough, but whether it has not, in some parts of India, been carried too far. There is reason to fear that there has been, not infrequently, a serious increase of illicit production which it is impossible to prevent, that the difficulty of obtaining liquor at a reasonable price has sometimes largely stimulated the consumption of drugs, especially hemp, that are more noxious, and that classes which have always been accustomed to the use of liquor have been forced into systematic evasion of the law.

The next head of Indian taxation is that of Provincial Rates, which I have already mentioned.

In 1859, the year after the transfer of the Government to the Crown, Mr. James Wilson was appointed financial member of the Governor-General's Council. The heavy charges incurred in the suppression of the mutinies and the reorganisation of the administration rendered the imposition of fresh taxation necessary, and in 1860, under the advice of Mr. Wilson, a general income tax was imposed. It was levied at the rate of 4 per cent, or rather more than 9½d. in the pound, on all incomes of 500 rupees and upwards, and at half that rate on incomes between 200 and 500 rupees. It yielded in 1861-62 a net revenue of nearly £2,000,000. Many changes have from time to time been made in the system thus introduced. The direct taxation of incomes has several times been wholly or partially abolished, and several times it has been restored. Sometimes there has been a general tax upon all incomes, sometimes a license tax on professions and trades, and sometimes on trades only. In 1877-78 the question of direct taxation was forced into prominence by the necessity of making provision against the financial dangers caused by the liability to famine to which the greater part of India is from time to time subject. Taxes which were called license taxes, but which were really in the nature of taxes on income, were then imposed throughout India on the commercial and trading classes, and additional rates were placed on the land in some of the provinces. In 1886 a further step was taken. An Act then imposed a tax on all incomes derived from sources other than agriculture, the latter being exempted. This Act affected no income below 500 rupees; on incomes of 2000 rupees and upwards, it fell at the rate of 5 pies in the rupee, or about 6¼d. in the pound; and on incomes between 500 and 2000 rupees at the rate of 4 pies in the rupee, or 5d. in the pound. In March 1903 the minimum taxable income was raised from 500 to 1000 rupees. The poorer classes are not touched. An income of £66 a year seems very small to us in Europe, but to a native of India, in his own country, it represents, not indeed wealth, but something far removed from poverty. I hope it may now be assumed, after many years of contest, that an income tax has been finally accepted as a permanent source of revenue in India.

There is no country where a tax upon incomes is more just than in India; but there has been difficulty in imposing and maintaining it, because it has been opposed by the richest and most powerful classes, who alone can make their voices heard. It has long been a reproach to our administration that they have borne no fair proportion of the public burdens. The official classes, in the absence of direct taxation, contribute almost nothing. The mercantile and professional classes derive, from the security which they enjoy, greater benefits from our government than any other part of the community, but they have paid almost nothing for its support, except when direct taxation has been imposed upon them. Even the land, although it provides so large a portion of the public revenues, sometimes fails to contribute anything like an adequate amount; the most notorious example of this fact is seen in Bengal, where the zemindars, in the richest province of the empire, not only, in consequence of mistakes made more than a century ago, pay an altogether insufficient sum as land revenue, but remain in great measure exempt from taxation. Much has been said about the unpopularity of an income tax in India. It is undoubtedly disliked by those who have to pay it; but out of the 232,000,000 people in British India, less than 300,000 are liable to the tax, and no such term as unpopular can reasonably be applied to it. I do not undervalue the fact that the small minority on which the income tax falls is politically the most influential section of the whole community, but its discontent is a less evil than the injustice of allowing it almost entirely to escape taxation. Temptations are never wanting in India for Governments to earn for themselves an apparent popularity by a refusal to impose taxes on the richer and more influential classes of the community, and while these, the only audible critics, approve, it is not difficult to find acceptable reasons for a course essentially impolitic and unjust. The real foundations of our power do not rest on the interested approval of the noisy few, but in justice and on the contentment of the silent millions.

The revenue under the head of Registration is not very important in amount. It is derived from fees levied on instruments brought for registration; in some cases, when immovable property above a certain value is affected, the registration of documents is obligatory, in other cases it is optional.

CHAPTER XII

REVENUES DERIVED FROM TAXATION (*continued*)

Customs duties—Duties before 1875—Duties on cotton goods—Free trade in India—Abolition of import duties—Indian tea—Export duty on rice—Re-imposition of import duties in 1894.

I HAVE gone through all the heads of taxation except Customs. I propose to give in some detail an account of past legislation on this subject. There have been, from time to time, great changes in the policy of the Government; of these changes it is not likely that we have seen the last, and their history is not unimportant.

Until 1860 nearly everything imported into India was taxed at the rate of 10 per cent *ad valorem*. On some articles the rate was much higher. Almost everything exported paid a duty of 3 per cent. In 1864, the general rate of duty on imports was reduced to 7½ per cent, and in 1875, under the Government of Lord Northbrook, to 5 per cent. Many exemptions from export duty were made from time to time, and in 1875 the only exports still taxed were rice, indigo, and lac.

The application to the Indian customs tariff of the principles of greater freedom of trade might have been long delayed but for the accident that the interests of a great British industry were affected. Cotton goods were among the articles on which import duties were imposed. The English manufacturers complained loudly that the practical result was to levy a protective duty to their detriment in favour of cotton manufactures rapidly growing up in India. After a long and acrimonious discussion, the question at issue, so far as the principles at stake were concerned, was decided on May 31, 1876, in a despatch to the Government of India from the Marquis of Salisbury, who was then Secretary of State for India. He said that there was no conflict between the interests of India and of England, and that while the abolition of these duties would give legitimate relief to a great British industry, it was a measure still more necessary in the interests of India; that while the duties had the effect of checking the import of British manufactures, they were at the same time exposing to future injury an Indian industry which it was of the first importance should rest upon sound foundations, which there was every reason to believe would rapidly increase, and which ought not to be allowed to grow up under influences which experience had shown must be injurious to its healthy and natural development. "Whether (he wrote) the question be regarded as it affects the consumer, the producer, or the revenue, I am of opinion that the interests of India imperatively require the timely removal of a tax which is at once wrong in principle, injurious in its practical effect, and self-destructive in its operation."

In the following year (July 11, 1877), a resolution was adopted by the House of Commons, without a division, that "the duties now levied upon cotton manufactures imported into India, being protective in their nature, are contrary to sound commercial policy, and ought to be repealed without delay so soon as the financial condition of India will permit."

Famine and other causes of financial difficulty

prevented immediate action, but in the financial statement, March 1878, an important step, not only towards the abolition of the duties on cotton goods, but towards the complete freedom of trade, was announced. A declaration was then made by myself, as Financial Member of the Council, of the principles which the Government of India intended to carry out gradually as circumstances allowed :—

"It is not necessary to discuss the advantages to a country of free trade, and the disadvantage of protective duties. It is sufficient to say that these have been admitted for many years by the statesmen who, of whatever party, have guided the policy of the United Kingdom. . . . The principles on which the customs legislation of the United Kingdom has been based are now admitted axioms by all who recognise the theoretic advantages of free trade. These principles are, as regards imports :

"1. That no duty should exist which affords protection to native industry ; and, as a corollary, that no duty should be applied to any article which can be produced at home without an equivalent duty of excise on the home production ; also, that no duty should be levied except for purely fiscal purposes.

"2. That, as far as possible, the raw materials of industry and articles contributing to production should be exempt from customs taxation.

"3. That duties should be applied only to articles which yield a revenue of sufficient importance to justify the interference with trade involved by the machinery of collection.

"As regards exports : That duties should be levied on those commodities only in which the exporting country has practically a monopoly of production.

"These principles are of general application, but in the case of India they possess a peculiar significance. India is a country of unbounded material resources, but her people are a poor people. Its characteristics are great power of production, but almost total absence of accumulated capital. On this account alone the prosperity of the country essentially depends on its being able to secure a large and favourable outlet for its surplus produce. But there is a special feature in the economic conditions of India which renders this a matter of yet more pressing and even of vital importance. This is the fact that her connection with England, and the financial results of that connection, compel her to send to Europe every year about £20,000,000 sterling worth of her products without receiving in return any direct commercial equivalent. This excess of exports over imports . . . is really the return for the foreign capital, in its broadest sense, invested in India, including, under capital, not only money, but all advantages which have to be paid for, such as the intelligence, strength, and energy on which good administration and commercial prosperity depend. From these causes the trade of India is in an abnormal position, preventing her from receiving, in the shape of imported merchandise and treasure, the full commercial benefit which otherwise would spring from her vast material resources. The comparatively undeveloped condition of the trade of India may be illustrated by the following figures:—The value of the imports and exports, taken together, per head of the population is in the United Kingdom about £20. In British India it is about 10s. The customs revenue on the few articles now retained in the import tariff of the United Kingdom is about 12s. per head, while that of India, on all the articles of its lengthy tariff, is about 3d., showing that, small as is the proportion of the foreign trade of India to that of England, the proportion of customs revenue derived from it is smaller still. Here then is a country which, both from its poverty, the primitive and monotonous condition of its industrial life, and the peculiar character of its political condition, requires from its Government, before all things, the most economical treatment of its resources, and, therefore, the greatest possible freedom in its foreign exchanges."

Excluding the duties levied on salt and liquors, which corresponded to the internal excise duties imposed on those articles, the Indian import duties yielded at that time (1876-77) £1,275,000; and £811,000 of this was derived from cotton goods. Apart from the latter sum there remained, therefore, only £464,000 levied from a multitude of articles, many of which yielded an insignificant revenue. It was clear that after the abolition of the duties on cotton goods it would be impossible to maintain the rest of the import tariff, and the intention was declared of getting rid of all import duties as soon as the state of the finances permitted. The first step was at once taken, in March 1878, by the remission of duties on a great number of articles, and on some of the coarser descriptions of manufactured cotton goods. The inland duties on the export of sugar across the great Inland Customs Line, to which I have already referred, were at the same time abolished. In the following year, in March 1879, the duty on all so-called grey cotton goods, except those of the finer qualities, was remitted.

None of the previous steps towards the abolition of customs duties had been taken by the Government without difficulty, and this further measure, which it was obvious must lead before long to the destruction of the whole fabric of the customs tariff, met with much opposition. Popular opinion in India had always, in regard to questions of fiscal reform, been obstructive and ignorant; and the fact that the abolition of customs duties would be favourable to English manufacturers was enough, in the belief of many, to prove that the party purpose of obtaining political support in Lancashire, and not any care for the interests of India, was the real motive of the Government. This foolish calumny deserved, and deserves, no notice or reply. The opposition to the reform of the cotton duties satisfied Lord Lytton that he must carry out the measure himself, or acquiesce in nothing being done at all. He believed that the interests of India required it, and he was not to be deterred by the imputation of base motives. The measure was held by Lord Lytton to be one which could not rightly be delayed, and it was carried into effect on March 13, 1879. This step was taken by Lord Lytton in opposition to the opinion of a majority of his Council, but on my own advice as member in charge of the Finances. It was approved, on April 4, 1879, by the House of Commons, in the following resolution :—

> "That the Indian import duty on cotton goods, being unjust alike to the Indian consumer and the English producer, ought to be abolished, and this House accepts the recent reduction in these duties as a step towards their total abolition, to which Her Majesty's Government are pledged."

The declared object of the Government of India being not merely the abolition of the duties on cotton goods but the complete freedom of the import trade, the measures actually adopted were taken with the knowledge and intention that they must lead to the speedy collapse of the whole fabric of the customs tariff. It was soon generally admitted that it was not reasonable that certain cotton goods should be free while others of almost the same character remained liable to duty. Both manufacturers and importers complained, and, as the condition of the Indian finances had by this time become highly prosperous, it was impossible to justify the retention of the remaining duties on the finer qualities of goods; and, as already explained, it was clear that, when the cotton duties were given up, the rest of the import duties must go with them.

The history of these proceedings, and the forecast of the future which had become inevitable, was summed up by myself in the year 1881 in the following passage which I quote from the *Finances and Public Works of India* :—

"The policy followed by the Government of India during the Viceroyalty of Lord Lytton was one of absolute free trade, without reservation or qualification, and financial necessities alone prevented that policy from being carried out to the fullest extent. These proceedings have rendered inevitable the almost total abolition of customs duties, which of all Indian taxes are probably the worst. The cotton duties are virtually dead, and the other import duties cannot long survive them. How long a period may elapse before such a consummation is reached cannot be predicted; but the time is not very far distant when the ports of India will be thrown open freely to the commerce of the world.

"The people of India consume at present hardly any foreign luxuries; and cotton goods, which are among the necessaries, and not among the luxuries of life, are the only articles of foreign production which come largely into their consumption. There is no present possibility of deriving a large customs revenue from anything else. . . . The reforms which have been described will be remembered hereafter in the economical history of India, and they will be set down among the honourable titles of Lord Lytton's and Lord Salisbury's administration. They will be remembered, not only because they were the first application to India of the principles of free trade, but also because they have been carried out in a manner which has made the adoption of any other policy virtually impossible in the future, and has rendered it almost a matter of certainty that, within a short period of time, the absolute freedom of Indian commerce will be accomplished.

"The authors of this book may be pardoned for recollecting the part they have taken in this work, and while on public grounds they must regret the almost universal opposition and disapproval in spite of which the policy they have so long maintained has been carried out, they cannot pretend that their personal satisfaction in the success which has been gained already, and in the greater future success which is inevitable, has been diminished by such considerations.

"Non tam portas intrare patentes
Quam fregisse juvat."[1]

This was written early in 1881, and in March 1882

[1] *The Finances and Public Works of India*, by Sir John Strachey and Lieut.-General Richard Strachey.

the anticipations of the authors were verified by the abolition, with two exceptions, of all the remaining import duties, on the advice of Lord Cromer, then Sir Evelyn Baring, by the Government of Lord Ripon.

The exceptions were two articles on which import duties must be imposed, because the same articles are subject to an internal excise duty. One of these is salt, liquors are the other. Arms and ammunition were afterwards also subjected to a duty which, on all the cheaper qualities, was prohibitory, but this was imposed for political reasons, it being inexpedient to allow the free import of arms into India.

In January 1886, Sir Auckland Colvin, who had succeeded Sir Evelyn Baring as financial member of the Council, gave the following summary of the results that followed the measures that have been described :—

"The value of imports of manufactured goods, treasure and Government imports apart, which in the ten years before 1878-1879 averaged £35,000,000, was, in 1884-85, £53,000,000. The average of the four years from 1878-79, when the first duties were remitted, to 1881-82, the year before the final abolition, was £47,000,000; the average of the three years from 1882-83 to 1884-85 has been £51,000,000. The percentage of increase from 1878-79 to 1881-82 was 28; from 1878-79 to 1884-85 it has been 45. If we remember that during this period prices have been steadily falling, and that these figures represent value, not quantities, the real increase will be much greater. I am not so foolish as to suppose that the great growth of our imports since 1878-79 is due solely or mainly to the abolition of the import duties. It is due to a variety of causes. It is partly due to the increase in our exports; it is partly due to the cause to which so much of the increase of our exports is due—namely, to the extension of our railways, and to the consequent improvement in the distribution and cheapening of commodities; it is due to the forcing of accumulated stocks, owing to the fall of prices in England, upon the Indian market; it is very largely due to the fall of prices in England; but, unquestionably, it is also partly due to the abolition of import duties."

The first serious remission of duty on cotton manufactures was made in March 1879. In the four years preceding that date, the average annual value of the imports of cotton goods was Rx.18,760,000; in the four years following the complete abolition of the duty, and ending with March 1886, it was Rx.24,690,000, and in the five years ending 1892-93 it was Rx.29,718,000. The prices of cotton goods fell greatly after the Indian import duties were remitted, and the increase in the quantities imported was more striking than the increase in value.[1]

With one exception, which will presently be mentioned, India had done everything in her power to establish complete freedom of commercial intercourse between the two countries. England could not say the same; she maintained, as she still maintains, her duties on Indian tea and coffee, deriving from the former, in 1901, £3,700,000.

In January 1888 a small import duty was imposed on petroleum, and assuming that it was necessary for financial reasons to increase the revenue derived from indirect taxation, there was no article of the import trade on which a customs duty might with less objection be imposed. There has been throughout a great part of India a very large and remarkable increase in the use of petroleum for lighting. It comes from Russia and America, and chiefly from the former. This duty has thus the merit of directly affecting no British industry.

[1] I have left these figures, as they were originally stated, in rupees, because the fluctuations in the gold value of the rupee between 1879 and 1893 were so great that the amounts cannot be given in pounds sterling.

So far as the import trade is concerned, the principles of free trade were, until March 1894, carried out in India more completely than in any other country. The same could hardly be said of the exports. One export duty remained, and still remains, that on rice, chiefly grown in Burma. The revenue taken from the land in Burma is very small, and Burma and India had, for many years, something approaching to a monopoly of the supply of rice to Europe. This rendered the results less injurious than they would otherwise have been; but the tax is one that cannot, on economical grounds, be defended. Since 1880 there has been no important increase in the trade, and the fall of prices in Europe has encouraged the use of other grains in place of rice in the manufacture of starch and for distillation. The only excuse for the maintenance of this tax has been its productiveness; during the five years ending with 1900-01, the average revenue yielded by it was nearly £600,000. The duty is levied at the rate of 3 annas per Indian maund of 82 lbs., or about 4d. per cwt.

In March 1894, the Government of India, in consequence of financial pressure caused by the fall in the gold value of the rupee, considered fresh taxation to be unavoidable, and the least objectionable method by which they could increase the public revenues appeared to them to be the re-imposition of duties upon imports. The tariff of 1875, under which, with the exception of the precious metals, almost everything imported into India was subject to a duty of 5 per cent, was with some modifications restored. Two important changes were made. Silver bullion was included among dutiable articles, and cotton goods were excepted. This exemption of cotton goods from taxation lasted, however, for a short time only. In December 1894 a 5 per cent import duty was imposed on cotton goods and yarns, and a countervailing excise duty of 5 per cent *ad valorem* was imposed on cotton fabrics manufactured at power mills in India. In February 1896 these duties were again revised. Cotton yarns were freed from duty. A duty of 3½ per cent *ad valorem* was imposed on cotton manufactured goods imported from abroad, and a corresponding excise duty at the same rate was imposed on goods manufactured at mills in India. In 1902 these duties were still levied.

In 1900-01, the total value of all imports by sea into India was £70,314,000. This amount included Government transactions, stores, valued at £3,078,000, and gold and silver valued at £5,409,000. The private imports were merchandise valued at £50,852,000, and gold and silver valued at £10,976,000.

If, excluding salt, we set aside those articles of private merchandise on which duties are necessarily levied, or which are levied for special reasons,—silver, arms and ammunition, petroleum, liquors, and sugar—the value of the remaining articles liable to duty was about £43,500,000. The value of the imports of cotton fabrics, almost entirely of British manufacture, was nearly £20,000,000, or, with the exceptions just mentioned, not far from one-half of the whole import trade. The customs duties on imports, in 1900-01, yielded altogether £2,670,000. Apart from the articles which I have placed in a separate category, cotton fabrics yielded nearly one-half of the total amount received, or £623,000. The Indian import tariff now comprises nearly 400 specified articles, but the actual number of dutiable articles is much larger, because duties are levied on all other articles, manufactured or unmanufactured, except a few specially exempted.[1] In the words of the latest Official Review of the Trade of India, issued by the Government of India, "though the Indian tariff comprises a lengthy list of dutiable articles, there are but few on which individually any revenue of importance is collected; these are spirituous liquors, petroleum, sugar, metals, including silver, and cotton piece goods. These yielded three-fourths of the whole revenue. Cotton piece goods are much the most important source of revenue in the tariff."

I have shown that at one time there was no country in which trade was so free from all burdens as India. Whether the re-imposition and maintenance of a multitude of customs duties, the majority of which yield practically nothing, and which fall principally on articles of British manufacture, has or has not been necessary or wise, is a question into which I do not now propose to enter. Personally I cannot be expected to approve the abandonment of a policy which I myself initiated, which was carried into complete effect by Lord Cromer, and which was declared by his successor, Sir Auckland Colvin, to have been successful and beneficial in its results.

[1] The more important among the articles exempted from duty are the following:—living animals, printed books, hops, grain, machinery, gold bullion and coin, coal, printing material, railway material, ships, raw wool. On certain manufactures of iron a duty of 1 per cent only is imposed.

CHAPTER XIII

FOREIGN TRADE—HOME CHARGES—CURRENCY—WEIGHTS AND MEASURES

Growth of Indian trade and of manufactures and other industries—Conditions under which trade is carried on—Imports of gold and silver—Excess of exports over imports—Home charges—The Secretary of State's Bills—The manner in which the Home charges are met—The currency—Fall in the gold value of silver—Loss by exchange—Serious consequences—The closing of the Indian mints to silver—The results—Weights and measures—Reforms proposed by the Governments of Lord Lawrence and Lord Mayo—Their importance and failure to carry them out.

THE development of the foreign trade of India during the last half-century has been very great, and it affords a remarkable illustration of the increase in the material wealth of the country. In 1840 the total value of the sea-borne trade was about £20,000,000; in 1857, the year before the transfer of the Government to the Crown, it was £55,000,000; in 1877 it was £114,000,000; in 1900-01 it was nearly £152,000,000. The foreign trade of India is now larger than that of the United Kingdom in the middle of the last century. It was carried in 1901 by nearly 9000 vessels, with a tonnage of 9,600,000 tons, of which more than 80 per cent were under the British flag. More than two-thirds of the foreign trade passes through the Suez Canal. The value of the coasting trade in 1901 exceeded £63,000,000.

I do not propose to give any account in detail of Indian trade, but there are some matters connected with it which must be noticed. Speaking in general terms, although there are some very important exceptions, it may be said that the imports into India consist chiefly of manufactured articles, while the exports consist almost entirely of agricultural products.

Among the imports, cotton goods are, as I have already stated, by far the most important, but great as this branch of trade now is, it has, for some years past, made little progress, and, among the causes to which this is to be attributed, the competition of Indian mills with those of England is not the least serious. Before 1851 there were no cotton mills in India, but there has been in later years a great and rapid growth, especially in Bombay, of the manufacture of all but the finer qualities of cotton goods. In 1877 the Indian mills employed 1,300,000 spindles. In 1901 there were 192 mills, and the number of spindles had risen to nearly 5,000,000, giving employment every day to some 156,000 persons. The products of these mills not only come largely into the local markets, but an extensive export trade in cotton piece goods and yarns has sprung up from India to Japan, China, and other countries of Asia. This is not the only case in which important industries have been established. The jute mills of Bengal have become not less important than the cotton mills of Bombay, and the exports of raw and manufactured jute have gone on rapidly increasing, until they constitute in value almost one-half of the exports from Calcutta. In Northern India there are mills which produce large quantities of woollen goods; the amount of malt liquors made in India is now larger than that imported from Europe; the greater part of the paper used in the Government offices is obtained from Indian mills; rice and timber mills in Burma give employment to a rapidly increasing number of workmen, and in the same province, oil-fields yield already considerable quantities of petroleum, and give great promise for the future. The production of coal, especially in Bengal, has made immense progress; Indian coal provides the greater part of the requirements of the railways and factories, and is becoming an important article of export. In 1901 more than 100 vessels laden with coal sailed from Calcutta, whereas twenty years before not a single ton was so exported.

The growth of mining and manufacturing industries in recent years is one of the most satisfactory signs of Indian progress. I quote from a memorandum by Mr. L. P. Shirres, of the Indian Civil Service, the following account of the progress in Bengal:—

"Great as has been the expansion of foreign trade at the ports of Bengal, it is altogether eclipsed by the outburst of mining and manufacturing activity, which is converting the metropolitan districts into a vast industrial tract. No mere enumeration of figures can convey the impression that would be derived from a voyage up the Hoogly, where the banks are studded with tall chimneys and every new reach of the river discloses a fresh vista of factories. . . . The total number of mills and works, exclusive of those connected with tea, classed as large industries, increased from 891 in 1891-92 to 1718 in 1900-01, or by 92·7 per cent, and the number of persons employed from 203,483 to 327,844, or by 61·1 per cent. These are classed under some fifty different heads, among these being bone-crushing mills, cement works, chemical works, lac factories, oil mills, potteries, tile factories, sugar factories, tanneries, rice and flour mills, silk mills and works, rope works, etc. The number of persons working at brass and iron foundries has doubled during the decade, and at its close the 25 largest foundries employed 11,600 persons. . . . The out-turn of the East Indian Railway Company's workshops at

Jumalpur has increased during the same period from £68,000 to £310,000. The quantity of paper produced has more than doubled, and the value has risen by 80 per cent. By far the most important industry, however, is that of jute. In the first nine years of the decade the number of mills increased by 10, the number of persons employed from 64,091 to 110,051 and the outturn from £1,333,000 to nearly £5,700,000. The area under cultivation amounted to nearly 2¼ million acres, or 3500 square miles, jute machinery to the value of £433,000 was imported, and the number of persons employed rose to 113,493. The exports of 'articles of Indian produce manufactured or partly manufactured' have risen in value from £2,567,000 to £7,267,000, or by 195 per cent."

Another Indian industry has attained extraordinary dimensions: the cultivation and manufacture of tea. About the year 1830, in the time of Lord William Bentinck, the Government began the attempt to introduce the cultivation of tea. Gardens were established in the Himálayan districts of the North-Western Provinces, and men were brought from China to superintend operations. For many years the results were doubtful, and if the experiment had been in hands other than those of the Government, which could afford to wait, and which was fortunately wise enough to persevere, it would have been abandoned as hopeless. At last, when experience had shown what was required and what was to be avoided, the success became so great that the action of the Government was no longer necessary, and the field was left entirely to private enterprise. This was the beginning of the great tea industries of India and Ceylon, which now supply almost the whole of the tea consumed in Great Britain. The hill districts of Eastern Bengal have since proved far more favourable to the abundant production of tea than those of Northern India. In

Ceylon, into which it was introduced from India, the progress of the cultivation of tea has been even more rapid and remarkable. There has perhaps never been a greater revolution in trade in so short a time than that which has occurred in the case of tea. Even as recently as 1886 China supplied two-thirds of the tea imported into the United Kingdom. In 1901, out of nearly 300,000,000 lbs., less than 18,000,000 lbs. came from China, 160,000,000 lbs. from India, and 105,000,000 lbs. from Ceylon. In the same year the British revenue derived from Indian tea was £3,700,000, while that derived from Chinese tea had fallen to £246,000.

A very different story has to be told of another branch of the export trade, of which India possessed almost a monopoly, that of indigo. The great and steadily-increasing development of the manufacture of artificial indigo, brought about by the application, chiefly in Germany, of scientific processes, has reduced the cultivation of indigo to such an extent that it has become a question whether this once important Indian industry will not perish altogether.

One of the most valuable products of India is that of cane sugar. The importation of beet sugar from Austria-Hungary and Germany at prices artificially and immensely reduced by the system of bounties threatened millions of Indian cultivators with losses similar to those suffered by the planters of the West Indies. In 1899, and again in 1902, in consequence of the rapid increase of these imports, countervailing duties were imposed, and the Government may be trusted to provide sufficient safeguards for the future.

The conditions under which the foreign trade of India is carried on are peculiar.

It is probable that out of nearly 300,000,000 people inhabiting India, at least 200,000,000 are more or less directly dependent upon agriculture for support. Great manufacturing industries have hardly any existence except when they have been established by European capital or under European influenee.

There is hardly one of the principal agricultural staples of the world which is not or may not be produced in India. The products both of the temperate and tropical zone find, in one or more of the regions within her boundaries, the climate, soil, and all other conditions that they require. The power of cheap agricultural production in India, and her capacity for supplying to other countries food-stuffs and raw materials for manufacture, are practically unlimited, while the capacity of Europe to consume is, or may become, as large as that of India to produce.

Almost everything that the people of India desire to meet their simple requirements is produced at home. This is true even of the comparatively rich, to the great majority of whom the wants and luxuries of European life are unknown. It is not so much the general poverty of the people, as the peculiar and slowly changing character of the social and industrial conditions under which they live, that confines within narrow channels their demands for the productions of other countries. The principal articles of general consumption which, in the absence of fiscal or other impediments, they can often obtain from abroad more cheaply than they can produce them, are clothing, simple metal manufactures, and metals as materials for their own industries. But there is one other important demand that cannot be supplied except from foreign sources. There has always been a flow into India of the precious metals, and centuries of disorder and oppression, the lessons of which are not soon forgotten, have led the people to invest their savings in what seems to them the safest form. Large quantities of gold and silver are thus constantly required for the purpose of hoarding. These hoards are kept for the most part in coin, but also in the shape of personal ornaments. It often surprises Englishmen to see the profusion of gold and silver bangles and other jewellery with which the women even of the humbler classes deck themselves on occasions of festivity. In the five years ending with 1902, the value of the net imports of gold and silver into India was about £37,500,000.[1]

In the same period, taking together the imports of merchandise and treasure, the average annual value of the imports into India fell short of the value of the exports by about £14,000,000. For this excess India receives no direct commercial equivalent, but she receives the equivalent in another form.

English capital to a very large amount has been, and is still being, invested in India by the State and by private individuals in railways, irrigation works, and industrial enterprises, and interest on these investments has to be remitted to England. In addition to this, large sums are required in England for what are really investments for India of another kind. It is an inevitable consequence of the subjection of India that a portion of the cost of her government should be paid in England. The maintenance of our dominion is essential in the interests of India herself, and, provided that she is not compelled to pay more than is really

[1] The production of gold in Southern India, chiefly in Mysore, has become important. In 1901 the mines yielded more than 500,000 ounces. The value of this gold was more than £2,000,000.

necessary to give her a thoroughly efficient Government, and in return for services actually rendered to her, she has no reason for complaint. The charges to be met in England are numerous: interest has to be paid on sterling debt incurred for India in England; there are, among others, charges for civil and military administration, interest and annuities on account of State railways and guaranteed lines, and on ordinary debt, furlough allowances, pensions, payments to the Government in England for British troops employed in India, stores of every kind, railway material for use in India, and the Secretary of State's administration at the India Office. The ordinary annual charge under the last-named head, exclusive of charges connected with the supply of stores to India, is about £130,000. The charges to be met in England necessarily vary from year to year; in 1900-01 they amounted to about £17,000,000.

I must briefly notice the manner in which the payments thus due by India to England are made. The average amount by which the exports from India annually exceed the imports was, as I have said, during the five years ending 1902, £14,000,000. This sum had to be paid in coin in India for the produce exported. The process by which these payments are effected is as follows:—The exporter from India sells his Indian produce in Europe; to pay for it in India the European importer must either send money to that country or he must purchase bills on India in London. The chief demand for remittances of money from India is that of the Secretary of State; he draws bills on the Government treasuries in India, which are paid in India out of the public revenues; and while the European importer obtains the money that he requires in India by the purchase of these bills, the Secretary of State at the same time receives the money that he requires in England. For the ten years ending with 1900-01, the average annual amount of the Secretary of State's bills was about £15,500,000.

It is this process which is sometimes represented as one by which India is being constantly drained of her resources, and forced to pay a crushing tribute to England. Such assertions are unfounded and ignorant. England receives nothing from India except in return for English services rendered, or English capital expended.

The time has passed in which it was deemed necessary to assume that it was always advantageous to a country that its imports should exceed its exports. This is one of the old opinions to which we may apply the words of Sir Robert Giffen: "The believers in such illusions are not entitled to any hearing as economists, however much they may be accepted in the market-place or among politicians. 'The balance of trade' and the excess of imports over exports are simply pitfalls for the amateur and the unwary."[1] The imports of Great Britain immensely exceed the exports; until very lately, on the other hand, the exports of the United States, probably the most prosperous country in the world, have, like those of India, greatly exceeded the imports. The obvious truth is that the accumulating wealth of Great Britain seeks useful employment all over the world, and that the legitimate returns on the capital thus invested flow back in the form of the excess imports, to which India and the United States, and other countries similarly situated, contribute. The payments made by India are the result and the evidence

[1] *Ency. Brit.* vol. xxv. 1902, art. "Balance of Trade."

of the benefits which she derives from her connection with England. In place of constant anarchy, bloodshed, and rapine, we have given to her peace, order, and justice; and, if our Government were to cease, all the miseries from which she has been saved would inevitably and instantly return. Her payments in England are nothing more than the return for the foreign capital in its broadest sense which is invested in India, including as capital not only money, but all advantages which have to be paid for, such as the intelligence, strength, and energy on which good administration and commercial prosperity depend. India derives from these investments benefits far outweighing in value the price that she has to pay, and it is through the excess of her exports over imports that she meets her liabilities.

The remittances on account of interest on English capital invested in useful public works in India involve no real charge to India, because such investments give to her a far larger profit than the interest sent away. Thus, for example, about £260,000,000 has been spent in India on railways and irrigation works, and that sum has been provided partly by State loans or from revenue, and partly through companies receiving a guarantee of interest, or other assistance from the State. The gross earnings of the railways amount to, say, £22,500,000, which is paid, in the first instance, into the Government treasuries; by far the greater portion of this sum is spent in India itself in wages and working expenses, and about £6,000,000 is sent to England as interest on the capital expended. The persons who voluntarily pay the £22,500,000 for the use of the railways are largely benefited by them, and would have had to pay much more had they been obliged to use ruder means of conveyance. It has been not unreasonably calculated that, in consequence of the greatly reduced cost of transport, India now derives from her railways, constructed for the most part with English capital, a benefit equivalent to £50,000,000 or £60,000,000 a year, while an immense trade has been created, which could not otherwise exist. To give one example, 5,000,000 tons of coal were carried in 1900 on the railways, which could not have been carried without them, and of this quantity 2,000,000 tons were exported. The payment of £6,000,000 in England indicates, in such circumstances, no drain upon India, but a transaction which has conferred upon her enormous benefits. The same may be said of the investments in tea, coffee, indigo, cotton mills, and other industries, mainly supported by British capital, the interest remitted on account of which implies the enrichment and not the impoverishment of the country.

There has, however, been one respect in which India has suffered serious injury from the necessity of having to make these heavy payments in England. This has resulted from the fact that the two countries have not had the same standard of value.

Gold being the standard of value in England, the payments which India has to make in this country must be made in gold, while the whole of her revenues are received in silver. Until June 1893 the standard of value in India was silver, and the mints were freely open for coinage; the metallic currency was exclusively silver, with subsidiary copper coins. The paper currency is established on a silver basis, notes being convertible on demand into silver coin.

Before 1873 the fluctuations in the value of silver

in relation to gold were comparatively small. The exchange value of the Indian rupee was seldom much less than two shillings. After 1873, in consequence, principally, of changes in the monetary systems of France and Germany, the causes which had maintained throughout the world, at an almost uniform ratio, the value of silver to gold, no longer operated. Of these causes I do not propose to speak, but, after they ceased to act, depreciation followed in the value of silver in relation to gold. One of the consequences was that when India had to buy the gold required for the discharge of her obligations in England, she had to give for it an increased number of silver rupees, for gold in India and silver in England were merely articles of merchandise. When the rupee was worth 2s., 1000 rupees would purchase £100 in England; when, as was the case in 1892, the rupee was worth 1s. 3d., the same number of rupees produced only £62 : 10s.

It is easy to understand what a serious matter this became when the Government of India had to purchase with depreciated silver the large amount of gold required for meeting its liabilities in England. In 1892-93 the amount remitted from India to meet the Home charges was £16,532,000, and this required a payment of 264,780,000 rupees. If this remittance could have been made at the rate of exchange prevailing in 1873-74, the payment would have been 177,520,000 rupees. Thus the fall in the gold value of silver involved an additional payment by India of more than 87,000,000 rupees from the revenues of the year. In other words, taxation to that amount, equivalent, at the rate of 1s. 4d. per rupee, to £5,800,000, had to be levied in India over and above what would have been necessary if these changes in the relative value of gold and silver had not taken place.

It was, at the same time, so impossible to foresee the course of the exchanges that the Government could not estimate, within many millions of rupees, the probable expenditure of the year. Its most careful anticipations were liable at any time to be completely upset by causes absolutely beyond its control. "The financial position," Sir David Barbour wrote in March 1893, "is at the mercy of exchange, and of those who have it in their power to affect in any way the price of silver. If we budget for the present deficit of 15,950,000 rupees, and Exchange rises one penny, we shall have a surplus; if it falls a penny, we shall have a deficit of more than 30,000,000 rupees; if we impose taxation to the extent of 15,000,000 rupees, a turn of the wheel may require us to impose further taxation of not less magnitude; another turn and we may find that no taxation at all was required. What we have got to consider in making our arrangements for next year is not so much the question of increasing the public revenue, or restricting that portion of the public expenditure which is under our control, but the chances of a settlement of the currency question."

Writing on this subject in 1888, I used the following language:—"No one can say where this continuous depreciation of silver is to stop, or when we shall see the end of the constantly recurring increase in the liabilities of the Government which follows as the inevitable result. Recourse has already been had to taxes that are economically objectionable, and which place fresh burdens upon the poorer classes, and we are perilously near the time in which we may be called on to adopt measures which may be politically dangerous or inexpedient. We have hitherto never introduced into India any strange and unpopular taxation affecting the masses of the population. If we were to change this policy, and were to impose heavy burdens of a kind hitherto unknown, our position might become very different from what it has been in the past. Our difficulties would be seriously increased if such burdens were to meet charges from which the Indian taxpayer derived no benefit, the nature of which he was unable to understand, and which were the direct result of the existence of a foreign dominion. But the truth is that, for such a state of things as that which exists, no readjustment of Indian taxation could afford a remedy. Even if India were a country like Great Britain, where the public revenues, in case of necessity, can almost at any moment be largely increased, she would find, while her standard of value differed from that of England, and while the gold value of silver continued to fall, no relief from pouring into the bottomless pit of her treasury constantly increasing supplies of silver. No language that I could use would be too strong to express my sense of the gravity of this question. There is no Indian authority who does not feel that, if it be allowed to drift on in the future as it has drifted in the past, we may some day find ourselves in a position not only of extreme financial difficulty but of political peril."

The serious anticipations thus expressed were soon fully verified, and in 1892 the Government of India submitted proposals to the Secretary of State for stopping the free coinage of silver in India, with a view to the introduction of a gold standard. The result was the appointment of a Committee, under the presidency of Lord Herschell, for the consideration of the whole subject. The inquiries of the Committee gave complete confirmation to the conclusion that the financial position of the Government of India had become, in consequence of the fall in the gold value of silver, extremely critical, and that it was probable that a further serious fall was impending. It was far from unlikely that the value of the rupee might before long not be more than one shilling. There was already a large deficit, and the Committee were of opinion that, if no remedy for the currency difficulty were applied, that deficit might be increased by as much as 100,000,000 rupees. It was not conceivable that any such sum could be provided by reduction of expenditure, and to provide it by fresh taxation would have been impossible, unless we were prepared to adopt measures that would not only have been economically disastrous, but which would have involved political dangers of the utmost gravity. The result of the Committee's deliberations was to agree with the Government of India that it had become necessary to establish a common standard of value between India and England; that the Indian standard should be gold; that the Indian mints should be closed to the public for the coinage of silver, but should be used by the Government for the coinage of rupees, if required by the public, in exchange for gold, at a ratio fixed, in the first instance, at 1s. 4d. per rupee; and that gold should be received at the Government treasuries at the same ratio in satisfaction of public dues.

In June 1893 an Act was passed by the Governor-General in Council to give effect to these recommendations. It was recognised that the first arrangements could only be regarded as provisional. The making of gold coins legal tender, and the other measures necessary for the final and effective establishment of a gold standard in India, were left to be provided by further legislation in the light of future experience.

It was not until four years had elapsed after the

closing of the mints that the value of the rupee approached the desired standard of 1s. 4d. Early in 1898 it was considered by the Government of India that the time had come for carrying to completion the measures initiated in 1893. Their proposals were referred to a Committee of which Sir Henry Fowler was chairman, and in 1899, in accordance with its recommendations, an Act of the Indian Legislature was passed (Act XXII. of 1899), declaring that English gold coin should be legal tender in India at the rate of one sovereign for fifteen rupees, and that the Indian mints should be open for the coinage of sovereigns to the public. Certain legal and technical difficulties have until now (1902) prevented the latter of these provisions from being carried into effect, but the former has been successful in causing an influx of gold into India for payment to the Government in exchange for rupees. Large amounts of gold have been reissued to the public in India for use as currency. Since 1898 the exchange value of the rupee has been maintained at 1s. 4d., practically without a break; a common standard of value between India and England has, it may reasonably be hoped, been permanently secured, and difficulties and dangers which were intolerable have been removed. The metallic currency of India, in ordinary use by the people, is now a silver token currency of enormous magnitude. Gold is the standard of value, but silver is a legal tender to an unlimited amount. The system in force is similar in principle to that which has prevailed for many years in France, and there seems no reason why it should not be equally successful. The profits on the coinage of silver are necessarily large; they are not treated as revenue, but are held as a special "Gold Reserve

Fund," available for the maintenance of exchange, and they are invested in sterling securities in England.

It was a great misfortune for India that this reform of the currency was so long delayed. In 1878, when Sir Richard Strachey was acting as Financial Member of the Council, he drew up an elaborate scheme dealing with this subject. It was adopted by the Government of Lord Lytton and sent to the Secretary of State with a strong recommendation that it should be adopted. Although differing in detail from the system established in 1893 and 1898, it was in principle the same, and where it differed its effect would have been more beneficial, because the gold value of the rupee was at that time much higher than that to which it subsequently fell. Unfortunately, the British Treasury, to which the proposals of the Government of India were referred, refused its sanction, and the Secretary of State could hardly act, if he had wished to do so, in opposition to its views. The result of this delay of fifteen years in carrying out a reform of vital importance was the needless imposition on India of an enormous burden which was felt in every branch of the administration, and of fresh and objectionable taxation.

There is one other matter, closely connected with the commercial interests of India, which I must notice before closing this chapter.

The loss and inconvenience caused to the commerce of Great Britain by the confusion and diversity of the existing weights and measures can hardly be exaggerated; it is denied by no reasonable man, and the time cannot be far distant, when the ignorant prejudices which have prevented the general adoption of the metric system will no longer be allowed to stand in

the way of a most urgent reform. In India, similar evils exist in an exaggerated shape; apart from the inconvenience in the larger transactions of trade, the poorer and more ignorant classes suffer constantly from the multiplicity of weights and measures, and from the want of all standards by which the operations of retail dealers can be tested and regulated. In 1867, when Lord Lawrence was Viceroy, a Committee was appointed to inquire into this subject throughout India. Its President was Sir Richard Strachey, and he thus described the general facts that were established :—
"The diversity among the weights and measures used in various parts of India is as great as is well possible. Not only do the weights vary from province to province, but from town to town, and even within the same town or rural district. Different weights are used in various trades in the sale of different commodities, and in wholesale and retail transactions."

The only system of weights at that time recognised by the Government, but never generally introduced for trade purposes, was created by Regulation VII. of 1833, a law which in fact served only as a basis for the currency. The *seer*, the weight in most common use, was declared to consist of 80 tolas, the tola being equal in weight to the rupee. This seer was commensurable only with English troy weights, on which the weight of the rupee was founded, and these being only used for the sale of drugs in retail and for gold and silver, it had no exact equivalent in avoirdupois weight, which is exclusively used in English commercial transactions. It was equal to $2\frac{2}{35}$ lbs. avoirdupois. Although to some extent introduced in Government transactions, and in towns containing a large English community, no serious attempt was ever made to bring the seer of 80 tolas into use in the country at large, and it was never generally used or known. It was inconveniently less than the weights of the same name commonly in use, and this reason was alone sufficient to make it disliked by the people and to prevent its more common adoption. Nor can it be said that the belief that loss is entailed upon purchasers by a diminution in the standard of weight is merely fanciful. That belief is an expression of the fact that prices often depend not only upon competition but on custom. Thus the Government seer had nothing to recommend it from an Indian point of view, while in relation to English commerce it was extremely inconvenient. There was nothing to render desirable any attempt to encourage its more general adoption.

The investigations made throughout India in 1867 established the fact that, although the diversities were almost infinite, the most generally known of all Indian weights was the seer, and that its average weight was about 2¼ lbs. avoirdupois. This being almost exactly equivalent to the kilogram of the metric system in force throughout the whole of civilised Europe, with the exception of the United Kingdom, it was proposed by Sir Richard Strachey, and the proposal was adopted by the Government of Lord Lawrence, that a seer of this value, or 2·205 lbs., should be the basis of the new Indian system. This weight differs little from the thousandth part of the English ton, the weight chiefly used in the Foreign trade, and from the fiftieth part of the hundredweight.

There never was a man less disposed than Lord Lawrence to pay much attention to reasons of a theoretical nature, nor one with profounder knowledge of India, or more absolutely devoted to the interests of its people. He wisely insisted that any conclusions must be based exclusively on a consideration of their convenience, and that we were bound to select a system which should be in all respects thoroughly and permanently beneficial to them. Believing this, he declared in a Despatch to the Secretary of State, in which all the members of his Government, myself included, concurred, that "the kilogram of the metric system at once provides a seer which would certainly be as acceptable to the people as any that could be chosen. On account of its simplicity and its symmetrical form, the metric system of weight, in its integrity, will be more convenient for India than any other. While it will be perfectly suitable for the internal wants of India, it will be in harmony with the system already adopted in the greater part of the civilised world, and which may ultimately be adopted by England herself. In any case it will be more convenient for commercial transactions between England and India than any other system not really commensurable with that of England."[1]

These conclusions were approved by the Duke of Argyll, who was then Secretary of State, and in 1870 a Bill was introduced by Sir Richard Strachey, and passed into law by the Government of Lord Mayo, who was then Viceroy. The measure received his warm approval, and it was passed by the Legislative Council, which had then the advantage of the presence of commercial members of much eminence, without a dissentient voice. It had been agreed by the Government of Lord Lawrence, and by the Secretary of State, that it was expedient, in the first instance, to deal with weights and measures of capacity only, and not with measures of length, the latter being a matter of less urgency.

[1] Despatch to Secretary of State, November 6, 1868.

The Government of Lord Mayo thought it desirable to take the opportunity of also defining in the new law the standard of length, on which, under the metrical system, the unit of weight depends. The Secretary of State, however, preferred the original conclusion, and a new Bill, introduced by Sir James Stephen, became law as the "Indian Weights and Measures of Capacity Act, 1871." It declared that it was desirable to provide for the ultimate adoption of a uniform system throughout British India; that the unit of weight should be the seer, equal to the kilogram of the metric system; that other weights and measures of capacity might be authorised by the Government, subject to the condition that they must be integral multiples or subdivisions of the prescribed units; that proper standards should be provided; and among other provisions, that, after a date to be fixed by the Government, these weights and measures should be used in the dealings and contracts of the Government, of municipalities, and railway companies.

It was from the first declared that no attempt would be made to force the new system, in regard to their private trade and dealings, upon any classes of the people. It was recognised that it was visionary to suppose, even if the Government had been inclined to do anything so foolish, that it was possible to force upon the people of India, within any definite period, the adoption of any new system of weights and measures.

"All," it was said, "who have studied the subject have agreed that the proper way of beginning the introduction of any new system would be to adopt it in all Government and municipal departments and on the railways. When we consider the manner in which a network of railways and canals will carry on an enormous proportion of the trade of the country, and when we remember the magnitude of the operations of the Government in the Public Works, the Commissariat, the Post-Office, the Customs, and other departments, it is reasonable to anticipate that in a not very distant future, the country would have become so far accustomed to the new units that the measures for their general introduction could no longer be called compulsory. It may be confidently said that not many years would elapse before this would be true at least of the wholesale traders in all the richest parts of India, and that they would gradually, for their own convenience, adopt the new system almost without pressure on the part of the Government. When the wholesale traders had become accustomed to the change, its gradual introduction into the operations of retail trade would be attended with comparatively little difficulty."

In accordance with this plan of proceeding, communications with the principal railway companies were opened by Lord Mayo. The East Indian and some other companies had gone so far as to alter their weighing-machines, to make them suitable to the new system, and Lord Mayo confidently expected to see the first steps towards this reform, in which he had taken a great and active interest, successfully carried out. His death put a stop to all further proceedings, and through causes on which I will not comment, matters remain in the same condition in which they were found by Lord Lawrence thirty-five years ago. Yet, the Regulation of 1833 having been repealed as obsolete, the Act of 1871 still remains on the statute-book, and, although treated as a dead letter, it is still the only law on the subject actually in force in British India. "We must be satisfied, for the present, with the knowledge that it is something even to have failed in the accomplishment of a wise undertaking, when the failure may help to prepare the way for success hereafter. It may confidently be asserted that the acceptance of a sound and uniform system of commercial weights and measures would be hardly less important and valuable to India than was the adoption of a uniform system of currency. The public inconvenience and injury caused by the neglect of this matter have gone on far too long, and must continue to increase as the country becomes richer and trade more active."[1]

[1] *The Finances and Public Works of India*, by Sir John Strachey and Lieut. General Richard Strachey, 1882.

CHAPTER XIV

PUBLIC WORKS—FAMINE

Mr. J. S. Mill on the duties of Governments—Famines in India—Necessity for roads, railways, and canals—Absence of roads under Native Governments—Their condition under the East India Company—Measures taken by Lord Dalhousie—Railway construction—Creation of Public Works Department—Progress up to 1887—Irrigation works in Northern India—Canals of Mohammedan sovereigns—The Ganges and other canals—Their value—Irrigation works in Central and Southern India and in Sind—Expenditure on railways and irrigation works—The manner of providing funds—Guaranteed companies—Policy of borrowing for investment in public works—Measures for the prevention and relief of famine.

THE duties of the Government in India go far beyond those which we expect from a Government in countries like our own.

"In the particular circumstances of a given age or nation," wrote Mr. J. S. Mill, evidently with India especially in his mind, "there is scarcely anything really important to the general interest which it may not be desirable, or even necessary, that the Government should take upon itself, not because private individuals cannot effectually perform it, but because they will not. At some times and places there will be no roads, docks, harbours, canals, works of irrigation, hospitals, schools, colleges, printing presses, unless the Government establishes them; the public being either too poor to command the necessary resources, or too little advanced in intelligence to appreciate the end, or not sufficiently practised in conjoint action to be capable of the means. This is true, more or less, of all countries inured to despotism, and particularly of those in which there is a very wide distance in civilisation between the people and the Government, as in those which have been conquered and are retained in subjection by a more energetic and more cultivated people."[1]

But for our Government, hardly any of these requirements of civilised life would now be supplied in India, and there are special reasons which make the duty which thus falls upon the Government extraordinarily urgent.

In India, the very existence of the people depends on the regular occurrence of the periodical rains, and when they fail through a wide tract of country, and, still worse, when they fail in successive years, the consequences are disastrous. It is, as the Government of India have observed, an obvious fallacy to suppose that any alterations of administration or in the system on which the assessments of the land are made can save an agricultural population, such as that of India, from the effects of failure of the rains. "The relation of cause and effect between a good rainfall, abundant crops, and agricultural prosperity, is not more obvious than that between a bad monsoon, deficient produce, and a suffering people. When the vast majority of the inhabitants of a country are dependent upon an industry which is in itself dependent upon the rainfall, it is clear that a failure of the latter must unfavourably, and in extreme cases calamitously, affect the entire agricultural community. The suspension of the rains means a suspension of labour; the suspension of labour means a drying up of the means of subsistence; and the latter is necessarily followed by distress and destitution. There is no industry in the world, the sudden interruption or the temporary destruction of which is not attended by

[1] *Principles of Political Economy*, vol. ii. p. 551.

impoverishment and suffering, and there is no country in the world, where the meteorological and climatic conditions are at all similar to those prevailing in India, that could by any land revenue system that might possibly be devised escape the same results. Nevertheless, if prevention of the inevitable consequences of drought be an ideal incapable of attainment, mitigation is manifestly an object worthy of the closest attention of the Government."[1]

The greater part of India is liable to this danger, but the country is so vast that it never happens that all parts of it suffer at the same time. Changes in the economical condition of the people, and especially greater diversity of occupation, can alone bring safeguards complete enough to render general famine, in its extremest form, through a great tract of country, impossible. But this must be a long and gradual process. Meanwhile, it has been found by experience that although the entire prevention of famines, the most destructive of all calamities, is beyond the power of any Government, we can do much to mitigate them by removing obstacles which hinder commercial intercourse, and by means which increase and secure the productiveness of the land. The instruments by which we can do this are roads, railways, works of irrigation, and wells. If, to give one illustration, we read the history of the Indian famines of 1876-78, and of 1896-99, we shall find ample proof of the incalculable value of such works. Without them, millions of people must have been left to perish without the possibility of relief.

Lord Macaulay did not speak too strongly when he said that, excepting only the inventions of the alphabet

[1] Resolution of the Government of India, January 16, 1902. Papers regarding the Land revenue system of British India presented to Parliament 1902.

and the printing press, no inventions have done so much for the moral and intellectual progress of man as those which abridge distance and improve the means of communication.

Until about the middle of the last century the duties which thus fall upon us were hardly recognised. Before that time India was, to a great extent, governed on principles that might have commended themselves to a beneficent Oriental ruler rather than to modern Englishmen. Even an enlightened man like Sir Charles Metcalfe could maintain in 1830 that India required no roads; and in fact there were none. No Native prince made a road. Before the establishment of our Government there was hardly a road deserving the name in all India. Under the Native Governments that preceded us (I am quoting from the Indian Famine Commissioners of 1880), nothing more was done than to plant trees along each side of the track used as a road, and occasionally to throw up earth on it when it passed through a depression; such bridges as existed were made at the private expense of civil magnates or governors desirous of leaving a name behind them.

The graphic description which Lord Macaulay has given of the highways of England in the time of Charles II. is almost exactly applicable to those of India as I remember them in my youth. On the best lines of communication in England, he tells us, it was often hardly possible to distinguish the road at all, or to avoid losing one's way in the dark; the mud lay deep on the right and left, and only a narrow tract of firm ground rose above the quagmire; it happened almost every day that coaches stuck fast until a team of cattle could be procured to tug them out of the slough; when the floods were out, passengers perished in the attempt to cross, or narrowly escaped being swept away, or had to wander across meadows, and ride to the saddle-skirts in water. The markets were often inaccessible during several months. "The fruits of the earth were sometimes suffered to rot in one place, while in another place, distant only a few miles, the supply fell far short of the demand." When Prince George of Denmark went to visit Petworth he was six hours in going nine miles, and it was necessary that a body of sturdy hinds should be on each side of his coach in order to prop it up; an unfortunate courtier who was one of the party complained that during fourteen hours he never once alighted, except when his coach was overturned or stuck fast in the mud. All this, which I have borrowed from Lord Macaulay, is precisely what might have happened to Indian travellers on the most frequented highways of the country some fifty or sixty years ago, if they trusted themselves to wheeled vehicles. But practically, for people who could afford it, the only means by which a long journey could be accomplished was to be carried by men in a palanquin. A dák journey, as it was called, of a thousand miles was, to an Englishman at least, a process of misery which in these days can hardly be understood. I remember Lord Lawrence telling me that when he was a young man he was thought to have performed an extraordinary feat, because, travelling day and night, he reached Delhi in a fortnight after leaving Calcutta—a journey, at the present time, of less than thirty hours. Throughout a great part of India it was only in the dry season that travelling was possible without extreme difficulty, and, during three or four months of the year, trade, excepting where water-carriage was available, came altogether to a standstill. As Sir George Chesney says in his *Indian Polity*:—

"The Court of Directors, until almost the termination of their existence, did not recognise the prosecution of public works as a necessary part of their policy. The construction of a road or canal was regarded by them, in their earlier days, much in the same light that a war would be—as an unavoidable evil, to be undertaken only when it could not be postponed any longer, and not, if possible, to be repeated."

Speaking in 1858, Mr. Bright said that in a single English county there were "more travelable roads than in the whole of India, and the single city of Manchester, in the supply of its inhabitants with the single article of water, has spent a larger sum of money than the East India Company spent in the fourteen years from 1834 to 1848 in public works of every kind throughout the whole of its vast dominions." I do not doubt that Mr. Bright's statement was substantially not far from correct.

In the last years of the East India Company, however, and especially during the Government of Lord Dalhousie, matters began rapidly to improve. Under the enlightened rule of their Lieutenant-Governor, Mr. Thomason, one of the wisest of Indian statesmen, great progress was made in the North-Western Provinces in the construction of metalled roads, and bridges, and other useful works; and his example was vigorously followed by his successor, Mr. John Colvin, and in the Punjab by the Lawrences. The grand trunk road from Calcutta to the North was rapidly pushed on. In 1854 the Ganges Canal, an irrigation work with which no similar works in the world, except those of the Punjab and Madras, can compete in magnitude and utility, was opened, though not completed.

People had become alive to the fact that without the material appliances which facilitate and cheapen the means of communication and production, there could be no rapid progress either in the condition of the people or in the efficiency of the Government. In 1853 the necessity of constructing railways to connect the chief provinces and cities of India was declared by Lord Dalhousie in a minute which laid the foundation of the existing system of railway communication. Three great lines were soon afterwards commenced: the East Indian Railway, from Calcutta towards the Northern Provinces; the Great Indian Peninsular Railway, and the Madras Railway, starting respectively from Bombay and Madras, and running through Western and Southern India. These lines were constructed by private companies, under a guarantee from the Government of a minimum return of 5 per cent on the capital expended.

In 1854 a separate Department of Public Works was for the first time created under the Government of India. In 1856-57 the outlay on public works, exclusive of the sums spent on railways by the guaranteed companies, had risen to nearly £2,250,000.

The mutinies of 1857 brought fresh and the strongest possible proof of the necessity for improved means of communication. When peace was restored, and the Government was transferred to the Crown, the construction of public works went on with increased speed, and from that time to this there has been constant progress. Considering the vast extent of India, and the fact that almost everything has been done by the Government or under its guarantee, or with its assistance, and little by unaided private enterprise, we may be well satisfied with the work that has been accomplished.

Railways now connect all the principal districts and cities; the great rivers are bridged; the country has been covered with roads, and there is no considerable town without its telegraph office. In 1901 nearly 28,000 miles of railway were open or under construction, and 195,000,000 passengers and 44,000,000 tons of goods were carried on them. Railways have given to the population throughout India an impulse of activity which in no other way could have been communicated. The time, however, is still distant when it will cease to be true that the provision of increased means of communication is one of the chief duties of the Government of India.

There is another result of the construction of railways in India that I must not omit to mention. They have increased, to a degree that is hardly calculable, our military strength; and so long as we retain our maritime supremacy, and the determination to maintain our empire, it will, we may reasonably believe, be impossible that any combination of hostile powers should dangerously threaten our dominion.

I must now refer to works of another kind, as important, in many parts of India, as those of which I have been speaking.

In Northern India, even in good seasons, artificial irrigation is a necessity for the successful cultivation of many of the more valuable crops, and when there is a general failure of the periodical rains there is no other means by which drought and scarcity can be prevented. A large portion of Northern India is now protected by canals of greater magnitude than any that exist in other countries of the world. In the United Provinces this is especially true of the tract called the Doáb, lying between the Ganges and Jumna. Owing to its geographical position, which made it the chief centre of the Moghal Empire, and to the industry of its numerous population, it has been for centuries one of the most important countries of India.

Long before our time some of the Mohammedan sovereigns had undertaken works on the western bank of the Jumna, with the object partly of irrigation, but still more with that of affording a supply of water to the city and imperial palaces of Delhi. A canal, the course of which is not very clearly known, was made by Firoz Toghlak, as far back as 1351 A.D., and more important works from the Jumna were constructed by Akbar and by Sháh Jehán in the sixteenth and seventeenth centuries. An elaborate system appears to have been in force for regulating the distribution of the water. The orders of Akbar provided "that all parties, rich or poor, weak or strong, shall share alike"; and directed, for the comfort of travellers, "that on both sides of the canal trees of every description, both for shade and blossom, shall be planted, so as to make it like the canal under the tree in Paradise, and that the sweet flavour of the rare fruits may reach the mouth of every one, and from these luxuries a voice may go forth to travellers, calling them to rest in the cities, where their every want will be supplied."[1] Not long after the death of Aurangzìb, when the empire was rapidly broken up, the canals of the Moghal sovereigns ceased to flow, and it was not until 1817, after these provinces had passed under the British Government, that their restoration and improvement was commenced. Later on an examination of historical records led to a result which deserves to be noticed. Describing the excavations for the canal of Firoz Toghlak, the historian Ferishta mentions incidentally that the work-people employed upon them found, near the foot of the hills,

[1] *Calcutta Review*, "Canals of Irrigation," 1849.

quantities of giants' bones. "To minds familiar with discoveries in fossil geology the old chronicle had a gleam of significance," and the investigations which followed led to the discovery, by Falconer and Cautley, of the gigantic fossil remains now in the British Museum.[1]

Little of the old irrigation works of our predecessors is retained in the existing canals. Practically, all of these have been made by ourselves, and the often-repeated statement, prompted, I suppose, by that strange inclination to depreciate their own achievements which often besets Englishmen, that the old canals have been more profitable than those constructed by ourselves, has not the least foundation of truth.

Among the irrigation works of primary importance in Northern India are those which distribute the water of the Ganges and Jumna. In the winter and spring, before the Ganges has been swollen by the melting of the snow in the Himálaya, and when water is urgently required for agricultural operations, nearly the whole visible stream of the great river at Hardwár, where it leaves the mountains, is thrown into an artificial channel. The works, due to the genius of Sir Proby Cautley, on the first twenty miles of its course are in a high degree remarkable, for the canal intersects the drainage of the lower Himálaya, and has to be carried across rivers which often become furious torrents, bringing down enormous floods. These obstacles have been overcome by various methods with a skill of which our Indian engineers may well be proud. One torrent flows harmlessly in a broad artificial bed over the canal which runs below; over another, still more formidable, with a bed more than two miles wide, the canal, which

[1] *Calcutta Review*, "Canals of Irrigation," 1849.

is virtually the whole Ganges, is carried by an aqueduct. Some 200 miles lower down the Ganges has again become a large river, and nearly all its water is again diverted into a second canal. The two canals together are capable of discharging more than 12,000 cubic feet of water per second; the ordinary supply of each is more than double the volume of the Thames at Teddington in average weather, and this great body of water is distributed over the country by a number of smaller channels for the irrigation of the land.

Three canals of smaller dimensions, but which in any other country would be looked on as works of great magnitude, distribute in a similar way nearly the whole of the water brought by the Jumna from the Himálaya. Altogether, in 1901, in the United Provinces, the length of the chief irrigation canals exceeded 1500 miles, the length of their distributories was nearly 11,000 miles; they irrigated nearly 3,000,000 acres of land, and more than double that area is capable of being served by them.

In Behár, the border province of the Bengal Lieutenant-Governorship, which in its physical character closely resembles the adjoining provinces of the north-west, irrigation works of considerable extent are taken from the river Són.

There are other important irrigation canals in Orissa and minor works in other parts of Bengal, but in that province irrigation is not ordinarily so essential as in countries farther north, where the climate is drier and the seasons are more precarious.

In the Punjab, where irrigation is even more necessary than in the United Provinces, great works have been constructed, or are in progress, to utilise the waters of the Sutlej, the Chenáb, the Rávi, the Jhelum, and other rivers. The Sirhind Canal, which distributes the water of the Sutlej through not only our own territories, but through the Native States of Patiála, Nábha, and Jhind, is a work hardly inferior in magnitude to the canals from the Ganges. It is capable of discharging 8000 cubic feet of water per second; the length of its main channel is more than 500 miles, and that of its distributories more than 5000 miles.

The canal from the Chenáb is not less important; it has brought and is bringing under cultivation a tract of country which was formerly little better than a desert. A canal of still greater magnitude is projected which, starting from Kalabagh on the left bank of the Indus, will afford irrigation to nearly two millions of acres.

Altogether, in 1901, the length of the main canals actually in operation in the Punjab exceeded 1600 miles, while the length of minor irrigation works was still greater. The canals of Northern India give to the State a good direct return on the cost of their construction, but the direct receipts are no index whatever to the benefits which are conferred by them upon the country. They give to great tracts complete protection against scarcity and famine, the wealth of the people is immensely increased, and it not seldom happens that the whole first cost of the works, although this is measured in many millions, is less than the value of the crops saved to the people in a single season.

Different systems of irrigation prevail in other parts of India. In Central and Southern India large tracts of country are dependent for their supply of water on lakes or reservoirs, known by the not very appropriate name of tanks. These are in some cases natural lakes, but oftener they have been formed by the construction of dams of masonry or earth across the outlets of valleys in the hills, and they are fed sometimes by rivers and sometimes by the rainfall of a more or less extensive area. They vary in size from ponds irrigating a few acres to lakes of several miles in circumference. In the Madras Presidency there are some 60,000 of these tanks. Some of them are works constructed in times of which we have no historical record.

These are not the only means of irrigation in Southern India. Works not inferior in importance to those of the United Provinces and Punjab, but on a different system, have been carried out by the British Government in the Madras Presidency for utilising the waters of the Godáveri and Kistna rivers. They constitute a noble monument to Sir Arthur Cotton, to whose genius they are mainly due. At the head of each of the deltas formed by the rivers before they reach the sea, a great weir, or, as it is locally called, an *anicut*, is thrown across the river, which is diverted into irrigation canals and distributing channels, some of which are also used for navigation. A large area, with a population of nearly 2,000,000, thus obtains complete protection against failure of rain; and these works have not only been in the highest degree beneficial to the people, but very profitable to the State. Without canal irrigation there would sometimes be no crops at all, and the value of the produce in a single year of scarcity has been four times as great as the whole of the capital expended on the canal works by the Government. Farther south, in Tanjore, works of a similar kind provide the means of utilising through a large tract of country, in the delta of the Káveri, almost the whole water-supply of that river. Another most remarkable work is in progress which pierces by a long tunnel the range of the Western Gháts, and brings the waters of the Perigar river, which fed by a copious rainfall ran uselessly to the sea, into the comparatively dry country on the eastern side of the mountains.

In Northern India the ordinary rental of land is doubled by irrigation, and it is often more than quadrupled in Madras.

In the province of Sind another system prevails. Little rain falls there, and without irrigation there would be no cultivation. In the same way that agriculture in Egypt depends on the inundation of the Nile, it depends in Sind on the floods brought down by the Indus in the season of the periodical rains. There is great room for further improvement, but the existing irrigation renders the province fairly prosperous, and gives or increases the means of subsistence to 3,000,000 people.

Altogether there are, in India, under the management or supervision of the British Government, some 43,000 miles of canals and other works, giving the means of irrigation to 20,000,000 acres of land. No similar works in other countries approach in magnitude the irrigation works of India, and no public works of nobler utility have ever been undertaken in the world. No year passes without some important extension of irrigation, but there are, unfortunately, many vast tracts of country in India where nothing in this direction seems possible, because there are no rivers that can be utilised; other means of storing and utilising water can, however, sometimes be adopted. No admiration can be too great for the Indian engineers to whom we owe these works. They have given fresh examples of their skill and science in the magnificent undertakings which, with similar objects, are being carried out in Egypt.

Up to the end of 1901, including not only the funds borrowed by the Government, but the capital raised by companies under the guarantee of the Secretary of State, or supplied from other sources, nearly £300,000,000 had been spent on railways and irrigation works in India. Nearly the whole of this outlay has taken place since the transfer of the Government to the Crown in 1858, and the greater part of it since 1870. In spite of all encouragement which the Government could legitimately give, there have not been many instances in which any large amount of private capital has hitherto been forthcoming without a guarantee of interest for railways in India. One of the most important causes of this disinclination on the part of English capitalists to invest money in these and other useful undertakings, has been the absence of a common standard of value between India and England. I have explained in a preceding chapter that we may reasonably hope that this obstacle has now been removed. Almost the whole cost of these works has been provided either directly by the Government, or by English companies aided by a guarantee.

I must briefly explain the system under which the funds for this great expenditure have been supplied.

When, after the mutinies of 1857, the obligation of providing numerous works of improvement had been recognised, it became evident that the ordinary revenue could not furnish the means of meeting the necessary outlay. The financial difficulties involved by the suppression of the mutinies were great, and for some years afterwards the necessity of providing barracks and hospitals for the largely increased force of British troops was so urgent that the progress of other works was crippled.

In 1864 the principle was accepted, that for the construction of works of irrigation it was right to supply by loan the funds which could not be otherwise provided, but it was not until 1867, during the Government of Lord Lawrence, that this conclusion took a practical shape under a scheme drawn up by General Sir Richard Strachey. It was clear that only a comparatively small part of the necessary outlay could be met from the revenues ; the rest was to be supplied by loans. No project was to be taken up which did not promise to be fairly remunerative within a reasonable time ; it was believed that the earnings would before long more than cover the interest on the borrowed capital, and that no ultimate charge would fall on the general revenues. In 1869 Sir Richard Strachey proposed to extend this system to the development of railways. His plans were adopted without reservation by Lord Lawrence, whose conclusions were recorded in a minute which it is now no breach of official reserve to say was drafted by Sir Richard Strachey. The scheme was substantially adopted by the Secretary of State, and the first steps were taken by Lord Mayo in 1870 for carrying them into effect.

I will not describe the various phases through which this policy has passed. The main principle, that railways and irrigation works in India may wisely, and without financial danger, be constructed with borrowed money, has been consistently carried out, partly by the Government directly, and partly through the agency of companies assisted by a guarantee of interest or by subsidies from the State. The complete financial success of this policy will be shown in the next chapter.

All this is closely connected with a subject which, for many years past, has constantly occupied the attention of the Government of India, that of the prevention and relief of famine.

Little is known in detail regarding the famines which devastated India before the establishment of British rule, but there is no doubt that they were numerous and terrible. The first great famine of which trustworthy records exist is that of 1769-70. It would be impossible for any description to exaggerate the frightful sufferings of that time, when it was believed that one-third of the population of Bengal perished. In the ninety years that followed, many serious failures of the periodical rains occurred, but, as the Famine Commissioners of 1901 tell us, there was no systematised and sustained action by the Government for their relief, "and amid the wars and distractions and financial difficulties that attended the building up of an empire, the claims of famine relief attracted small attention." The first serious attempt to deal with the subject was made in the North-Western Provinces in 1861, but when the great famine of 1866, commonly known as the Orissa famine, occurred, "the principles and methods of relief administration were still unsettled and unformed. That famine may be regarded as the turning-point in the history of Indian famines, for in the course of the inquiry conducted into it by the Commission presided over by the late Sir George Campbell, the foundations were laid of the humane policy which the Government of India have now adopted." After the great famine of 1876-78 a Commission, under the presidency of Sir Richard Strachey, with Sir Charles Elliott as secretary, was appointed by Lord Lytton to inquire into the whole subject of famines in India, and to advise the Government on the measures to be taken for their prevention and relief. "Their inquiries," in the words of the Famine Commissioners of 1901, "for the first time reduced to system the administration of famine relief, and their report has powerfully influenced for good agrarian and administrative reform in India. The labours of the Commission of 1880 were of two kinds: on the one hand they formulated general principles for the proper treatment of famines, and, on the other, they suggested particular measures of a preventive or protective character. In regard to the general principles with which we are immediately concerned, the Commission of 1880 recognised to the full the obligation imposed on the State to offer to the necessitous the means of relief in times of famine. But it was the cardinal principle of their policy that this relief should be so administered as not to check the growth of thrift and self-reliance among the people, or to impair the structure of society, which, resting as it does in India upon the moral obligation of material assistance, is admirably adapted for common effort against a common misfortune. 'The great object,' they said, 'of saving life and giving protection from extreme suffering may not only be as well secured, but in fact will be far better secured, if proper care be taken to prevent the abuse and demoralisation which all experience shows to be the consequence of ill-directed and excessive distribution of charitable relief.' In this spirit the Provincial Famine Code was framed, and the modern policy of famine relief administration was determined. That policy was first brought to a crucial test in the famine of 1896-97, and the very elaborate inquiry into its results conducted by the Commission of 1898 completely vindicated the principles laid down in 1880, and demonstrated the success which a system of relief based upon them could achieve. Wherever there was failure, it was due not so much to defects in the system of relief, as to defects in the administration of it."[1]

In 1899 another serious famine occurred, and a Commission under the presidency of Sir Antony MacDonnell was appointed by the Government of Lord Curzon to re-examine, in the light of the further experience that had been gained, the whole question of measures for the relief and prevention of famine. Sir Antony MacDonnell had himself, in 1897, when Lieutenant-Governor of the North-Western Provinces and Oudh, shown with admirable ability and conspicuous success the manner in which serious famine must be combated. The Report of this Commission, issued in 1901, will prove hereafter of inestimable value to the Government of India in dealing with these great calamities.

The result of the labours of these three Commissions has been the preparation of elaborate codes of instructions for every province, laying down the principles and the practice to be followed on every occasion of threatened or actual scarcity. We cannot expect that there will be no recurrence of these disasters. India will still be subject from time to time to widespread and lamentable suffering, but we may reasonably hope that we shall not again see in their most aggravated form the horrors and the terrible mortality which attended the famines of former times. Large tracts of country which were, not long ago, isolated by physical obstacles, and, by the want of means of communication, almost inaccessible to trade, and dependent on the food produced in their own borders, are now easy of access. Whereas millions formerly perished from the physical

[1] Since the famine of 1876-78 there have been three Famine Commissions, that of 1880, of 1898, and of 1901, presided over respectively by Sir Richard Strachey, Sir James Lyall, and Sir Antony MacDonnell.

impossibility of providing them with food, Sir Antony MacDonnell's Commission of 1901 was able to state that in the famines of 1897 and 1899 there was never a dearth of food in any famine-stricken tract. "To the policy," the Commission wrote, "of protective railways such ample effect has now been given that the final horror of famine—an actual dearth of food—need no longer be a source of apprehension. In inaccessible mountain country or in some remote valley the local officers may have, upon occasion, to bring food for the people, or to subsidise private trade to do so, but in the continent at large there is, for the future, no anxiety as to the ability of private trade to deliver food where it is needed. There is, indeed, necessity for improving the means of transport by an increase of the rolling stock, but, generally, railway construction has, in our opinion, played its part in the policy of famine insurance. To put the food-supply of the country in circulation was necessarily the first object of a wise famine policy; to protect and develop the supply itself should be its second object; and this is the function of agricultural development generally, and of irrigation in particular. This subject was dealt with at considerable length by the Commission of 1898, and the evidence which we have taken, and our own experience, show that there is a wide field for the construction of irrigation works. All provinces do not, indeed, present practicable schemes for the construction of great canals, but the possibilities of smaller protective works have in no province been exhausted, while in some provinces they have as yet hardly been examined. For storage tanks, reservoirs, and, above all, irrigation wells, the scope and the necessity are very great. As the whole subject of irrigation has now been taken up by the

Government in pursuance of the recommendations of the Commission of 1898, we need do no more than point to the confirmation which our inquiries afford to the conclusions of the last Commission, and express our cordial approval of a new departure in famine policy which would place irrigation works in the place that protective railways have hitherto occupied in the famine insurance programme."

Between 1896 and 1901 India suffered to an extent, happily altogether unusual, from repeated failure of the periodical rains, but, while the distress thus caused was in the highest degree lamentable, there is much in the history of that time which gives hope and encouragement. Speaking with an authority and personal knowledge greater perhaps than that of any man in India, Sir Antony MacDonnell, after the famine of 1897 in the North-Western Provinces, "drew the general conclusion that the cultivating classes, whether tenants or proprietors, have displayed a command of resources, either in the shape of capital or credit, and a power of resistance which has not been paralleled in any period of scarcity." The same conclusion was declared by the Commission of 1898 to be applicable to India generally. "The general conclusions," they wrote, "we are disposed to draw are that it may be said of India as a whole that of late years, owing to higher prices, there has been a considerable increase in the incomes of the land-holding and cultivating classes, and that their standard of comfort and expenditure has also expanded. During the recent famine these classes, as a rule, have therefore shown greater power of resisting famine, either by drawing on savings, or by borrowing, or by reduction of expenditure, than in any previous period of scarcity of like severity."

I cannot leave the subject of famine without referring to the truly noble work of the Englishmen entrusted with the management of relief operations during the scarcities of former and recent years. No language of respect and admiration for them could be too strong. Often they gave not only their health but their lives, dying at their posts, or working to save the people entrusted to them until no possibility of work remained.

CHAPTER XV

THE PUBLIC DEBT—FAMINE INSURANCE

The Public Debt—Its amount—Division into Ordinary and Public Works Debt—Increase of Debt owing to the Mutinies of 1857—Subsequent decrease of Ordinary Debt—Investments of the Government in Railways—Railways constructed by guaranteed Companies—The financial results of the policy of borrowing for public works—Expenditure from revenue on public works—Insurance against Famine—The policy adopted.

It will be understood from what has been said in the last chapter that the subject of public works is closely connected with that of the public debt.

The permanent public debt of India amounted in 1900-01 in India and in England to £205,300,000. The debt is divided for purposes of account into two parts—the Ordinary debt, similar in character to the public debt of other countries, and the Public Works debt, consisting of money invested in productive works, that is, in railways and works of irrigation. The ordinary debt was, in 1900-01, £69,996,000, and the public works debt was £135,327,000.

In 1857, just before the outbreak of the mutinies, the public debt of India was about £51,000,000. The task of suppressing the mutinies and the reorganisation of the administration added more than £42,000,000 to the debt; and in 1862 the total amount of the debt was £97,000,000. Thus in the thirty-eight years that elapsed after the suppression of the mutinies and the cessation of the extraordinary expenditure immediately due to them, that is, from 1862 to 1900, the debt was apparently increased by £108,000,000. This increase resulted entirely from the policy of borrowing for investment in railways and irrigation works, and I call it an apparent increase, because that policy now involves no burden, but a profit to the State. Apart from such investments, the public debt in the period I have mentioned not only received no increase, but was reduced by about £27,000,000. This will appear the more remarkable when it is remembered that India during this time suffered from a succession of serious famines, for the relief of which, and for protective works, an expenditure of more than £23,000,000 was incurred, that a net sum of £12,250,000 was spent on war, that heavy expenses had often to be met on account of military operations against the frontier tribes, and that a very large increase of charge has been caused by the fall in the gold value of silver.

The existing railways have either been constructed directly by the Government or through companies guaranteed or otherwise assisted by the State. In the latter case the Government has reserved, under the original contracts, the power of purchasing the lines after a certain period has elapsed. This power has been exercised in nearly every case in which it was possible to do so, the payments being made in the form of terminable annuities, carrying with them a sinking fund for the redemption of capital. The railways thus become State lines, and, in the course of the next half-century, the Government of India will come into full possession of a magnificent property, yielding every year a great revenue. The most important of the undertakings purchased in this way was the East Indian Railway, the great line connecting Calcutta with Delhi and the Northern Provinces. The transaction has already proved very advantageous to the State. In the ten years ending with 1901 it brought to the public revenues, after meeting all charges, including interest on borrowed capital, a clear profit of about £6,300,000, and, in addition, a further sum of £650,000, representing capital debt paid off through the operation of the terminable annuity by means of which the purchase of the line was made. At the end of seventy-four years from 1880, when the annuity expires, the Government will come into the receipt of a clear yearly income which is not likely to be less than £2,700,000, equivalent, after making allowance for all outgoings, to the creation of a capital of upwards of sixty or seventy millions sterling. It is not now possible to say what will have been the total capital expenditure on the railway at that time, but up to the end of 1901 it had not exceeded forty millions, and whatever additional capital may be required, it is reasonable to assume that there will be simultaneously an increase of net revenue at least sufficient to cover the additional interest to be paid. In this and in some other cases the working of the line has not been managed directly by the Government, but through a company under a working lease.

The rate of interest guaranteed on the capital of the railways first constructed by companies was 5 per cent, and the Government bound itself to make good any sum by which the net traffic receipts, after paying all working expenses, fall short of the amount necessary to provide interest at that rate. The later contracts have been more favourable to the Government.

The true measure of the burden of public debt is the

annual charge thrown upon the revenues by the payment of interest. The financial results of the policy of borrowing for investment in public works, judged by this test, have been highly satisfactory. It was inevitable that a considerable period must elapse before railways and irrigation works in India could yield an income sufficiently large to meet the charges incurred for their construction, and this for many years was actually the case. It is not easy to state with accuracy the total amount that had to be paid between the time when the construction of railways commenced and the time when they ceased to be any burden on the revenues, nor is this now a question of much importance. According to some estimates it exceeded £50,000,000. Whatever was the amount, it is certain that it was much less than the amount now saved to the country in a single year on the cost of transport alone, and when the direct charge on the revenues was the heaviest, there can be no doubt that it was far more than compensated by the advantages which were being conferred upon the country by the improvement in the means of communication. Its wealth grew steadily, the people were protected against the extreme consequences of famine, and there was no branch of the public administration the efficiency of which was not increased. As I shall presently show, the burden on the revenues necessarily incurred for a time has now, we may hope, finally disappeared.

The direct financial results would have been, and would still be far more favourable, but for the fact that many of the railways and canals are incomplete, and that there are many on which the receipts have not nearly reached the amount which may ultimately be expected. Some of them have been constructed for the special purpose of giving protection to poor and remote districts, with little prospect of profit. Some other railways are required for military reasons connected with the defence of the North-Western frontier; no works are more necessary, but they are not likely to give much commercial return. Another cause has largely diminished the direct profit from these works. The effect of the fall in the gold value of the rupee has been very serious. The earnings of all these works are in silver, but the greater part of the interest on the capital expenditure, the annuities paid in respect of guaranteed railways purchased, and nearly the whole of the payments to guaranteed companies, have had to be paid in gold. In 1891-92, for example, these gold payments amounted to £5,652,000. To provide this sum India had to pay nearly 25,000,000 rupees more than would have been required if the rupee had retained its old value of two shillings. But for such charges the Indian railways and canals would long ago have yielded a large income to the State.

The railways—and the same is true of the irrigation works of India—yielded in 1900-01 an income which more than covered all the expenditure incurred upon them. The debt incurred for public works was a debt which involved neither the obligation of repayment nor charge for interest, but which brought a direct profit to the State. After charging against revenue all interest charges not only on the open lines but on lines under construction from which no revenue was obtained, all expenses of every kind incurred in working the open lines, the amount paid annually by means of sinking funds and annuities for the redemption of the commuted capital of railways purchased by the State, and charges of every other description, there was in 1900-01 a clear profit to the State of £325,000. In the words of the Railway Administration Report of the Government of India for 1901, the railways have not only ceased to be a burden on the general revenues of the country, but may be expected in future to be one of the most certain and increasing sources of State revenue. The general truth of this conclusion cannot be doubted, although it must, from the nature of the case, be expected that the receipts will be liable to many vicissitudes, and it may happen in particular years that the results may financially be less favourable than those that I have described.

Up to the end of 1900-01 the total capital expenditure on irrigation works had been £28,246,000. The net receipts more than covered all charges on revenue of every description, and gave a surplus of £236,000.

In 1862 the public works debt was not separated, as it is now, from the ordinary debt. In that year the total net charge to the State on account of debt of every description, and including the sums paid as guaranteed interest to railway companies, was £6,585,000. In 1900-01 the total net charge to the State was £1,487,000, the amount of the interest on the ordinary debt and on other obligations; the payment of the interest on the public works debt, amounting to £5,298,000, involved, as I have shown, no charge at all, but, on the other hand, the railways and works of irrigation constructed with borrowed money gave to the State a profit of £561,000.[1] The ordinary debt of India was much less than the revenue of a single year.

I have hitherto spoken only of those public works

[1] It may be noted that "commercial services," as they have been called, *i.e.* Railways, Irrigation works, Post Office, and Telegraph, gave altogether, in 1900-01, a profit of £809,000.

which give a direct return in cash on the capital outlay, and which have been mainly constructed with borrowed money. Since the transfer of the Government to the Crown there has also been an immense expenditure from revenue on works of a different class, but not less useful, such as roads and bridges, telegraphs, hospitals, barracks and military works, colleges, schools, and other public buildings, and minor works of irrigation and navigation.

Before leaving the subject of public works and debt there is another matter to which reference must be made.

It has already been pointed out that, in addition to the reasons which in other countries render the construction of railways necessary, they are required in India because without them it is not possible to give adequate relief on the occurrence of the famines to which India, an almost purely agricultural country, has always from time to time been exposed through the failure of the periodical rains. In many parts of the country the provision of irrigation works is still more important.

It was not until 1874, when Lord Northbrook was Viceroy, that it was recognised that, since famines could not be looked on as abnormal and exceptional calamities, it was essential that provision against the grave financial obligations which they involve should be made as one of the ordinary charges of the State. "Whatever means," Lord Northbrook said, "we may take to obviate or mitigate them, it must, under present circumstances, be looked upon as inevitable that famines will from time to time occur"; he concluded that to meet them merely by borrowing would be financially ruinous, that it was necessary to reserve in prosperous times a substantial surplus of revenue over expenditure, and that, if this surplus were devoted to the reduction of debt, or to the construction of productive public works, thereby preventing the increase of debt, there would be no objection, when famine occurred, to meeting from borrowed money charges to the full extent to which debt had been reduced or prevented.

In 1877-78 measures were proposed by myself and adopted by the Government of Lord Lytton for giving practical effect to these principles.

Between 1873 and 1878 the actual expenditure on the relief of famine, including remissions of land revenue, was more than 160,000,000 rupees. This was a period of exceptional disaster, and it was concluded that it might safely be assumed that the average annual charge for relieving famine was not likely to exceed 15,000,000 rupees. It was determined, therefore, that in addition to that necessary margin of revenue over expenditure which a prudent administration always desires to maintain, a surplus of 15,000,000 rupees must every year be provided on account of famine relief alone, and that this sum, when the country was free from famine, must be regularly devoted to the discharge of debt, or to the prevention of debt which would otherwise have been incurred for the construction of railways and canals. The practical result of such a plan would be to store up, in times of prosperity, resources by means of which, when famine occurred, it would be possible to meet the inevitable requirements of the future and the heavy obligations of the State. If, for example, this policy were followed during a period of ten years in which there was no famine, debt at the end of that time would have been reduced or prevented to the extent of 150,000,000 rupees, and, if serious famine then occurred, the same amount might be borrowed for its relief without placing the country in a worse position financially than that of ten years before.

The original scheme was subsequently modified, and it was determined that a portion of the sum set aside every year as an insurance against famine might be directly expended on the construction of railways and canals required for the protection of districts specially liable to drought and consequent scarcity.

This policy of insurance against famine was simple in its nature, but it has been constantly misunderstood and persistently misrepresented. It has often been supposed that a separate fund was constituted into which certain revenues were to be paid, and which could only be drawn upon for a specified purpose. No such unreasonable and impracticable notion was ever entertained, and every idea of the kind was from the first repudiated by the Government and by myself, the author of the original scheme. The "Famine Insurance Fund," of which people have often talked, never existed. The intention was nothing more than the annual application of surplus revenue to the extent of 15,000,000 rupees to the purposes that I have described. The sum now allotted annually is £1,000,000. Although, in some years, financial pressure has made it impossible to make the full annual grant under the Famine Insurance Scheme, the system has been substantially maintained. The sum expended from revenue under the head of Famine Relief and Insurance, either on the actual relief of distress, or on protective irrigation works and railways, or on the reduction of debt, from the time when the scheme came into operation up to the end of 1900-01, exceeded £23,000,000; of this more than one-half was spent on the actual relief of famine.

CHAPTER XVI

EDUCATION IN INDIA

First establishment of colleges in Bengal—Controversy between advocates of Oriental and English study—Lord Macaulay in 1835—His contempt for Oriental literature — Mountstuart Elphinstone on Indian education—System established under Macaulay's influence—Neglect of primary education—System laid down by Lord Halifax in 1854—Its main features—Proportion of population able to read and write—Female education—Lady Dufferin's Association—Mr. Baines on illiteracy of the people—The Indian Universities—Colleges—Number of Natives knowing English—Collegiate Instruction—Education of Mohammedans—Sir Syad Ahmad Khán—His College—Medical Colleges—Technical and Art Schools—Secondary Education—Small number of educated Natives—Neglect of study of Science—Sir Henry Maine on study of English classical literature—The teaching of false history—Inaccuracy and bad faith of James Mill—Books and newspapers—Their general character—Mr. Baines on influence of the literate class—Liberty of the Press in India.

It was only during the later times of the East India Company's Government that the promotion of education in India was considered one of the duties of the State. The encouragement, however, of Oriental learning had long, to some extent, been acknowledged to be a matter of importance, both for its own sake, and because a knowledge of Mohammedan and Hindu law was necessary in the civil and criminal courts. To Warren Hastings belongs the honour of having founded, in 1782, the first college in Bengal, and it was maintained for some years at his expense. It was especially intended to encourage the study of Arabic and Persian literature and Mohammedan theology, "to qualify the Mohammedans of Bengal for the public service, chiefly in the courts of justice, and to enable them to compete on more equal terms with the Hindus for employment under Government." In 1791, a college, with similar objects, but "designed to cultivate the laws, literature, and religion of the Hindus, and specially to supply qualified Hindu assistants to European judges," was established at Benares. A few more institutions of a similar kind were founded, and as time went on the demand for other forms of education increased. A long controversy took place between the advocates of Oriental and English study: the former desired to give more liberal help to students of Sanskrit, Arabic, and Persian, to encourage the production of literary and scientific works in Oriental languages, and to provide for the translation of valuable books from the languages of Europe into those of India; the latter maintained that all the higher branches of knowledge should be taught through the medium of English alone. The controversy virtually ended in 1835 with a Minute by Lord Macaulay, who was then a member of the Governor-General's Council in Calcutta. Nothing could exceed the contempt which in his picturesque sentences he poured forth on the languages and literature of the East. That India, and Arabia, and Persia possessed great literatures of their own, that they have produced poets and philosophers whose works hold no mean place among the enduring monuments of human genius, these were facts which Lord Macaulay totally ignored.

"The question before us," he wrote, "is simply whether, when it is in our power to teach this language—English—we shall teach languages in which, by universal confession, there are no books on any subject which deserve to be compared to our own; whether, when we can teach European science, we shall teach systems which, by universal confession, wherever they differ from those of Europe, differ for the worse; and whether, when we patronise sound philosophy and true history, we shall countenance, at the public expense, medical doctrines which would disgrace an English farrier, astronomy which would move laughter in the girls at an English boarding-school, history abounding with kings thirty feet high and reigns thirty thousand years long, and geography made up of seas of treacle and seas of butter."

It is interesting to compare the scornful utterances of Macaulay with, as I believe, the wiser views which a great and accomplished Indian statesman, Mountstuart Elphinstone, expressed in a Minute on education in India not many years before.

"Sanskrit poetry," he wrote, "has called forth the enthusiastic admiration of no mean judges among ourselves. Even without the example and assistance of a more civilised nation, the science possessed by every people is gradually superseded by their own discoveries as they advance in knowledge, and their early works fall into disuse and oblivion. But it is otherwise with their poetry; the standard works maintain their reputation undiminished in every age, they form the models of composition and the fountains of classical language, and the writers of the rudest ages are those who contribute the most to the delight and refinement of the most improved of their posterity."

In the same Minute he deplored the fact that we had dried up the sources of Native talent, that the existing learning of the country was being lost, and the productions of former genius forgotten.

"A class of men," he said, "was formerly maintained whose time was devoted to the cultivation of their understanding; their learning may have been obscure and degenerate, but still it bore some affinity to real science, into which it might in time have been improved. They were not, perhaps, much inferior to those monks among whom the seeds of European learning were long kept alive;

and their extinction, if it did not occasion the loss of much present wisdom, would have cut off all hope for the future. . . . When once the college had become an established place of resort for Brahmans, it would be easy to introduce by degrees improvements into the system of education, and thus render the institution a powerful instrument for the diffusion of civilisation. Some such alterations must be the fruit of time, and cannot be adopted until we have instruments better fitted to impart instruction, as well as auditors better prepared to receive it. At no time, however, could I wish that the purely Hindu part of the course should be totally abandoned. It would surely be a preposterous way of adding to the intellectual treasures of a nation to begin by the destruction of its indigenous literature, and I cannot but think that the future attainments of the Natives will be increased in extent as well as in variety by being, as it were, engrafted on their own previous knowledge, and imbued with their own original and peculiar character."[1]

No one was more desirous than Elphinstone to encourage the study of the English language. For a native of India there is no other key by which he can unlock the richer stores of Western science and knowledge, and without it he cannot hope to take any prominent part in the higher branches of the public administration. Whether it was right to assign to English and the classical literature of England the almost exclusive position which they have been made to hold in our system of education in India, and almost to ignore the existence of the vernacular languages of the country and the literature of the East, is another matter. For my part I do not doubt that the views of Warren Hastings, and Sir William Jones, and Wellesley, and Elphinstone were far wiser than those of Macaulay, and that for Hindus and Mohammedans the study of their own languages and the literature of their own people

[1] Forrest's "Selections from the Minutes of the Hon. Mountstuart Elphinstone"—Minute on Education, March 1824.

and kinsmen was not less essential than the study of English.

The influence of Macaulay was irresistible. The Government of Lord William Bentinck decided that "the great object of the British Government ought to be the promotion of European literature and science among the natives of India, and that all the funds appropriated for the purpose of Education would be best employed on English education alone." Although some of the old institutions were allowed to go on teaching in a feeble way the classical languages of the East, the conclusion virtually arrived at was that Oriental studies required no encouragement from the State. During the next ten or fifteen years progress was made in the establishment of English colleges and schools. Very little was thought at that time about primary education for the masses of the people. Education, it was said, would "filter downwards."

So far as higher education is concerned, the principles laid down in 1835 have been in the main adhered to ever since. The learning and literature of the East are practically as completely ignored in our Government Colleges and Universities at the present time as they were in the time of Lord Macaulay. All higher education, whether scientific or literary, is given in English, and a young man may go through nearly the whole of his University course without having occasion to make use of the language of his own country. The bare statement of the fact that little can be learned in our colleges except through the medium of a foreign tongue, goes far to explain their comparative failure. But the subject of the results obtained by our system of education is one to which I shall return.

There were some exceptions to the general neglect

of primary education which followed the measures taken in 1835. In the North-Western Provinces, in particular, their wise and enlightened Lieutenant-Governor, James Thomason, laid the foundations of a system of village schools; but it was not until 1854 that the duty of the State in regard to this matter was distinctly recognised. In that year orders, for which Lord Halifax (then Sir Charles Wood) was mainly responsible, were sent by the Court of Directors to India. The despatch containing them has been called "the charter of education in India." I shall quote, from the Report of the Indian Education Commission of 1883, a summary of its contents; it will show the system on which the Government has been working ever since:—

"The immediate aims of the Government were the same as those to which the attention of every European State was first directed when organising its system of public instruction. The existing schools of all kinds were to be improved and their number increased, systematic inspection was to be established, and a supply of competent teachers was to be provided. But in India the attitude of the State to national education was affected by three conditions to which no European State could furnish a parallel. In the first place, the population was not only as large as that of all the European States together that had adopted an educational system, but it presented, in its different provinces, at least as many differences of creed, language, race, and custom. Secondly, the ruling power was bound to hold itself aloof from all questions of religion. Thirdly, the scheme of instruction to be introduced was one which should culminate in the organisation of a literature and science essentially foreign. While, therefore, on the one hand, the magnitude of a task before the Indian Government was such as to make it almost impossible of achievement by any direct appropriation from the resources of the empire, on the other, the popular demand for education—so important a factor in the success of the European systems—had to be created. The Government adopted the only course which circumstances permitted. It was admitted that 'to imbue a vast and ignorant population with a general desire for knowledge, and to take advantage of the desire when excited to improve the means for diffusing education among them, must be the work of many years; as a Government, we can do no more than direct the efforts of the people, and aid them wherever they appear to require most assistance.'"

Under the orders of 1854, supplemented by later instructions, a separate Department of Public Instruction was constituted. Universities were to be founded in Calcutta, Madras, and Bombay; institutions for training teachers for all classes of schools were to be established; the number of Government colleges and high schools was to be increased; new middle schools were to be created; efforts were above all to be devoted to the development of elementary education with the object of "conveying to the great mass of the people, who are utterly incapable of obtaining any education worthy of the name by their own unaided efforts, useful and practical knowledge, suited to every station in life." The English language was to be the medium of instruction in the higher branches of education, and the vernacular languages of the country in the lower, and English was to be taught wherever there was a demand for it. The extension of education in the higher branches would, it was thought, be mainly effected by applying the system of grants-in-aid; the resources of the State were to be so devoted as to assist those who could not be expected to help themselves, while it was hoped that the richer classes would gradually be induced to provide for their own education. The system of grants-in-aid to private institutions was to be based on entire abstinence from interference with the religious instruction given in the schools; aid was to be given, within certain limits, to all schools which imparted a good secular education and were under competent management; all aided schools were to be open to inspection by Government officers. This system has been put into practice throughout British India. Every province has its separate Educational Department under an officer called the Director of Public Instruction, with a large staff of officers, colleges, schools, and grants-in-aid. Very much in this system was, undoubtedly, admirable, but there are many respects in which the results have obviously been far from satisfactory.

There were formerly many advocates in India of "the downward filtration" theory of education, to which reference has already been made. There can be no country in which the expectation that education would "filter downwards" was more impossible to be fulfilled. Apart from the fact that all higher education was given in a foreign language, the literary classes—if we are to give them so inappropriate a name—whether they are Brahmans learned in the sacred literature of ancient India, or men primed with the most modern knowledge that our English Colleges can impart, agree for the most part in rejection of the idea that education ought to be extended to the masses of the people. But for many years past the Government has adhered to the principle affirmed in 1854, that the main duty of the State lies in providing means of primary instruction to the classes which can make no provision for themselves. I need hardly enlarge on the magnitude of such an undertaking in India. Anything like compulsory education is out of the question. Even if unlimited funds were available, it would be impossible to succeed, except by slow degrees, and by steady perseverance through a long course of years, in educating any large proportion of two hundred and thirty millions of people, nearly the whole of whom are now totally illiterate, and filled to a degree which can hardly be exaggerated with the prejudices of ignorance, and caste, and superstition. It was an almost inevitable consequence of the difficulty of such an undertaking that the Government, notwithstanding the principles that it had laid down for its guidance, should continue to spend the greater part of its available funds on higher education, the results of which were more immediately apparent, and comparatively little on the extension of elementary instruction.

In some parts of India there have been, from time immemorial, considerable numbers of village and local schools, in which instruction of a very elementary kind is given. In the Hindu schools the instruction is chiefly or wholly secular; the Mohammedan schools have a religious character. In Bengal and in Madras the existing system of primary instruction is in a great measure based on the indigenous schools, which receive grants-in-aid from the State; in Bombay, in the United Provinces, and the Punjab, on the other hand, the primary schools are mostly provided by the Government at the cost of local funds, raised by rates on the land. In Burma, where a far larger proportion of the population can read and write than in any part of India, primary education, according to the ancient custom of the country, is almost entirely in the hands of the Buddhist monks.

Reading, writing, arithmetic, and sometimes a little mensuration, are taught in the primary schools.

Although progress has undoubtedly been made, the proportion of the population of India which has received even elementary instruction is almost infinitesimally small.

The census returns of 1901 showed a total population of 294,360,000, of whom 149,951,000 were males, and 144,409,000 were females. Out of the male population, 134,752,000 were illiterate. Out of the female population, no less than 142,976,000 were illiterate, and 1,433,000 could read and write. In other words, about 90 per cent of the male and 99 per cent of the female population were illiterate. Excluding Burma, the differences in these respects between the various provinces of British India and the Native States are not very great. In the United Provinces, for instance, the male population, in 1903, was 24,617,000, of which number 23,194,000 were illiterate. The female population was 23,078,000, of whom the number who could read and write was less than 56,000. In the Punjab and North-West Frontier Provinces, out of 14,512,000 males, 13,578,000 were illiterate, and out of 12,369,000 females the number not illiterate was 42,000. Even in Madras, where education has made greater progress, more than 80 per cent of the male and more than 95 per cent of the female population are illiterate.[1]

Even these figures do not adequately represent the real illiteracy of the mass of the people, for, as Mr. Baines showed in his Report on the Census of 1891, and this is equally true now, more than half of the whole number returned as literate are found among a few classes, comprising less than 20 per cent of the whole population. The Brahmans, as might be expected, head the list; although they were estimated in 1891

[1] Many of these figures can only be looked on as approximately correct. Apart from other causes which, in dealing with such vast numbers in such a country as India, make strict accuracy impossible, there were no returns for nearly a million persons out of the total population of India to show whether they were or were not illiterate. The term "illiterate" in the Indian census returns signifies "unable to read and write."

to constitute only 5 per cent of the total population, they included 17 per cent of the literate class, and more than 20 per cent of those who know English. Percentages of this kind must not, however, be taken for more than they are worth, in dealing with a population larger than that of civilised Europe, and classes grouped under similar names differ greatly in different Indian countries. For instance, a large proportion of the Brahmans of Madras appear in the census returns as literate, and a very small proportion of those of the United Provinces, the Brahmans in the latter case, unlike those in the former, being very largely agricultural.

Women in India take a larger and more active share in the practical business of life than is usually supposed; in the management of family and household affairs they probably exercise almost as great an authority and influence as women in Europe; they often manage estates and large commercial concerns, and show extreme acuteness and intelligence. An example of their practical ability is seen in the Native State of Bhopál, which, four times in succession, has been ruled by women. But the idea that women, or at any rate respectable women, ought to receive a school education, or any of the instruction that is proper for boys, is one that is entirely new in India, even among that small section of the population which has been powerfully affected by Western habits of thought. It is true that some of those who have received an English education feel that it is hardly tolerable that the women with whom they pass their lives should be totally illiterate, and that, in the absence of all female teachers, they have taken upon themselves the duty of instructing their wives and daughters. But among the small number of those who are conscious of the prevailing evil, and would be glad to see it remedied, the majority cannot overcome the repugnance of their families to female education, nor the opinion of the society that surrounds them, and they prefer to follow the customs of their people and the example of their forefathers. As a general rule, even those who have received the highest training that our English schools and colleges can give, are opposed to the education of women, and hold the traditional Indian view that to be able to read and write is an accomplishment which a modest woman had better be without. While such opinions as these continue to be generally held, it is impossible that the Government can take any very successful steps for the promotion of female education.

In spite of these difficulties, there has been some progress. Remarkable instances have occurred in which Native ladies have attained literary and academic distinction; several have passed the University Entrance Examinations, and a few have obtained degrees. With very rare exceptions, however, the instruction afforded has been purely elementary. The chief progress has been in Southern India, where women are less secluded than in the North. While in 1871 there were about 10,000 girls receiving school instruction in Madras, the numbers had risen to 128,000 in 1901.

Such progress as there has been, is in a great measure due to the missionary societies. The girls in their schools are more numerous than in those of the Government, and zanána missions connected with the societies give more or less secular instruction in a considerable number of Native families. The example given by English ladies who have devoted themselves to teaching in the zanánas has, to some extent, been followed by Natives themselves, who are often unwilling to admit avowed Christian influences into their families. The Report of the Indian Education Commission states that—

> "In Calcutta, Madras, and Bombay, and in many large cities of India, it is now possible for a wealthy native to obtain instruction for the ladies of his family within his own house. A distinct class of zanána agencies on a secular basis is springing up, conducted by committees of native gentlemen, or by mixed committees of Natives and Europeans, with the object, in some cases, of imparting education in zanánas without any element of religious teaching; in others, of testing by periodical examinations, and encouraging by records, the home education of governesses. These agencies are already doing useful work, although on a comparatively small scale, and the commission trusts that they will receive a still larger measure of sympathy and co-operation from English ladies in India."[1]

In connection with the subject of female education I must mention the truly admirable scheme initiated by the Marchioness of Dufferin and Ava, and actively encouraged ever since by the wives of the Viceroys, for supplying female medical aid to the women of India. I have referred to the success of the medical colleges established by the Government, and to the great aptitude shown by Natives of India in the practice of surgery and medicine. The country is covered with hospitals and dispensaries; but the women of India are shut off from the benefits brought by European science to their doors, because their customs make it impossible to allow the professional attendance of men. A lamentable amount of unnecessary suffering is the consequence. The association that has been founded, and which has made remarkable progress, has for its object the provision, on a large scale, of the means of teaching and training women in India to act as doctors, hospital

[1] *Report*, p. 535.

assistants, nurses, and midwives; the establishment, under female superintendence, of dispensaries and hospitals for the treatment of women and children; the opening of female wards, under female superintendence, in existing hospitals and dispensaries; the provision of female medical officers and attendants for existing female wards; and the supply of trained nurses and midwives for women in hospitals and private houses. It has been laid down as a fundamental rule of the association that it shall be absolutely unsectarian in its aims and conduct, and that no one of its servants shall ever be allowed to proselytise or interfere in any way with the religious belief of the people. This excellent movement has received active encouragement both from our own Government and from the rulers of Native States. Connected with this association there were, in 1900, 235 hospitals and dispensaries, and more than 1,500,000 women and children received relief. There were 33 highly educated lady doctors, 73 assistant surgeons, and a large number of hospital assistants, while 354 women were studying in the various medical schools in India.

The figures that have been given show how small an impression has hitherto been made on the enormous mass of Indian ignorance. There are, as Mr. Baines has pointed out, two facts to be remembered. The first is the fact that the great mass of the population is agricultural, and in far more civilised countries this is not the class among which education flourishes. "The second influence antagonistic to a more general spread of literacy is the long-continued existence of a hereditary class, whose object it has been to maintain their own monopoly of all book-learning as the chief buttress of their social supremacy. Sacerdotalism knows that it can reign over none but an ignorant populace. The opposition of the Bráhman to the rise of the writer castes has been already mentioned, and the repugnance of both, in the present day, to the diffusion of learning amongst the masses can only be appreciated after long experience. It is true that the recognition by the British Government of the virtue and necessity of primary education has met with some response on the part of the literary castes, but it is chiefly in the direction of academic utterances, which cannot, in the circumstances, be well avoided. It is welcomed, too, in its capacity of affording the means of livelihood to many of these castes, as they have to be engaged as teachers, and are bound accordingly to work up to the State standard of efficient tuition. The real interest of the castes in question is centred on secondary education, of which they almost exclusively are in a position to reap the advantage." [1]

Discouraging as the actual condition of primary education may seem, things are far better than they were, and the progress that has been made must not be undervalued. In the whole of India, excepting the North-Western Provinces, when the Government was transferred to the Crown there were only some 2000 Government and aided elementary schools, with less than 200,000 scholars, while in 1901 there were 147,000 schools and 4,400,000 scholars. Nor should it be forgotten how short a time has elapsed since our own country, under far less difficult circumstances, began practically to recognise the necessity of elementary education. Four years before the accession of Queen Victoria no public money was granted in England for elementary schools.

[1] *General Report on the Castes of India*, 1891, p. 211.

Reference must now be made to the means provided for higher education and to the results that have been obtained.

The three universities of Calcutta, Madras, and Bombay were established in 1857; a fourth was established at Allahabad for the North-Western Provinces in 1887. Their constitution is similar to that of the London University: they have a Chancellor, Vice-Chancellor, and Senate, with a governing body; they are examining bodies only, but by their examinations they control the course of study throughout the greater part of India, in the colleges affiliated to them. In 1882 a university was established at Lahore for the Punjab, and this, though in the main an examining body, like the older Universities, devotes a portion of the income which it derives from examination fees to the maintenance of a college for Oriental learning.

The entrance examinations for matriculation are open to all. The subjects are English, a classical or vernacular language, history, geography, mathematics, and, in Madras and Bombay, elementary physical science. The usual age of the candidates is between sixteen and eighteen, and, according to the estimate of the Education Commission, the standard of knowledge required is about that which at the age of sixteen an English boy of average intelligence will be found to possess. Success in this examination admits a student to any of the affiliated colleges.

The college course does not much differ in the various provinces. After two years, a student may present himself for the first examination in Arts, the subjects being English, a classical language (Oriental or European), history, mathematics, logic, and, if he so desires, a branch of natural science. Two years later he may present himself for the B.A. degree. Degrees are conferred in Arts, Law, Medicine, and Civil Engineering. The M.A. degree completes the college course; the examination is held in one or more of the following subjects: languages, history, mental and moral philosophy, mathematics, pure and mixed, and physical science. The proportion of students who go beyond the entrance examination is not large, and the number who obtain degrees is small.

Taking the Arts Colleges of all the universities together, in the five years ending with 1901-02, 37,946 candidates passed the entrance examination. During the same period 15,207 candidates passed the First Arts Examination: there were 6605 B.A. and 655 M.A. graduates. It is a significant fact, illustrating the neglect of Oriental studies, that in the same five years there were two "Masters" and twelve "Bachelors of Oriental learning." In his General Report on the census of 1891, Mr. Baines observed that the main points brought out appeared to be, "first, the insignificant number of pupils that carry instruction beyond the rudiments; secondly, the remarkably unprepared state in which the minute remainder appear for matriculation; and, lastly, the relatively infinitesimal number that obtain a University degree."

The number of Natives possessing a knowledge of English was, in the whole of India, in 1891, only 386,000, and this included boys under instruction. The number seems extraordinarily small, and can apparently, as Mr. Baines says, only be explained by the fact that the study of English ends in a very rudimentary stage, and that the class is numerous "that learn a certain amount of English at school, but carry the use of it no further than the last examination. and cease to be able to read and write it after the lapse of a few years."

In regard to the general scope and character of collegiate instruction in India, I may quote the account given in the Report of the Indian Education Commissioners :—

"The system is now almost uniform throughout India. Purely Oriental colleges must be excepted. These, however, are so few in number that they scarcely enter into a consideration of collegiate education in its modern development. The college of to-day aims at giving an education that shall fit its recipient to take an honourable share in the administration of the country, or to enter with good hope of success the various liberal professions now expanding in vigorous growth. The English and Oriental classes occupy an important place in the collegiate scheme. In history, philosophy, mathematics, and physical science, English is the medium of instruction, and the passport to academic honours. . . . The affiliated colleges are of two grades: those whose students go no farther than the First Arts Examination, and those in which they proceed to the B.A. and M.A. degrees. The strength of the teaching staff varies with the wealth of the institution, the number of the students, and the class of examinations for which candidates are sent up. Thus, the Presidency College in Calcutta has a Principal, eleven Professors, and two teachers of Sanskrit and Arabic. This staff provides for lectures being given in all the various subjects of all the examinations. A smaller college will be content with a Principal, two Professors, a Pandit, and a Maulavi. In their scheme of discipline, and in the academic life of their students, Indian colleges have but little analogy to those of the older of the English universities, their resemblance being closer to those of Scotland and Germany. Residence in college buildings is not only not generally compulsory, but the colleges are few in which any systematic provision is made for control over the students' pursuits out of college hours. Boarding-houses are indeed attached to certain institutions, and their number increases year by year, but unless the student's home be at a distance from the collegiate city, and he have no relatives to receive him, it is seldom that he will incur the expense which residence involves. Two principal reasons account for this feature in our system. First, the initial outlay upon buildings is one from which Government and independent bodies alike shrink. For so poor is the Indian student that it would be impossible to demand of him any but the most moderate rent—a rent perhaps barely sufficient to cover the cost of the annual repairs. The second obstacle lies in the religious and social prejudices which force class from class. Not only does the Hindu refuse to eat with the Musalman, but from close contact with whole sections of his own co-religionists he is shut off by the imperious ordinances of caste. Experience, however, has already proved that the barriers of custom are giving way. In the North-Western Provinces and the Punjab, where the residential system has been widely tried, the success has been considerable, and nothing but want of funds stands in the way of a fuller development. In the more important Bombay colleges, also, a considerable number of the students are in residence; in Bengal and Madras the system has been less fully recognised."[1]

In the years that have elapsed since the above words were written, the results of our system of education have come into clearer relief, and few Englishmen would now be found to take so optimistic a view as that expressed by the Education Commissioners of 1883. It cannot be said that our Indian Colleges have fostered a genuine desire for learning; the students seldom pursue learning for its own sake, but for the most part solely to acquire a degree, and the object of a degree is that it constitutes a qualification for Government service or a profession. Nor can it be denied that the knowledge which an Indian graduate possesses is at best shallow; he has a smattering of several subjects, but he can hardly acquire in our Colleges that mastery of any subject which would make his knowledge of it really valuable. No native of India, educated solely in his own country, has yet produced any work of original merit in any of the subjects taught in our Colleges, nor

[1] *Report of the Indian Education Commission*, p. 273.

has our teaching brought forth fruit in the application of Western ideas and Western science to Indian problems. Indian history and Indian archæology have been enriched by no contributions from Indian students, nor has any native of the country adapted and applied the experience of the West to the development of the material resources of India.

If, however, all this be admitted, and if the fermentation of ideas which the new learning has generated has not led to the results which were hoped for, it has on the other hand undoubtedly produced other results, the value of which must not be ignored. Speaking generally, the English-educated generation differs from that which preceded it rather on the moral than on the intellectual side. As public servants the higher integrity of those who have received an English education is a matter of common observation. The past of India has not been favourable to the cultivation of civic virtues, but to whatever extent movements for the suppression of undesirable customs, for the spread of education, or for other enlightened purposes, have been encouraged by Natives of the country, it has been by those who have some tincture of Western learning. These are results of importance, and it is remarkable that they have been gained from an education which is purely intellectual, and which strictly abstains from interference in morals or religion.

On the whole, and without undervaluing the many advantages that have followed, it must be confessed that a sense of disappointment is the prevailing opinion with regard to our system of College education in India. The last public inquiry into this subject was made in 1902, when a Commission was appointed by Lord Curzon to inquire into the whole question of the conduct of examinations by the Indian Universities. It pronounced a somewhat guarded and not very encouraging verdict.

Although an important share in higher education is taken by the institutions established by private effort, with the help of grants-in-aid from the State, there is no present probability of the arrival of the time when it may be possible for the State to devote its principal efforts to the encouragement of primary instruction, leaving the main provision of the means of higher education to private institutions, aided and supervised by the Government. But much honour is due to the work of secular education undertaken by private agencies, and especially to that of Protestant and Roman Catholic missionaries. In 1890 there were in British India nearly 300,000 scholars in their colleges and schools.

The success of the measures for the promotion of higher education has been more marked among Hindus than among Mohammedans. In many parts of India, Mohammedans, especially those of the upper classes, have always been disinclined to accept the education offered in our schools and colleges, and frequent complaint has been made that they are consequently unable to compete on equal terms with Hindus for employment under Government. Feelings of religious intolerance sometimes tend to make the Mohammedans refuse to admit the necessity of Western knowledge, but there are other reasons which affect them, and which have been described as follows by the Indian Education Commission :—

"Apart from the social and historical conditions of the Mohammedan community in India, there are causes of a strictly educational character which heavily weigh it in the race of life. The teaching of the mosque must precede the lessons of the school.

The one object of a young Hindu is to obtain an education which will fit him for an official or a professional career. But before the young Mohammedan is allowed to turn his thoughts to secular instruction, he must commonly pass some years in going through a course of sacred learning. The Mohammedan boy, therefore, enters school later than the Hindu. In the second place, he very often leaves school at an earlier age. The Mohammedan parent belonging to the better classes is usually poorer than the Hindu parent in a corresponding social position. He cannot afford to give his son a complete education. In the third place, irrespectively of his worldly means, the Mohammedan parent often chooses for his son while at school an education which will secure for him an honoured place among the learned of his own community, rather than one which will command success in the modern professions or in official life. The years which the young Hindu gives to English and mathematics in a public school, the young Mohammedan devotes in a Madrasa to Arabic and the law and theology of Islam. When such an education is completed, it is to the vocation of a man of learning rather than to the more profitable professions that the thoughts of a promising Mohammedan youth naturally turn."[1]

It must not be assumed from the fact that the Mohammedans look with little favour on our system that they are always less alive to the value of education than Hindus. In the United Provinces, for instance, the Mohammedan section of the population furnishes, in proportion to its numbers, more pupils than the Hindu. In spite of the disadvantages under which the Mohammedans are placed by their dislike of the education given in our colleges, they hold, in those Provinces, in proportion to their numbers, a larger number of offices in the service of the Government than the Hindus. But this is not the case in the greater part of India; as a rule, the share of the Hindus in public employments much exceeds that of the Mohammedans.

[1] *Report*, p. 505.

These difficulties in regard to the higher education of Mohammedans have been similar in kind to those which have frequently arisen in our own country. That education should be severed from religion is an idea as repugnant to a good Mohammedan as it is to many Christians. There is little use in discussing whether our Government could have done otherwise than hold itself rigidly aloof from all concern with the religious education of the Mohammedans. Similar questions hardly arise in regard to the education of Hindus, for their religion is not one that can be taught, or that they desire to see taught, for it has no fixed dogmas and tenets. It may be true that it would have been politically wise to show greater sympathy with the belief and habits of thought of our Mohammedan subjects, and to treat more respectfully a religion and literature which they highly and naturally prize, but it was and is practically impossible for an English Government to act in these matters on any other rule than that which has been adopted. It cannot teach in its own schools and colleges the doctrines of Islam.

Thus it has come to pass that the colleges of the Government, as well as those conducted by missionaries, are all unacceptable to the Mohammedan who desires that his son shall be instructed in his own faith, and in the classical languages of his people.

There was a man among the Mohammedans of Northern India who believed that this difficult problem could be solved, and the results of his efforts have been so great that I must somewhat fully explain them. He has shown, in my opinion, and, so far as I know, it has been shown nowhere else in India, how this difficult question of education, in some at least of its phases, should be treated.

Sir Syad Ahmad Khán belonged, as his name betokens, to an ancient family that claims to be descended from the Prophet. His ancestors came into India from Central Asia, and held high office under the Moghal Emperors. I was proud to call him my friend, and there was no man of any creed or country for whom I felt a more true respect. It was soon after the mutinies of 1857 that I first knew him at Morádabad. He was then one of the most distinguished of our Native judges, bearing, at a time when Native courts of justice were often far from immaculate, a character as high as that of any Englishman. He was in the prime of life, a man of noble presence, honoured by all our countrymen for the loyalty and courage with which he had devoted himself to our cause, when our Government had been swept away, and not one Englishman remained in Rohilkhand.

Sir Syad Ahmad Khán, although he did not possess the power of fluent speech in English, had made himself well acquainted with our language. He was in every respect a thoroughly enlightened man, fully alive to the value of European knowledge, and to the fact that unless the Mohammedans could accept the results of Western civilisation there was no hope for them in the future. He felt that after a century of British rule there was still little sympathy between the Mohammedans and ourselves, and that nothing but the better education of his countrymen could bring the two into more friendly relations. This education could not be supplied by the State; it must be supplied by the Mohammedans themselves, in a manner consistent with the dictates of their religious belief.

Sir Syad Ahmad Khán, like the friends of knowledge and progress in other countries, had to bear the open or covert opposition of many of his countrymen. His doctrines were declared to be unorthodox and dangerous, nor were Englishmen wanting whose opinions had been cast in moulds of a sort similar to those approved by Mohammedan bigotry, and who looked with little favour on his innovations. For he, a Musalman, not only declared that he reverently accepted the authority of the Christian Scriptures, but had dared to enter into critical dissertations of their meaning, and to appeal to them for evidence of the mission of Mohammed.

Sir Syad Ahmad Khán was a sincere believer in his own religion. He claimed for it that it should not be judged by the opinions of the ignorant and the bigots of his own faith, or by those of hostile critics of another, but that it should be interpreted in the liberal spirit in which wise Christians interpret theirs. According to his belief, the faith of Islam, properly understood, would be the friend of truth and progress in every branch of human knowledge.

With this conviction Sir Syad Ahmad Khán devoted himself to the establishment of a college for the higher education of Mohammedans. He gave to this object for many years every effort of his life, and the whole of his worldly means. He was joined by some influential friends; as time went on, hostile prejudices and opposition diminished; munificent endowments were offered, and help and encouragement came not only from Mohammedans, but from Hindus and Englishmen. In 1883, the college founded by him at Aligarh, in the North-Western Provinces, had made such progress that the Indian Education Commissioners wrote of it in the following terms:—

"It is in some respects superior to any educational institution in India, and one which bids fair to be of the greatest importance from a political as well as from an educational point of view. . . . It is the first expression of independent Musalman effort which the country has witnessed since it came under British rule. The Aligarh Society has set an example which, if followed to any large extent, will solve the problem of national education: and it is difficult to speak in words of too high praise of those whose labours have been so strenuous, or to overrate the value of the ally which the State has gained in the cause of education and advancement."

The College receives grants-in-aid from the Provincial Government and from the Nizam of Hyderabad. In 1902 its income from all sources did not exceed £6000. It has an English Principal and three English Professors, graduates of the University of Cambridge, and six Native Professors, four of whom have taken degrees in Indian Universities. The school attached to the College has an English headmaster, an English assistant master, and sixteen Native masters, many of whom were formerly pupils in the College, and who from devotion to its interests have remained at Aligarh rather than seek more lucrative careers elsewhere.

The great majority of the students live in the quadrangles which are built round the College; the number in residence in 1902 was nearly 500. Religious instruction and the observation of religious rites are part of the daily exercise; but although the College was primarily intended for Mohammedans, and is essentially a Mohammedan institution, so much sympathy and generosity were shown by Hindu friends that its secular classes are open to Hindus also. In regard to scholarships and prizes the rules of the College show no partiality to Mohammedans, and separate boarding-houses are provided for Hindu students. The College is affiliated to the Allahabad University, and, judged by the results of University examinations, there is no

College in the United Provinces that has been so successful. Students have come to it not only from distant provinces but from countries beyond the borders of India. Manly sports of all kinds are encouraged to an extent nowhere else known in India. The College has its gymnasium, its riding-school, its teams for hockey, football, and cricket. Its cricketers have beaten the best English eleven that Simla could produce.

In January 1877, Lord Lytton laid the foundation stone of new college buildings at Aligarh, and Sir Syad Ahmad Khán, in words addressed especially to the Viceroy and to his numerous English friends, spoke as follows :—

> "The personal honour," he said, "which you have done me assures me of a great fact, and fills me with feelings of a much higher nature than mere personal gratitude. I am assured that you, who upon this occasion represent the British rule, have sympathies with our labours, and to me this assurance is very valuable, and a source of great happiness. At my time of life it is a comfort to me to feel that the undertaking which has been for many years, and is now, the sole object of my life, has roused, on the one hand, the energies of my own countrymen, and, on the other, has won the sympathy of our British fellow-subjects and the support of our rulers; so that when the few years I may still be spared are over, and when I shall be no longer amongst you, the College will still prosper, and succeed in educating my countrymen to have the same affection for their country, the same feelings of loyalty for the British rule, the same appreciation of its blessings, the same sincerity of friendship with our British fellow-subjects as have been the ruling feelings of my life."

Sir Syad Ahmad Khán closed his long and noble life in March 1898. The bitter theological animosity which his religious teaching at first aroused had already begun to give way before the growing respect which his exertions on behalf of his people had called forth, and, since his death, even where his religious views have not been specifically accepted, the influence of his work has been great. Even the opponents of some of his tenets confess with admiration the purity and nobility of his motives, and there can be no question that his teaching and his influence have had a profound effect upon a very important class of the Mohammedans of Northern India. There are now many ardent workers in the cause of Mohammedan progress, a large proportion of whom were once students in the College at Aligarh.

To the end of his life Sir Syad Ahmad Khán laid the greatest emphasis upon the maintenance of a high moral character in the students of his College. He required that the young men trained in it should be virtuous in private life and upright in the public service, and always urged upon them the imperative duty of forwarding to the utmost of their capacity the welfare of their people.

It was the hope of Sir Syad Ahmad Khán that the Aligarh College might, as the Indian Education Commissioners wrote in words already quoted, help by its success and example to "solve the problem of national education" in India. He saw in imagination a time which he could not hope to see himself, in which the Mohammedans of India would possess, perhaps in Aligarh which he himself had chosen, an intellectual capital, a centre not only of learning and knowledge but of a purified and tolerant and progressive faith. His successors in the work that he initiated entertain the same aspirations. They urge that there are large sections of the Mohammedans, and not improbably other branches of the Indian community, which will never accept a system of secular education from which the religious element is sedulously excluded. They maintain that residence in College ought to be an essential condition for obtaining a degree, and that this condition can only be organised in India by the members of a community acquainted with all the requirements of its own co-religionists, for every class has its peculiar ordinances in regard to food and methods of life, for which parents will demand strict safeguards. To fulfil completely the objects which led to the foundation of the College at Aligarh, the establishment of denominational Universities would be necessary, and it is suggested that as a beginning this College might be developed into a teaching University for Mohammedans. I believe, for my part, that this would be a measure of great utility, likely to lead to results of the utmost value. If the experiment proved successful, other bodies might obtain hereafter teaching Universities of their own, each of them an educational centre, attracting to itself the members of its own religious belief, with its own traditions and intellectual life. Thus the difficulty connected with religious education might be solved, and solved by those who would be the most likely to make such education enlightened. These are aspirations which would require for their development much larger funds than those which the Aligarh College can now command, and the Mohammedan community is generally poor. There are many people in England anxious to assist, if they knew how, the work of Indian progress. Let them send their help to the Mohammedan Anglo-Oriental College at Aligarh: they could find no more certain way of doing good.[1]

[1] Sir Syad Ahmad Khán was for some years a member of the Council of the Governor-General for making laws and regulations. He was also a member of

I shall refer in a subsequent chapter[1] to the Colleges that have been established for the education of young Chiefs and nobles.

Very useful colleges have also been established for special objects, such as the study of medicine and surgery, and engineering.

The Medical Colleges deserve particular notice, for no educational institutions in India have been more remarkably successful. There are more than 1700 hospitals and dispensaries in British India, in charge of Native surgeons educated in our colleges and schools. Among all the benefits conferred upon the people by our rule, there is perhaps no one more highly and universally valued than this. Many of the Native surgeons are extremely skilful, and perform operations in a manner that would not discredit the surgeons of London or Paris. More than 10,000,000 patients are treated every year at the Indian hospitals and dispensaries.

Science has, for the most part, received in India, as in England, scant encouragement from the State, but that it has not been altogether neglected is shown by the work performed by the Departments of Survey, Geology, Botany, Meteorology, Forest, and Agriculture. Lord Curzon has spared no efforts for the promotion of

the Legislative Council in the North-Western Provinces, and Queen Victoria recognised his services by conferring on him the dignity of Knight Commander of the Star of India. Towards the end of 1902, an association was founded in London, under the name of the Mohammedan Anglo-Oriental College, Aligarh, Association, with the object of promoting the cause of education among Mohammedans, and the interests of the Aligarh College, and at the same time of assisting and advising any Natives of India desiring help in regard to their manner of life and course of study in England. It has been formed by a number of Mohammedan gentlemen, many of them students in this country, and other Natives of India who sympathise with its objects and many distinguished Englishmen are among its honorary members.

[1] See Chapter XXIV.

scientific research. Mining experts have been appointed; posts have been created for the study of economic chemistry, of the diseases of cattle, of plants and insect pests, and a Board of Experts has been nominated to act as the permanent scientific adviser of the Government of India.

One other admirable institution must be noticed, the Pasteur Institute at the Hill Station of Kasauli below Simla. It is performing a noble work in the service of humanity. In 1902 more than 500 persons were saved by it from the peril of a terrible death. A similar institution has now (1903) been established in Southern India.

Little has hitherto been done for technical instruction, but a useful beginning has been made, especially in Bombay. This is a want which in England is being slowly supplied, and we see in India the reflection of English indifference. The establishment of Agricultural Departments has, however, given recognition to the importance of applying scientific knowledge to agriculture, the chief of the industries of India.

In several provinces schools of art have been established, and presided over by highly accomplished men. Their utility is more than doubtful. India has nothing to learn from us in the matter of decorative art. We have done much to debase her beautiful and still living arts, and almost all the influence that we have exercised has been destructive. A wide field, on the other hand, is open for practical training in many handicrafts and manufactures.

The systems followed in different provinces in respect of secondary education vary so much that no description would be generally applicable. There is usually in every district a Government Higher school, where English and the subjects required for the entrance examinations at the Universities are taught. Many schools of a similar kind have been established by missionaries, and receive grants-in-aid. In most of the smaller towns there is a Middle school, giving an education intermediate between that given in the higher and primary schools, and English is sometimes taught.

Although the number of the Natives of India who are good English scholars is small, there are many who have learned enough of our language for the ordinary clerical work of the public offices, and they hold almost all the minor appointments of this kind. They are a very useful and efficient class, but they have seldom any pretensions to be called educated men. The great majority of the young men at our higher schools and colleges go there because it is a certain way of getting on in life. It is a very successful way both for themselves and for their employers, but, with rare exceptions, they are content with the smallest amount of English education which enables them to perform their work. A few are more ambitious, and qualify themselves for higher employment. In some provinces they hold important offices in the executive service, and supply a large proportion of the Native Judges. Some of them have reached, as Judges of the High Courts, the highest judicial rank which any one, whether he be Native or English, can attain in India. Many practise with great success at the bar; others are professors and masters in the colleges and schools, or in charge of the numerous hospitals and dispensaries.

Although our educational system has been, in some important respects, successful, the number of Natives of India who can be called highly educated, according to a European standard, is almost infinitesimally small in proportion to the vast population of the country. Sir Henry Maine, commenting on the fact that in the twenty years ending with 1883 not more than 5000 M.A. and B.A. degrees were given altogether, wrote as follows:—"I will assume that every man who has taken a Bachelor of Arts degree is sufficiently educated to have valuable ideas on politics; and for the purpose of including all who, in any sense, can be called educated men, I will multiply the total by five. That gives 25,000 Indian gentlemen of an education and age to take an interest or a part in politics."[1] Sir Henry Maine added that he thought it probable that his estimate of 25,000 was much above the mark. Since that opinion was given the number of graduates has largely increased. In the ten years ending with 1901-02, the number of M.A. degrees given in India was altogether 1185, and the number of B.A. degrees was 12,533. Notwithstanding this increase of numbers, I do not doubt that the conclusion stated by Sir Henry Maine remains substantially true. I doubt whether out of the almost infinitesimally small proportion of the population of British India who possess any education at all, there are as many as 25,000 men who, judged by a high European standard, can be called educated. Nor can it be doubted that the assumption that every man with a B.A. degree can properly be called educated is, in India, far too sanguine. The female population of India exceeds 144,000,000, and among them there are probably not 1000 women to whom the term educated could properly be applied.

The number of Brahmans who are more or less learned in ancient Sanskrit literature is considerable, although there are not many great scholars. With rare

[1] "The Reign of Queen Victoria," *India*, vol. i. p. 526.

exceptions, they have no acquaintance with any branches of Western knowledge, nor any desire to obtain it.

I have spoken of the controversy of 1835, which, under Lord Macaulay's influence, ended with the decision that English literature and science, taught through the medium of the English language, must be the basis of higher education in India. Very little science was taught in those days even in England, and still less in India; it was the study, not of English science, but of English classical literature, that was practically encouraged, and so it has been ever since. As Sir Henry Maine has often pointed out, the strict and sober tests of truth which modern science can alone supply were exactly the element that was wanting in the education of Orientals, and especially of Hindus. Native thought and literature, as he says, "is elaborately inaccurate; it is supremely and deliberately careless of all precision in magnitude, number, and time." "The Indian intellect stood in need, beyond everything else, of stricter criteria of truth. It required a treatment to harden and brace it, and scientific teaching was exactly the tonic which its infirmities called for." Even at the present time, although matters in this respect are somewhat better than they were, science holds an altogether secondary place in the Indian Universities. We may find an illustration of the truth of Sir Henry Maine's remarks in the remarkable success achieved by Natives of India whose professions have a more or less scientific, exact, and practical basis. This is especially the case with those who have devoted themselves to the study and practice of European surgery and medicine, and to that of Anglo-Indian law, the character of which is eminently accurate and precise. The best results of English education in India are seen in the Native surgeons and in the

Native judges, not in those whose education has been merely literary. Natives have not been successful as engineers. As a rule, they dislike physical exertion that can be avoided. A good engineer must be himself a master of mechanical arts, always ready in case of necessity to make use of his own hands, and this is usually not agreeable to the educated Native.

Almost nothing of our knowledge of ancient or modern India, whether of its history, its languages, or its people, or which can help us in the arduous task of administering this vast empire, has been contributed by men who have been educated in our Indian schools and colleges. These institutions give, in the English language, a more or less good imitation of the purely scholastic part of an ordinary English education, but the young men of India learn in them almost nothing about their own country, or about the Government under which they live, and, least of all, are they taught to be good and loyal citizens.

Sir Henry Maine has pointed out with admirable truth the mischievous results to India of the fact that the English classical literature of the end of the eighteenth century, which we teach in our Colleges, was "saturated with party politics," and that its views are often absolutely false.

> "This," he says, "would have been less serious if at this epoch one chief topic of the great writers and rhetoricians—of Burke and Sheridan, of Fox and Francis—had not been India itself. I have no doubt that the view of Indian government taken, at the end of the century, by Englishmen whose work and speeches are held to be models of English style, has had deep effect on the mind of the educated Indian of this day. We are only now beginning to see how excessively inaccurate were their statements of fact and how one-sided were their judgments."[1]

[1] "The Reign of Queen Victoria," *India*, vol. i. p. 506.

The prevailing burden of this literature is, as another eminent man has observed, the duty of "resistance to authority, the doctrine that Governments are always oppressive and unwise, and the canonisation of those who have built up the shrine of liberty with stones plucked from the fortress of tyranny. Much of the hostile attitude we meet with in India is due to the books we have placed in the hands of schoolboys; we have fed them with the invectives of Milton and Burke, and they, with their great imitative faculty, have conceived that we stand to the people of India in the position of the Stuarts and the Georges towards the people of England." This sort of education, in the words of M. Harmand, "is dangerous fare for Asiatic brains. It seems to dislocate all the foundations of what they know and what they feel, to deprive them of moral stability, and to perturb their souls with irresolution to their very depths."[1]

In late years valuable contributions have been made to the history of British India, but it still remains true that the old stories of the crimes by which the establishment of our power in India was attended have been passed on as articles of faith from one author to another. A few students know that for the most part these stories are false, and (to use the words of Sir Alfred Lyall) that "the hardihood and endurance of the men who won for England an empire, were equalled only by the general justice and patience with which they pacified and administered it." These calumnies have caused, and still are causing, no little mischief both in England and in India. Thousands of excellent people are filled with righteous indignation when they read of the atrocious acts of Clive and Hastings, the judicial murder of Nand-

[1] *L'Inde*, Préface de M. Jules Harmand.

kumár, the extermination of the Rohillas, the plunder of the Begums. No suspicion reaches them of the truth that these horrors never occurred, and the fear can hardly be repressed that there may be some foundation even now for charges of Indian misgovernment and oppression. Disparagement of their own countrymen has always been one of the common failings of unwise Englishmen, those "birds of evil presage who," as Burke has told us in a passage that I have already quoted, "have at all times grated our ears with their melancholy song." They find in the supposed crimes of the founders of our Indian empire an unfailing source of invective and obloquy. This false history has been taught by our schools and colleges and universities, and believed by the educated Natives of India to be true. It is impossible that this should not have a serious effect on their feelings towards their English rulers.

We owe to Sir James Stephen, to whom India owes many other debts for good service, "the first attempt (I am quoting the words of Sir Henry Maine) to apply robust, careful, and dispassionate criticism to this period of history." One at least of the imaginary crimes to which I have referred—the judicial murder of Nandkumár by Impey and Hastings—will hardly again appear in sober history.

The great criminal in this matter was James Mill, whose history, "saturated," if history was ever so saturated, "with party politics," is ordinarily accepted to this day as a veritable history of British India. His "excessive dryness and severity of style," Sir James Stephen says, "produce an impression of accuracy and labour which a study of original authorities does not by any means confirm. . . . His want of accuracy is nothing to his bad faith. My experience is that when he makes imputations, especially on lawyers, he ought always to be carefully confronted with the original authorities."[1] I should have hesitated even on such authority as that of Sir James Stephen, to accuse an historian not only of inaccuracy but of bad faith, if I did not feel that I had qualified myself to form an independent opinion on the subject.

I have personally had occasion to investigate the facts of perhaps the worst of the crimes of which Hastings has been accused, the sale and extermination of the Rohillas.[2] Several years of my Indian service were passed in the province of Rohilkhand. When I was first sent there, men were still living who remembered having heard in their childhood the story of Háfiz Rahmat, the great Rohilla chief, of his defeat by the English, and his death. I went to Rohilkhand without a doubt of the truth of the terrible story told by Burke and Mill, and by Lord Macaulay in his famous essay, but I soon changed my opinion. I found myself in the midst of a population by which the history of those times had not been forgotten, and of which an important and numerous section consisted of Rohillas, the children and grandchildren of the men whose race was supposed to have been almost exterminated. I was in frequent communication with a Rohilla prince who ruled over a considerable territory which his ancestor owed to Warren Hastings, and which had been in the possession of his family ever since. No one had ever heard of the atrocities which to this day fill Englishmen with shame. Later in life I was able to undertake an examination of the original authorities on the Rohilla

[1] *The Story of Nuncomar and the Impeachment of Sir Elijah Impey*, vol. ii. p. 149.

[2] *Hastings and the Rohilla War*, by Sir John Strachey, 1892.

war, and I can hardly express in moderate language my indignation at the misrepresentations, the suppression of truth, the garbling of documents of which I found that Mill had been guilty. The English army was not hired out by Hastings for the destruction of the Rohillas; the Rohillas, described by Burke as belonging to "the bravest, the most honourable and generous nation on earth," were no nation at all, but a comparatively small body of cruel and rapacious Afghán adventurers who had imposed their foreign rule on an unwilling Hindu population; and the story of their destruction is absolutely fictitious. It was unfortunate that Lord Macaulay accepted Mill as an authority deserving the fullest confidence. There is hardly an important statement of fact in his essay on Warren Hastings which is not taken from Mill's History, or from the equally inaccurate charges and speeches of Burke. I share the admiration which Sir James Stephen has expressed for the services rendered to India by Lord Macaulay, and of him I shall speak no word of disrespect. But it is a misfortune that he was thus misled. I fear that the time is distant when English people will cease to accept his brilliant essays as the chief sources of their knowledge regarding the establishment of our empire in India.

A few words must be added on the subject of the books and newspapers published in India. The number of books that appear every year is large, but the number of new works of permanent value by Native authors, issued from the Indian press, is infinitely small. In 1890-91 there were 5595 publications, of which 2157 were in various vernacular languages, 424 in Sanskrit, Arabic, or Persian, and 650 in English. "According to the Official Reporter (I am quoting from Mr. Baines), a few works on Sanskrit texts, with an occasional drama on a historical occurrence or a subject of the day, are all that are likely to survive the year of their birth. A good deal of this infant mortality, so to speak, seems to be attributable to the very high proportion of the publications which deal with the text-books prescribed for University or School Examinations, or other ephemeral works designed for the same market. . . . A more favourite outlet for budding talent is found in journalism, of which we find 490 exponents in the list. The largest circulation is stated to be 20,000 in the case of one paper in Bengal; about 6000 is the maximum in Bombay, and 5000 in Madras. Elsewhere it seems to rarely reach a thousand. This does not represent, of course, nearly the number of readers."

It is a serious misfortune that discredit should often have been thrown on the results of English education by the foolish talk and disloyal writing of a section of the English-speaking Natives of India. This is chiefly true of the Bengális. Many of them are gifted with a remarkable faculty of fluent speech and writing. Although to our taste their English is often antiquated and magniloquent, few foreigners master so completely the difficulties of our language. Some of their newspapers, published in English, are, so far as the style is concerned, well written, but, with honourable exceptions, little else can be said in their favour. The vernacular press of Bengal has been sometimes distinctly seditious and shamefully scurrilous. This is by no means equally true of some of the other provinces, where many of the newspapers, although they may have little or no value, have at least been conducted with propriety and decorum.

To every one who desires to learn the truth regarding the progress of education in India, the excellent statement of the facts contained in the Report by Mr. Baines on the census of 1891 cannot be too highly commended. Many references have already been made to it, but I may quote also the words with which he concludes his chapter on the "Literacy of the Population." "Where so much is heard as at present of the literate claims of India, it is just as well to define the limitations of that term. It may thus be judged how far the φῶς ἀφεγγής of the handful of people to whom, under the most liberal interpretation, the term can be said to apply, is to be held capable of illuminating the thoughts and conditions of the vast mass from whom the very education, apart from the traditions, of that close corporation, inclines them to stand aloof."

I do not propose to describe how it came to pass that no means were for many years provided by the law in India for punishing the authors of publications that were unquestionably seditious, which stirred up dangerous strife between men of different religions, or were used as the means of levying blackmail from Native princes and Native officials. I doubt whether there is any civilised country in the world where the things would be tolerated which, until a few years ago, were tolerated in India, or where liberty of the Press was interpreted as it was interpreted there. When, in 1835, Lord Macaulay rightly and successfully advocated the abolition of the restrictions then existing on the Press in India—restrictions which no reasonable man would desire to see restored—he said that if the law that he proposed were adopted, "no person would be able to print or publish sedition or calumny without imminent risk of punishment." Lord Macaulay's anticipations were far from being fulfilled. For many years there was no sedition however flagrant, and no calumny however virulent, that could not be published in India with no risk at all. The Government of Lord Lytton attempted to deal with this subject by a legislative measure of extreme moderation, which placed no real restrictions on the freedom of the Press. Soon afterwards there was a change of Government in England, and all the checks imposed on seditious publications were removed. The evil became worse than ever, until, in 1898, after seditious writing in the public Press, especially in Bombay, had become intolerable and politically dangerous—when serious riots had occurred and British officers had been murdered—it was admitted by all reasonable men that action could no longer be delayed. The Penal Code and the Code of Criminal Procedure were amended by the Government of Lord Elgin in a manner which placed no restrictions on the absolute freedom of the Press to criticise or condemn, in language consistent with loyalty to our rule, any of the proceedings of the Government, but which at the same time brought the law into a shape in which it fulfilled the requirements declared, more than sixty years before, to be necessary by so true a friend to the liberty of the Press as Lord Macaulay.

CHAPTER XVII

RACES—LANGUAGES—CASTES—RELIGIONS AND SUPERSTITIONS

Races—Aryans—Dravidians—Languages of India—Distribution of population among various Religions—The Hindus—Animism—Religion of the Hindus—Illustrations of the Religion of an Indian province—Brahmanism—Caste—Reverence for Brahmans—Caste not confined to Hindus—The Mohammedans in India—Their distribution—Animosity between Hindus and Mohammedans—Causes of political anxiety—Increase of Mohammedanism in Bengal—Buddhists—Christianity in India—Jains—Sikhs—Parsis.

I DO not propose to say more than a few words regarding the ethnographical history of India. Knowledge of the subject is still in its infancy. There can, however, be no doubt that some, at least, of the conclusions drawn from modern philological and physiological research, and from the ancient literature of India, must contain a considerable amount of truth.

It appears that in times of which we have no historical record, there came into North-Western India from Central Asia a race of men called Arya. Their language was Sanskritic, closely allied to the languages of Greeks, Romans, Celts, and Germans. Gradually they spread themselves over Northern India, expelling or enslaving the races with whom they came into contact. These were dark-coloured people, inferior in all the arts of civilised life to the Aryan immigrants.

In the North, under Aryan domination, the Hindu polity and religion grew up as they are described in ancient Sanskrit literature. Many vestiges of the lower races still remain, especially in the wilder and more inaccessible tracts, but throughout the Indo-Gangetic plain their subjugation was complete. In the southern parts of India the Aryans never established themselves in general possession, but the Brahmans succeeded in obtaining recognition for their claim to universal veneration, and in including the local religions within the pale of Hinduism. The so-called Dravidian races of Southern India differ greatly in physical characteristics from the peoples of the North.

Throughout almost the whole of the countries of Northern and North-Western India, containing a population of some one hundred and sixty millions, Aryan supremacy, although not necessarily Aryan origin, for language is no test of race, is shown by the languages of the people. Although these differ greatly among themselves, the vocabulary of all of them is mainly Sanskritic. The most widely spoken of these, and of all the languages of India, although its dialects are very numerous, is Hindi. It is spoken, in various forms, by some ninety millions of people. Eighteen millions speak Punjábi, eleven millions Gujaráthi, nineteen millions Maráthi, and more than forty millions Bengáli.

The Dravidian languages of Southern India have no affinity to those of the Aryan group. They are spoken by more than fifty millions of people. The chief of them are Támil, Telugu, Kanarese, and Malayálam, but there are many dialects.

Other distinct classes of languages are those known as Kolarian, spoken by various tribes, of which the Santháls, in Bengal, are the most numerous; the languages allied to Tibetan; and Burmese. The last-named language is spoken by about six millions of people.

Altogether, seventy languages are enumerated in the census returns of 1891 as spoken in India, but many of these are dialects rather than distinct languages. Europe does not present, in this respect, greater diversity than India.

According to the census of 1901, the two hundred and ninety-four millions of people, for whom returns were furnished, were distributed among the principal religions as follows:—

Hindu	207,146,000
Animistic	8,711,000
Sikh	2,195,000
Jain	1,334,000
Parsi	94,000
Buddhist	9,477,000
Jew	18,000
Christian	2,923,000
Mohammedan	62,458,000

In regard to the religion of the Hindus in ancient times, or as it is described in ancient Sanskrit literature, and in regard to the forms in which it is professed by the less ignorant classes, who constitute a comparatively very small proportion of the population, I shall say nothing. The subject is one on which it is easy to find information. I propose now to refer only to the religion of the masses of the people, which, until not very long ago, had hardly been noticed in books professing to describe the religious beliefs and practices of the Hindus.

The religion of the masses of the agricultural population, which includes the great majority of the inhabitants of the Indian continent, has little resemblance to the more orthodox forms of Hinduism. I have laid much stress on the fact, which lies at the very root of all knowledge about India, that neither India as a whole nor any Indian country possesses, according to European ideas, any sort of unity. This is especially true of religion. There are more than two hundred millions of people that we call Hindus, but the term Hindu is one of which no definition is possible.

Excepting the wild tribes which have not yet been engulfed in the ocean of Brahmanism, every one in India is called a Hindu who is not a Mohammedan or a Christian, or a professor of some other recognised creed. "The faith of the masses," as Mr. Baines says, "is purely local," and "saturated with Animistic conceptions."

Before going farther, this term "Animistic," which was adopted in the census of 1891, and in that of 1901, must be noticed. I quote, from the report of Mr. Baines, Dr. Tiele's interpretation of the word :—

"Animism is the belief in the existence of souls or spirits, of which only the powerful—those on which man feels himself dependent, and before which he stands in awe—acquire the rank of divine beings, and become objects of worship. These spirits are conceived as moving freely through earth and air, and, either of their own accord, or because conjured by some spell, and thus under compulsion, appearing to men (*Spiritism*). But they may also take up their abode, either permanently or temporarily, in some object, whether lifeless or living it matters not; and this object, as endowed with higher power, is then worshipped or employed to protect individuals or communities (*Fetishism*). Spiritism, essentially the same as what is now called Spiritualism, must be carefully distinguished from Fetishism, but can only rarely be separated from it."

"In the stage of development (Mr. Baines continues) in which we find Animism in India, it has passed from its archaic and indeterminate shape into a collection of polydaimonistic tribal religions, in which spells, magic, and exorcism are all prominent. In this stage the malevolent spirits are considered the more important, and little notice is taken of the good. The main object, in the first place, is to get power over the spirits by magic, and, in a higher stage of belief, by gifts or homage. These notions are to be found in every stage of evolution in different parts of India, but the term Animistic has been restricted, in the census tables, to a certain class of the community. As in the case of several other forms of creed in that country, it is necessary to define the scope of the title negatively, or by explaining what is not included under it, rather than what is. In anticipation, therefore, of an explanation of the term Hindu, it may be stated that it was the intention of the framers of the rules for enumeration, that under the head of Animistic should come all members of the forest tribes who were not locally acknowledged to be Hindu, Musalman, Christian, or Buddhist by religion. . . . The distinction between the tribal form of faith and that of the lower grades of Bráhmanic community is very elastic. . . . But the distinction is really of little moment, because every stratum of Indian society is more or less saturated with Animistic conceptions, but little raised above those which predominate in the early stages of religious development." [1]

Sir Alfred Lyall has given, in his *Asiatic Studies*, an interesting account of modern Hinduism.

"The term 'Hindu' is not," he writes, "a national, or even a geographical denomination, but signifies vaguely a fortuitous conglomeration of sects, tribes, hereditary professions and castes." The Hindu religion is "a religious chaos." . . . "I doubt whether any one who has not lived among Hindus can adequately realise the astonishing variety of their ordinary religious beliefs, the constant changes of shape and colour which these beliefs undergo, the extraordinary fecundity of the superstitious sentiment." Hinduism is "a tangled jungle of disorderly superstitions, ghosts, and demons, demi-gods, and deified saints, household gods, tribal gods, local gods, universal gods, with their countless shrines and temples, and the din of their discordant rites—deities who abhor a fly's death, and those who delight still in human victims." [2]

[1] *General Report on the Census of India*, 1891, p. 157. [2] *Asiatic Studies*, p. 2.

If a religion be a creed with certain distinctive tenets, the Hinduism of the mass of the people is not a religion at all. Their religion is in no way represented by the sacred books of Sanskrit literature. The sanctity of the Vedas is an accepted article of faith among Hindus who have heard of their existence, but they have nothing to do with the existing popular beliefs. The Purânas, and other comparatively late works, which Elphinstone says may be called the scriptures of modern Hinduism, have no practical connection with the religion of the great majority of the population. Some of their gods and goddesses and heroes, indeed, have almost everywhere, in one form or another, places among the recognised deities. Millions of pilgrims flock to the shrines of Vishnu and Siva, for, as Mr. Baines says, "pilgrimages are the substitutes for most other religious observances, always excepting those connected with the propitiation of local spirits, whether family or attached to the house or village." Krishna and Ráma are loved from one end of India to the other, and the popularity of Hanumán is universal, but the everyday life of the ordinary Indian peasant is usually very little affected by thoughts of Hindu mythology. I am now speaking of the rural population. In the larger towns there is much more of the Hinduism that we read about in books.

Sir Alfred Lyall, in his first chapter, has described the religion of an Indian province, taking his illustrations mostly from Berár, in Central India. I will not refer to them because they are easily accessible, but I will quote some passages from a very instructive and valuable report by Sir Denzil Ibbetson, of the Civil Service, on the census of 1881 in the Punjab. It follows closely on the lines of Sir Alfred Lyall's work, and its facts are applicable in their general character, although not in all their details, to a very great part of India.

Hinduism—or, to give it its more appropriate name, Brahmanism—is, as Sir Denzil Ibbetson says, a sacerdotalism rather than a religion.

> "The veneration for Brahmans runs through the whole social as well as religious life of a Hindu peasant, and takes the practical form of either offerings or food. No child is born, named, betrothed, or married; nobody dies or is burnt; no journey is undertaken, or auspicious day selected; no house is built, no agricultural operation of importance begun, or harvest gathered in, without the Brahmans being feed and fed; a portion of all the produce of the field is set apart for their use; they are consulted in sickness and in health, they are feasted in sorrow and in joy. But with the spiritual life of the people, so far as such things exist, they have no concern. Their business as Brahmans is to eat and not to teach. . . . The sacerdotal despotism has altogether overshadowed the religious element, and the caste system has thrust its roots so deep into the whole social fabric that its sanction is social rather than religious. A man may disbelieve in the Hindu trinity; he may invent new gods of his own, however foul and impure; he may worship them with the most revolting orgies; he may even abandon all belief in supernatural powers, and yet remain a Hindu; but he must reverence and feed the Brahmans, he must abide by caste rules and restrictions, he must preserve himself from ceremonial pollution, and from contact and communion with the unclean, on pain of becoming Anathema Maranatha."

This general veneration of Brahmans, and the recognition of their divine right to be fed by the rest of the community, is the main link between the countless shapes of Hinduism; this, to the great majority of Hindus, constitutes in practice the chief part of their religion. But there is another bond of union which must not be forgotten—the universal belief in the holiness of the cow. The Hindu is by no means remarkable for humanity in the treatment of his cattle, but their lives are sacred. Kine-killing has often been a capital offence in Native States. In Kashmir it was, until not long ago, punished either with death or with imprisonment for life.

Sir Alfred Lyall was the first to explain clearly the process which has been going on, and which, wherever opportunity offers, goes on still, by which Brahmanism brings within its pale almost all the forms of worship with which it comes into contact, and adopts without objection all sorts of strange gods and demons. There has been, in his words, "a gradual Brahmanising of the aboriginal, non-Aryan, or casteless tribes," and nothing in Hinduism is more remarkable than the manner in which it has gone on, and still goes on, increasing the number of its adherents.

Mr. Risley, of the Indian Civil Service, has given from his own observation, in his work on *The Tribes and Castes of Bengal*, a work that is the most important contribution hitherto made to Indian ethnography, illustrations of the processes by which these conversions to Hinduism are accomplished. Sometimes, as he shows, the leading men of an aboriginal tribe, desirous of increased dignity, manage to enrol themselves in one of the recognised castes.

"They usually set up as Rajputs, their first step being to start a Brahman priest, who invents for them a mythical ancestor, supplies them with a family miracle connected with the locality where their tribes are settled, and discovers that they belong to some hitherto unheard-of clan of the great Rajput community. In the earlier stages of their advancement they generally find great difficulty in getting their daughters married, as they will not marry within their own tribe, and Rajputs of their adopted caste will of course not intermarry with them. But after a generation or two their persistency obtains its reward, and they intermarry, if not with pure Rajputs, at least with a superior order of manufactured Rajputs, whose promotion into the Brahmanical system dates far enough back for the steps by which it was gained to have been forgotten. Thus a real change of blood may take place; while in any caste the tribal name is completely lost, and with it all possibility of accurately separating this class of people from the Hindus of purer blood, and of assigning them to any particular non-Aryan tribe. They have been absorbed in the fullest sense of the word, and henceforth pose, and are locally accepted as high-caste Hindus. All stages of the process, family miracle and all, can be illustrated by actual instances taken from the leading families in Chota Nagpur.

"In other cases whole tribes or sections of tribes (Mr. Risley tells us) may become enrolled in the ranks of Hinduism as members of a caste claiming an origin of remote antiquity, or they may become gradually converted without abandoning their tribal designation." He gives an illustration of the latter case in the Bhumij tribe of Western Bengal. "Here a pure Dravidian race have lost their original language, and now speak only Bengali; they worship Hindu gods in addition to their own (the tendency being to delegate the tribal gods to the women), and the more advanced among them employ Brahmans as family priests. They still retain a set of totemistic subdivisions, but they are beginning to forget the totems which the names of the subdivisions denote, and the names themselves will probably soon be abandoned in favour of more aristocratic designations. The tribe will then have become a caste, and will go on stripping itself of all customs likely to betray its true descent. The physical characteristics of its members will alone survive."[1]

By these and by similar processes which have certainly been in operation for many centuries, the non-Aryans of India have gone on being absorbed into Hinduism. To become a Hindu by any of the methods of conversion by which other religions are recruited is impossible. Every orthodox Hindu will tell us that no one can become a Hindu who was not born one. There can be no proselytism, and no one becomes a Hindu by

[1] *The Tribes and Castes of Bengal*, Introduction, pp. xvi. xvii.

religious conviction. It is not the less true that there is no religion that obtains from outside its borders a larger number of fresh votaries. It works, as Mr. Risley says, in a different and more subtle fashion.

> "It leaves existing aggregates very much as they were, and so far from welding them together, after the manner of Islam, with larger cohesive aggregates, tends rather to create an indefinite number of fresh groups; but every tribe that passes within the charmed circle of Hinduism inclines sooner or later to abandon its more primitive usages or to clothe them in some Brahmanical disguise. One by one the ancient totems drop off, or are converted by a variety of ingenious devices into respectable personages of the standard mythology; the fetish gets a new name, and is promoted to the Hindu Pantheon in the guise of a special incarnation of one of the greatest gods; the tribal chief sets up a family priest, starts a more or less romantic family legend, and in course of time blossoms forth as a new variety of Rajput. His people follow his lead, and make haste to sacrifice their women at the shrine of social distinction. Infant-marriage, with all its attendant horrors, is introduced; widows are forbidden to marry again; and divorce, which plays a great and, on the whole, a useful part in tribal society, is summarily abolished. Throughout all these changes, which strike deep into the domestic life of the people, the fiction is maintained that no real change has taken place, and every one believes, or affects to believe, that things are with them as they have been since the beginning of time." [1]

Mr. Risley adds that it is curious to observe that the operation of these tendencies has been quickened, and the sphere of their action enlarged, by the extension in India of railway communication. Pilgrimages become easier and more pleasant, and "Siva and Krishna drive out the tribal gods as surely as grey shirtings displace the more durable hand-woven cloth."

With regard to the worship of the gods, the important matter to the Hindu peasant is the propitiation of the

[1] *The Tribes and Castes of Bengal*, Introduction, p. xxviii.

tribal or other deity who attends to the affairs of his own particular caste or occupation, and of the local gods and ghosts and saints and demons who haunt every hill and grove and village. Their names are often unknown, or little cared for, outside the limits of their personal or territorial authority, and their numbers are countless. These powers, for the most part malevolent, go on multiplying or perishing; they are maintained or degraded according to their deserts; frequent miracles, the stream of which in India is never-ending, support the faith of their devotees or transfer it to some new object; and all of them are readily accepted as worthy of veneration or fear by the Brahmans; the gates of the Hindu Pantheon are never shut. These local gods and evil powers are at all times on the alert to resent and punish neglect and disrespect. Little is to be hoped from them, but everything is to be feared. Every disease and every misfortune is more or less dependent on their influence, and the life of the Indian peasant is bound up with the observances required to give a certain amount of security against this ever-present danger. In Southern India, and in Lower Bengal, the number and power of local deities and malevolent spirits are even greater than in the north. "It almost seems (Mr. Baines observes) that the weaker the race the more numerous and bloodthirsty are its gods, and the greater the influence of the sacerdotal system of caste."

In the Indian superstitions there is almost always a grotesque element. I will give a few examples of them; they will not be applicable to any one extensive tract, for custom in regard to these matters is infinitely various, but they will not on this account be less characteristic.[1]

[1] I have taken these illustrations of local superstitions from Sir Denzil Ibbetson's "Report on the Census of the Punjab," from Sir Henry Elliot's *Races*

The most dreaded of the minor deities in Northern India are those who cause special diseases. The smallpox goddess, Sítala, is the eldest and most formidable of seven fatal sisters. She is worshipped by women and children only, and enormous numbers of them attend her shrines. She usually rides on a donkey, and therefore it is proper to give a feed of grain at her shrine to the donkey of the village potter, first waving the grain and white cocks over the head of the child to be protected. At the same time black dogs are fed, fowls, pigs, goats, and cocoa-nuts are offered. An adult who has had smallpox must let a pig loose for Sítala, or he will be attacked again. If an epidemic of smallpox appears in the village the goddess is punished by the cessation of all worship and offerings, but so long as the disease is absent nothing is too good for her. She is easily frightened or deceived, and when a woman has lost a son by smallpox, and fears that another may be attacked, it is desirable to let the goddess understand that the second son is of no value, and, as evidence of this, to send him round the village in a dust-pan, or to dress him in old rags borrowed from the neighbours.

Everything is to be feared from the malevolent dead. A man who has died a violent death, or without sons, is dangerous, and it is prudent to erect a shrine to him. One of these ghosts of great fame in the Delhi territory is Teja. He was taking milk to his aged mother when a snake bit him on the nose. He begged to be allowed to take the milk to her, and then came back to be again

of the North-Western Provinces, and from the *Report on the Settlement of Bareilly*, by Mr. Moens. I have often given the words of the original authors, but so much has been omitted or altered that I have not marked all my borrowings as quotations, and it has therefore to be explained that nearly all that is said on this subject is due to the authorities that I have named, and especially to Sir Denzil Ibbetson's interesting Report.

bitten and killed. These evil ghosts are especially dangerous to women and children after eating sweetmeats, and a pinch of salt should be taken as a precaution. They are fond of going down your throat when you yawn. They cannot set foot on the ground, so it is wise in haunted places to sleep on the ground and not on a bed. Very often they take up their abode in animals dangerous to human life.

The Evil eye is more common and dangerous than the jettatura of Naples. Malignant influence is often exercised by inanimate objects. I have myself been officially obliged, in one of the Hill districts, to interfere on behalf of a considerable population, to give protection against a small white house newly built in a conspicuous situation, the owner of which sorrowfully admitted that, through no fault of his own, it was undoubtedly bringing ruin on his neighbours. Sir Alfred Lyall has given examples of the worship of inanimate objects of strange appearance. I knew a case in which the sight of a distant mountain peak of peculiar form had caused for many years the complete abandonment of a village and of a rich tract of cultivated land. Good and bad omens are innumerable. Two water-pots, one on the top of the other, are especially fortunate if they be left to the right in passing; and the same rule is applicable to cows and antelopes; a snake, on the other hand, should be passed on the left.

I will give, merely as illustrations, a few examples of local superstitions:—

"If," writes Sir Denzil Ibbetson, referring to the Punjab, "a boy be born, a net is hung over the doorway, a chain stuck on to the wall, and a fire lighted on the threshold, which is kept up night and day to prevent evil spirits from passing. The swaddling-clothes should be borrowed from another person's house. On the night of the sixth day the whole household sits up and watches over the child, for on that day his destiny is determined, especially as to immunity from smallpox. If he go hungry on that day he will be stingy all his life. None of these precautions are taken on the birth of a girl."

No agricultural operations can be carried on without the performance of certain ceremonies, and the superstitions connected with them are endless. I will give one or two illustrations taken from the Agra Province and the Punjab. This is the manner in which the planting of sugar-cane is commenced in parts of Rohilkhand. When the ground is ready the plough is worshipped and decorated. This goes first, and is followed in the same furrow by a second. Behind this comes the sower, wearing silver ornaments, a necklace of flowers, a red mark on his forehead, and lamp-black on his eyelids. Before beginning his work he is regaled with ghee and sweetmeats. He strews the bits of sugar-cane into the furrow at intervals of about a foot. He is called the elephant. Behind him comes a second man, called the crow, who picks up any bits which have not fallen into the furrow. A third man, called the donkey, supplies the elephant with sugar-cane from a basket tied to his waist. It is a fortunate omen if a man on horseback comes into the field while this is going on. When the work is done, all who have been engaged in it go to the house of the cultivator of the field and have a dinner, composed of pulse, milk and spices, rice, and cakes of unleavened bread. In some districts the wife of the elephant follows with a ball of cotton. At some unexpected moment he turns on her, and after a sham contest bears her to the ground. The cotton, being forced out of her hand, spreads upon the ground, and the parties present exclaim, "May our sugar-cane grow and spread like this cotton." Not the least essential part of this and all other proceedings is that the Brahmans must be fed and proper offerings given to them.

Sir Denzil Ibbetson gives some examples of superstitions in the Punjab regarding cattle. Nothing connected with them, such as butter or leather, must be bought or sold on Saturday or Sunday. The manner in which, when cattle-plague first appears in a village, it can be cast out, and transferred to the next village in the East, is curious. All field work, grinding, and cooking are stopped on Saturday morning, and on Sunday night a procession takes a buffalo skull, a lamb, sticks of the *siras* tree, butter-milk, fire, and sacred grass to the boundary, over which they are thrown, while a gun is fired three times to frighten away the disease. "Last year a man was killed in an affray resulting from an attempt to transfer the plague in this manner. A villager in Gurgáon once captured the cattle-plague in its material shape, and would not let it go till it promised never to remain where he or his descendants were present; and his progeny are still sent for when murrain has fastened on a village, to walk round it and call on the plague to fulfil its contract."

Great power over milch-cattle is exercised by the Singhs, or snake-gods, and the milk of the eleventh day after calving is sacred to them. These Singhs have a widespread reputation among the villagers of Northern India. Those best known are the black, green, and grey Singhs; but dead men have a way of becoming snakes, so their numbers multiply, and shrines must be erected to them. If a peasant sees a snake he will salute it, and if it bites him he or his heirs will build a shrine to prevent similar occurrences in future.

Among the conditions in which India differs from every other country in the world there is nothing more prominent and remarkable than the institution of caste. The Hindu population of India is extraordinarily diverse, but it has almost everywhere this common characteristic, that it is divided into castes, each of which is governed in all the relations of social life by its own customs. The number of these castes is almost infinite. Many of them may often be included under the same or a similar designation, but even the highest castes are constantly divided into sections, the members of which are separated by wide differences of custom, who cannot intermarry and cannot eat together without pollution. The one thing in which they all agree is in the reverence due to Brahmans.

It is one of the delusions about modern India that although there have been many changes in the system of caste, it remains true that the Hindu population is divided into the four great classes described by Manu: Brahmans, Kshatriyas, Vaisyas, and Sudras. In India itself this notion is often fostered by the more learned among the Brahmans, who love to make themselves and others believe in the continuous existence of a divinely constituted organisation. To what extent the religious and social systems shadowed forth in the ancient Brahmanical literature of India had an actual existence it is difficult to say, but it is certain that little remains of them now. The Brahmans, indeed, maintain their exceptional position.

The interesting but most difficult and complicated question of the origin of caste in India is one into which I cannot attempt, even in the most cursory manner, to enter. To the ordinary observer caste appears at the present time to mean for the most part hereditary occupation. India, in the words of Sir Henry Maine, is seen to be divided into a vast number of independent, self-acting, organised social groups—trading, manufacturing, cultivating—and in the majority of instances caste is only the name for a number of practices which are followed by each one of a multitude of groups of men. "As a rule, every trade, every profession, every guild, every tribe, every class, is also a caste; and the members of a caste not only have their special objects of worship, selected from the Hindu Pantheon, or adopted into it, but they exclusively eat together, and exclusively intermarry." This, however, represents only a portion of the facts. Occupation is far from being necessarily a sign of caste. There is no caste, not even the highest, that of Brahmans, members of which are not to be found in almost every occupation, provided only that it involves no personal or ceremonial pollution. Although very often an indication of caste, occupation cannot have been its origin. Mr. Risley, whose work I have already quoted in speaking of the closely connected subject of religion, has thrown by his researches much new light upon this question. Starting with the well-established fact that although religion, language, and custom may give, in the words of Professor Flower, valuable indications, they are no true tests of race, and that these can only be found in physical characteristics; and observing that obvious and persistent physical differences can often be seen between the various castes of India, Mr. Risley applied to the castes and tribes of Bengal, and of other provinces, those scientific methods of comparing and recording typical physical characteristics, which in other countries have added so greatly to ethnographic knowledge. Elaborate anthropometric investigations led him to the conclusion that the true origin of caste is to be found in race. His researches have shown that "the race sentiment of the Aryans, which runs through the whole course of Indian tradition, and survives in scarcely abated strength at the present day . . . so far from being a figment of the intolerant pride of the Brahmans, rests upon a fact, which scientific methods confirm, that it has shaped the intricate groupings of the caste system, and has preserved the Aryan type in comparative purity in Northern India."[1]

Among the almost innumerable castes there is none that has so many members as that of the Brahmans. According to the census of 1891 they numbered 14,800,000. Besides these there were only three castes each of which had more than 10,000,000 members: Rájput, Kunbi (agriculturists), and Chamár (workers in leather). About 16 per cent of the inhabitants of India were included in these four castes. There were between forty and fifty others, each of which had more than a million members.

The distinctions and subdivisions of all these castes are innumerable, and even the Brahmans are as much divided among themselves as the rest. They are usually said to consist of two great divisions, but according to Mr. Sherring, in his work on *Hindu Tribes and Castes*, there are more than 1800 Brahmanical subdivisions; and it constantly happens that to a Brahman of some particular class or district the pollution of eating with other Brahmans would be ruinous. They are numerous almost everywhere; Oudh is one of their

[1] *The Tribes and Castes of Bengal*, Introduction, p. i. To those who desire to study this difficult question of caste in India, Mr. Risley's important work cannot be too strongly recommended. A very interesting book on the same subject, whether or not all the conclusions of its author be accepted, is M. Émile Senart's *Les Castes dans l'Inde*, published in the *Annales du Musée Guimet Bibliothèque de Vulgarisation*.

especial strongholds. In that province in 1881 they constituted one-seventh of the Hindu population.

"Every one of them," writes Mr. Benett, "is invested with a reverence which no extreme of abject poverty, no infamy of private conduct, can impair, and which is beyond anything which a mind not immediately conversant with the facts can conceive. They are invariably addressed with the titles of divinity or highest earthly honour. The oldest and highest of the members of other castes implore the blessing of the youngest and poorest of theirs; they are the chosen recipients of all charity, and are allowed a licence in their private relations with the inferior castes which would be resented as a deadly injury in any but themselves."

The Brahmans have become so numerous that only a small proportion can be employed in sacerdotal functions, and the charity which it is a duty to bestow upon them could not, however profuse, be sufficient for their support. They are found in almost every occupation. They are soldiers, cultivators, traders, and servants; they were very numerous in the old Sepoy army, and the name of one of their subdivisions, "Pánde," became the generic term by which the mutineers of 1857 were commonly known by the English in India. The number of Brahmans in the public service is very large. "Their number"—I am quoting from the Report of the Public Service Commission—"is sixfold that of any other Hindu caste, except the Kayasths—who, however, are only half as numerous as the Brahmans—and it represents a proportion of about 35 per cent on the total number of persons employed in the executive and judicial branches of the public service. This is especially noteworthy when it is remembered that the number of males of the Brahman caste bears a proportion of only between 7 and 8 per cent to the total male Hindu population of British India."

It is remarkable that the Brahmans, with rare exceptions, have never aspired to actual sovereignty.

The ordinary assumption that caste in India is an institution entirely peculiar to Hindus is erroneous.

Sir Denzil Ibbetson, in his Report on the census in the Punjab, shows how completely it is true that caste is now a social and not a religious institution. Conversion to Mohammedanism, for instance, has often no effect on the caste of the convert. The same is sometimes true of converts to Christianity. Mr. Baines tells us, for example, of a Christian apothecary in Madras who asked that a wall might be built round the yard of the dispensary of which he had official charge, in order that the women of his family might take exercise in the seclusion due to their caste.

There has often been much misapprehension about the Indian Mohammedans, of whom there are more than 62,000,000. Among all the countries of India there are only two in which the Mohammedans are very numerous, and many of them are so ignorant of the religion to which they nominally belong, and so little devoted to its tenets, that they might almost as properly be counted among the innumerable classes of Hindus.

Throughout the long strip of country, for the most part scantily peopled, in the valley of the Indus, below the mountains of Afghanistán and Baluchistán, that form the western frontier of India, the great majority of the population has been for many centuries Mohammedan. This tract, varying in breadth to a maximum of about 400 miles, extends for some 800 miles, from beyond Pesháwar on the north, through the plains of the Western Punjab and Sind to the sea. Although within the geographical limits of India it is very distinct from any other Indian country. The dominant races of Patháns and Baluchis are of foreign origin, but the majority of the population consists of the descendants of Hindu or aboriginal tribes, who long ago accepted, more or less, the religion of their conquerors. The North-West Frontier Province contained, according to the census of 1901, nearly 2,000,000 Mohammedans and only 134,000 Hindus.

In the eastern and richer and more populous parts of the Punjab, Mohammedans, real or nominal, descended mostly from converts from Hinduism, are also very numerous. There are altogether more than 12,000,000 Mohammedans in the Punjab and its subordinate States, and they constitute about one-half of the whole population. More than 70 per cent of the people of Kashmir are Mohammedans.

Excepting these countries, on the northern and western frontiers of India, the only great Indian province in which a very large proportion of the populationed has embraced Mohammedanism is Bengal. Out of a total population of 74,700,000 there were, in 1901, 25,250,000 Mohammedans and 46,700,000 Hindus. In the eastern districts of the delta of the Ganges, and beyond the Bráhmaputra to the eastern limits of India, they constitute the great bulk of the agricultural population. Nothing is known historically of the time or manner in which this religious conversion occurred. But the conversion was in a great measure nominal rather than real.

Thus, out of a total Mohammedan population of 62,500,000, some 40,000,000, or nearly two-thirds of the whole number, are found on the western and eastern borders, and principally in the Punjab, the North-West Frontier Province, and Bengal. In the rest of India, containing about 232,000,000 people, there are only about 22,000,000 Mohammedans. The progress of the Mohammedan religion in India generally has therefore been smaller than might be supposed from the bare statement of the numbers that profess it, and that progress will seem still smaller when the true character of a large section of Indian Mohammedanism is understood.

A large proportion of the Mohammedans of India hardly deserve that name. They differ little from their Hindu neighbours in their customs, and often not very much in their religion, and they maintain similar distinctions of caste. The following description is given by Sir Denzil Ibbetson of the Mohammedans of the Eastern Punjab, and a similar story might be told for Bengal and other parts of India :—

"The Musulman Rájput, Gujar, orJát is, for all social, tribal, political, and administrative purposes, exactly as much a Rájput, Gujar, orJát as his Hindu brother. His social customs are unaltered, his tribal restrictions are unrelaxed, his rules of marriage and inheritance unchanged; and almost all the difference is that he shaves his scalp-lock and the upper edge of his moustache, repeats the Mohammedan creed in a mosque, and adds the Musulman to the Hindu wedding-ceremony. . . . The local saints and deities still have their shrines, even in villages held wholly by Musulmans, and are still regularly worshipped by the majority, though the practice is gradually declining. The women especially are offenders in this way, and a Musulman mother who had not sacrificed to the smallpox goddess would feel that she had wantonly endangered the life of her child. The Hindu family priests are still kept up and consulted as of old, and Brahmans are still fed on the usual occasions, and in many cases still officiate at weddings side by side with the Mohammedan priests. As for superstitions, as distinct from actual worship, they are wholly untouched by the change of faith, and are common to Hindu and Musulman. A brother officer tells us that he once entered the rest-house of a Mohammedan village in Hissar, and found the headmen refreshing an idol with a new coat of oil, while a Brahman read holy texts alongside. They seemed somewhat ashamed of being caught in the act, but, on being pressed, explained that their Mulla had lately visited them, had been extremely angry in seeing the idol, and had made them bury it in the sand. But now that the Mulla had gone they were afraid of the possible consequences, and were endeavouring to console the god for his rough treatment. The story is at any rate typical of the state of the Mohammedan religion in the villages of the Delhi territory."[1]

In these matters the Hindus are ready to meet the Mohammedans more than half-way. The Brahmans have no sort of scruple in accepting Mohammedan saints as proper objects of veneration, and nothing is commoner than to see Hindus taking an active part in Mohammedan ceremonies, and beating their breasts at the Moharram like good Musalmans. This is true of the lower classes only, but centuries of Mohammedan supremacy have also left their mark on the higher classes of Hindus. The general seclusion of their women is one of the instances in which they still follow Mohammedan custom.

The great majority of the Musalmans of India are the descendants of Hindu converts. The Mohammedan sovereigns usually treated their subjects, in matters of religion, with great tolerance; but more or less pressure was from time to time brought upon Hindus to induce them to embrace the faith of the ruling power. This was especially the case in the time of Aurangzíb, the most bigoted of the Mohammedan emperors. The change of faith was often little more than nominal, and took place to an extent just sufficient to save the joint property of the village community from molestation. One section of the brotherhood would become Mohammedan, while the rest remained Hindu. The change of

[1] *Report on the Census of 1881 in the Punjab*, p. 143.

religion had little practical result, nor did it affect the rules of caste or the social life of the community.

There is, of course, in India a large and very important body of Mohammedans of a different type, descended, with little or no admixture of the Hindu element, from the servants and soldiers of the Mohammedan rulers, and from former invaders or immigrants, who hold with more or less orthodoxy the tenets of their faith. They are especially to be found in Northern India. The Mohammedan population of the towns is usually far less Hinduised than that of the country villages. In the Agra Province only 7 per cent of the Hindu population live in the towns, while 25 per cent of the Mohammedans are found there. In the agricultural districts about 10 per cent of the people are Mohammedan, but in the towns the Mohammedans constitute more than one-third of the inhabitants. This fact tends to make their political importance greater than it would otherwise be. In many of the towns much religious animosity prevails between Mohammedans and Hindus, and this often leads to serious and sanguinary affrays. Among the agricultural population the members of the several creeds usually live together more peaceably. This, however, is not always the case, nor does it by any means follow that Mohammedans who know little or nothing of the tenets of the religion they profess are on that account less fanatical in their hatred of Hindus. When a Mohammedan rises in the world he becomes more orthodox, and begins to assume foreign titles to respect. He calls himself Khán, or Shaikh, or even Saiyad, a descendant of the Prophet.

"In the Punjab," writes Mr. Beames, "where the process of conversion has been carried out on a very large scale, there used to be a proverbial couplet to this effect, supposed to be spoken by a convert—

> Last year I was a weaver, this year I am a Shaikh,
> Next year, if grain is dear, I shall be a Saiyad—

meaning that if he sold his crops well he should be wealthy enough to assume this latter title." [1]

The chief classes of Mohammedans claiming foreign descent are the Saiyad, Moghal, Pathán, and Shaikh. Among these the Shaikhs are the most numerous, but the great majority of them are the descendants of Hindu converts. Politically, the Patháns of Afghán origin are the most important. During the Mohammedan dynasties, and especially while the empire was breaking up, they poured into India as adventurers and soldiers of fortune, ready to sell their swords to the highest bidder. Their unscrupulous violence and courage gave them great influence, and they were the only Mohammedan foreigners who permanently established themselves in the plains of India in large numbers. These were the people who, under their Indian name of Rohillas, fought against us in the time of Warren Hastings. The story of their cruel extermination has, I fear, become an accepted fact of history; but, as I have shown, it is purely fabulous.

Recollections of their old dominion, and the splendid monuments which testify to the magnificence of their former sovereigns, have exercised a powerful influence in keeping alive among the higher classes of Mohammedans in Northern India feelings of pride in their religion and race; but their social and political importance was seriously diminished by the mutinies of 1857, when many of their chief families became implicated in rebellion and suffered in consequence. They

[1] Elliot's *Races of the North-Western Provinces*, vol. i. p. 185.

still, however, hold a more influential position in the country than their mere numbers would give them; they are more generally energetic than Hindus, and possess greater independence of character. In perfection of manner and courtesy a Mohammedan gentleman of Northern India has often no superior.

It is not possible to say what proportion of the 62,500,000 Mohammedans may be held to represent the classes once dominant in India. Sir George Campbell, whose knowledge entitled him to speak with unusual authority, thought that on an outside estimate we might assume them to be 5,000,000. Whatever be the actual number, it is comparatively small. It doubtless includes many who feel for us and our Government a deep and fanatical dislike, but it also includes a large number of men who deserve our confidence and respect. It is a mistake to suppose that the better classes of Mohammedans are as a rule disloyal. English education, which not unfrequently seems to develop and bring into prominence the least admirable qualities of the feebler races, often tends to make Mohammedans more manly and self-reliant, and more loyal citizens.

The fears that have sometimes been expressed that we may see in India a general outburst of Mohammedan fanaticism, and a simultaneous rising of millions of Mohammedans against our Government, are altogether groundless. If Mohammedanism contains any elements of political danger, they are nullified by the fact that the feelings of true Mohammedans towards idolatrous Hindus are more hostile than towards Christians, and that Hindus will never desire the restoration of Musalman supremacy. Nothing could be more opposed to the policy and universal practice of our Government in India than the old maxim of divide and rule; the maintenance of peace among all classes has always been recognised as one of the most essential duties of our "belligerent civilisation"; but this need not blind us to the fact that the existence side by side of these hostile creeds is one of the strong points in our political position in India. The better classes of Mohammedans are a source to us of strength and not of weakness. They constitute a comparatively small but energetic minority of the population, whose political interests are identical with ours, and who, under no conceivable circumstances, would prefer Hindu dominion to our own.

I have laid much stress on the fact that the majority of Indian Mohammedans differ in some respects little from Hindus; but there has undoubtedly been a growing tendency during the last half-century towards the purification of their faith. We must hope that with the increase of knowledge and civilisation this progress will continue, but it is not likely, within any time that we can foresee, to bring with it increased harmony of feeling between Mohammedans and Hindus. The more orthodox a Mohammedan becomes, the wider becomes the gulf that separates him from every form of idolatrous worship.

Although there is no danger to our Government from Mohammedan disaffection, the animosity, which is so easily aroused between Mohammedans and Hindus, is often a cause of serious anxiety. In past times it has frequently led to violent conflicts, and in late years it has shown itself with much virulence. Outbreaks of religious exasperation, attended with destructive rioting and bloodshed, have often occurred; in some instances they have assumed large proportions, nor have they been confined to the towns where the population is, as a rule, more disposed to be fanatical and turbulent. In

1893, for example, widespread disturbances of a most serious character, affecting a considerable tract of country and a large population, occurred in the district of Azimgarh, in the Agra Province. They were traced to the influence of cow-protecting societies which had, for some years, been carrying on their propaganda. In the same year, the great city of Bombay, containing more than 800,000 people, was for three days the scene of furious conflict. Eighty persons were killed and some hundred were wounded, and mosques and temples were desecrated and ruined. Order was not restored until a large force of troops, including British Cavalry and Infantry and Artillery, had been called out. In this, as in almost all similar cases elsewhere, the chronic hostility between Hindus and Mohammedans had been stimulated by the agitation against cow-killing. There was, the Bombay Government reported as the result of its inquiries, "an uneasy feeling among Mohammedans that they and their faith were suffering at the hands of the Hindus, that they were being gradually but surely edged out of the position they have hitherto held, and that their religion needed some special protection." This question of cow-killing has been a cause of frequent trouble throughout a great part of India, and while Hindu agitation has been primarily directed against Mohammedans, it has obviously a serious significance for ourselves. Indian statesmen ought not to forget that this is a subject—and it is almost the only one that exists—which forms a bond of union among the 230 millions of the countless castes and classes of Hindus throughout the whole continent of India, on which they all hold the same belief and have the same sympathies.

In some parts of India, and especially in Bengal

Proper, there has been a large increase of Mohammedanism during the last thirty years. In 1872 in that province the Hindus outnumbered the Mohammedans by half a million; in 1901, these proportions were reversed, the Mohammedans being more numerous by half a million than the Hindus. On this subject Mr. O'Donnell, who superintended the census of 1891 in Bengal, wrote as follows:—"It is known that a powerful Mohammedan propaganda is at work, and that the preaching of the ubiquitous Mullahs and Mirs is directed not only to instil the precepts of a higher life, according to the doctrines of the Kurán, on Musalmans, but to gain over followers for its teachings. That converts should result seems natural, but, however this may be, it is certain that the great growth of Musalmanism in Bengal Proper is connected with physical rather than doctrinal forces. The Musalman with his more varied and nutritious dietary is probably a more vigorous man than the Hindu. Moreover, the universal practice of widow marriage, which the Bengali Hindu holds in abhorrence, adds very largely to the reproductive class amongst Mohammedan women. On the other hand, ill-assorted marriages are far more common amongst Hindus, men well advanced in years being united to girl-wives, who in the natural course of human life are left widows, debarred from further maternity, at a comparatively early age."

Nearly all of the 9,500,000 Buddhists of the census are found in Burma. Buddhism no longer exists as one of the religions of the peoples of the Indian continent. Even in Burma, Mr. Baines writes, "the popular belief is little but Animism, and the attachment to the higher creed is largely due to the educational influence of the religious orders, because every boy has to be sent, if only for a short period, to one of the monasteries as a novice or lay brother. Like the Neo-Brahmanism, too, it is gradually absorbing within its sphere the forest tribes who are professedly Animistic in their belief, and like its former rival, it places no embargo on their tutelary gods, whilst through the monastic system it tends to raise them in the social scale. Considerably more than half the males in Burma can read and write, a feature in which the difference between the two systems is very clearly denoted."

Out of 2,900,000 Christians, in 1901, in British India and the Native States, 170,000 were Europeans, of whom a little more than one half were in or connected with the Army. The other half included the civil employés of the Government and their families, the railway servants, and the whole of the non-official European community. There were about 89,000 Eurasians. The Christians of Indian origin numbered 2,660,000. Of these nearly two millions are found in Madras and in the Native States of Malabar, the great majority of them belonging to the Church of Rome, descendants of the converts made in the sixteenth century by St. Francis Xavier and by his followers. The Native members of the various Protestant sects throughout India numbered 970,000, those of the Roman Catholic Church 1,123,000, and those of the Syrian Church 571,000. These figures are exclusive of the French and Portuguese possessions, where the Christian population is almost entirely Roman Catholic. The total increase of the Christian population in the ten years between 1891 and 1901 in British India and the Native States, was about 639,000. The number of Native members of the Roman and Syrian Churches increased by 250,000, and that of the various Protestant sects by 378,000. The greater part of the increase was in Southern India, but there was no province in which the number of Christians was not larger in 1901 than ten years before. Although the Christians in India constitute only one per cent of the whole population, these figures are remarkable.

Judged by even a low standard, the religion of the great majority of the Native Christians, especially those of Southern India, is Christianity in little more than name. There are many noble exceptions, but it cannot be professed that Indian Christians have gained for themselves, as a rule, an exceptional measure of respect either among their own countrymen or among Europeans. There has been no apparent connection between the increase in the number of Christians and the progress of education. The effect of higher English education on the religious beliefs of educated Hindus has doubtless been very great, but it has had little tendency to make them Christian. Converts from Mohammedanism to Christianity are very few. The large majority of converts are drawn from the lowest castes of Hindus and from the Animistic tribes, and this goes far to explain the fact, stated in the Report on the Census of 1901 in the United Provinces, that "to the great mass of converts the change in religion causes little change in outward relations; it was reported from one district that families had been converted without the rest of the villagers knowing it. What change is made is on the whole for the better."

The only other Indian religions that need be noticed are those of the Jains and the Sikhs. Jainism is, in its doctrines, very similar to the more orthodox forms of Buddhism. There is, Mr. Baines tells us, in parts of India, a tendency for it to become virtually a sect of Brahmanism. "In the north and west of India the Jains are still a cultivated class, mostly engaged in commerce, whilst in the south they are, as a rule, agriculturists."

The Sikhs are politically important, but in matters of religion there is no great difference between them and Hindus. "In the present day," writes Mr. Baines, "peace has relaxed the bonds of discipline, and the distinction between Sikhs and the rest of the Brahmanic community is mainly ritualistic. For example, it was found by experience that at the census, the only trustworthy method of distinguishing this creed was to ask if the person in question repudiated the services of the barber and the tobacconist, for the precepts most strictly enforced nowadays are that the hair of the head and face must never be cut, and that smoking is a habit to be absolutely avoided."[1]

The Parsis form a very small but highly respectable community, devoted for the most part to mercantile pursuits. Their enterprise as traders, and their freedom from prejudices of caste, take them into all parts of India, but the great majority of them are found in Bombay. They have gained for themselves by their character, their superior education, and their wealth, a somewhat exceptional position, but they have so little in common with anything Indian, and their numbers are so small, that they can only be mentioned as an interesting group of foreigners, who for many centuries have retained their ancient creed, and have kept themselves apart from the people of all Indian countries.

[1] *General Report on the Census of India*, 1891, p. 164.

CHAPTER XVIII

AN INDIAN PROVINCE

The United Provinces of Agra and Oudh—Area, population, language, and history—Aspect of the country—The agricultural population—Cities — Manufactures — Architectural monuments — Erroneous beliefs regarding food of the people—The agricultural year—The rainy season—Summer, autumnal, and winter crops—Irrigation—Methods of agriculture.

If any one were to propose to give in a single volume a description of all the countries of Europe—their geography, their climates, their governments, and systems of administration, the character and customs and languages and religions of their inhabitants—his undertaking would not be more impossible than that of giving within the same limits an adequate description of India; nor, however much those limits might be exceeded, do I believe that any one possesses the necessary knowledge. I think that if I endeavour to give some account of one of the great provinces, noting, as I go on, points which in other Indian countries differ or correspond, I may be able to convey more accurate information than by any other plan that I could follow. This will be especially true in regard to the public administration; for notwithstanding my frequent warnings about the danger of generalisations, the main structure of the government throughout British India has been built up on not very various lines.

I propose to take as my example of an Indian province the United Provinces of Agra and Oudh. I choose them because I know them best. A large part of my Indian service was spent in them, and I have been, as Lieutenant-Governor and Chief Commissioner, at the head of their administration.

The Agra Province, known until 1901 as the North-Western Provinces, lies within the great Indo-Gangetic plain, the main features of which have been already described in the second chapter of this work. It comprises nearly all the upper portion of the basin of the Ganges and Jumna, from their sources in the Himálaya to the borders of Bengal. It is one of the most homogeneous of the great provinces of India, in the aspect of the country and in the condition and character of its inhabitants. It includes two small Native States, Tehri, as distinguished from British Garhwál, a purely Himálayan district, and Rámpur, in Rohilkhand. The latter, by far the more important of the two, has a special interest to Englishmen in being, as it has been since the time of Warren Hastings, to whom it owed its preservation, a flourishing Rohilla State—a standing comment on the totally fictitious stories to which I have already referred, and which I fear most of us still believe, told by Burke and James Mill and Macaulay, of the cruel extermination of the brave Rohillas.

Including these Native States, the Agra Province covers about 88,000 square miles, and contains 35,700,000 people.

Oudh, excepting on the north, where its boundary is the Himálayan State of Nepál, is surrounded by districts of the Agra Province. It contains 24,000 square miles, and 12,800,000 people.

Physically, there are no important differences between the two provinces, the whole, excepting the districts bordering on the tableland of Central India, and the Himálayan districts of Kumáon and Garhwál, forming one continuous alluvial plain, broken only by the rivers which intersect it ; but politically, they have been, until some years ago, under separate administrations. Oudh became British territory in 1856 ; it was partially amalgamated with the North-Western Provinces in 1877. Although there are still many differences in the revenue and judicial systems of the two provinces, they are now virtually a single province under a Lieutenant-Governor, whose headquarters are at Allahabad. In 1901, in consequence of the formation of the North-West Frontier Province, and to avoid confusion from the similarity of names, the North-Western Provinces became the Province of Agra, and, with Oudh, they are now known as the United Provinces of Agra and Oudh. They cover 112,000 square miles, with a population of 48,500,000. Their area is not much smaller, and their population is much larger than that of Great Britain and Ireland. There are no countries in Europe, excepting Belgium and England, in which the population is so dense. No other Indian province, with the exception of Bengal, is so thickly peopled.

It must be remembered, however, that comparisons between the density of population in India and in countries like England are apt to be very misleading, unless we bear in mind the great differences that exist in the distribution of the people. In England more than half of the whole population is congregated in large towns, while in India the corresponding population is extremely small. According to the census of 1901, the total urban population of India was only 29,200,000 out of a total of 294,300,000, or about ten per cent of the whole.[1]

[1] It may usefully be borne in mind that people generally are too much in

Throughout the United Provinces, although there are many and great differences of dialect, the general language of the people is, in one form or another, Hindi. The mixed language called Urdu, or Hindustani, which has become a *lingua franca*, very generally understood, especially by Mohammedans, throughout a great part of India, grew up in the Northern Provinces in the time of the Mohammedan sovereigns. Its grammar is mainly Hindi, while in its vocabulary there is a large admixture of Persian and Arabic, the languages of the Musalman invaders. Urdu is the literary and official language of the United Provinces; it is commonly spoken in the towns and by the upper and more educated classes.

This has been for ages the most famous part of India. In prehistoric times it was the Central or Middle land, the Madhya-desha of the sacred books of the Hindus and of the ancient poets, the abode of the solar and lunar races, and of the gods and heroes of the Máhábhárata and Rámáyana. To say nothing of the more or less mythical cities of which little but the names remain, this tract contains the most holy places of India—Benares, Ajodhya, Kanauj, Muttra, and many others. It was here that Buddha was born and preached and died, and it was from this centre that his creed

the habit of assuming that average or mean results have necessarily a real signification, and represent facts. Very often this is far from being the case. An average or mean is strictly an abstract arithmetical idea, and in that sense every such mean, properly calculated, is correct, but when this abstract idea is applied to facts, it may often have no useful meaning whatever. Thus, if we had before us a hundred objects, one of which was 1001 feet high, while the remaining ninety-nine were each 1 foot high, we should say correctly, in one sense, that the average height of the whole was 11 feet. But, in fact, the height of none of the objects would be at all near to 11 feet; the arithmetical idea would have no useful significance, but would confuse and lead us wrong. This is constantly true in dealing with statistics of population, and a multitude of other matters.

spread over a great part of the Eastern world. In more modern times Hindustan, the name, properly speaking, of these provinces only, and not of the whole of India, was the chief seat of the Mohammedan power. Delhi and Agra became the capitals of the Afghán and Moghal sovereigns, and although the great majority of the population always remained Hindu, there was for many centuries no part of India in which Musalman authority and organisation were so complete. In our own times Northern India has been politically the most important portion of our Indian Empire. "To the native imagination," as Mr. Keene has observed, "Hindustan is still the centre of India, and Delhi is still the metropolis."[1]

The North-Western Provinces came into our possession between 1775 and 1803. Until 1833 they were governed from Calcutta as a part of the so-called Bengal Presidency. By an Act passed in that year (3 and 4 Will. IV. c. 85), Bengal was divided into the two Presidencies of Bengal and Agra, and a separate Governor was to be appointed for the latter. The Agra Presidency was, however, not constituted, but by an amending Act passed in 1835 (5 and 6 Will. IV. c. 52) its territories became the North-Western Provinces, under a Lieutenant-Governor without a Council. These provinces and Oudh were the principal scene of the mutinies of 1857. Before that year the seat of the Government of the North-Western Provinces was at Agra; it was then transferred to Allahabad, and has remained there. Delhi, which until 1857 had belonged to the North-Western Provinces, has been since that time under the Government of the Punjab.

Sir Henry Maine, referring to Northern India, has spoken of the monotony of life and ennui "caused by

[1] Keene's *Moghul Empire*.

its ungenial climate and the featureless distances of its plains," and he quotes the words of the Emperor Baber, the founder of the Moghal dynasty, on closing the history of his conquest :—

> "Hindustan is a country that has few pleasures to recommend it. The country and towns are extremely ugly. The people are not handsome. The chief excellency of Hindustan is that it is a very large country, and that it has abundance of gold and silver."

It cannot be denied that great tracts in Northern India, and precisely those of which English travellers see the most, deserve, for a portion of the year, the epithets of monotonous and featureless and ugly. There is, for the most part, no luxuriance of vegetation; during the hot dry months, when the crops have been cut, everything is burnt up by the fiery winds; the ground is almost everywhere highly cultivated, but all is brown and arid. At other seasons, although a country so absolutely flat can hardly escape being monotonous, there is, the towns apart, as much to admire in the plains of Northern India as in those of Northern France, and more than in those of Northern Germany.

I referred in my first and second chapters to the great physical differences between this part of India and Bengal, and to the causes to which these differences are due. In the rainy season and winter, travelling along the railway through the central parts of these Provinces, a distance of more than 500 miles, the whole country through which we pass is a continuous sheet of cultivation, studded with groves of mango, the most valuable of the fruit-bearing trees of India, a constant succession of villages, many towns, and not a few great and famous cities. If, judging by a European standard, the traveller sees few signs of wealth, he sees few of extreme poverty. Nearly the whole of the agricultural population is collected in villages, between which stretch the wide unbroken fields. There are few of those scattered homesteads which are so often seen in Europe. This feature of rural life, a consequence of the universal insecurity which until the last century had prevailed from time immemorial, is common throughout India.

In 1901, out of 48,500,000 people in the United Provinces, 41,300,000 were Hindu and nearly 7,000,000 were Mohammedan.

As everywhere else in India, the mass of the population is agricultural, and the number of non-agriculturists is smaller than would be supposed from the figures of the census. A large proportion of the people returned as engaged in trades and employments are village servants and village shopkeepers who belong in fact to the agricultural community. It is probable that 90 per cent of the whole population are so closely connected with the land that they may properly be called agricultural.

There is, however, no part of India in which large cities and towns are so numerous. In the Agra Province, Benares has 209,000 inhabitants; Cawnpoor, 197,000; Agra, 188,000; Allahabad, 172,000; Meerut, 118,000; and eight other towns have populations of from 50,000 to 100,000. Oudh is more entirely agricultural. It has only two large towns: Lucknow with 264,000, and Fyzabad with 75,000 inhabitants. Trade is active. The exports consist almost entirely of agricultural produce, wheat and other food-grains, ghee, oil-seeds, sugar, and (but this is the product of a dying industry) indigo; the imports are chiefly European manufactured articles, cotton-goods, metals, drugs, petroleum, and salt. Manufactures of general commercial importance there are none, excepting in some instances, as at Cawnpoor, in which they have been established by Europeans, but large numbers of people throughout the country are employed in domestic handicrafts. The coarser cotton cloths which form the ordinary clothing of the poorer classes are chiefly of home manufacture. Some of the textile fabrics, as the kinkhábs, or gold brocades and embroideries of Benares and of Agra, are costly and beautiful.

I cannot speak at any length of the splendid works of architectural and decorative art which are found in these provinces. They are unequalled in India, and are not surpassed in any country in the world. Except in Athens, nothing has ever been built more beautiful than the Táj, erected at Agra by Shah Jehan as a mausoleum for his wife, and in which he himself is buried.

> "Perhaps in the whole world," says Mr. Fergusson, "there is not a scene where nature and art so successfully combine to produce a perfect work of art as within the precincts of this far-famed mausoleum. . . . No words can express the chastened beauty of that central chamber, seen in the soft gloom of the subdued light that reaches it through the distant and half-closed openings that surround it. Used as a Barah Durrie, or pleasure-palace, it must always have been the coolest and the loveliest of garden retreats; and now that it is sacred to the dead it is the most graceful and the most impressive of the sepulchres of the world." [1]

I doubt whether any European palace can show anything equal in beauty to the audience-halls of the Moghal emperors in their capitals of Delhi and Agra. No portals approach in magnificence those of Fatehpur Sikri and Delhi. The tower of Giotto at Florence is not a more perfect work than the noble minaret of the Kutb.

[1] Fergusson's *History of Indian and Eastern Architecture*, pp. 575, 598.

In this part of India the most splendid architectural monuments are those left by the Mohammedan sovereigns. Simple and admirable in general design, they are still more remarkable for the faultless taste of their decoration. Nothing has ever surpassed the surface ornamentation of stone-carving with which some of the buildings of the Afghán dynasties are covered, or the later and still more beautiful inlaid work of the Moghals. There seems no doubt that the art of pietra-dura decoration was introduced into India by Italians, but the masters were surpassed by their pupils. The process was applied in a new and independent style, and there is nothing in Italy in this sort of decoration that can be compared, in beauty of design, or colour, or effect, with the work found in the palaces and tombs of India. The Oriental artists of the Mohammedan sovereigns had at their disposal unbounded wealth, unlimited labour, and the most lavish profusion of precious materials, but nothing is more remarkable in their finest works than the sobriety and refinement of their taste.

I will not dwell on the stories of British vandalism which has ruined or suffered to perish some of the most admirable works of Oriental architecture, or on the general decadence in which European influences have helped, and still help, to involve the beautiful arts of India. I trust that we have seen the worst. Our English governors have become generally alive to the disgrace which, in past times, our countrymen have too well and too often deserved for their barbarous destruction or ignorant neglect of admirable works of artistic or historic value. Whatever may once have been the case, no such reproach now attaches to these or, I hope, to any other provinces. I may perhaps be pardoned if

I add that when I look back upon my long career in India there are few things that I remember with more personal satisfaction than the fact that I was able to do something towards preserving for future generations some priceless works, such as the Táj, the Agra Palace, and the tomb of Akbar.

Among Lord Curzon's titles to honour one that ought not to be forgotten has been his constant and practical recognition of the fact that there is no country the antiquities and arts and monuments of which are more precious than those of India.

During the winter a large part of Northern India has a climate as cold as that of spring in the South of Europe, and the time between October and April is sufficiently long to bring to maturity many of the chief agricultural products of the temperate zone. During the summer months, on the other hand, the crops are those of the tropics, or of a kind that do not suffer from excessive heat. There is thus in the productions and processes of agriculture a variety of which we have no example in Europe.

I am afraid that the belief that the people throughout India live generally upon rice is almost as prevalent in England as ever. There could be no more complete delusion. Rice, in the greater part of India, is a luxury of the comparatively rich. It is grown where the climate is hot and damp, and where there are ample means of irrigation; it is a valuable crop in the greater part of India, but it is only in Lower Bengal, in parts of Madras and Bombay, in Burma, and in districts where the conditions of soil and climate are suitable to its abundant production, that it forms the ordinary food of the people, or enters to an important extent into the consumption of the poorer classes. Out of the whole population of India, it is probable that not more than a fourth part live upon rice.

The mistaken notions that prevail on this subject doubtless had their origin, as Sir Henry Maine has observed, in the fact that the English in a great measure obtained their first ideas about India from what they saw or heard on its coasts. Because the ordinary food of the people in Lower Bengal is rice it was assumed that it was the ordinary food throughout India. Sir Henry Maine has drawn from this an instructive illustration of the danger of over-bold generalisations — a danger, as I have more than once remarked, which cannot be too carefully guarded against in regard to a multitude of Indian questions. "Mr. Buckle," he says, "in the general introduction to his *History of Civilisation*, has derived all the distinctive institutions of India, and the peculiarities of its people, from their consumption of rice. From the fact, he tells us, that the exclusive food of the natives of India is of an oxygenous rather than a carbonaceous character, it follows by an inevitable law that caste prevails, that oppression is rife, that rents are high, and that customs and laws are stereotyped." This is as if an Indian traveller, landing on the west coast of Ireland, and finding that the people lived on potatoes, were to assume that potatoes were the ordinary food throughout Europe, and were to base upon the imaginary fact conclusions regarding the conditions of society in Germany and Spain.

Excepting in the rice-consuming countries that have been named, millets form the chief food of the population throughout almost the whole of India, and they furnish also the most important of the crops used as fodder for cattle. Pulses of various kinds are largely consumed. Little or no meat is eaten by the poorer classes, and the pulses supply the nitrogenous element which is required. Meat, however, is commonly eaten by Mohammedans when they can afford it, and many of the Hindus who abstain from it do so because it is an expensive luxury, rather than from religious scruples.

The millets and pulses which form the chief food-supply of the people flourish throughout the greater part of India. In the damper and more tropical regions they are cultivated in the drier months of the warm winter; in the drier countries where the winter is comparatively cold, they are the principal crops of the summer.

In Northern India the agricultural year begins with the periodical rains which, as I explained in my second chapter, are established towards the end of June or the beginning of July. The crops of the cold season are cut in March and April, after which comes a period of about two months, when, owing to the intense heat and drought, agricultural operations are almost at a standstill. Towards the middle or end of June the heat reaches its extremest point. Midnight is hardly less oppressive than mid-day, except that during the day a fiery wind blows strongly from the west. Vegetation is burnt up; hardly a sound of animal life is heard. All day and all night, except for a short time about sunrise, when the temperature is at its lowest, you will, if you are wise, keep every door and window closely shut to bar out the raging heat. Sometimes at this season, but less frequently in these Provinces than in the Punjab, there sweeps up one of those remarkable atmospheric disturbances known as dust-storms, when the day becomes as dark as the darkest night, with violent winds which occasionally bring with them destructive hail or torrents of rain.[1]

Among all the phenomena of nature, there are few more impressive than those which usher in the rainy season in Northern India. It is not only of heat and discomfort that one has to think. Until rain falls the fields cannot be ploughed for another harvest, and the danger of drought and famine, if the coming of relief should be too long delayed, cannot be forgotten. The telegrams with news of the progress of the monsoon from the sea are every day eagerly expected, as in time of war news of the progress of a campaign.

In India, and in regions of the earth lying under similar geographical conditions, within the tropics or in their neighbourhood, the changes of the seasons recur with a regularity and an intensity unknown in Europe, and, if their normal course be seriously interrupted, the consequences have a significance which in temperate climates it is not easy to appreciate. The vital importance for good or evil of the variations of the seasons is, of course, obvious in other countries, but in India it is brought home to every one with extraordinary strength and vividness. Not a year passes in which it is not clear to almost the whole population that the very existence of the country as a dwelling-place for man depends on the regular sequence of the seasons. In Europe drought or floods may cause misery and loss, but they can hardly lead to absolute ruin over thousands

[1] "Non altrimenti fatto che d' un vento
Impetuoso per gli avversi ardori,
Che fier la selva senza alcun rattento;
Li rami schianta, abbatte, e porta fuori:
Dinanzi polveroso va superbo,
E fa fuggir le fiere e li pastori."

DANTE, *Inf.* ix. 67.

of square miles, and to many millions of people, such as that which has not unfrequently happened in India from failure of the periodical rains.

In favourable years the rains have usually set in about the middle of June on the Bombay coast and in Bengal; they travel up gradually towards Northern India, where they arrive about a fortnight later, and their advance may often be traced from one day to another. At last, when the heat has become greater than ever, the clouds begin to collect, and there comes down a deluge, almost always accompanied by thunder and lightning. When the rain is plentiful and all goes well, nothing can be more wonderful than the change which comes almost instantaneously over the whole face of nature. Under the influence of the tropical heat and abundant moisture, within a time that may be measured by hours rather than days, the country that was like a desert begins to look like a garden. The rapidity of the progress of vegetation is astonishing, and the manner in which animal life suddenly reappears is not less wonderful. We are reminded of the description of Aaron and the magicians stretching forth their hands over the streams and over the ponds and bringing up frogs which covered the land of Egypt.

As soon as the rain has sufficiently moistened the ground, the fields are ploughed and the summer and autumnal crops are sown. All these are included under the general name of *kharíf.* The most widely cultivated, and the most important to the poorer classes, since they furnish to them and to their cattle the principal means of subsistence, are the millets called *juár* and *bájra* (*Sorghum vulgare*, and *Pennisetum typhoideum*). In districts where the climate is damp and irrigation easy, rice is extensively grown at this season. Sugar-cane is another crop of much importance; in no other part of India is it so valuable as in these provinces; it may be classed among the hot-weather crops, since it remains on the ground nearly throughout the year, and its growth mainly depends on the heat and moisture of the summer. Some of the pulses, maize, and cotton are also largely cultivated at this season of the year. In parts of the provinces indigo is still an important crop, but as I have already noticed, the future of this product has become very doubtful.

The rains are over in Northern India towards the end of September, and in the following month the autumn crops are for the most part cut.

In October and November, when the excessive heat and moisture have passed away and the cold season has begun, the soil and climate become suitable for the agricultural products of temperate latitudes, and the winter crops, known under the general name of *rabi*, are sown. Between November and March it would be difficult to find a more delightful climate for Englishmen than that of Northern India. The nights and mornings are cold and even at times frosty, and the days pleasantly warm. After Christmas there is almost always a short season of moderate rain, which is of much importance to the growing spring crops.

The chief agricultural staples of Northern India at this period of the year are wheat and barley. They occupy nearly 60 per cent of the whole food-producing area in the United Provinces. Wheat from Northern India has been, in some years, an important source of supply to England, and, as the means of communication are extended and cheapened, it may become more important hereafter. Whether, to any great extent, it is possible that Indian wheat may hereafter compete in the English market with wheat from America is a question on which I will not speculate, but there is no doubt that India is capable, under favourable conditions of price, of providing a very large and increasing supply. Wheat in the Punjab is a still more important crop than in the United Provinces. It is also extensively grown in parts of Central India, Bombay, and the Northern Deccan, and in those countries, as well as in Northern India, it forms the chief article of food among the richer classes. Barley is largely consumed by those who cannot afford to eat wheat. Various kinds of pulses, tobacco, opium, linseed, and mustard are widely cultivated at this season. Oil-seeds are one of the chief articles of export from India to Europe. The principal winter crops are harvested in March and April.

Although, as furnishing the chief means of subsistence to the mass of the population, the first importance must be assigned in this part of India to the summer crops, which are dependent on the periodical rains, the more valuable products, on which the people have mainly to rely for increase of wealth and prosperity, and for the means of paying their revenue and rent, are those grown in the winter. Even in favourable seasons artificial irrigation is necessary for their successful cultivation. The rental of irrigated land in Northern India is usually double that of land dependent on the season alone.

I have already given some account of the magnificent irrigation canals constructed by the British Government, surpassing in magnitude and usefulness all other works of the kind in the world, and I have especially noticed those of the United Provinces.[1] In Northern India it is for the crops of the cold season that they are especially valuable. Important as they are, the wells constructed

[1] Chapter XIV.

by the villagers themselves are more important still. In the great alluvial plain, water can almost everywhere be found from ten to forty feet from the surface of the ground. If the soil be solid, a well can often be dug for a few shillings; if sandy strata have to be passed through, the well must be lined with masonry, and costs much more. Very often, when water is not far from the surface, the wells are only intended to last for a single season. In the United Provinces, a large proportion of the cultivated area is constantly irrigated from wells during the winter months, and the number of wells is usually a good index to the condition of the agricultural population. Unfortunately, although the value of well-irrigation, in ordinary circumstances, cannot be over-estimated, the supply of water in extremely dry seasons often fails, and wells cannot give the complete protection against drought and famine which is afforded by canals drawn from the great rivers.

Little need be said about Indian methods of agriculture. The implements are simple, but the persevering industry of the people is great. Wheat and barley, under good cultivation, yield a produce equal in quality and quantity to that usually obtained without artificial manure in Europe or America, although the result is of course inferior if the comparison be made with the produce of land to which costly and scientific methods have been applied.

As Dr. Voelcker, speaking with high authority and personal knowledge, has observed, "there can be no question that the ideas generally entertained in England, and often given expression to in India, that Indian agriculture is, as a whole, primitive and backward, are altogether erroneous. . . . Taking everything together, and especially considering the conditions under which

Indian crops are grown, they are wonderfully good." The Indian cultivator, Dr. Voelcker assures us, is at his best quite as good as the average British farmer, and in some respects superior to him. "Taking," he says, "the ordinary arts of husbandry, nowhere would one find better instances of keeping land scrupulously clear from weeds, of ingenuity in device of water-raising appliances, of knowledge of soils and their capabilities, as well as of the exact time to sow and to reap, as one would in Indian agriculture, and this not at its best alone, but at its ordinary level. It is wonderful, too, how much is known of rotation, the system of mixed crops, and of fallowing. I have never seen a more perfect picture of careful cultivation, combined with hard labour, perseverance, and fertility of resource, than I have seen at many of the halting-places in my tour." [1]

The system of rotation of crops in Northern India is simple. In the richer and better-manured lands two crops are often raised from the same land within the year. On the greater part of the land the usual plan is to raise one crop only. In the first year millets are grown in the rainy season, and after the crop has been cut the land will be left fallow for nearly a year, until the following October, when it is ready for sowing wheat or barley. This will be cut in March or April, and when the rains begin in June or July it will be followed by another crop of millets. To another product of Northern India, tea, I have referred in a former chapter. [2]

[1] *Report on the Improvement of Indian Agriculture*, by J. A. Voelcker, Ph.D., etc. etc., Consulting Chemist to the Royal Agricultural Society of England.

Dr. Voelcker was appointed, at the request of the Government of India in 1889, to investigate the whole subject of Indian Agriculture and to report on the measures that might be taken for its improvement. He spent thirteen months in India, the whole of which time was devoted to practical and scientific inquiries in the various provinces.

[2] Chapter XIII.

CHAPTER XIX

AN INDIAN PROVINCE (*continued*)

The land revenue — Tenures — Settlements — Village communities — Classes of cultivators—Settlements in Northern India—Surveys—Principles of assessment—The settlement officer—Record of rights —Village accountants — Recent reforms — Settlement reports — Settlements in Oudh—The Tálukdárs—Lord Canning's Proclamation — Measures of Lord Lawrence — Recent improvements — Condition of Oudh — Agricultural departments — The Government of India on the principles of administering the land revenue.

EXCEPT where the State has alienated its rights in favour of individuals, or of religious or charitable institutions, or otherwise, private rights in land have always been subject in India to the superior rights of the sovereign.

A description has been given in a former chapter[1] of the nature of the land revenue. It has been shown that it must not be looked upon as taxation properly so called, but as the share of the produce to which, from time immemorial, the State, as the chief proprietor of the land, has been entitled; that no Government in India has ever taken so small a share as that which we demand; and that the rate at which the land revenue falls has gone on constantly diminishing. It has been the policy of our Government to encourage, by the limitation of its demand, the growth of private property

[1] Chapter IX.

in land; to create such property where no private rights of ownership could be found; to define for a term of years or in perpetuity the shares of the produce or rent which the private landholder and the State shall respectively receive, and to give security to the former that improvements made by him on the land shall not lead to an increased demand by the Government. The interests connected with the land possess an altogether paramount importance. The variety of tenures and agricultural customs is infinite, but there is no part of India in which the condition of the people and the success or failure of the administration are not intimately affected by the manner in which the rights and responsibilities of the State and of individuals in the land are regulated.

One warning in connection with these subjects must be borne in mind. Such terms as "property in land," "proprietor," and "tenant" have to be used in default of others more appropriate; but since private proprietorship in land has hardly existed in India in the form in which it exists in England, misconception easily arises. It has happened not unfrequently that English ideas of property, derived from a different condition of things, have exercised a pernicious influence on the interests of the actual occupants of the land.

What is technically called a "Settlement of the land revenue" consists in the determination of the share of the produce or rental to which the State is entitled, and in the record of all private rights and interests in the land.

The systems for the assessment of land revenue may, speaking generally, be said to fall into two great divisions, one being in force in Southern and the other in Northern India.

In the Madras and Bombay provinces, the land is for the most part in the possession of peasant proprietors, with every one of whom the Government enters into a separate engagement. The tenure is called *ryotwári*.[1]

"The tenure of the ryot in Southern India (I am quoting from the Report of the Indian Famine Commissioners of 1880) is as secure and simple as can well be conceived. He holds his land in proprietary right, subject to the payment of the assessed revenue, which is fixed for a period of thirty years. He has the option of resigning his entire holding, or any individual field, at the end of the agricultural year. His improvements cannot be made a ground for increasing his assessment at the time of the periodical settlement. He can sell, mortgage, or let his land to any one without requiring the consent of the Government, and at his death the land descends to his children according to the rules of inheritance."

The land is marked off by the Survey department into fields or blocks, on each of which the Government demand is assessed. In Bombay a valuation is made of every field, under a minute system of investigation, in regard to soil, produce, situation, markets, prices, past history, selling and letting value, and other particulars, and the average demand of the Government is fixed at a rate estimated to fall at about 7·6 per cent of the gross produce.[2] The assessments are made for thirty years.

In Madras, by an elaborate system of classification,

[1] The meaning of the term *ryot* in Southern India is different from that which it bears in the North. In the former case it means the private owner of the land; in the latter case it means a cultivating tenant who has often no permanent rights at all.

[2] No estimates of the proportion which the Government demand bears to the gross produce of the land can pretend, in this or other cases, to be anything but rough approximations to the truth, and this is one of the numerous instances in which arithmetical averages often mean little and are altogether misleading.

experiment, and inquiry, an estimate is made of the average annual value of the produce of the plot to be assessed. After deducting the cost of cultivation and making large allowances for vicissitudes of season, distance from markets, and other considerations, one half of the net profit is assumed to be the share or revenue of the Government—an amount held to be equivalent to an average rate of about 6·3 per cent of the gross produce. The share actually taken is usually less. The settlements are made for thirty years.

In Northern India the system is different. The Government revenue is assessed, not on each field or block, but on the whole of the land included within the boundaries of the village. The village is the unit of assessment.[1] The Government has usually no dealings with individual cultivators. There is often a class of landholders intermediate between the Government and the cultivator; they receive rent in cash, or in a share of the produce, and they pay a portion of this rent as land revenue to the Government. These proprietors, especially in Oudh, under the name of Zemindars, or Tálukdárs, often hold very large estates.

In a large part of the Agra Province, and still more

[1] The term "village" has, in the official language of Northern India, a technical meaning. By "village," as Mr. Baden Powell explains in his *Land Systems of British India*, "we do not mean a small collection of houses, with a green, a few shops, and a church-spire rising above the immemorial elms; we mean always a group of landholdings aggregated in one place; there is generally one, or more than one, group of dwellings situated somewhere in the area, and the 'village' has a common tank, graveyard, and cattle-stand, and probably an area of scrub jungle and grazing ground attached to it." Wishing to avoid, as far as possible, the use of unfamiliar Indian words, I have said that the village is the unit of assessment, but this is not technically accurate. The actual unit is the "mahál," a word usually translated "estate," but which has really no English equivalent. It signifies "a local area held under a separate engagement for the payment of the land revenue, and for which a separate record of rights has been made." There may be several villages in a "mahál," and there may be more than one "mahál" in a village.

commonly in the Punjab, the land is held by small proprietors, cultivating their own land wholly or in part, and associated together in village communities.

"These communities are represented by an elected or hereditary head, and are jointly responsible for the payment of the Government revenue due from the entire village. Sometimes all the land is held in common, and the proceeds are thrown together and divided among the sharers by village custom. Sometimes the proprietors all have their separate holdings in the estate, each paying the quota of revenue due from his plot, and enjoying the surplus profits of it."[1] Although I speak of village communities, it must be understood that communities of the ancient type, interesting descriptions of which have been given by Sir Henry Maine and others, can hardly or never be found at the present time.

It has been already explained that the share of the rental to which the State, as chief proprietor of the land, is held to be entitled, was formerly much larger than it is now. At the beginning of the last century, in the North-Western Provinces, it was 90 per cent; it was afterwards 66 per cent; and since 1854 it has been nominally 50 per cent. This is considered equivalent to about 7·8 of the gross produce. The amount actually taken by the Government is almost always less.

The manner in which the Government revenue, assessed on the village as a whole, is to be distributed among the shareholders is usually settled by themselves. Any proprietor may demand the separation of his property from the rest of the village, but so long as the village estate remains undivided, the ultimate responsibility for the payment of the Government revenue rests jointly on the whole community. The present

[1] *Report of Indian Famine Commission of 1880*, Part II. p. 110.

tendency, as Mr. Baden Powell says, "is to divide, and for each man to bear his own burdens, and take the benefit of his own industry and exertion. The advantages of the system of union and exclusion of strangers were more felt in times of war and trouble, when defence against a raid had to be continually prepared for, and when common exertion was necessary to bear up against a heavy assessment, than they are now. The happy pictures of self-governing communities, careless of the world outside, that our books draw are more visionary than real."[1] In the Punjab the village proprietors themselves cultivate the greater part of the land. In the United Provinces a larger proportion of it is cultivated through tenants paying rent. It is a consequence of this fact that the average standard of comfort among the agricultural classes is lower than in the Punjab.

Whatever be the tenure of land, the system of agriculture throughout India is one of *petite culture*. In the words of Sir Edward Buck, we may consider that almost the whole country is split up into millions of five-acre farms. The holders of these farms are small proprietors or tenants, either paying revenue directly to the State or rent to an intermediate landlord.

Tenants, technically so called, but who, it must be remembered, hold a very different position from tenants in England, are almost everywhere divided into two classes. A large proportion of them possess, according to immemorial custom, a right of permanent and hereditary occupancy in the land so long as they pay the rent that is due. The amount of their rent mainly depends on local custom, not on competition. In some cases they are entitled to hold at permanently fixed

[1] *Land Systems of British India*, vol. ii. p. 153.

rates, and their right is heritable and transferable. In other cases the rent can only be enhanced on certain grounds specified by law. Such tenants can only be ousted by decree of Court, on proof of non-payment of rent, and without a decree of Court the landlord cannot obtain a higher rent. The principal ground of allowable enhancement is that the tenant is paying at a lower rate than that usually paid by neighbouring tenants of the same class for land of equal value. Cultivators of this description are, in fact, co-sharers in the land, possessing limited rights of property. They often derive their present position from the fact that they or their ancestors were once proprietors; a man who loses his proprietary right is still, according to ancient custom, allowed to retain his occupancy as cultivator. Similar rights may, under certain conditions, accrue by mere lapse of time. A tenant who, by himself or his ancestors, has held during twelve years uninterrupted occupation of the same land acquires a permanent right of occupancy.

Cultivators of this class are usually far better off than those who have no such privileges. "Wherever," say the Indian Famine Commissioners of 1880, "inquiry has been made, it has been found that in all matters relating to material prosperity, such as the possession of more cattle, better houses, and better clothes, the superiority lies on the side of the occupancy tenant, and as a rule they hold larger areas of land. About 70 per cent of the cultivated land in the Agra Province is tilled either by the proprietors themselves, or by tenants with these rights."

Below this class come the tenants-at-will. They constitute a very large class, but they are less numerous in the Agra Province than the tenants with occupancy rights. The tenant-at-will can be evicted at the close of any agricultural year, and the amount of his rent depends on the bargain he can make with his landlord. Whenever a tenant is evicted, a claim may arise for compensation for improvements which he has made. Below the tenants come the agricultural labourers, the poorest section of the community, depending on wages usually paid in kind. Although they constitute a large class, they are happily far less numerous than the tenants.

The land revenue in the United Provinces of Agra and Oudh amounted in 1901 to £4,200,000.[1]

The first step towards a settlement of the land revenue is an accurate survey. The great Trigonometrical survey was commenced early in the last century, and has now extended its network of triangles over the whole of India. Its operations, in the measurement of an arc of the meridian, and in affording data for determining the figure of the earth, have possessed the highest scientific value, and have served as the basis of innumerable useful undertakings. On it has been founded the Topographical survey, which delineates the geographical features of the country, and the Revenue or Cadastral survey, which provides maps of villages and estates, and demarcates them with permanent boundary marks. This is the basis of every settlement of the land revenue. Each village has its maps, showing its boundaries and principal features and every field. These are made sometimes by professional surveyors, but more often by men belonging to the village, who have been trained to the work. There are, it is said, more than 30,000,000 fields and plots in the Agra Province, all of which have been measured and mapped.

[1] The average incidence of the land revenue per cultivated acre is about 2s. in the Agra Province, and a little more in Oudh.

The settlement of the amount to be paid annually as land revenue in the United Provinces, and in the greater part of British India, excepting Bengal, is usually made for a term of thirty years, during which time there can be no increase, under any circumstances, in the Government demand. Of the permanent settlement in Bengal, made more than a century ago, I shall have to speak again. It was also applied in 1795 to Benares and to three other districts of the North-Western Provinces, bordering on Bengal, and it is still in force. In the rest of Northern India this misfortune has been escaped. In this case, however, the loss in the permanently settled districts has been that of the State alone. It does not obtain the full amount of land revenue which it would otherwise have been receiving, but the people have not suffered, as in the greater part of Bengal, from the absence of a Cadastral survey and record of rights. There is no difference in this respect between the permanently and temporarily settled districts of the Agra Province.

The thirty years' assessment was formerly made on the assumption that the amount payable to the State was a fair average sum which, taking one year with another, could be paid without difficulty during the term of the settlement, the profits of good years covering the losses of bad; but the assessments are now made on a principle more favourable to the owner of the land. Their basis is the actual rental or assets at the time when the settlement is made, so that the owner enjoys the full benefit of any future advantage which may accrue either from his own exertions or from any other cause until the term of the settlement expires. In practice, when unusual calamities of season occur, the Government is never backward in allowing the temporary suspension or permanent remission of its demand.

The responsibility for the proper supervision of all arrangements connected with the periodical assessments of the land revenue rests, in the first instance, on the settlement officer. His duty is both fiscal and judicial; he has to determine the amount of the Government demand, and to make a record of all existing rights and responsibilities in the land. He has a staff of experienced subordinates, almost all of whom are natives of the country, and the settlement of the district assigned to him is a work which formerly required several years of constant work. The establishment of agricultural departments and other reforms have, however, led to much simplification of the settlement officer's proceedings, and to much greater rapidity in the completion of the settlements. All the work of the settlement officer is liable to the supervision of superior officers; the assessments proposed by him require the sanction of the Government before they become finally binding; and his judicial decisions may be reviewed by the civil courts.

It is the duty of the settlement officer to make a record of every right which may form the subject of future dispute, whether affecting the interests of the State or of the people. The intention is to alter nothing, but to maintain and place on record that which exists.

One of the necessary results of these proceedings is the prevention of litigation and of crime. In the words of Mr. Thomason, the settlement officer

"comes among the people as their friend and peacemaker rather than as their judge. He does not ordinarily interpose between two parties when their passions are inflamed by the animosity of a fierce dispute or the anxiety of a protracted lawsuit; his first object has been to fix a moderate assessment, and to lay restrictions on a right possessed by the Government, which they all acknowledge and consider sacred, and for moderation in the exercise of which they are grateful. Having successfully accomplished this, and thereby conferred on them a new and valuable property, he calls upon them, whilst their minds are calm and their best feelings brought into action, to come to an agreement on all points likely to produce disputes among them; he then reduces the terms of the agreement to record, and gives to the record the stamp of judicial authority."[1]

An elaborate system was long ago established for the preparation and maintenance of the record of rights. Every field, as I have explained, is shown in the village maps, and it has a number corresponding with a register or field-book. In this are entered the area of the field, the crop, whether or not it is irrigated, the rent payable for it, the names of the proprietor and tenant, and other particulars. A rent-roll is prepared for every village, showing the fields and area of each cultivator's holding, the length of time for which he has held, the rent which he has to pay, and the person to whom it is payable. A list is also drawn up showing the proprietors of land in the village, the share of each, and the amount of revenue for which each is responsible.

It was formerly a weak point in the land revenue system of Northern India, that no sufficient provision existed for maintaining the accuracy of the records prepared at the time of the settlement with so much labour. It is obviously not enough to make a record of facts connected with the land at any given time; the constant revision of the record is necessary, so that it may always represent the actual condition of things.

[1] Directions to Revenue Officers.

Every village or circle of villages in Northern India has, according to ancient custom, among the servants of the community, a local accountant or notary called the Patwári, and on him the responsibility primarily rests for the maintenance of the village records. In the United Provinces there are about 30,000 patwáris, each of whom has usually charge of three or four villages. It was found extremely difficult in practice to ensure the accuracy of the patwári's papers. Maps and records, prepared at the cost of the State with the utmost care, frequently lost the greater part of their value by failure to maintain them up to date. This had long been recognised as a serious evil. Public and private interests alike suffered from the frequent inaccuracy of the official registers.

The establishment in 1875 of a separate department of Land Records and Agriculture, to which reference will again be made, has gone far to remedy these defects, and to ensure the constant correction of the village records.

I quote from an official report the following account of the manner in which this is done :—

"Changes occur every year under nearly all the heads of the record which the patwári has to prepare. Field boundaries are altered; waste land is brought under cultivation; parts of holdings are relinquished by tenants; tenants are ejected; new tenancies are created; rents are raised or lowered; proprietors die and their lands are divided among the heirs; sales and mortgages take place; irrigation and crops vary perpetually with season and market. All such changes are carefully noted every year by the patwári in the map and in his annual record. Abstracts of each year's record are made for each village and tabulated, and these again are compiled for each sub-division of the district. In this way the agricultural resources of every village, sub-division, and district can at any time be ascertained.

"To render these records accurate, and to enforce their punctual preparation, a very rigorous system of supervision and testing is necessary. This is effected through Native inspectors called Kánungos. There is in each district a staff of these officers, whose duty it is to supervise and check the field work of the patwáris, to test their annual entries, and verify changes recorded by them. There are nearly 1200 kánungos of various grades in these provinces. In every district there is a special training school, through which the patwáris are required to pass and qualify according to prescribed standards."

These measures for ensuring the accuracy of the village records have also led to very important improvements in the system under which settlements are periodically revised.

The policy of fixing for all time the demand of the State upon the land has been—we may trust, finally—abandoned. We have had sufficient evidence of the folly of such a policy in the consequences to which, after more than a century's trial, it has led us in Bengal. It has nevertheless always been felt that there were serious evils connected with the system under which settlements were made in Northern India for a term of years. Whatever care was taken, operations of survey and inquiry and record could not be carried on continuously for long periods of time without harassment of the agricultural classes, and without causing uneasiness and discontent. When the term of the settlement approached its close, not only was a check placed on improvements, but positive deterioration was to be feared, because the people were apprehensive that signs of prosperity might lead to enhancement of the Government revenue.

The necessity for elaborate local investigations ceases when the village records are accurately maintained, and in a great part of the United Provinces these are now so trustworthy that when a new settlement is necessary they can be used as a sufficient basis for the revision of the assessment.

An official paper gives the following account of the system under which settlements are now made :—

"These most valuable and successful reforms, carried out under the direction of the Department of Land Records and Agriculture, which have laid the foundations of all the recent improvements in the revision of land assessment, were originally devised and inaugurated by Sir Edward Buck. In the districts about to be brought under settlement, the annual correction of the village maps has made them so nearly accurate as to render a fresh survey unnecessary, and the rent-rolls compiled by the Patwáris, under the supervision of the Kánungos, are sufficiently correct to serve as the basis of assessment. For the costly and troublesome temporary establishments which used to be employed has been substituted this ordinary and permanent agency, and the results have been, that proceedings which would have lasted at least ten years under the old system will now be carried out in three years, and probably at less than a quarter of the expense. The first duty of the settlement officer is to verify the rent-roll drawn up by the village accountant; and unless he has grounds for believing that the rents are fraudulently understated, or that for any other reason they are very much below the rents paid in similar circumstances in the same neighbourhood, he accepts them as the basis of his assessment, and fixes the Government revenue at half the rental. He is forbidden to take prospective assets into account, and in every case the assessment will rest on the ground of actuals. In assessing land cultivated by the proprietors themselves, for which no true rent is paid, he applies a rate which is 25 per cent lower than the rent paid by tenants in the same village."

No enhancement of the Government demand can be made on account of increased value given to the land by wells or other permanent improvements made at the expense of the owner or occupier.

This is a rule which was altogether unknown under any of the governments that preceded us. In Bombay its observance is secured by law; in the other provinces, in one form or another, the same principle is followed, and the Government of India has insisted on the necessity of everywhere making the assessment of the land revenue in a manner which shall stimulate the expenditure of private capital upon the improvement of the land, and secure to the owners the benefits of their enterprise.

The importance of the reforms that have thus been carried out, and which are mainly due to the formation of the provincial Agricultural departments, can hardly be overstated. They have brought about a revolution in the system under which settlements were formerly made. The administration has been strengthened; the interests of the agricultural population are better protected; the efficiency of the courts has been increased, because they have access to trustworthy records of the rights of all persons interested in the land; the expenses of litigation have been reduced; and the saving of money to the Government will be very large.

The Reports of the settlement officers constitute, in the words of Sir Henry Maine, "a whole literature of very great extent and variety, and of the utmost value and instructiveness." I have now before me one of these Settlement Reports, a folio volume of more than four hundred pages. I doubt whether there is any English county of which, physical science apart, so minute a description could be found. Geography, climate, history, castes, religions, communications, population, commerce, condition of the people, education, agricultural statistics, systems of cultivation, tenures of land, history of past and present settlements, rates of rent and revenue—there is hardly a subject of interest in regard to which the results of long and patient investigation have not been recorded. This is the class of authorities to which we must go if we desire to learn the truth about the condition of the people.

Excepting in Bengal, where more than a century ago a permanent settlement of the land revenue was made without surveys, and on data to which at the present time we should attach no value, systems of settlement as careful and elaborate as that which I have been describing exist in all the chief provinces of British India. The plans followed in the Punjab and in the Central Provinces are similar, for the most part, to those of the United Provinces. In Southern India, where the prevailing tenures of land are different, the systems of assessment are, as I have already said, different also. Under one system or another, cadastral surveys have been made and registers of rights and possession have been prepared, which, notwithstanding inevitable imperfections, are probably more complete than any that exist in any other country. Much in the existing land revenue system of Northern India is due to the great Akbar; it assumed almost its present form under the East India Company; it owes much of its perfection to James Thomason,[1] one of the most enlightened men that have administered an Indian province, and its efficiency has gone on constantly increasing since the transfer of the Government to the Crown. No greater and more beneficent work has ever been undertaken than these vast operations, extending over several hundred thousands of square miles, designed to protect the interests of more than 150,000,000 of people.

I shall have occasion to refer again to the condition of Oudh in 1856, when it became British territory. The

[1] Mr. Thomason was Lieutenant-Governor of the North-Western Provinces from 1843 to 1853.

Tálukdárs were the great landlords, and about two-thirds of the province were included in their estates. Some of them belonged to families which had been in possession for centuries, and their claims to be recognised as proprietors could not rightly be denied. Some had been officials or revenue contractors, intermediate between the Native Government and the village proprietors; by their ability or rapacity they had often become holders of large estates, and had managed to appropriate to themselves more or less completely the rights of the old occupants.

On the annexation of Oudh in 1856, the Tálukdárs were treated with neither discrimination nor justice. In the first settlement of the land revenue, claims were often ignored which ought to have been admitted, and when the mutinies of 1857 occurred the majority of the Tálukdárs went into open rebellion. I will not give in any detail the history of what followed. A proclamation was issued by Lord Canning, confiscating to the British Government, with a few exceptions, all landed property in Oudh. His object, regarding which there was at first much misunderstanding, was to get rid of all the obligations involved by the settlement of 1856, to obtain a *tabula rasa* which would give the opportunity of repairing the injustice with which many of the Tálukdárs had been treated, and of restoring their estates on condition of loyal submission. This purpose was effectually carried out, but unfortunate consequences followed. After the mutinies there came over the British Government and its officers, almost throughout India—happily, for a short time only, but long enough to do much injury—a flood of reactionary opinions, and the experience of the past seemed forgotten. Permanent settlements of the land revenue were to be introduced;

great landlords were to be created or their growth encouraged, in the belief that they would become devoted supporters of our Government; the system of dealing with small village proprietors and communities was pronounced politically unwise; the rights of tenants were declared to have no existence, or at any rate must not be strengthened to the detriment of the landlord.

When Oudh was reoccupied after the mutinies, in 1858, it offered a fine field for the application of such opinions. "The maintenance," the Government of India wrote to the Secretary of State in November 1859, "of a landed aristocracy in India, where it exists, is an object of such importance that we may well afford to sacrifice to it something of a system which, while it has increased the independence and protected the rights of the cultivators of the soil, has led to the exhaustion or decay of the old nobility." India is doubtless a country in which it would be more than ordinarily foolish to ignore the consideration due to families whose position and claims may have been recognised for centuries, and which in the eyes of the people still retain their titles to honour, and in the settlement of 1856 many of the Tálukdárs received scant justice. But the injustice that followed the new arrangements was worse. The ancient rights of multitudes of small proprietors and cultivators, rights often older and more undoubted than those of the Tálukdárs, were swept away or ignored; the Tálukdárs not only recovered their estates, but they received, in many cases, extravagant privileges to which they themselves had made no pretensions, and solemn promises that those privileges should be maintained were given by the Government. It is true that, under the orders of Lord Canning, all subordinate rights in the land which had been actually enjoyed before the annexation of the province were to be preserved; but the onus of proof lay upon those who claimed them. In consequence of the orders of confiscation, followed by the grant of full rights of property to the Tálukdárs, the legal presumption was *primâ facie* that the right of the Tálukdár was complete and that other rights in the land had been extinguished. Anarchy prevailed in Oudh before annexation, and it was difficult for an ignorant peasant-proprietor to prove that he had enjoyed at that time rights independent of those of the Tálukdár. The fate of the tenants was no better. With rare exceptions, rights of occupancy in the land were declared to have no existence in Oudh. Lord Lawrence, when he became Viceroy, was anxious that remedies should, so far as was possible, be applied, to diminish the injustice which had been done. I was myself, as Chief Commissioner of Oudh, one of the agents through whom he acted, but I look back with little satisfaction on such amount of success as was gained. Public opinion in India was still going through the phase of admiration for artificially created aristocratic institutions; and, both in his own Council and in England, Lord Lawrence met with such strong opposition that it was impossible to do much. He did all that seemed at the time practicable, but it may be a question whether it would not have been better to have done nothing; for although protection was given to an important class of small proprietors, and to a small class of tenants, it may be feared that the measures that were taken tended, in some respects, to give greater strength to a vicious system.

About two-thirds of the land in Oudh are now owned by great landlords, the Tálukdárs, and one-third by proprietors of small estates, or by the sharers in village communities. The greater part of the province is cultivated by tenants possessing no permanent rights. Custom has gradually been giving way to competition in the determination of rents. Much, however, has been done in recent years to improve the position of cultivators. The Tálukdárs have concurred in legislation to render the condition of tenants less precarious. Under an Act passed in 1886, important checks have been placed on enhancement of rent and eviction. Sitting tenants are now, as a general rule, entitled to continue in undisturbed occupation of their holdings, at present rates, for periods of seven years; and on the expiry of each period they are entitled to renewal at a rent not exceeding by more than 6¼ per cent that formerly paid. In all cases compensation is due to tenants before they can be evicted. Measures have also been taken for the preservation of the estates of old families which had become involved in pecuniary difficulties. Act II. of 1890 enabled a Tálukdár to entail the whole or a portion of his estate, and to place it beyond the danger of being lost to his family by the extravagance of his heirs.

In spite of all our mistakes and shortcomings in Oudh, the condition of the people generally is beyond all comparison better than it was before the establishment of our Government. There has been a great increase of cultivation, the means of communication have been immensely improved by the construction of roads and railways, new markets have been opened, the prices of agricultural produce have risen, and the cultivators, although usually very poor, are better fed, better clothed, and better housed than they were.

In speaking of the system under which the assessments of land revenue are periodically revised, and under which land records are maintained, I referred to the improvements that have followed the creation of separate departments for the control of this branch of the administration. I must return for a moment to this subject.

Lord Mayo was the first Governor-General who gave practical recognition to the value of the study of questions connected with Indian agriculture.

"For generations to come," the Government of India wrote in 1870 to the Secretary of State, "the progress of India in wealth and civilisation must be directly dependent on her progress in agriculture. Agricultural products must long continue the most important part of the exports, and the future development of Indian commerce will mainly depend upon the improvement in the quantity and quality of existing agricultural staples, or on the introduction of new products, which shall serve as materials for manufacture and for use in the industrial arts. . . . There is perhaps no country in the world in which the State has so immediate and direct an interest in such questions. The Government of India is not only a Government but the chief landlord. The land revenue is derived from that portion of the rent which belongs to the State and not to individual proprietors. Throughout the greater part of India, every measure for the improvement of the land enhances the value of the property of the State. The duties which in England are performed by a good landlord fall, in India, in a great measure, upon the Government. Speaking generally, the only Indian landlord who can command the requisite knowledge is the State."

In 1870, a separate Department of Agriculture and Commerce was created under the Government of India.

It was foreseen by Lord Mayo that this central department of control would be able to do comparatively little until working departments with similar objects had been established under the local Governments. In 1875, when I was myself Lieutenant-Governor, the first provincial department of Agriculture was created in the North-Western Provinces. The honour for the successful initiation and subsequent progress of this excellent reform is mainly due to the enlightened and untiring energy of Sir Edward Buck. Similar departments have since been established in the other provinces of British India. They are still in their infancy, but they have already led to valuable results. I do not doubt that much will ultimately be done, by the application of more scientific methods, towards the actual improvement of Indian agriculture, but up to the present time the chief work undertaken has been the improvement of the land revenue administration, the better organisation of the system for maintaining accurate land records, and the reform of the methods under which the land revenue is assessed.

The necessity of everywhere organising Departments of Agriculture was strongly urged by the Famine Commission of 1880, and the recommendations then made were accepted, and to a great extent carried out, by the Government of India. Sir Antony MacDonnell's Famine Commission of 1901 wound up its Report by the following reference to this subject:—"Much progress has been made in the last twenty years, but the progress has been unequal, and the time has, in our opinion, now come for a further advance. These Agricultural Departments have a double function to discharge, and this is expressed in their designation as Departments of Land Records and Agriculture. They have on the Land Records side to register all facts connected with the tenure of land, with questions of rent and revenue, and with agricultural statistics. On the Agricultural side they have to deal with the condition of the cultivating classes, with agriculture, and with agricultural methods and the various questions connected with their efficiency. We are, indeed, far from thinking that the Indian cultivator is ignorant of agriculture; in the mere practice of cultivation, Agricultural Departments have probably much to learn from the cultivator. But in the utilisation of his hereditary skill, in economy of the means of production, and in the practice of organised self-help, the Indian cultivator is generally ignorant and backward. It is in correcting these deficiencies that Agricultural Departments will find their richest fields of labour. Without pretending to exhaust the number of subjects on which these departments may usefully employ themselves, we may mention the following: improved agricultural teaching to the better classes; the promotion of Mutual Associations; agricultural research and experiments; inquiries regarding tillage and manure; the investigation of crop diseases and their remedies; the provision of improved seed; the experimental introduction of new staples; the improvement of cattle breeding; the investigation of cattle diseases; and the development of the fodder supply. To some of these subjects more or less attention has, we know, been already given, but they all claim greater and more systematic attention. To this end the employment of a stronger expert staff in every province is necessary. The steady application to agricultural problems of expert research is the crying necessity of the time."

In 1900 and 1901, an elaborate inquiry was made by the Government of Lord Curzon, and by the Provincial Governments, into the subject of the land revenue system of British India. It had been contended by some of the critics of the Government that the intensity and frequency of famines in India had been largely due to poverty caused by over-assessment of the land revenue demand, and the Government of India determined to take the opportunity of instituting fresh inquiries into all the more important questions connected with the land revenue administration. The conclusions of the Government were embodied in a Resolution dated the 16th January 1902. It deserves the attention of every one who desires to learn the truth on this subject, for nothing could be more complete,[1] and I may fitly close this chapter with the following extract in which the Government stated the propositions which it claimed to have established.

"(1) That a permanent settlement, whether in Bengal or elsewhere, is no protection against the incidence and consequences of famine.

"(2) That in areas where the State receives its land revenue from landlords, progressive moderation is the keynote of the policy of Government, and that the standard of 50 per cent of the assets is one which is almost uniformly observed in practice, and is more often departed from on the side of deficiency than of excess.

"(3) That in the same areas the State has not objected, and does not hesitate, to interfere by legislation to protect the interests of the tenants against oppression at the hands of the landlords.

"(4) That in areas where the State takes the land revenue from the cultivators, the proposal to fix the assessment at one-fifth of the gross produce would result in the imposition of a greatly increased burden upon the people.

"(5) That the policy of long term settlements is gradually being extended, the exceptions being justified by conditions of local development.

"(6) That a simplification and cheapening of the proceedings connected with new settlements, and an avoidance of the harassing invasion of an army of subordinate officials, are a part of the deliberate policy of Government.

"(7) That the principle of exempting or allowing for improvements is one of general acceptance, but may be capable of further extension.

"(8) That assessments have ceased to be made upon prospective assets.

"(9) That local taxation as a whole, though susceptible of some redistribution, is neither immoderate nor burdensome.

[1] This Resolution was published in the *Papers regarding the Land Revenue System of British India*, presented to Parliament in 1902.

"(10) That over-assessment is not, as alleged, a general or widespread source of poverty and indebtedness in India, and that it cannot fairly be regarded as a contributory cause of famine. The Government of India have further laid down liberal principles for future guidance, and will be prepared, where the necessity is established, to make further advance in respect of—

"(11) The progressive and graduated imposition of large enhancements;

"(12) Greater elasticity in the revenue collection, facilitating its adjustment to the variations of the seasons and the circumstances of the people;

"(13) A more general resort to reduction of assessments in cases of local deterioration, where such reduction cannot be claimed under the terms of settlement.

"In thus defining their policy, the Government of India would not desire to claim for the land revenue system of British India an exactitude or a freedom from blemish to which it cannot pretend. Historically it owes its immediate origin to practices inherited from the most decadent period of native rule, and its form to changes made slowly and not without mistakes by men who were aliens to the country, and could only with difficulty, and by slow degrees, assimilate the requirements or enter into the feelings of the people. Where habit and precedent count for more than wisdom, there has been need for caution in reform; and logical completeness or simplicity could not be expected of a system, born amid such surroundings, applied to such manifold conditions and to so heterogeneous a population, and subject, in the various stages of its development, to considerations of practical expediency rather than of abstract symmetry or scientific perfection. . . . Assessments cannot be dictated by the theorist in his study; they elude dogmatic treatment, and can only be safely worked out by the Settlement Officer in the village and on the fields. While they may admit of statistical analysis, they are liable to be hampered by premature statistical definition. The true function of Government is to lay down broad and generous principles for the guidance of its officers, with becoming regard to the traditions of the province and the circumstances of the locality, and to prescribe moderation in enhancement, and sympathy in collection. Above all, it is its duty to exercise discrimination in the choice of the agents whom it employs for this most critical and responsible of tasks. The Governor-General in Council acknowledges with gratitude the services that have been rendered to Government in this respect by a long line of devoted and capable officers, and he believes that the existing system, if pursued upon the lines that have been indicated, is both well suited to the present conditions of the country and compatible with its future development, and that the revenue which it provides, and which is more lenient in its incidence than at any previous stage of Indian history, is capable of being levied from the people with surprisingly little hardship and without discontent."

CHAPTER XX

AN INDIAN PROVINCE (*continued*)

Administration of an Indian Province — An Indian district — The Magistrate and Collector or District Officer—His functions—Sub-divisions of districts—The Tahsildárs—Executive and Judicial Powers —The Joint, Assistant, and Deputy Magistrate and Collector —The Police—Jails—Hospitals—Sanitation—Vaccination—Public works—Education—General illiteracy—Municipalities—Local self-government—Commissioners of divisions—The Revenue Board—Heads of departments—The Lieutenant-Governor—The Legislative Council—The Judicial Courts.

I NOW propose to give a sketch of the manner in which the administration of an Indian province is carried on, taking, as before, the United Provinces of Agra and Oudh as my example. In regard, however, to many matters little need be added to what has been already said. An account, more or less generally applicable to the whole of British India, has already been given of the constitution of the Provincial Governments, of the Civil Services, of the system under which justice is administered, of the measures taken to encourage education, of the railways and works of irrigation, and of the principal sources of the public income. I shall now refer more particularly to some of the executive branches of the provincial administration, to which little reference has hitherto been made.

Throughout British India the District, technically

so called, is the unit of administration. Every province is divided into Districts, each of which has its separate organisation. A province is a collection of Districts, and without a clear conception of a District no one can understand how the actual government of India is carried on. In the details of District organisation there are great differences in different provinces, but the general principles on which the administrative system is based are much the same everywhere, and the account which I am about to give of a District in the United Provinces is, in many respects, generally applicable to the whole of British India.

These Provinces are divided into forty-eight districts, each of which is a compact tract, having usually an area of 1500 or 2000 square miles, and a population of 750,000 to 1,500,000. This is about the area and population of one of the larger English counties. In several provinces, and especially in Madras, the districts are much more extensive.

In India, where an absolute government is administered by a small body of foreigners far more advanced in civilisation than the people of the country itself, the most essential condition of safety to the rulers, and of good government to the people, is that authority should be strong, and authority cannot be strong unless it is concentrated. In every district of British India the Government has its representative in whom all executive civil authority centres. This officer, in the province of Agra, in Bengal, in Madras, and in Bombay, is called the Magistrate and Collector, or Collector alone; in the Punjab, in Oudh, in the Central Provinces, in Burma, and in the other so-called Non-Regulation provinces, he is called the Deputy Commissioner. The term "District Officer," by which he is often known, is applicable in both cases. The name Collector conveys to English ears a very false idea. A collector in England is a petty officer who collects rates and taxes; in India, he is, in many respects, the most important officer in the whole administrative hierarchy.

I borrow from Sir William Hunter the following description:—

"The district officer, whether known as collector-magistrate or as deputy commissioner, is the responsible head of his jurisdiction. Upon his energy and personal character depends ultimately the efficiency of our Indian Government. His own special duties are so numerous and so various as to bewilder the outsider; and the work of his subordinates, European and native, largely depends upon the stimulus of his personal example. His position has been compared to that of the French *préfet*, but such a comparison is unjust in many ways to the Indian district officer. He is not a mere subordinate of a central bureau, who takes his colour from his chief and represents the political parties or the permanent officialism of the capital. The Indian collector is a strongly individualised worker in every department of rural well-being, with a large measure of local independence and of individual initiative. As the name of collector-magistrate implies, his main functions are twofold. He is a fiscal officer, charged with the collection of the revenue from the land and other sources; he is also a revenue and criminal judge, both of first instance and in appeal. But his title by no means exhausts his multifarious duties. He does in his smaller local sphere all that the Home Secretary superintends in England, and a great deal more, for he is the representative of a paternal and not of a constitutional Government. Police, jails, education, municipalities, roads, sanitation, dispensaries, the local taxation, and the imperial revenues of his district are to him matters of daily concern. He is expected to make himself acquainted with every phase of the social life of the natives, and with each natural aspect of the country. He should be a lawyer, an accountant, a financier, and a ready writer of state papers. He ought also to possess no mean knowledge of agriculture, political economy, and engineering."[1]

[1] *The Indian Empire*, p. 513.

All this signifies, not that he is expected to be omniscient, but that the Magistrate and Collector is the principal officer of Government in every branch of the executive administration of the district. As the local representative of the Government, through whom all the orders and measures of the ruling power are issued and made known to the people, and on whom the Government depends for information of every serious matter that occurs, he holds a position of great and exceptional importance. If the District officer is weak and incapable, authority and law in the district are weak also; if he is strong and competent, they are respected. Every cause which tends needlessly to diminish his influence lessens the authority of the Government. At the same time, it must not be supposed that he has any irresponsible and arbitrary power: all his more important duties are strictly regulated either by law or by rules laid down by the Government, and all his proceedings are subject to supervision and, when necessary, to correction.

His duties as Collector differ in different provinces, according to the system on which the land revenue is assessed, the prevailing tenures of land, and other local circumstances. Thus, in Bengal, where the Government demand has been fixed in perpetuity, and where comparatively few measures have been taken to maintain accurate records of existing rights in the land, the duties of the Collector are less important and difficult than in the temporarily settled provinces.

In Northern India the District officer, as Mr. Thomason wrote, "in order properly to discharge his duties, must possess the most complete knowledge of the landed tenures in his district, and of everything which tends to affect the interests of the agricultural population." He has to act in many capacities. He supervises the arrangements for securing the payment at the appointed times of the land revenue, the excise upon spirits, the revenue derived from stamps, and the assessment and collection of the income tax. He is personally responsible for the care of the Government treasury at the headquarters of the district, and for the punctual preparation and submission of the public accounts. The records and registers affecting landed property are deposited in his office; and, in connection with the Agricultural Department, to which reference was made in the last chapter, the duty rests upon him of maintaining in a condition of efficiency the elaborate system laid down for their preservation and correction. He decides judicially, subject in many cases to an appeal to the Civil courts, disputes regarding rent and other questions between landlords and tenants.

> "Nothing can pass in the district of which it is not his duty to keep himself informed, and to watch the operation. The vicissitudes of trade, the state of the currency, the administration of civil justice, the progress of public works, must all affect most materially the interests of the classes of whom he is the constituted guardian. Officious interference in matters beyond his immediate control must be avoided, but temperate and intelligent remonstrance against anything which he sees to be wrong is one of his most important duties."[1]

It need hardly be said that the District officer cannot administer personally the details of all this business. He has at his disposal a large staff of officers, only a few of whom are English, through whom the work is carried on. An efficient District officer watches every department of the administration; he is always ready to intervene, but he does not occupy himself with

[1] *Directions for Collectors, N.W.P.* p. 184.

the details of business which his subordinates are as competent as himself to transact. His duties of supervision are so onerous and important that he ought, as Mr. Thomason has said, to do nothing that he can make others do for him.

Every district is partitioned, for the convenient administration of business, into a number of subdivisions, often corresponding with those that existed before our time. Each revenue subdivision is in charge of a Native officer of high standing, called in the Northern Provinces a Tahsildár, and in Southern India a Mamlatdár. He superintends the collection of the revenues, and all business connected with the land. The Tahsildárs are the principal agents of the Collector in the interior of the district, and their duties, on a smaller scale, are almost as various as those of the Collector himself. They are chosen with care, and are an intelligent and excellent class of public servants. "The satisfactory administration of the subdivision" (the Famine Commissioners of 1880 wrote), "the proper carrying out of the details of government, the protection of the people from hardships and oppression, the detection of abuses, and the general well-being of the community, very greatly depend upon the integrity, zeal, and ability of the Tahsildár." There are usually five or six Tahsildárs in each district of the United Provinces.

The District officer is also the chief Magistrate of the district; the powers which he possesses in this capacity have already been described. His title of Magistrate is hardly, according to English ideas, more appropriate than that of collector. He exercises, it is true, magisterial and judicial functions, but he is a great deal more than a magistrate. The responsibility for the protection of life and property throughout the district, for the maintenance of the public peace, and for ensuring obedience to the laws, rest ultimately upon him. He has, in the United Provinces, supreme authority over the police, and all the magisterial courts and the gaols are under his supervision. In one capacity or another, he possesses all the authority necessary to make him, in the eyes of the people, the representative of the Executive Government.

We often hear demands for the more complete separation of the executive and judicial functions of the District officer, but they are demands based on the assumption that a principle necessary for England must be good for India also. There could be no greater error. The first necessity of good administration in such a country as India is that it should be strong, and it cannot be strong without the concentration of authority. In the everyday internal administration there is no office so important as that of the District officer. He is one of the mainstays of our dominion, and few steps could be taken in India which would be more mischievous and dangerous than to weaken those powers which enable him to maintain his position as the local representative of the Government.[1]

[1] In the discussion on the Financial Statement for 1902-1903, which took place in the Council of the Governor-General on the 26th March 1902, one of the most enlightened and respected among the Native gentlemen of India, the Hon. Syad Husain Bilgrami, made an interesting speech, in which he referred to the position of the District officer. "The Viceroy," he said, "represents the might and majesty of the Empire, but the Viceroy is not so potent as the District officer who has found his way to the hearts of the people by taking an interest in their affairs, listening to their little grievances, and treating their faults and shortcomings with that good-humoured tolerance which is one of the characteristics of born rulers of men. The Indian people love an autocratic official provided he is sympathetic and just. They even prefer a high-handed man if he is accessible and kind. Above all, they love a gentleman, and will do anything for him. Many an English administrator has left behind

The first place on his staff is held by the Joint Magistrate and Deputy Collector; in the Non-Regulation provinces he is called Assistant Commissioner. He is always an officer of considerable length of service and experience. The territorial or other limits of his jurisdiction are determined by the District officer; the extent of his executive authority mainly depends on the amount of confidence placed in him by his superior; but in respect of cases heard by him as a magistrate, his powers are almost the same as those of the District officer himself. Next below him, in the Regulation provinces, comes the Assistant Magistrate and Collector; if the district be large and the work heavy, there may be more than one officer of this grade. No Assistant is invested with any powers or receives promotion until he has given evidence of his competency by passing examinations in the Native languages and in law. The Magistrate and Collector, the Joint Magistrate and Deputy Collector, and the Assistant, are, as a rule, Englishmen belonging to the Covenanted Civil service, but, as I have already explained, a certain proportion of these offices have been thrown open to the Native members of the Provincial service.[1] The other chief officers of the executive staff are the Deputy Collectors and Deputy Magistrates; they are almost always Natives. There are several in each district, some of them at the headquarters, and others in the interior of the district.

Reference has been made in a previous chapter[2]

him a name which is a household word in our villages and towns, and is written indelibly on the hearts of the people."

It must be understood that the remarks made above regarding executive and judicial functions are only intended to refer to the District officers in the so-called Regulation provinces. In some of the other provinces the existing system would be much improved by relieving the District officer of some of his judicial powers.

[1] Chapter VI.

[2] Chapter VII.

to the Code of Criminal Procedure, which defines the various classes of magisterial and other criminal courts, and the powers which each class of officers can exercise.

The system under which the police is administered differs in different provinces, but its general organisation throughout India is based on a law passed in 1861, and the manner in which its duties are to be performed is laid down in great detail in the Code of Criminal Procedure. Every district is divided into a number of police divisions, each of which is in charge of a police officer, almost always a Native, with a force of constables, clerks, and other subordinates. Every village or circle of villages has, according to the ancient custom of the country, its chaukidár, or watchman, whose duty it is to report all occurrences falling within the cognisance of the police.

Under the Native Governments that preceded us there was, outside the towns, hardly any police at all, and the responsibility for preserving the peace and for the detection of serious crime rested on the proprietors of land. This responsibility still attaches to them by law, and various old regulations define their obligations for reporting, preventing, and detecting crime. It was inevitable that as the administration became more regular, and more completely organised, the difficulty of enforcing general responsibilities of this kind would become greater, and the assistance practically given by the landholders in matters of police is usually small.

At the headquarters of every district there is an officer called the District Superintendent of police. He is, with rare exceptions, an Englishman. He supervises, with the help of his staff of inspectors and others, and subject to the general control of the Magistrate of the district, all police arrangements, and is responsible for the efficiency and good behaviour of the force. The law gives to the District officer a general power over the police of the district, but the interference which he practically exercises varies in different provinces. In the United Provinces his supreme authority and responsibility have been carefully maintained; but in some other provinces (unfortunately, as I think) his powers have been so strictly limited that the police has become virtually a separate department, administered by the District Superintendent, under the orders of the Inspector-General of police, at the headquarters of the Provincial Government.

The character of the police in India varies very much. Before the transfer of the Government to the Crown, no branch of the administration was in greater need of reform. The police was often oppressive and corrupt. The traditions of police management in India tended to encourage much that was bad. Under almost all Native Governments, past and present, torture has been avowedly or tacitly permitted, and has been looked upon as a natural and legitimate means of obtaining evidence. The people, for the most part, will not protect themselves, but have been accustomed, from time immemorial, to submit unresistingly to all official action. Under such circumstances it has always been difficult to guard against abuses. The improvement has been great. There is little violent crime, and the protection to life and property is, in the greater part of British India, as complete as in almost any European country. But there can be no doubt that Sir James Stephen was right when he gave, as a result of his personal experience in India, the opinion that "no part of the Institutions by which India is governed requires more careful watching in order to prevent the police, which is designed for the protection of the people, from becoming a means of petty oppression. The Code of Criminal Procedure is full of provisions intended to guard against this and at the same time to make the police efficient for their purpose."[1] Although, compared with the state of things which formerly prevailed, the progress has been great, it is still true that steadily to maintain an honest and efficient police is one of the standing difficulties of our administration, and that there is still very much room for improvement.

Every district has its gaol, and there are central prisons in convenient situations. Although not in all respects managed on the system adopted in England, there are few countries in Europe where the gaols are so well looked after. A great Indian prison is a model of cleanliness and good management. Every district has also its engineer establishments for the construction and maintenance of roads, bridges, and other public works and buildings; its telegraph and post offices; its schools and hospitals. In 1901 there were 484 hospitals and dispensaries in the United Provinces, and some 3,800,000 patients were treated in them. I have already referred to these institutions, and to the great skill of many of the Native surgeons. They are highly valued by the people, and for the most part are supported from local funds or by voluntary local subscriptions, the Government supplying the Native doctor and European medicines. There were also, in 1901, twenty-seven separate hospitals for the exclusive use of women. These belonged, for the most part, to the admirable institution founded, when she was in India, by the Marchioness of Dufferin and Ava, of which some

[1] *History of the Criminal Law of England*, vol. iii. p. 331.

account has been given in a previous chapter,[1] and which has rendered invaluable service to the women of India. Each district has a European officer, called the Civil Surgeon, who supervises all the medical establishments.

I wish that I could give a satisfactory account of the progress of sanitary improvement, but the prejudices and ignorance of the people make even simple reforms difficult. There are not many parts of India which are not liable to frequent epidemics of cholera, and in late years bubonic plague, which, except in the remote Himálayan districts, had long been almost unknown, has become lamentably destructive. Much, however, has been done to improve the sanitary condition of the larger towns, and in many cases important works for water supply and drainage have been constructed. There is another respect in which much progress has been made. Smallpox has always been extremely fatal in Northern India, but the prejudices and suspicions of the people have gradually been giving way, and vaccination has been extended with increasing success. In the Himálayan districts of the Agra province, in particular, smallpox, which formerly sometimes decimated the population, has been almost extirpated. A staff of vaccinators is maintained by the Government in every district of the United Provinces, and in 1901 more than 1,500,000 persons were vaccinated. It is only in a few of the larger cantonments that vaccination has been made compulsory. The registration of vital statistics becomes every year more trustworthy. The whole sanitary department of the province is under the control of an officer called the Sanitary Commissioner.

[1] Chapter XVI.

I will not again speak of the public works constructed by the British Government in Northern India. Some account has been already given of the great canals of irrigation, and of the immense improvement that has taken place in the provision of means of communication.[1] The principal towns and districts are now connected by railways, and the country is well supplied with roads and bridges.

An account was given in a previous chapter[2] of the system of education followed in the Indian universities, colleges, and schools. The villages in the districts of the United Provinces are grouped together in small circles, each of which has its Government school, affording elementary instruction to the poorer classes of the agricultural population. These schools teach, in the language of the country, reading, writing, arithmetic, and a little geography and mensuration. They numbered in 1901 nearly 7000, and contained 276,000 scholars.

In regard to female education, these, like other provinces, are, in the words of the Government, "lamentably backward. There is no general wish for female education, and so long as that is the attitude of the popular mind, little can be done. For the progress that has been made, the Government is indebted mainly to missionary efforts." In 1901 there were 152 primary schools for girls maintained by the Government or by municipalities, with 4000 scholars; and 165 aided schools, with 7000 scholars. There was also a considerable number of boys in so-called indigenous schools which have no connection with the Educational Department of the Government.

In each revenue subdivision there is a school,

[1] Chapter XIV.

[2] Chapter XVI.

teaching, in the vernacular language, grammar, geography, Indian history, arithmetic, algebra, geometry, mensuration, and the elements of natural science. At the headquarters of each district there is a Government school of a superior kind, in which English is taught, and in many of the larger towns there are good schools conducted by private agencies, chiefly by missionaries, receiving grants-in-aid from the Government. These schools often give an education up to the standard of the entrance examination of the University.

Reference has already been made to the colleges. Until 1887 the direction of higher education was in the hands of the University of Calcutta, but in that year a university was established at Allahabad, to which the colleges of the United Provinces have been affiliated. Like the other Indian universities, with the exception of that at Lahore, it is not a teaching body.

I have shown in a previous chapter[1] how vast a proportion of the population of the countries of India remains altogether illiterate, and that the United Provinces are no exception to the rule. In 1901 the male population was 24,617,000, of whom 1,423,000 could read and write. The female population was 23,078,000, and the number that could read and write was 55,900. But the subject of education in India is one to which I must not return.

For the management of local affairs every large town has its municipality, the members of which are chiefly natives of the place not in the service of the Government. There are 104 of these municipalities in the United Provinces, and 3,290,000 people live within their limits. These non-official bodies co-operate usefully with the Government authorities in the management

[1] Chapter XVI.

of the roads, conservancy, schools, hospitals, and in all the local business. Many of the Native members are honorary magistrates, often associated in Benches. A large proportion of the less serious criminal cases brought to trial are decided by the unpaid Native magistracy.

In almost all cases a large majority of the members of the municipal boards are elected by the townspeople. The voting qualification depends on amount of income, house-rating, and contribution to municipal taxation. The rules under which elections are conducted are framed by the Provincial Government, and vary according to local circumstances. The chairman is usually the District officer, but in this matter the boards have generally the power of making their own choice. The income of the municipalities of the United Provinces amounted in 1901 to £331,000, more than half of which was raised by octroi duties on articles brought into the towns for consumption.

There are similar boards in the rural districts. An electoral body is nominated by the Government, and this body chooses from its own members not less than three-fourths of the board. The District officer is the chairman. These boards levy no rates, but local funds and grants from the provincial revenues are assigned for the local duties entrusted to them.

Although much has been done throughout India for the encouragement of local self-government, the systems in force are still to a great extent in a tentative stage. It cannot be said that the people usually take much interest in such matters; they care, for the most part, nothing for sanitation, or for any of the modern improvements to which we attach importance, and if they were left to please themselves they would ordinarily prefer that their towns and villages should remain in the condition with which their forefathers were content. No taxation is more unpopular in India than direct taxation for local purposes. People can understand that they must contribute towards the expenses of the State, for the maintenance of the army, for the courts of justice, and so forth; but that they should be made to pay for the drainage of their streets, and for so-called improvements which we tell them will diminish mortality and disease, is a thing of which, for the most part, they fail to see the necessity or justice. Nevertheless men are often found among the Native members of the municipalities who are sufficiently enlightened to understand the value of the work in which they are engaged, and glad to help in performing it.

Including the cities of Calcutta, Bombay, and Madras, there were in 1901 in British India 760 municipalities, with an income of nearly £5,000,000 and a population, within municipal limits, of about 16,000,000.

I must now speak of the manner in which the executive authorities of the districts are brought under the control of the Provincial Government.

The forty-eight districts of the United Provinces are grouped together into nine Divisions, technically so called, each of which is in charge of an officer called the Commissioner. In matters connected with the revenue in all its branches, and with the executive administration generally, he exercises powers of supervision over the proceedings of the District officers, but he does not interfere in the details of the business entrusted to them. In certain cases appeals lie to him, and nothing of importance can happen without his knowledge, because all communications between the District officers and the Government pass through his hands.

A similar system prevails in other parts of British

India, with the exception of Madras, where there are no Commissioners. In that province the District officers communicate directly with the Government, except in revenue matters, on which they make their reports through the Revenue Board.

Besides the Commissioners of divisions, there is a large staff of officers, through whom the executive business of the province is supervised, reported on, and submitted for the orders of the Lieutenant-Governor. The members of the Revenue Board are entrusted with the duty of supervising the proceedings of the Collectors and Commissioners in matters connected with the land, and the collection and management of the public revenues. The term "board" has become, in this and other provinces, somewhat of a misnomer. It has been found in India, as elsewhere, that, as Bentham expressed it, almost every board, entrusted with executive duties, is a screen, efficient for hiding what ought to be known, and for avoiding individual responsibility. Each member of the Revenue Board has now his own separate duties.

The departments of Police, Jails, Education, Medical Services, Public Health and Vaccination, Agriculture and Commerce, Forestry, Meteorology, Registration, Stamps and Excise, and Public Works have all, under one title or another, their respective heads, who act as the advisers of the Lieutenant-Governor. They make their reports and receive their orders through the Secretaries to the Government.

The headquarters of the Government of the United Provinces are at Allahabad, but they are removed during the hottest months of the year to Naini Tál, in the Kumáon Himálaya. Each of the great Indian provinces has had, for many years past, its Hill Station.

I have already referred to the benefit to the public service which attends the annual migration of the Supreme Government to Simla, and there can be no question that the efficiency of the Provincial Governments is also greatly increased by the custom of allowing officers under their own immediate orders, and who have no local duties to perform, to carry on their work in a cool climate, instead of remaining in the enervating heat of the plains.

Authority, in every branch of the public service excepting the judicial, is centralised in the Lieutenant-Governor, subject only to the paramount authority of the Governor-General in Council. Excepting the Viceroy, no officers in India are entrusted with so large a measure of personal power as the Lieutenant-Governors of the great Indian provinces. They have no executive councils. Their nominal dignity is less than that of the Governors of Madras and Bombay, but the territories ruled by the Lieutenant-Governors are in no way inferior in political importance, and, in the case of Bengal and of the United Provinces, they have larger populations and larger revenues. The checks against the wrongful exercise by the Lieutenant-Governor of arbitrary power, are, however, complete. There is no branch of the administration in which he is not bound either by positive law, or by the standing orders of the Supreme Government, or by the system which has gradually grown up under his predecessors. Any great changes which he may desire to introduce must first receive the approval of the Governor-General in Council. He can impose no new taxation; his powers of sanctioning fresh expenditure, although large, are carefully restricted; and he has no control over the military forces.

Until 1887 the Lieutenant-Governor of the North-Western Provinces had no Council for legislative purposes, and all laws required for the North-Western Provinces and Oudh were passed in the Council of the Governor-General. The Lieutenant-Governor of the United Provinces has now a Legislative Council similar to those in Madras, Bombay, and Bengal, the constitution of which was described in a former chapter.[1]

Under the Indian Councils Act of 1892, the number of Councillors must not exceed fifteen, and the Rules passed under the Act provide that not more than seven of these shall be officials. The appointments to the Council are made by the Governor-General on the nomination of the Lieutenant-Governor. Six of the non-official members are nominated on the recommendation of various bodies. The Senate of the University of Allahabad recommends one member. Five members are recommended by groups of Municipal Boards, groups of District Boards, Associations of landholders, whether landlords or tenants, and Associations of merchants, manufacturers, or tradesmen. It is provided that the nomination to the remaining two non-official seats shall be made by the Lieutenant-Governor in such a manner as will, in his opinion, secure a fair representation of the different classes of the community.

There are other departments of the administration which, as before explained, are under the control of the Supreme and not of the Provincial Government, because they deal with matters of imperial interest, common to the whole of India; among these are the Post Office and Telegraph, the Survey, the Public Accounts and Currency.

Before leaving this part of my subject I must repeat

[1] Chapter IV.

that no one can understand how the actual government of India is carried on until he has obtained a proper appreciation of the facts which are stated in the earlier part of this chapter. The unit of administration in every province of British India is the district; every district has its own organisation; the province is a collection of districts, with the addition of the strong central authority of the Provincial Government which controls and gives unity to the whole; the machinery by which this central authority is exercised is efficient and complete; nothing of public importance can occur in any district or in any village, information regarding which is not immediately laid before the Government of the province.

I have hitherto referred to the executive administration only. The courts of justice, as in other countries possessing civilised systems of government, are independent of the executive power; the Government, like its subjects, is amenable to the law, and, like them, may be sued in the courts.

A general account has already been given of the system under which the administration of justice in India is carried on.[1] In the United Provinces each district has a Civil Judge, who also presides over the court of session.

The district is divided into a convenient number of sections, in each of which there are courts of civil jurisdiction, subordinate to the court of the Judge. There are two classes of these courts: those of the Munsifs, who try suits up to the value of 1000 rupees, and those of the Subordinate judges, who try them, with certain restrictions, to any higher amount. Appeals lie in the smaller cases to the Judge, and in cases for more

[1] Chapter VII.

than 5000 rupees to the High court. There are also Small-cause courts, which decide petty cases without appeal. Out of more than 200 Subordinate judges and Munsifs in the North-Western Provinces there are only two or three who are not Natives.

The High Court of the North-Western Provinces,[1] which has its seat at Allahabad, consists of a Chief Justice and five Puisne Judges, all appointed by the Crown. One of the Judges and the Chief Justice are chosen from the English Bar, three of the Judges are members of the Covenanted Civil Service, and one of them is a Native gentleman. In Oudh the principal court is that of the Judicial Commissioner; it consists of Judges appointed by the Lieutenant-Governor, with the previous approval of the Governor-General.

The Lieutenant-Governor appoints the district judge, and possesses in criminal cases the power of pardon, but he has no control over the judicial administration.

[1] Although the North-Western Provinces are now called the Province of Agra, the High Court, having been constituted by an Act of Parliament, which has not been altered, retains its old title.

CHAPTER XXI

AN INDIAN PROVINCE (*continued*)

Condition of the people—Increasing wealth and prosperity—Indebtedness of the agricultural classes—Increase of population—Emigration—Character of the people—Their great honesty—Cruel customs—Crime—Infanticide—Criminal Tribes.

REFERENCE will be made hereafter to some of the results of the elaborate system of government which I have been describing. Something must now be said regarding the material condition of the people.

It is easy in almost every country to find examples of extreme poverty, and it is easy in India. The day labourer is often little better than an hereditary bondsman, and in bad seasons his condition may be miserable. It would be hard to discover people living in a worse state of moral and physical degradation than that of the lowest classes of Mohammedans in many of the towns of Northern India. It is easy for the Indian pessimist to take cases of this kind, which are not rare, and then, by a bold generalisation, to assume that extreme poverty and misery are the normal condition of the agricultural population throughout India. We might as reasonably, on evidence of the condition of the poorest classes in the West of Ireland, or in the worst slums of the great cities of England, conclude that the rural and town population of our own country are universally wretched and degraded.

I have laid much stress on the progress of India in material prosperity; but that India is a poor country is a fact which no one could think of denying, and so it will inevitably remain while the country is almost purely agricultural. In the words of an eminent economist, it has been proved by experience, everywhere and at all times, that a purely agricultural country is never rich, even from an agricultural point of view. Where other industries and commerce also flourish, it is through their means that agricultural wealth is developed.[1] But it by no means follows that because an agricultural country is not rich its people are miserable.

Referring to Northern India, I have already said that there is perhaps no country in which more complete and trustworthy information has been placed on record in regard to every subject affecting the agricultural population.

The great majority of Indian agriculturists have the advantage of possessing, either as peasant proprietors or as cultivators with occupancy rights, permanent interests in the land. The condition of the people mainly depends on the degree in which these interests exist. This is always shown in a striking manner when seasons of drought occur. The first to suffer are the field-labourers, who live on the wages of their labour. If the rainy season fails, the land cannot be cultivated, and they are thrown out of employment. The next to suffer are the tenants-at-will, with no fixed rights and little credit. Where, on the other hand, the land is cultivated by the proprietors themselves, or by tenants with hereditary rights, it is only when drought is unusually severe and

[1] "L' esperienza di tutti i luoghi e di tutti i tempi ha dimostrato che i paesi puramente agricoli non sono mai ricchi, neppure sotto l' aspetto agrario, e che invece dove fioriscono i commerci e le industrie il tornaconto privato crea la richezza rurale."—Jacini, *Relazione sull' Inchiesta agraria.*

prolonged that these classes require help, for they have stocks of food and money to fall back upon, and they have credit with the money-lenders.

The field-labourers, when they have no permanent and hereditary employment in their villages, and who depend on wages paid usually in kind, are the only class in the condition of which it is probably true that there has been no general improvement. They are often worse off than in the times when there were no roads and railways, and when the value of agricultural produce was lower. To the menial servants of an Indian village a rise in prices does not necessarily bring increased wages, and they are usually too ignorant and helpless to think of bettering their condition by going elsewhere for employment, which would not in these days be difficult to find. But these are exceptions. Unless the seasons be especially unfortunate, the ordinary life of the Indian peasant is far from unhappy. The immediate requirements of life are easily satisfied in the climate of India, and if we compare the physical ease of the average Indian agriculturist with that existing among the same class in a great part of Europe, I do not doubt that "the advantage would probably be greatly in favour of the former, although his life may be shorter and subject to greater risks." This is the conclusion stated by the Famine Commissioners of 1880, and they wrote with a knowledge, an experience, and an authority to which very few can pretend. There can be no question that in times of ordinary prosperity there is, in proportion to the population—and the population of India is more than seven times as large as that of the United Kingdom—more want and extreme misery in our own country than in India; and, if in this matter comparision were possible, we should have to make it not with

India in its normal condition, but with India, I do not say in time of famine, but in time of scarcity.

Elaborate calculations, based really upon no facts, and in themselves valueless, are put forth from time to time to prove that the average income of the Indian agriculturist does not exceed a few farthings a day, and that the masses of the population have no sufficient means of obtaining the bare necessaries of life. Such statements often arise from simple ignorance, but at other times from that unfortunate inclination which makes Englishmen not unfrequently seem to rejoice in anything which can bring discredit upon their country-men. These assertions are not only unfounded, but transparently absurd.

It is a fact that the Indian peasant has very little money, and that measured in money his income is very small, and this fact may easily lead to totally mistaken conclusions. But his income is not and cannot be measured in money. It is a very ordinary supposition of English writers that the Indian, like the English peasant, buys all that he requires for his support, but nothing could be more erroneous. As a rule, he derives from the land which he himself owns or cultivates most of the necessaries of life for himself and his family.

"He retains," in the words of Mr. T. H. Thornton, "so much of his produce as he requires for seed and home consumption, and disposes of the surplus only, and this surplus he does not ordinarily sell in open market, but makes over to the village *banya*, or shopkeeper, with whom he has an account current for cash advanced and goods supplied. The attempt to give a money value to these primitive transactions, and formulate the financial condition of the peasantry in terms of cash receipts and payments, must be a very hazardous undertaking."

I may add, in regard to those classes of the population which have incomes that can properly be stated in money, that we are apt in this country to forget that an income which would here mean absolute poverty would often denote ease and comfort in India. The term poverty has no absolute and invariable signification; it depends on the relation between a man's wants and the means of supplying them. Every one acquainted with India knows that almost everywhere a man who possesses five or six rupees a month, or say 3d. a day, is looked upon as a comparatively well-to-do person, able to provide, in something more than comfort, not only for himself but for his family.

Little money passes through the hands even of the well-to-do Indian peasant. He need buy little or nothing except the simple implements of husbandry, cooking-vessels, clothing, sweetmeats, and tobacco; and all these together will not cost him many shillings in the year. In the provinces to which I have more particularly referred, his cottage affords clean and, according to his ideas, comfortable shelter. He has not much clothing, but much is not wanted; in the winter he suffers little from the cold. In ordinary circumstances, he has sufficient food of the only kind that he desires, the produce of his own fields or garden, his millets and lentils, his barley or his rice, his much-appreciated *ghee*, made from the milk of cows or buffaloes, the vegetables, spices, and condiments of which in a hot climate there is no lack, and as much tobacco, sugar, and sweetmeats as he can afford to buy. The more valuable products of his land, such in Northern India as the wheat which he does not himself consume, give him the means of meeting the demands for rent or revenue. His wife has often her holiday attire and her silver ornaments, for after providing the necessaries of life there is frequently something left for simple luxuries and for buying jewellery, the latter a common form of hoarding. If, as is usually the case, he drinks no spirits, the only tax that he has to pay is about fivepence a year for salt, for himself and each member of his family. The improvement in the condition of the people in Northern India within my own recollection and observation has been obvious. As one of the settlement officers says, the vessels used by the peasantry fifty years ago were almost always earthen—now they are of brass; their clothing is better and they have more of it—"now every tenant dresses like a Brahman or zemindar of old days." One of the most experienced officers of the Agra Province has declared, as the result of his inquiries and observation, his belief that the landowning classes are, speaking generally, four or five times as rich as they were early in the last century. "Everywhere," he says, "there has been an extraordinary rise in the value of land, and the great advance in wealth and prosperity of the agricultural classes is too plainly evident to be called in question."

It has been estimated by competent observers that in the Punjab the value of land has more than sextupled in value since it became a British province. On this subject, I may quote the interesting remarks made in the Council of the Governor-General on 26th March 1902, in the discussion of the Financial Statement for 1902-03 by Sir Denzil Ibbetson. I suppose that there is no Englishman who possesses more intimate and personal knowledge of the people, or one whose ability and experience entitle him to speak with greater authority regarding their general condition. After referring to statements that during the past fifty years the Indian peasant had been growing poorer, he thus proceeded:—

"The Honourable Syad Husein Bilgrami tells us from his personal observation that the peasant is, as a fact, better off. In such a matter I attach greater weight to personal experience than to *a priori* reasoning. And my honourable friend's testimony will carry special weight as based upon an intimacy of knowledge to which no one who is not a native of the country can pretend. At the same time, I have spent twenty years of my service in India, in work which has brought me into intimate daily contact with the people, and I also have formed a very definite opinion as to their condition. We have heard a great deal of late about the poverty of India, about its impoverishment under British rule, and about the reduction of the average income within the last fifty years. As for the diminution of average income, the best and shortest answer that I have seen to the assertion has been given by the *Hindu Patriot*. It is, briefly, that the assertion is *sheer nonsense and opposed to common knowledge*. As the *Patriot* observes, 'the day labourer who used to get only one anna a day now receives more than two annas.'[1] There is not a Member of this Council who cannot of his own personal knowledge confirm the statement.

"But, as the *Patriot* very truly remarks, increased wages do not necessarily mean increased comfort, and the charge of impoverishment remains to be dealt with. In the great cities there is, no doubt, poverty amounting to destitution, as in all the great cities of the world. In the villages and small towns the labouring classes are poor enough in all conscience, more especially in backward or unprogressive tracts, where no development of industries or of communications has brought assistance to the labour market, and most of all in purely agricultural areas, where the change, to which the Honourable Syad Husein has alluded, that is slowly taking place under the solvent influences of occidental ideas and institutions, has substituted cash payments for work actually done, for the old customary payments in grain. But if their incomes are small, their needs are small also. The margin between the two is narrow, and when prices rise, as they do rise in years of stress, there is no doubt that the pinch of hunger is widely and severely felt. But, so far as my knowledge

[1] The *Hindu Patriot* is the most ably conducted and important Native newspaper in Bengal, written entirely by Natives of the country, and always independent and unsparing in its criticisms of British administration.

and experience carry me, there is in ordinary seasons far less of that carking, grinding poverty, that uncertainty of how the day's food is to be provided, that certainty that on some days it will not be forthcoming at all, which eats into the heart of man—there is far less actual destitution than there is in wealthy England, the only country with which I am able to make a comparison. The fact is partly due, no doubt, to that practice of universal charity which is in its details so small as almost to escape observation, but as a whole so splendid as to constitute, in my eyes at least, the chief glory of the Indian people.

"We are told that India is being slowly bled to death, that its agriculture, its commerce, and its industries are ruthlessly exploited for the benefit of England, that the British rule has been one long continuous process of impoverishment, under which the old prosperity of the peasantry has steadily decayed till they stand tottering on the brink of famine, and that even in the best of years many of them hardly escape starvation. My Lord, I am not so rash as to predicate anything of India as a whole. I dare not frame an estimate for a whole nation. But I should like to send those who believe this thing (for I recognise that some, though not all, of those who say it do sincerely believe it)—I should like to send them to a district in the Punjab, where I spent eight years in the beginning of my service, which I settled, which I know by heart, and which I revisited only ten years ago; a district only fifty miles from Delhi, which while it is traversed by a great canal, and includes some of the finest well cultivation in the province, includes also great jungle areas, where the people live chiefly upon the produce of their herds, and wide plains where the crops of industrious cultivators are dependent upon the uncertain rains of heaven. I should like then to tell the people of that district what they tell us, and to ask them whether they agree. There are men there who have heard from their fathers, or perhaps I should now say from their grandfathers, and who would tell them, as they were never tired of telling me, of the state of affairs which preceded our advent. I will not weary the Council by any attempt to describe that state of affairs in detail. Suffice it to say that in the early years of the last century, when we took over the district, the royal canal had long dried up, that more than four-fifths of the area was over-run by thick forest, which afforded shelter to thieves, vagabonds, and beasts of prey, and its inhabitants either removed or exterminated, and that out of 221 villages in a single *pargana*, the people of no fewer than 178 had been wholly driven from their homes and fields.

"I believe the history of our early administration of that district to be typical. It would have been impossible to 'impoverish' what had already been laid desolate. But at first we made many and grievous blunders. We misunderstood the local tenures; our assessments, founded upon the rates which we inherited from our predecessors, were oppressive, and our police and criminal administration was stern and rude, though perhaps not more so than the unsettled state of the district demanded. But the mistakes did not long remain undiscovered or unrectified. The country gradually settled down in the early 'thirties, a rough survey afforded a basis for a more reasonable revenue system, and from that time to the present, or at any rate up to 1892 when I last saw it, the history of the district has been one of continuous advance in prosperity. In 1871, when I first went there, its condition was that of an ordinary fairly prosperous British district, though it included tracts which had suffered from the too prodigal use of canal water. When I revisited it in 1892 the change for the better that had taken place in the interval was marvellous. The canal had been re-aligned at great expense so as to extend and improve irrigation; the supply of water had been rigorously limited to what was needed, rather than to what was asked for; the swamps had been drained, so that I found waving sheets of wheat where I had been accustomed to shoot snipe; the saline efflorescence which had thrown hundreds of acres out of cultivation was slowly but steadily disappearing; villages which I had been obliged to assess with extraordinary leniency on account of their water-logged and depressed condition had become prosperous, and their people were no longer unable to marry their daughters because they were barren with malaria; new branches of the canal had been carried through arid tracts of which the produce had been notoriously insecure; and a railway had been constructed right through the heart of the district. I either marched through or saw people, not merely from the canal tract, but every part of the district, including the driest and the most precarious. They had their grumbles and their grievances, without which no properly constituted husbandman is complete, but their general story was one of increasing contentment and prosperity; nor was outward evidence lacking. It was impossible to ride across the old familiar fields and through the well-known villages without realising the progress that had been made. To mention three small but significant facts: brick houses, which had formerly been confined to the *sáhukár* of the village, had become much more common; small factories for ginning and baling cotton had sprung up all through the cotton-producing tract; and when I wished to show my daughters one of the picturesque old-fashioned cane-presses to which I had been accustomed, I was told that, except in two villages, they had been superseded throughout the district by the iron mill invented by Mr. Milne of Behea. I know this, that if any one were to tell these people whom I know so well that their history under British rule has been one of continuous deterioration and impoverishment, they would simply laugh in his face. I have chosen to speak of this particular district, because I have known it as I have never known any other, and because I visited it again after an interval of fifteen years. But I have served in many other districts of the Punjab, and from all that I have seen and heard, I believe that what I have said of this district is in the main true of all."

There can be no question that the story which Sir Denzil Ibbetson has told us of the Punjab is equally true of other provinces of British India.

In a previous chapter[1] I showed the progress of the commerce of India—progress which it is not possible should have taken place without a corresponding development of the wealth and industry of the country. This increase of the external and internal trade has occurred simultaneously with an equally remarkable increase in almost every branch of the public income, although the burdens of the people have been reduced. The statistics of the railways, the telegraphs, the post office, and the savings banks all tell the same story. That all this should be compatible with anything but a great and rapid improvement in the material

[1] Chapter XIII.

condition of the people is contrary to reason. It is, unhappily, true that there is one respect in which the growing wealth of the country is sometimes liable to a terrible shock. All that has been said of the ordinary prosperity of the people is indisputably true, but the danger cannot be forgotten to which I have repeatedly referred, and to which, in the greater part of India, they are exposed when there is a failure of the periodical rains, a danger against which no efforts that a Government can make can provide more than partial remedies. This is a question which has been fully noticed in other chapters, and I have described what has been done to protect the country against famine or to mitigate its consequences.

Much has often been said regarding the general indebtedness of the agricultural classes to money-lenders, and the evil results that often follow cannot be denied. It is no peculiarity of India that agriculture can hardly be carried on without credit, but the great vicissitudes of season to which the country is liable often increase the risks that are a consequence of that fact. There is no reason whatever for supposing that Indian agriculturists have ever been an exception to a very general rule, but it can hardly be doubted that their indebtedness is greater now than it was before the establishment of our Government. This has been one of the results which, in the words of the Famine Commissioners of 1880, have followed "in the progressive development of social life from a simple to a more advanced stage. . . . There has been a considerable increase in the incomes of the landholding and cultivating classes, and their standard of comfort has also risen. With a rise in the transfer value of their tenures, their credit has also expanded." We have given to the agricultural classes, as I have shown in a previous chapter, rights which formerly had little or no existence. The right of private property in land has been virtually almost created by ourselves. When there was practically no such right, there was, comparatively speaking, no credit; there was no adequate security that a landholder desirous of borrowing could offer, and there was therefore less indebtedness. As the standard of comfort has risen, wants of every kind and demands for expenditure have increased also, and with this increase has come more frequent necessity for recourse to the money-lender. It would be a complete mistake to suppose that the pressure of the land revenue has been the principal cause of the difficulties into which the owners of land have often fallen, but I do not doubt that among the contributory causes we must count the manner in which the Government demand has been not unfrequently levied. Although in actual amount it is far more moderate than that of any former Government, or of any Native Government at the present time, it is collected, under our existing system, with greater rigidity, and has thus, in unfavourable seasons, tended to increase the difficulties of the proprietor of land. The fact that greater elasticity ought, in this respect, to be given in the application of our revenue system is now fully recognised and acted upon by the Government.

Frequent attempts have been made, and laws have been passed, in the hope of protecting the agricultural classes from the exactions of money-lenders and from their own improvidence. Whether these attempts have had any useful effect is more than doubtful. Efforts are in progress in many parts of India to establish Agricultural Banks which, it may be hoped, may be successful. Meanwhile it cannot be too confidently stated that, in spite of all drawbacks, there has been great and indeed extraordinary improvement in the general condition of the people.

Gloomy forebodings have been .not uncommon in regard to the difficulties to which India may be exposed in a not very distant future from the pressure of population on food. In some Indian countries the population is already denser than in almost any part of Europe, and it is rapidly increasing. Among the checks on the growth of population which formerly existed—war, pestilence, and famine—the first has ceased, and the last has at least lost much of its power. Of pestilence, I can say nothing. I fear that cholera and plague and fever are as destructive as ever. No obligation, both for men and women, is more universally recognised than that of marriage at the earliest possible age. Although emigration across the sea has made considerable progress, the time must be distant in which it can afford an outlet of much importance to the surplus population of India.

In spite of all this, it is probable that before the growth of population becomes a serious question, increase in the productiveness of the soil, increase of cultivation, which goes on rapidly, and above all the growth of a non-agricultural population, and greater diversity of occupation, will have supplied a remedy. Railways, and improved communications, and increasing wealth are bringing about great changes. Not long ago it was hardly possible to emigrate from one part of India to another; in 1901 there were more than 200,000,000 passengers on the railways. Bengal and other provinces furnish the labourers required by Assam for its tea-plantations, and Burma receives every year a large number of immigrants from Southern India. When the people become less unwilling to leave their own provinces for countries where the conditions of life are easier, and when diversity of occupation increases, they will find ample space within the limits of the Indian continent. Exclusive of Bengal, for which there are no statistics, there are said to be in India some 80,000,000 acres of unoccupied land fit for cultivation —an area exceeding the whole area of the United Kingdom. The land actually under cultivation would often, with improved methods, support a far larger population, and already, in some parts of India, important manufacturing industries are growing up.

The people are eminently fitted for industrial occupations, and the natural resources of the country afford abundant opportunities for their development. The supply of coal is unlimited, its quality is good, and its cost is small. It has been shown by experience that almost all the requirements of the railways can be satisfactorily supplied by Indian mechanics. There is no apparent limit to the extension of many manufactures, or to the means of subsistence which will thus be provided for very large numbers of the population.

Something must now be said about the character of the people in the provinces which I have been attempting to describe.

English officers tell us that they would not hesitate to lead their Sikhs and Patháns and Gúrkhas against any European enemy. We could not go so far as this in speaking generally of the population of the United Provinces of Agra and Oudh; but the people are by no means wanting in manliness and courage, and some classes furnish excellent soldiers. In regard to their other qualities it is dangerous to generalise. There is no country in Europe in which the differences between the various sections of the population are so great.

A Hindu gentleman of great intelligence once said to me that while he fully admitted the superiority of the English not only in the arts of civilised life, but in many noble qualities, there was one virtue, on which the English especially prided themselves, in which they seemed to him inferior to his own countrymen. "The English," he said, "seem to think that honesty consists in not telling a lie in answer to a direct question. Almost all of us tell lies when it seems convenient to do so; but, in my opinion, in the particular quality of honesty we are better than the English."

There was a good deal of truth in the contention of my Hindu friend. If lying be the test of dishonesty, it would be hard to equal the dishonesty that you meet with in India. I have heard one of the most eminent of our judges doubt whether the perjury that goes on in his court in England could be surpassed in India; but I think he was wrong, and that in this matter the Indian courts would easily carry off the palm. Nevertheless, if I were asked what was the most striking characteristic of the people of Northern India, I should say it was their honesty. Mr. Benett of the Indian Civil Service has well expressed what I believe to be the truth on this subject:

"Writing two centuries before Christ, of the Hindus in the kingdom of Patna, an educated Greek selected as the leading feature in their character their honesty and integrity in the ordinary relations of life; and, paradoxical as it may sound to most English ears, it is probable that this is almost as true of the Hindu village of to-day as it was of the Buddhist court of two thousand years ago. Even among our own servants no one can fail to have been astonished at the absolute safety with which large sums of money may be entrusted to their keeping, when theft would be almost impossible of detection and would secure them comfort for the remainder of their lives. In the higher ranks, the well-paid and educated office-clerks are faithful and trustworthy beyond any other class of men who can be procured for their responsible duties. What has been said applies to their relations with foreign masters, for whom they can rarely feel any affection, and who not unfrequently regard them with a suspicion which would be itself enough to make most men dishonest. In their relations with their own people the quality is far more conspicuous. Trade transactions involving enormous sums are carried through with a want of precaution which we should consider idiotic, but which is justified by the rarity of breaches of faith. In a country where writing is an art as common as it is with us, large debts are contracted every day on nothing but the verbal security of the borrower; and if there may be occasional repudiation in our courts, the fact that that security is still considered sufficient is ample proof that the debts are honourably acknowledged among the parties themselves. In such cases limitation is never thought of, and families who have emerged from poverty will discharge debts contracted by their ancestors a century back, of which no other record exists but an entry in the money-lender's private ledger. Their whole system postulates an exceptional integrity."[1]

No people are more charitable. It is true that the Indian idea of charity is often very different from ours, and it is affected so strongly by caste considerations that it sometimes seems to us to pass into cruelty. But there is hardly any class that is not, according to its means and according to its own ideas, kind-hearted and benevolent. Nothing is more remarkable in times of scarcity than native charity, although it is often too indiscriminate to be wise. The people generally are extremely industrious. Although uneducated and superstitious, the agricultural classes are certainly not inferior in intelligence to the peasants of many of the countries of Europe.

All classes are polite but not servile in their manners; it would be impossible to surpass the finished courtesy of a Mohammedan gentleman.

[1] *Introduction to the Oudh Gazetteer*, by Mr. W. C. Benett, C.S., p. 28.

I must leave this part of my subject. I spent in Northern India the best and most interesting portion of my life. It is impossible to live among its people without feeling for them a deep regard, and, assuming that our dominion does not perish before the proper time has come, I cannot doubt that their future will be fortunate.

I have been describing a peaceful, contented, and well-disposed society, deserving in a high degree the respect and affection of its rulers, but it must not be forgotten that we shall have a very incomplete idea of India if we look only at what we see upon the surface. The more we learn about India the more we become alive to the fact that we are, to use Sir James Stephen's expression, the representatives of a belligerent civilisation, which has to wage constant warfare against strange barbarisms, horrid customs, and cruel superstitions, ancient survivals, ready at any moment to start into activity.

If we look at the criminal statistics of Northern India, which are as carefully collected as in any country of Europe, it will appear that there is less crime than in England, and that the people are astonishingly peaceable and honest. The conclusion will be true; but if we inquire more deeply we shall find strange facts that these statistics do not show. We shall find, for instance, that in the United Provinces there were, not many years ago, more than 300,000 people belonging, not to barbarous tribes like the Patháns on the Afghán frontier,[1] nor to the outcasts and scum of the community, but to classes of honourable and comparatively civilised men, who were living under the restraint of special penal

[1] The following is extracted from an official report of 1887:—"According to the Pathán code of honour, murder under certain conditions is not a crime but an obligation. Two thousand murderers are believed to be at large in the Peshâwar district." In this case also a special law has been put in force.

laws, because from time immemorial they had killed their female children. Among all the races of India, there is none more noble than the Rájput; and among the Rájputs, the first rank belongs to the Chauháns—the *sangre azul*, as they have been called, of Indian chivalry. No men in India are so proud of their lineage, and they trace their descent, not from mortal ancestors, but from the sacred fire called forth on the summit of Mount Ábu, by one of the sages of the Vedas, to destroy the demons who were persecuting the Brahmans and depriving the gods of their sacrifices. These people are numerous in the United Provinces. In the district of Mainpuri there are more than 30,000 of them, and not fifty years ago it was discovered that among them there was not a single girl. Every daughter that was born was killed. The higher the rank of the family the more constant and systematic was the crime.

"There is at Mainpuri," wrote Mr. Raikes, the magistrate of the district in 1850, "an old fortress which looks far over the valley of the Eesun River. This has been for centuries the stronghold of the Rája of the Mainpuri Chauháns, whose ancient blood represents the *crême de la crême* of Rájput aristocracy. Here, when a son, a nephew, a grandson, was born to the reigning chief, the event was announced to the neighbouring city by the loud discharge of wall-pieces and matchlocks; but centuries had passed away and no infant daughter had been known to smile within those walls." [1]

This is not rhetoric but the statement of a fact. In 1856 special inquiries were instituted. It was found that this practice of infanticide, although especially prevalent among the Rájputs, was by no means confined to them, and it was common not only in the North-Western Provinces but in Oudh, the Punjab, and in parts of the Bombay presidency. Numbers of villages

[1] *Notes on the North-Western Provinces of India*, 1852.

were visited where there was not a single girl, and where there had never been one within the memory of man. Of one large Rájput community on the borders of Oudh it was officially reported that "not only are there no girls to be found now, but there never have been any, nor has such an event as the marriage of a daughter taken place for more than two hundred years." In 1869 another investigation showed that there was little change for the better. This was the sort of report:—In seven villages, 104 boys, and 1 girl; in twenty-three villages 284 boys, and 23 girls; in other villages, the marriage of a girl an entirely unknown ceremony.

There is an interesting account of the marriage customs of the Rájputs in Sir Alfred Lyall's *Asiatic Studies*. A Rájput cannot marry a woman who does not belong to a Rájput family, but at the same time he cannot marry one of his own class.

> "The custom makes marriage difficult by narrowing the field of selection; for neither can a man go very far among strange tribes to seek his wife, nor a father to seek a husband for his daughter; so that a poor man often does not marry at all, while a rich man of high birth is besieged with applications for his hand, in order that the stigma of an unmarried daughter may at least be formally removed."[1]

Thus, while an unmarried daughter is looked upon as hopelessly disgraced—and this is true of almost all classes throughout India, and not of Rájputs only—a son-in-law cannot always be found unless the father of the girl is prepared to pay highly, and the marriage of a daughter may mean the ruin of a family. Rather than incur this danger, the Rájput prefers that his daughter should perish. But a still more powerful reason is immemorial custom, which Manu declares to be "trans-

[1] *Asiatic Studies*, p. 220.

cendent law and the root of all piety." These people have gone on killing their children generation after generation because their forefathers did so before them, not only without a thought that there is anything criminal in the practice, but with the conviction that it is right.

For many years past measures have been taken for the prevention of this crime. For a long time, in the days when our civilisation was less belligerent than it has since become, it was thought that the best hope of success lay in the removal of the causes which appeared to lead to its commission, and especially in the prevention of extravagant expenditure on marriages; but although these benevolent efforts were undoubtedly useful, their practical results were not great, and it became clear that it was only by a stringent and organised system of coercion that these practices would ever be eradicated. In 1870 an Act of the Legislature was passed which enabled the Government to deal with the subject. A system of registration of births and deaths among the suspected classes was established, with constant inspection and enumeration of children; special police-officers were entertained at the cost of the guilty communities, and no efforts were spared to convince them that the Government had firmly resolved that it would put down these practices, and would treat the people who followed them as murderers. Although the time may be distant when preventive measures will cease to be altogether necessary, great progress has been made, and there are now thousands of girls where formerly there were none. In 1874 the population living under special regulations numbered 359,000; in 1887 it was more than 200,000; in 1891 the population under supervision had fallen to 62,000; in 1901 the Act was still in force in 264 villages, but in many of these it was hoped that the practice of infanticide had been abandoned. In the Mainpuri district, where, as I have said, there was once hardly a single Chauhán girl, nearly half of the Chauhán children at the present time are girls.

In those districts in which the Rájput clans are scattered and greatly mixed with other classes of the population, and where the support of clan feeling and clan custom is comparatively weak, there is reason to think that infanticide has almost ceased. In other districts where the Rájputs are found in large and homogeneous communities, the suppression of the crime is more difficult. There can be little doubt that if vigilance were relaxed the custom would before long become as prevalent as ever.

Another illustration may be given of the strange conditions that still exist in India, and of the difficulties with which we have to contend. Much of the crime that is committed is carried on by tribes of criminals as their regular and legitimate occupation, not only with no thought of criminality, but in the belief that in following the custom of their forefathers they are acting in the only way that is right. I will not repeat the well-known story of the Thugs, the professional murderers who practised their trade over a great part of India. They have been extirpated by the British Government. Another class of murderers, poisoners by profession, still exists in our own provinces, but in greatly diminished numbers. We have not altogether succeeded in stamping out the professional Dacoits, associated for the purposes of violent gang-robbery, but it is in the Native States that they now chiefly have their headquarters, from which they carry on their marauding expeditions. Other criminal organisations, with which it is more difficult to deal, abound to this day.

The following quotation from an official report will show what these professional criminals are. They have no resemblance to the habitual criminals of Europe.

"We all know that trades go by castes in India; a family of carpenters will be a family of carpenters a century or five centuries hence, if they last so long; so with grain-dealers, blacksmiths, leather-makers, and every known trade. If we keep this in mind when we speak of 'professional criminals,' we shall realise what the term really means. It means that the members of a tribe whose ancestors were criminals from time immemorial are themselves destined by the usages of caste to commit crime, and their descendants will be offenders against the law until the whole tribe is exterminated or accounted for in the manner of the Thugs. Therefore, when a man tells you he is a Badhak, or a Kanjar, or a Sonoria, he tells you, what few Europeans ever thoroughly realise, that he is an offender against the law, has been so from the beginning, and will be so to the end; that reform is impossible, for it is his trade, his caste—I may almost say his religion—to commit crime."

Here is an account of one of these tribes called Barwárs. Their headquarters are in the district of Gonda, in Oudh, where they inhabit forty-eight villages, and number a thousand families. They have little to do with agriculture; they live quietly and honestly at their homes for some months of every year, and the rest of their time is spent in wandering, in small gangs, over distant parts of the country, plundering everything they can find. But they may not steal cattle; they may despoil the temples of the gods; they may rob even the goddess Debi, one of the special objects of their worship. The only sacred places that they may not touch are the temple of Jagannáth in Orissa, and the shrine of a certain Mohammedan martyr. They have a regular organisation, under duly chosen chiefs; every child goes through a form of religious initiation on the twelfth day of his life; if a man of the tribe gives up his thieving profession he is excommunicated and disgraced. The time for starting on their predatory expeditions is settled by the astrologers, and the plunder brought home is divided according to fixed rules, after 3¾ per cent has been set aside, to be distributed in certain proportions among their gods. Each family has in its house an altar, dedicated to the special tutelary god of the tribe, Panch Puria, a god not recognised by other classes; on a certain day in August a fowl must be sacrificed on the altar, and thin cakes of bread must be baked, and these offerings have then to be given to a Mohammedan fakeer, who goes from house to house beating a kettledrum. It was stated, in 1901, by the Government of the United Provinces that "very little advance had been made in reforming the Sonorias and Barwárs."

Other criminal tribes are devoted to cattle-stealing, others are dangerous robbers. In Gurgáon, one of the frontier districts of the Punjab, official reports tell us of a large isolated British village, surrounded by Native territory, inhabited almost exclusively by some 2000 people of the Mina tribe. Their sole occupation is, and always has been, plunder in the Native States, and in distant parts of British India; they give no trouble at home, and, judging from criminal statistics, it would be supposed that they were an honest community. They live amid abundance, in substantial houses, with numerous cattle, fine clothes and jewels, and fleet camels to carry off their plunder; and, it is added, "there is no end to their charity." When

I was myself a District officer, I knew personally an almost exactly similar case in Rohilkhand.

In the Agra Province alone there are said to be twenty-nine different tribes who, without any notion of criminality, have from time immemorial made crime their sole serious occupation; and they are probably not less numerous in other parts of India where less is known about them.

There is a special law for dealing with these classes. Registers are kept showing all the members of the tribes; they can be compelled to live within certain local limits, and prevented from leaving those limits without permission, and they may be arrested if they are found beyond them. In some cases, the measures taken have been more or less successful, but the difficulties are great, and a long time must elapse before we see the end of the criminal tribes of India. In 1890 the Government of India declared that it was clearly established that improved communications, railways, and telegraphs had greatly facilitated the operations of the classes who are in the habit of leaving their homes to commit crime at a distance and returning with their plunder.

CHAPTER XXII

BENGAL

Exceptional character of Bengal and its people—The Bengal Lieutenant-Governorship—Natural features, area, and population—Products—Scenery—Climate—Cities—Art—Hindus and Mohammedans—Lord Macaulay's description of the Bengalis—The Mohammedan peasantry—The Permanent Settlement—Zemindars and ryots—Loss of public revenue—Confiscation of the rights of the peasantry—Weakness of the Government—Absence of records of agricultural rights—Former constitution of the Bengal Government—A separate Government constituted—Improvements in the administration—Great increase in rentals of the Zemindars and loss by the ryots—Maintenance of conditions of the Permanent Settlement—Claims of the Zemindars for exemption from taxation—Rates on the land—Changes in the Bengal Rent Law—Condition of the people in Behár—The Tenancy Acts—Cadastral Surveys—Lord Curzon's Government on the results of the Permanent Settlement.

I NOW propose to give a few sketches of another great British Province—Bengal. I am the more desirous of doing this because Englishmen are frequently under the impression that Bengal and Bengális are types of India and its people, the truth being that there is no province which is in all respects more exceptional, and no people more distinct. But these sketches must be very brief, and many important matters must remain unnoticed.

I have explained the various significations which the name Bengal has had at different times. It now usually means the country included within the Bengal

Lieutenant-Governorship, but this again includes four provinces—Bengal Proper, comprising the tracts between the Ganges and Bráhmaputra and the deltas of those rivers, and bounded on the west by the river Kosi; Behár, on the north-west of Bengal Proper, adjoining the United Provinces of Agra and Oudh, to which in its physical character a great part of it is very similar; Chutia Nágpur, a wild and hilly country between Bengal Proper and Central India; and Orissa, south-west from Calcutta, the country of the river Máhánadi, with the sea on its eastern side.

A description of any one of these four provinces would be wholly inapplicable to the rest. Their physical conditions, the character of their population, and their languages are all different. Including the subordinate Native States, the Lieutenant-Governorship of Bengal covers an area of 189,837 square miles; it is almost as large as France, with double its population: Bengal at the census of 1901 contained 78,500,000 people. As Sir William Hunter has observed, "Its elements exhibit every stage of human enlightenment and superstition, from the sceptical educated classes, represented by the Hindu gentleman who distinguishes himself at a London Inn of Court, to the hill chieftain, who a few years ago sacrificed an idiot on the top of a mountain to obtain a favourable decision in a Privy Council appeal."[1] Although I shall have to make some references to Behár, it is almost solely of Bengal Proper that I now propose to speak. It is the largest and most populous and richest of the provinces that make up the Lieutenant-Governorship. It has an area of more than 82,000 square miles, and a population of nearly 46,000,000.

[1] *Imperial Gazetteer of India*, art. "India."

Bengal Proper is everywhere intersected by the channels and tributaries of the Ganges and Bráhmaputra. The Ganges at one time reached the sea through the channel of the Bhágirathi, which in the lower part of its course is known as the Hugli, on which Calcutta is situated. The Bráhmaputra flowed formerly far to the eastward in a separate stream, but in the earlier part of the last century it changed its course, and rolling westward joined the Ganges about two hundred miles from the sea. Their mingled waters now flow together to the Bay of Bengal through countless large and small channels. Sir William Hunter has given a graphic description of this part of the province :—

"The delta of the Ganges" (he says), "and with it the delta of the Bráhmaputra is indistinguishably mixed up, where it borders on the sea, becomes a labyrinth of creeks and rivers, running through the dense forests of the Sundarbans, and exhibiting during the annual inundations the appearance of an immense sea. Higher up, the rice-fields, to the extent of thousands of square miles, are submerged. The scene presents to a European eye a panorama of singular novelty and interest—the crops covered with water; the ears of grain floating on the surface; the stupendous embankments, which restrain, without altogether preventing, the excesses of the inundations; and peasants in all quarters going out to their daily work with their cattle in canoes or on rafts. The navigable streams which fall into or diverge from the Ganges intersect the country in every direction, and afford abundant facilities for internal communication. In many parts boats can approach, by means of lakes, rivulets, and water-courses, to the door of almost every cottage. The lower region of the Ganges is the richest and most productive portion of Bengal, and abounds in valuable produce." [1]

The rivers in Lower Bengal render, to a great extent, the services which are rendered in other countries by the roads. In many parts of the province a

[1] *Imperial Gazetteer of India*, art. "India."

well-to-do man keeps his boat as elsewhere he would keep his cart. Railways have penetrated into most of the districts: their development during the last ten years of the nineteenth century has been great, and there are now only five of the thirty districts which compose Bengal Proper through which a railway does not run. The other districts are mostly those in which it is difficult for railways to contend with the cheap water-carriage; they do not diminish the usefulness of the rivers or materially lessen the traffic which they carry. The great marts and entrepots of internal commerce, especially in the eastern parts of Bengal Proper, are situated at convenient places on the chief rivers, and the agricultural produce of the country is carried off in all directions by the navigable channels. The list of the useful products of Bengal would be a long one. Almost everything is provided in abundance that a people in a tropical climate requires. Rice, jute, timber, bamboos, indigo, opium, oil-seeds, and tea are the principal agricultural products which come into the export trade from Calcutta, but tea is only cultivated in the mountainous borders of the province, and not in Bengal Proper, and the indigo and opium come from Behár and the United Provinces of Agra and Oudh. I have already referred in some detail to the great and remarkable growth of industrial and mining interests in Bengal.[1] A great business is done in hides and skins, and in coal, the output of which has increased largely in recent years, and shows every sign of further development. The great agricultural staple, more important than any other, is rice, which constitutes the chief food of the people.

Although the endless stretches of the rice-fields are

[1] Chapter XIII.

monotonous, few flat countries can be more beautiful than parts of Bengal. A constant succession of admirable pictures is afforded by the reaches of the rivers, busy with traffic; the boats with their great sails; the clumps of feathery bamboos, the climbing canes and cocoanuts, "the pillared shade" of the sacred figs, the tamarinds and mangoes, tall rushes and plantains; the villages, with tanks green with weeds and water-lilies; neat cottages covered with creeping gourds and cucumbers and melons; the emerald greenness of the grass—these, and a thousand picturesque details, and the colouring of its hot and steamy atmosphere, make Bengal one of the most beautiful countries of India. Nor is it so disagreeable for Englishmen to live in as might be supposed. Although it has not the advantage of the pleasantly cold winter of Northern India, the heat of the summer is tempered by the greater prevalence of cloud and rain, and by the nearness of the sea. Heat like that of June at Agra or Lahore is unknown, and for three or four months in the winter the climate is very agreeable. The rainfall in Lower Bengal has seldom failed; excellent crops are almost always secured, and the whole of this portion of the province is as nearly as possible free from the danger of famine.

Although there is hardly any part of India where trade is so active, there are few cities and important towns. Calcutta, with its immediate suburbs, and the large transpontine suburb of Howrah, which is to Calcutta what Southwark is to London, contained in 1901 more than 1,105,000 people. It is in population the second city in the British Empire, but with this exception there are few towns in Bengal which, according to a European standard, can be called large. Patna, with 134,785 people, and Dacca, with 90,542, are the largest. In addition to these three towns, Calcutta, Howrah, and Patna, there are only four besides Dacca which have more than 50,000 inhabitants. Almost the whole population is rural. Near Calcutta and Dacca many factories, chiefly of jute and cotton, have been established, but away from these centres there are scarcely any manufactures, except of common cloth and other articles, made by the ordinary village artisans. Bengal has never, within historical times, been distinguished, as other Indian countries have been, for excellence in art, except in textile fabrics, and its population is, for the most part, devoid of that admirable sense of colour which prevails in many parts of India. The difference in the appearance of the crowds that throng the streets of Bombay and Calcutta is remarkable, the former clad in bright and variously coloured garments, the latter in an almost uniform garb of dirty white. The native portion of Calcutta, although full of wealth, can hardly be surpassed in mean ugliness; people who are comparatively rich are often content to live in hovels; and among the zemindars and rájas of Bengal, with incomes which even in England would be thought great, there is hardly one who lives in a house which in its architecture and decoration is not detestable. In this respect the modern native city of Bombay is a striking contrast to that of Calcutta. The western and eastern capitals of India have grown up under not very dissimilar circumstances, but while the latter in its native quarter is little better than a collection of huts, the former can show streets which are sometimes strikingly picturesque. The admirable Indian styles of architecture which are living arts in other provinces are seldom represented in Bengal.

Throughout nearly the whole of Bengal Proper the

language of the people is Bengáli, but with much variation from place to place. "Bengal," Mr. Baines wrote in 1891, "is the province of all others in which there is the widest gap between the small literary castes and the masses of the people. The vernacular has been split into two sections: first, the tongue of the people at large, which changes every few miles; secondly, the literary dialect, known only through the press, and not intelligible to those who do not also know Sanskrit. The latter form is the product of what may be called the revival of learning in Eastern India, consequent upon the settlement of the British on the Hugli. The vernacular was then found rude and meagre, owing to the absence of scholarship, and the general neglect of the country during the Moghal rule. Instead of strengthening the existing web from the same material, every effort was made in Calcutta, then the only seat of instruction, to embroider upon the feeble old frame a grotesque and elaborate pattern in Sanskrit, and to pilfer from that tongue whatever in the way of vocabulary and construction the learned considered necessary to satisfy the increasing demands of modern intercourse."[1] The result is that books published in Bengáli are, for the most part, quite unintelligible to the people at large.

I have already referred to the great progress of the Mohammedan religion in Bengal.[2] In 1901, in Bengal Proper, the Mohammedans were more numerous than the Hindus, the former numbering 22,287,061, and the latter 21,731,482. In some of the eastern districts the Mohammedans constitute three-fourths of the whole population. Although often fanatical in their religion,

[1] *General Report on the Census of India*, 1891, p. 143.
[2] Chapter XVII.

they are generally totally ignorant of its history and abstruser tenets. The chief effect of their conversion has been to give them a more independent bearing and character than the Hindus of the classes to which they belong, and not unfrequently a disregard of life and the rights of property which leads to the commission of heinous and cruel crimes. The religion of multitudes of them is so interfused with local superstitions that it might almost be classed among the varieties of Hinduism. Changes, however, have been in progress in this respect during the last half-century, and there has been a tendency among the Mohammedans of Bengal, which is still maintained, towards the purification of their faith from Animistic superstitions and from Brahmanical influence. The great mass of the Musalman population is agricultural, but, even where it is most numerous, wealth and property in land are chiefly in the hands of the Hindus. If we look merely to numbers, the Lieutenant-Governor of Bengal is, as Sir William Hunter says, "as great a Musalman power as the Sultan of Turkey himself," but in our political speculations we need not alarm ourselves about the millions of Mohammedans in Bengal. They lack the capacity, the religious fervour, and the personal vigour which have at other times and in other places swept everything away before the onset of Islam. They have of late years been more and more awakened to the necessity of marching with the times, and of obtaining the advantages of English education, so that they may not be hopelessly defeated in all walks of life by the Hindus. This new development is increasing steadily, and much of the bigotry of former generations has already passed away.

The educated Mohammedans deserve to be named

with respect. They are not very numerous or wealthy, and cluster chiefly about Calcutta, Dacca, and Patna.

Many years ago Lord Macaulay gave a description of the Natives of Bengal. There is good reason, as I have already said, for calling in question the accuracy of some of his historical pictures, based on fallacious records, which have taught to thousands of Englishmen almost all that they know about India; but when Lord Macaulay wrote his character of the Bengális he was describing, from personal knowledge and observation, a people among whom he had himself lived. Its accuracy has hardly been denied by the Bengális themselves, and will be disputed by no Englishman.

"The men," he wrote, "by whom this rich tract was peopled, enervated by a soft climate and accustomed to peaceful employments, bore the same relation to other Asiatics which the Asiatics generally bear to the bold and energetic children of Europe. The Castilians have a proverb that in Valencia the earth is water and the men women; and this description is at least equally applicable to the vast plain of the Lower Ganges. Whatever the Bengalee does he does languidly. His favourite pursuits are sedentary. He shrinks from bodily exertion; and, though voluble in dispute, and singularly pertinacious in the war of chicane, he seldom engages in a personal conflict, and scarcely ever enlists as a soldier. There never, perhaps, existed a people so thoroughly fitted by habit for a foreign yoke."[1]

In another passage Lord Macaulay has passed upon the Bengális a similar judgment. I will quote a portion of it:—

"The physical organisation of the Bengalee is feeble even to effeminacy. He lives in a constant vapour-bath. His pursuits are sedentary, his limbs delicate, his movements languid. During many ages he has been trampled upon by men of bolder and more hardy breeds. . . . His mind bears a singular analogy

[1] Macaulay's *Essays*—"Lord Clive."

to his body. It is weak even to helplessness for purposes of manly resistance; but its suppleness and tact move the children of sterner climates to admiration not unmingled with contempt. . . . Nor does he lack a certain kind of courage which is often wanting to his masters. To inevitable evils he is sometimes found to oppose a passive fortitude, such as the Stoics attributed to their ideal sage. An European warrior who rushes on a battery of cannon with a loud hurrah will sometimes shriek under the surgeon's knife, and fall into an agony of despair at the sentence of death. But the Bengalee, who would see his country overrun, his house laid in ashes, his children murdered or dishonoured, without having the spirit to strike one blow, has yet been known to endure torture with the firmness of Mucius, and to mount the scaffold with the steady step and even pulse of Algernon Sidney."[1]

Lord Macaulay would have been the first to declare that we might find Bengális of a different stamp. Courage is no more an invariable virtue among the hardiest races of Europe than cowardice an invariable infirmity among the population of Bengal. There have been many changes since Lord Macaulay wrote, and among signs of increasing vigour, one that is not without significance has been, in late years, the development of a taste for athletic sports among the educated classes and in the Government schools and colleges. Gymnastics are often practised with some enthusiasm, and the Bengáli schoolboy has taken to cricket, hockey, and football, especially to the latter, which is now played all over the province. This, however, is true of a small section only of the population, and the general character of the people throughout the greater part of the province remains as Lord Macaulay represented it. It cannot, however, be applied to the northern and eastern districts, where the majority of the population is Mohammedan. The Mohammedan peasantry of the eastern portion of

[1] Macaulay's *Essays*—"Warren Hastings."

the province are men of far robuster character than the Bengális of the western districts; it was among them that the sepoys who fought under Clive at Plassey were chiefly recruited, and the maritime districts supply thousands of intrepid boatmen and lascars to the mercantile marine.

It has often been said, and it is probably true, that Bengal is the only country in the world where you can find a great population among whom personal cowardice is looked upon as in no way disgraceful. This is no invention of their enemies; the Bengális have themselves no shame or scruple in declaring it to be a fact. Even in the western parts of Bengal Proper and in Calcutta there can, however, be little doubt that English education, which has taken so deep a root, is encouraging the growth of manliness among other virtues, and is producing effects which are not limited to the young men trained in our colleges. The writers in the popular vernacular newspapers have begun to speak of patriotism and courage as qualities which should be presupposed to be present in characters worthy of respect. Even the academic admiration of such things is a mark of progress. The people generally are acute and intelligent, patient and industrious, and when they get more knowledge they may become more self-reliant and less helpless against wrong.

Leaving speculations on possible changes that may come to pass if our dominion should last sufficiently long, and looking to present facts, it is difficult to conceive for such a people as that of Bengal any independent political future. Neither in our own great Native army nor in the army of any Native State is there a Bengáli soldier; it would be impossible to induce Bengális to enlist, and equally impossible that the recruiting officers should accept them. Even the Darwán or door-keeper, who guards the entrance to a well-to-do Bengáli's house, is invariably a man of the more vigorous races of one of the northern provinces; no Bengáli would credit a countryman of his own with possession of sufficient courage to keep out a bold intruder. But for the presence of our power, Bengal would inevitably and immediately become the prey of the hardier races of other Indian countries.

The condition of the people of Bengal has been profoundly affected by action taken more than a century ago by the British Government. In 1793 the so-called Permanent Settlement of the Land Revenue was introduced.

We found in Bengal, when we succeeded to the Government, a class of middle-men, called Zemindars, who collected the land revenue and the taxes, and we continued to employ them. As a matter of custom and expediency, but not of right, the office of zemindar was generally hereditary. In a few cases, especially in Behár and Chutia Nágpur, the zemindars were the heads of large clans, or the descendants of conquering families, but even then they had never been in any sense recognised as the owners of the land. It was supposed, however, by Lord Cornwallis and the English rulers of the time, that it would be an excellent thing for Bengal to have a class of landlords something like those of England; the zemindars were the only people that seemed available for the purpose, and they were declared to be the proprietors of the land. It was by no means intended that injustice should thus be done to others. Nor, when the Settlement was made, did it appear that any great boon had been conferred upon the zemindars, for the Government demand was assessed on what we should now consider the extravagant basis that 90 per cent of the rental belonged properly to the State.

Excepting the State, there was only one great class, that of the ryots or actual cultivators, which, according to immemorial custom, could be held to possess permanent rights in the land. The existence of those rights was recognised, and, as it was supposed, guarded by the law. It was provided that "the Governor-General in Council will, whenever he may deem it proper, enact such regulations as he may think necessary for the protection of the dependent talookdars, ryots, and other cultivators of the soil." There has been much dispute as to the exact nature of the rights given to the zemindars, but every one agrees that it was not the intention of the authors of the Permanent Settlement to confiscate anything which, according to the customs of the country, had belonged to the cultivators. The right of property given to the zemindars was a portion of those rights which had always been exercised by the State, and of which the State was at liberty to dispose; it was not intended that they should receive anything else. The land revenue, representing the share of the produce or rental to which the State was entitled, was fixed in perpetuity. The ryots were to continue to hold their lands permanently at the "rates established in the purgunnah"; when the amount of those rates was disputed it was to be settled by the courts; so long as rents at those rates were paid, the ryot could not be evicted. The intention of the Permanent Settlement was not only to fix for ever the land revenue of the zemindars, but, at the same time, to secure to the ryot fixity of tenure and fixity of rent. There was in those days a great area of waste land, and the zemindars were entitled to the profit derived from its reclamation, but, unfortunately, the rights which it had been intended to secure for the ryots were only secured upon paper, and have been grievously disregarded.

If the intentions with which the Permanent Settlement was made had been carried out, the result would, at any rate, have been beneficial to the ryots of Bengal, whatever might have been the effect on the interests of the State. I described in a former chapter[1] the nature of the right, which the ruling power has always exercised in India, of reserving for its own purposes a portion of the rent of the land. It was a right which had been exercised in Bengal from time immemorial. This resource, which would have gone on growing with the increasing prosperity of the country, has been thrown away in Bengal. The consequences at the present time are these:—Even if it be assumed that the share of the rent which the State can wisely take is smaller than the share which any Government, Native or British, has ever taken or proposed to take in India, the amount now received by the State from the land in Bengal must be held to fall short of what it might have been by a sum that can hardly be less than £3,500,000 a year; this is a moderate computation—probably the loss is much more. This is given away in return for no service to the State or to the public; the zemindars are merely the receivers of rent; with rare exceptions they take little part in the improvement of the land, and, until not many years ago, they bore virtually no share of the public burdens. The result of these proceedings of 1793, to the maintenance of which the faith of the British Government has been pledged, is that the poorer classes in poorer provinces have to make good to the State the millions which have been given away in Bengal.

[1] Chapter IX.

More serious evils have followed in the train of the Permanent Settlement. The crowning misfortune has been the destruction or non-recognition of those rights of the masses of the agricultural population which the authors of the Settlement undoubtedly intended to preserve.

"The original intention of the framers of the Permanent Settlement" [I am quoting from Sir George Campbell] "was to record all rights. The Canoongoes (District Registrars) and Putwarees (Village Accountants) were to register all holdings, all transfers, all rent-rolls, and all receipts and payments; and every five years there was to be filed in the public offices a complete register of all land tenures. But the task was a difficult one; there was delay in carrying it out. English ideas of the rights of a landlord, and of the advantage of non-interference, began more and more to prevail in Bengal. The executive more and more abrogated the functions of recording rights and protecting the inferior holders, and left everything to the judicial tribunals. The putwarees fell into disuse or became the mere servants of the zemindars; the canoongoes were abolished. No record of the rights of the ryots and inferior holders was ever made, and even the quinquennial register of superior rights, which was maintained for a time, fell into disuse. When a regular police was established, the zemindars were in practice freed from any effective responsibility for the suppression of crime, or other administrative functions. They became in every sense mere rent-receivers."[1]

The consequences of the Permanent Settlement did not become immediately prominent. At the beginning of the last century the population was far smaller, there was much waste land to be occupied, and there was little disposition or power on the part of the zemindars to disregard the old customary terms on which the land was held. But, as time went on, and population and

[1] *System of Land Tenures in Various Countries*, published by the Cobden Club, p. 176.

wealth increased, as cultivators were more readily found, and custom began to give way to competition, the position of the ryots became worse and that of the zemindars became stronger. Other circumstances helped the process of confiscation of the rights of the peasantry. For more than half a century after the Permanent Settlement was made, the Executive Government in Bengal was extremely weak. The English principle that in the ordinary affairs of life the less the State interferes with individual action the better, and that for the protection of private rights little more is required than the maintenance of order, with good courts of justice accessible to all, is admirable when applied to the government of Englishmen, but it is unsuitable to India, and there could be no people to which it was less applicable than the people of Bengal. This principle of non-interference was carried out in that province to an extent unknown in any other part of India. Nothing would have so much helped the timid people of Bengal in social and political progress as the just and active and masterful administration of Englishmen, resolute that the rights of the weak should be respected, determined to satisfy themselves by personal knowledge that this was done, and possessing power to interfere effectively on behalf of those who could not protect themselves. A system of administration which left it to the courts of justice to remedy any oppression of which the sufferer might complain, or which he might be able to prove, practically resulted in providing no remedy at all.

I showed in a former chapter[1] that in other provinces of India an elaborate machinery has been spread over the whole country, extending its ramifications into every

[1] Chapter XIX.

village, for the purpose of maintaining an accurate record of the rights and liabilities of all classes of the agricultural population. In the greater part of Bengal nothing of the sort exists. There has been, until lately, no cadastral survey and no record of agricultural rights, but within the last ten years these have been introduced throughout North Behár, and in the greater part of Orissa, as well as in parts of other districts and in estates under Government management. Under the arrangements of the Permanent Settlement, the Government has no anxiety about the collection of its land revenue. The whole responsibility for punctual payment falls upon the zemindar. If he does not pay at the district treasury on the appointed date, no questions are asked; there may or may not have been causes which make immediate payment difficult; these are matters with which the Government does not concern itself; it is enough that the revenue is due; the estate is put up to public auction, and the demand of the State is the first claim on the proceeds of the sale. In consequence of this system, the Executive Government, so far as the collection of the land revenue is concerned, has little to do in the interior of a Bengal district, and financially there is little direct reason for interference with any interests in the land.

There were other causes for the weakness of government in Bengal. This being the province in which British authority was first established on that side of India, and from which our chief conquests were gradually made, the Government of Bengal was for a long time the Supreme Government in British India. Until 1833, the Governor-General was called the Governor-General of Fort William in Bengal, not the Governor-General of India, and it was not until 1853 that he was relieved from the duty of governing Bengal. While the empire was being constantly extended, he could spend comparatively little time in Calcutta. When he was there, he was by law Governor, but it was impossible for him to attend personally to the details of Bengal administration. When he was absent from Calcutta, the senior member of Council for the time being became Deputy Governor. Thus there was a frequent change of rulers, and no one man was long responsible for the good government of the province. At last, the contrast between the condition of Bengal and that of other parts of India became too obvious to be neglected. This was especially seen when Bengal was compared with the neighbouring province on the north, which in 1835 had been placed under a separate Government. When the North-Western Provinces, under their admirable Lieutenant-Governor, Mr. Thomason, were becoming a model of good and vigorous administration, Bengal was the most backward of the great provinces of India. There were almost no roads or bridges or schools, and there was no proper protection to life and property. The police was worthless, and robberies and violent crimes by gangs of armed men, which were unheard of in other provinces, were common not far from Calcutta.

By the Act of 1853 a separate provincial Government was constituted for Bengal, and a Lieutenant-Governor was appointed. From that time a great change began, and constant improvement has been going on ever since. The courts have been purified, the police has been organised, crimes of violence have almost ceased, public works have been constructed, education has made great progress, and, although still weak when judged by the standard of other provinces, the executive administration has become stronger. Not the least beneficial of these changes were the measures which soon began to be adopted, but of which we have not seen the end, for the protection of the rights of the agricultural population.

The difficulty of the problems to be solved in Bengal has been great. In 1793 the rental left to the zemindars under the Permanent Settlement, after payment of the land revenue, is supposed not to have exceeded £400,000; according to some estimates it was less. If the original intentions of the Government had been carried out, it was to the ryots that the greater portion of any future increase in the annual value of the land would have belonged, in those parts at least of the province which were at that time well cultivated. It is not possible to state with confidence the present gross annual rental of the landlords. According to an official valuation admitted to be imperfect, it was said, in 1891-92, to be about £10,000,000, and in 1901 to be about £11,200,000. It is certainly much more. However this may be, it may be safely assumed that after deducting the land revenue, which is now about £2,700,000, the net rental is thirty or forty times larger at the present time than it was a century ago. In some parts of Bengal the increase has been far greater, and this has mainly resulted from the destruction of the rights of the peasantry. Hardly any of it has been due to the legitimate action of the zemindars. That part of it which has not been due to worse causes has been due to the increase of population, to the industry of the ryots, and to the expenditure of the State, an expenditure defrayed, in great measure, from the taxation of poorer provinces. If ever there was an "unearned increment" it is this.

It must not, however, be supposed that the land

of Bengal now belongs to a small and wealthy class of proprietors. Although some of the estates of the zemindars are great tracts of country, yielding immense incomes to their owners, a constant process of subdivision has been going on. In 1901 the number of estates in the whole province had increased to 186,583, of which 152,824 or nearly 82 per cent were petty estates paying less than 100 rupees as revenue, with an average area of only 51 acres and an average assessment of 24 rupees per annum.

We cannot now restore to the State the large revenue which has been sacrificed; we cannot replace the ryots in the enjoyment of the property of which they have been deprived, and give to them again the rates of rent which have been so enormously increased, but we can at least secure to them protection for the rights they still retain, and prevent the further illegal enhancement of their payments.

I am far from suggesting that pledges given at the time of the Permanent Settlement should be set aside, or that the zemindars should be deprived of privileges which, however they may have been acquired, have been enjoyed through a long course of years. So far, however, as it is now possible, without breach of engagements which we are bound to maintain, to remedy evils such as these which I have been describing, it is our obvious duty to do so.

The zemindars have repeatedly put forward the claim that in consequence of the stipulations of the Permanent Settlement they are entitled to exemption for ever from all taxation upon profits derived from the land. In 1859, when an income tax was first imposed on every kind of property throughout India, they protested that the conditions of the Settlement were violated, and that the Government had been guilty of a breach of faith. In 1871, and again in 1877, they demanded, on similar grounds, exemption from liability to rates imposed on land and other immovable property for local and provincial roads and public works, for sanitation, education, and other local objects. These claims have always been rejected, and the time has passed in which there was danger that any British Government would listen to the pretension that it was the design of the framers of the Permanent Settlement that no taxation should ever fall upon profits drawn from the land. The intention of that Settlement was simply to fix permanently the share of the produce or rental to which the State, in its capacity of superior landlord, intended to limit its demand. No questions of taxation were touched or involved. In the words of Sir James Stephen, the Permanent Settlement "reduced to a certainty one particular charge on the land, which had previously been of variable amount, and so freed the landholders from uncertainty which had previously hung over them in respect of it. . . . Since the Permanent Settlement the proprietary right of the zemindars has been undoubted, and the line between their property and that of the State has been clearly defined, and is no longer subject to increase 'in consequence' (to use the words of the Permanent Settlement itself) 'of the improvement of their respective estates.'"[1] As Sir James Stephen went on to say, to affirm, that because this has been done, the land has been freed from that liability to taxation which is the common liability of all property in all countries, is a confusion of thought against which it is superfluous to argue. Under Acts passed in 1871 and 1877, and consolidated by Bengal Act IX. of 1880,

[1] Speech in the Legislative Council, 6th April 1871.

rates were imposed upon the land, and they yielded in 1900-01 about £620,000. By these rates, and by the previous imposition of the income tax, the principle that profits derived from the land are liable to taxation both for local and imperial purposes was affirmed. Within the last few years proposals have been made to impose a cess for the payment of patwáris, and also an educational cess, and though these measures have not in fact been enforced, the reason for abstention was not that they would have infringed the conditions of the Permanent Settlement, but that the necessity for them had passed away for the time.

The first serious effort for the improvement of the rent-law of Bengal was made in 1859, when an Act dealing with the subject was passed. Its chief object was to place restrictions on the landlord's powers of enhancement, distraint, and eviction, and to declare the conditions under which occupancy rights accrued to the ryots. It was described by Lord Canning as "a real and earnest attempt to improve the position of the ryots of Bengal, and to open to them a prospect of freedom and independence which they have not hitherto enjoyed, by clearly defining their rights, and by placing restrictions on the power of the zemindars such as ought long ago to have been provided." The intentions of the Legislature were excellent, but the Act proved imperfect and insufficient, and in some respects made matters worse than they were before. As time went on the difficulties increased. In Eastern Bengal the state of affairs became highly unsatisfactory; combinations of ryots to refuse the payment of any rent occurred, and violent collisions took place between them and the zemindars, aggravated by the fact that the former were mostly Mohammedans and the latter Hindus. In 1876 it became necessary to legislate for the prevention of agrarian disputes.

In Behár the case was more serious. This great province of Bengal has an area of 32,000 square miles, and a population of more than nineteen and a half millions. There is hardly any part of British India possessing greater natural advantages of soil and climate, and no part where the condition of the agricultural population is more precarious, or the margin of subsistence smaller. This was a cause of much anxiety to Lord Lawrence when he was Viceroy, and he stated his belief that legislation would become necessary for the protection of the ryot, "and make him what he is now only in name, a free man." In 1878, Sir Ashley Eden, then Lieutenant-Governor of Bengal, described the ryots of Behár as "poor, helpless, discontented men, bound down to a state of extreme depression and misery, tenants of the richest province in Bengal, yet the poorest and most wretched class we find in the country. . . . The loose system of zemindari accounts, the entire absence of leases and counterparts, the universal prevalence of illegal distraint, the practice of amalgamating holdings so as to destroy evidence of continuous occupation, are evils which necessarily prevent any possible development of agricultural prosperity among the tenant class, and place them entirely at the mercy of their landlords." The Indian Famine Commissioners of 1880, not long afterwards, pressed the same subject on the attention of the Government.

"Where," they said, "as in Behár, the relations of landlord and tenant are those of a high-handed proprietary body on the one hand, habitually disregarding the law, and on the other a tenantry, ignorant, very helpless, and sunk in the most abject poverty, the onus of bringing complaints ought not to be laid on the tenants, and the first and most important duty of the Bengal Government and of the officials would seem to be to guard zealously against infringements of the law by the rich, and to put them down as if they were offences against the public peace." "It was proved," writes Mr. Finucane, the head of the Agricultural Department in Bengal, "by indisputable evidence, that the rents of ryots in Behár have during the past fifty years been illegally and arbitrarily enhanced out of all proportion to what the landlords were under the law entitled to demand, and to what the tenants were legally liable to pay. Though the rent law gave the ryot certain rights, he was so helpless or so ignorant that he was unable to assert these rights out of court, or to go into court to enforce them."

I will make a few more extracts from official reports regarding the condition of the people in parts of Behár.

"The gross rental of permanently settled estates being at the lowest estimate five times the amount payable by landholders as Government revenue, there can, as a matter of course, be no difficulty in realising that revenue under the sunset law. But there are certain tracts in which, though the permanently settled land revenue may be realised, yet the sums realised by the Government have had again to be expended, many fold increased, on charitable relief which became necessary in order to prevent mortality by starvation. Such pre-eminently is the province of Behár, and specially the three northern districts of Darbhanga, Mozaffarpur, and Sáran. Within a period of seventeen years there have been five in which a portion of the people of this part of the province have died of starvation. The whole conditions of agricultural industry are such as to render it precarious. It is impossible for the people to fall back in one year of partial failure of crops on the accumulated reserves of a previous year, whether of grain, property, money, or credit. Thus, in the one district of Darbhanga, which is taken as being the worst of all in these respects—a district which is one of the most fertile, best cultivated, and highly favoured by nature in all India—it was necessary for the Government to expend in one year, on one famine in 1874, by way of charitable relief, no less than £370,000 in cash, and 118,000 tons of grain, valued in Burma at £9 per ton. If to this be added the cost of transport, and cost of famine establishment, it will not be too much to put down the net cost of famine to Government in this single district at £1,500,000, the Government revenue being less than £50,000 per annum. The famine expenditure in this district, in one year, was more than thirty times the amount of the Government revenue, and far more than its capitalised value. . . . Yet the rental of the district was no less than twelve times the amount of the Government revenue. It is not alone on famine relief that enormous sums have been expended in this part of the country. There has been also a great outlay on State railways, which, though they may facilitate the importation of grain in times of distress, can in ordinary times be of little benefit to the mass of the peasantry ; for it is evident that so long as landlords are permitted to take advantage of the local competition for land in order to enhance rents illegally, it is they, and they only, who appropriate the profits resulting from that rise in prices which attends the opening up of means of communication. Besides £200,000 expended on a temporary famine railway to Darbhanga in 1874, there has been an expenditure on the Tirhut State railway of £1,300,000 within the past ten years."[1]

Much, however, has been done, since the facts just quoted were described, to ameliorate the condition of the peasantry in Behár. The Tenancy Act which became law in 1885 defined the position of tenants, and this has been still further consolidated by the institution, still in progress, of a cadastral survey and record of rights. In the famine of 1897 it was found that only a small proportion of the tenantry accepted relief, and the extent of their resources surpassed the general expectation ; those who were employed on relief works belonged almost entirely to the class of landless day labourers, the numbers of whom were large.

Some of the zemindars of Behár are among the richest men in India. The estates of the Rája of Darbhanga, in

[1] *Report of the Agricultural Department in Bengal for 1886.*

the district just mentioned, have an area of 2400 square miles, a population of more than 750,000, and a rental exceeding £130,000 a year. The increase in the net rental of the zemindars of North Behár in the last three generations has been immense. At the time of the Permanent Settlement it was about £3000, and in 1893, a hundred years later, it was about £2,400,000, or eighty times greater.[1] If the intentions of the framers of the Settlement had been carried out, the larger part of this vast sum would have been in the possession of the unfortunate peasants whose rights have been swept away.

Happily, the condition of the agricultural population in the greater part of Bengal is much better than in Behár; the necessity for their protection was urgent, but they were not reduced to a condition such as that common in Behár; climatic conditions are such that the productive powers of the land are not precarious, and they live, as a rule, in reasonable comfort.

The discussion of the measures required for placing the law of landlord and tenant throughout Bengal on a better footing continued for many years. In 1885 the "Bengal Tenancy Act" was passed by the Governor-General in Council, mainly with the view of benefiting the tenantry of Behár. I will not attempt to describe all its provisions, but its value cannot be doubted. It aimed at giving protection to the ryots without interfering with the rights of landlords. It defined the position of the various classes of landlords and tenants, the incidents of the various tenures, the conditions under which rights of occupancy in the land could be acquired and maintained, the manner in which rents were to be

[1] "Minute by Sir Antony MacDonnell, Officiating Lieutenant-Governor of Bengal, 21st September 1893."

regulated, enhanced, and reduced, the circumstances under which evictions might take place; it imposed penalties for illegal exactions, laid down rules regarding compensation for improvements, gave power to the Government to order surveys and the preparation of records of rights, and dealt with a multitude of other matters of importance. There has undoubtedly been in recent years immense improvement. In the words of a paper which has been already quoted, "the rise in the price of agricultural produce has benefited all who have such produce to sell. For a long time the landlords contrived to appropriate the greater part of the benefit, but partly owing to the increase in the number of districts and the creation of subdivisions, which have let the light of day into the remotest parts of the country, and partly owing to the Bengal Tenancy Act and the operations under it, a fair share has at last been secured to the ryot."[1]

The passing of the Tenancy Act was an excellent measure, and its results have been most valuable. More is required, but much progress has been and is being made. I have shown that in other parts of British India there has been a survey of every field, and that a permanent record is maintained of all rights and interests in the land. This, in other provinces, is the basis of our system of administration. Without such basis, in a country where nearly the whole population is agricultural, neither the executive authorities nor the courts of justice have the means of obtaining the knowledge essential to the protection of the most important interests of the people. In land disputes the first essential is to know accurately where the land is situated,

[1] "Memorandum on the Material Condition of the People of Bengal," by L. P. Shirres, C.S.

and its area; in all questions of transfer, or sale, or rent, or tenure, this knowledge is required, and there are, in the greater part of Bengal, no means of supplying it. In this province, until a few years ago, there were virtually no detailed surveys, no revenue maps, no records of rights; there was universal ignorance of almost all facts connected with the greatest industry of the country, which it was the most necessary to know.

The first steps, however, have been taken to wipe away this disgrace. A cadastral or field survey was begun in 1892 in the province of Behár, accompanied by a record of all existing rights in land, and this is still being carried out under the provisions of the Bengal Tenancy Act. The Government contributes towards the cost of these operations, but the greater portion of it is apportioned between the zemindars and ryots, who directly benefit by the survey. This measure at first met with much opposition from the zemindars. The traditions of administration in Bengal, to which I have referred, had not accustomed them to such an interference on the part of the Government, although this was no more than has been done in every other province of British India, and they not unnaturally disliked payment of the cost. In other provinces the expenditure on cadastral surveys is defrayed from the Imperial treasury, but they are accompanied by a re-settlement of the land revenue, and the result is usually an enhancement of its amount. In Bengal, the settlement being permanent, the State receives no such advantage, and it would be unreasonable to call on the general Indian taxpayer to provide the means of meeting an expenditure the objects and benefits of which are purely local. But as time has passed, the zemindars equally with the tenantry have recognised the value of these operations, and they have learned to appreciate the great advantages which an accurate record brings to them. While this important work has been carried on in the permanently settled districts of Bengal, a work of not less importance to the good of the people has been brought to a conclusion in the province of Orissa, of which two-thirds are temporarily settled. This province had not known settlement operations for sixty years, but the present settlement was concluded in the space of ten years (1890-1900), and has resulted in a substantial increase of assessment, with practically no friction or opposition whatever.

Every measure of political importance is discussed by the organs of the educated classes. Not long ago there could be no doubt as to what would be the reception of any measure that seemed to threaten the interests of the zemindars. No taxation affecting them could be imposed without the cry being raised that the solemn pledges of the Permanent Settlement were being violated by an unscrupulous Government. Every measure which has had for its object the more just distribution of the public burdens has, as a rule, met with nothing but opposition. We were told that to reduce the salt tax was folly; let it be increased if the Government wants more money. The abolition of customs duties on cotton goods was solely prompted by the desire to benefit the manufacturers of Manchester, and by the base political purpose of gaining votes in Lancashire. Educated Bengális were not to be deceived by the profession that we desired to give to the people of India cheaper salt and cheaper clothing. It is, I fear, impossible to deny that English education in Bengal has given frequent aid to the perpetration of injustice and to the prevention of reform.

It has sometimes been loudly asserted by persons imperfectly acquainted with the facts, that in Bengal, in consequence of the Permanent Settlement, the country has been preserved from famine, that the cultivators are more prosperous than in other parts of India, that agricultural enterprise has been fostered, and private capital accumulated which has been devoted to useful industries and to public works and industries. I have already referred to the exhaustive inquiry made by the Government of Lord Curzon in 1901 into the whole subject of the Land Revenue administration throughout India. The conclusions arrived at were established by a mass of unimpeachable evidence. It was shown that there was no foundation whatever for any such contentions as those which had been urged. Failure of the periodical rains is far less common than in the greater part of India, but when it has occurred, Bengal has suffered like other provinces. As regards the condition of cultivators there is, the Government of India demonstrated, not only no ground for the contention that their position, owing to the Permanent Settlement, has been converted into one of exceptional comfort and prosperity, but such assertions are directly contrary to the fact. "It is precisely because this was not the case, and because, so far from being generously treated by the zemindars, the Bengal cultivator was rack-rented, impoverished, and oppressed, that the Government of India felt compelled to intervene on his behalf, and by the series of legislative measures that commenced with the Bengal Tenancy Act of 1859 and culminated in the Act of 1885, to place him in the position of greater security which he now enjoys. As for the allegation that the Permanent Settlement has been the means of developing in Bengal an exceptional flow of public-spirited and charitable investment, while the Government of India are proud of the fact that there are many worthy and liberal-minded landlords in Bengal—as there are also in other parts of India—they know that the evils of absenteeism, of management of estates by unsympathetic agents, of unhappy relations between landlord and tenant, and of the multiplication of tenure-holders or middle-men between the zemindar and cultivator in many and various degrees, are at least as marked and as much on the increase there as elsewhere; and they cannot conscientiously endorse the proposition that, in the interests of the cultivator, that system of agrarian tenure should be held up as a public model which is not supported by the experience of any civilised country, which is not justified by the single great experiment that has been made in India, and which was found in the latter case to place the tenant so unreservedly at the mercy of the landlord that the State has been compelled to employ for his protection a more stringent measure of legislation than has been found necessary in temporarily settled areas. It is not, in fine, in the Permanent Settlement of Bengal that the ryot has found his salvation; it has been in the laws which have been passed by the Supreme Government to check its license and to moderate its abuses."[1]

[1] *Papers regarding the Revenue System of British India*, presented to Parliament, p. 3

CHAPTER XXIII

THE ARMY IN INDIA

The ultimate basis of our dominion—Indian interests beyond the limits of India—The advance of Russia—Defence of North-West Frontier —The Frontier tribes—Formation of the North-West Frontier Province—Results of the advance of Russia—The armies of India before 1857—The Mutinies—The reorganisation of the Native Army—Its present constitution—Its fighting qualities—The Bengal Army—The Officers of the Indian Army—The Police—Increase of the army in 1885—Present strength—The British troops—Improvement in their health—Hill stations—Frontier and Port defences—Volunteers—Changes in 1893 in constitution of Army—Existing commands—Armies of the Native States—Special contingents for Imperial service.

In this book I profess to speak of nothing except of India itself, its internal administration, and its progress under British rule. There are other subjects, of the utmost gravity, with which Indian interests are intimately connected, of which, although I am silent regarding them, it must not be supposed that I fail to recognise the importance, believing, as I do, that the position of England as the greatest Power of the world, with which, indeed, her national existence in a form worthy of her is inseparably bound up, depends upon the maintenance of her Indian Empire. The ultimate basis of our dominion in India is obviously our military or, to speak more accurately, our naval power, and this to be efficient must be capable of being exercised on sea and land not only within India itself but far beyond her borders. The problems connected with the advance of Russia to the frontiers of Afghánistán, and our relations with the latter country are far from their final solution. In Persia and the Persian Gulf, in Arabia, in Africa, in Tibet, in China, and in Siam there are great Indian and Imperial interests which, let us trust, British statesmen will never forget, and which they will defend with all the power of the empire. By the military positions that we now occupy and by the construction of railways, we have gained for the north-western frontiers of India a great accession of military and political strength, and a not less important step towards that end has been the adoption of wiser methods in dealing with the wild and warlike tribes which have given to us such constant causes of anxiety. These causes still remain, but those most competent to judge now look forward hopefully to the time when they may cease to be, as they have been in the past, a serious source of military weakness. A most important step towards that end was the formation, in 1901, of the North-West Frontier Province, by which the frontier districts were severed from the Punjab, and placed under a separate administration under the immediate control of the Supreme Government. This measure, advocated long ago by Lord Lytton, although in a different form, as a matter of urgent necessity, was at last successfully accomplished by Lord Curzon.

All these are subjects into which I cannot enter, but it must never be forgotten how profoundly the proximity of a great European Power has altered our position in India, and that it is not only our military position that has been affected. The change has been felt throughout India. It has thrown into the minds of men uncertainties regarding the future; it has disturbed the finances, and thus has retarded the progress of works essential to the prosperity of the country, and checked improvement in the administration. No Englishman who deserves the name will for a moment doubt our resolution to maintain our Empire, or that we can render India invulnerable, but statesmen will do well to remember that nothing can save us, sooner or later, from attack, except the certainty on the part of those who may desire to assail us, that every hostile attempt must end in disastrous failure. The condition among all others obviously essential to our success is one on which I need not dilate: absolute supremacy at sea gave to us our empire, and without it the maintenance of that empire in India or elsewhere will be impossible.

Although I can say nothing more on the serious subjects to which I have been referring, some account must be given of the constitution of the army in India.

In the earlier times of the East India Company, a military force grew up in each of the three presidencies of Bengal, Madras, and Bombay. Three distinct armies came into existence, and until not long ago they still remained.

The principal extensions of territory having occurred, since the beginning of the nineteenth century, in the presidency of Bengal, the army of Bengal became the most important of the three; in 1856, the year before the mutinies, it was more numerous than the other two armies together. In that year the British forces in India consisted of 39,000 Europeans and 215,000 Natives, besides several contingents, as they were called, maintained for the protection of Native States, and at their expense.

The Native army of Bengal, consisting in 1856 of

seventy-four regiments of infantry, with ten regiments of regular and eighteen of irregular cavalry, was mainly recruited, especially for the infantry, from the Brahmans and Rájputs of Oudh, and in a lesser degree from the North-Western Provinces. A part of the Bombay army and of the contingents was supplied from the same classes. The army of Madras was recruited from its own presidency. Besides the regular army, and various local corps, there was a strong force of so-called irregular cavalry and infantry, the most important part of which was raised in the Punjab from Sikhs, Patháns, and other warlike races. This body of troops, known as the Punjab Frontier Force, guarded the northern frontier, and was under the orders of the Provincial Government. The greater part of the artillery in India was manned by Native soldiers.

About one-third of the European infantry, and all the European artillery were local troops, raised by the East India Company for permanent service in India. They numbered about 14,000 men.

In 1857 almost the whole of the Bengal Native army, a part of that of Bombay, and the contingents in Northern India, mutinied. The Madras army remained faithful. The Punjab Frontier Force was not only faithful, but rendered admirable service in the suppression of the revolt.

Before peace was restored the old Bengal army had ceased to exist. The Government was transferred to the Crown, and the whole military organisation was altered. The local European army was abolished. The artillery, which had been chiefly Native, became almost wholly British. The place of the local European infantry was supplied by British regiments of the line. The total strength of European troops was largely increased, while that of the Native army was largely diminished. Three distinct armies—those of Bengal, Madras, and Bombay—were still maintained. After the new arrangements had been completed, the army in India consisted of about 62,000 British and 135,000 Native troops.

I quote from the Report of the Indian Army Commission of 1879 the following summary of the changes made after the mutinies; but, as I shall show, it became necessary in 1885 to increase the numbers both of British and Native troops:—

"On the reorganisation of the army, after the mutiny was quelled, it was decided that the proportion of Native and European troops in India should never greatly exceed two to one, and that the field and other artillery should be exclusively, or almost exclusively, manned by Europeans. . . . All the fortresses in the country are now served by British artillery. All the heavy batteries and all the batteries of field artillery are manned by Europeans. The lessons taught by the mutiny have thus led to the maintenance of the two great principles of retaining in the country an irresistible force of British troops, and of keeping the artillery in the hands of Europeans.

"Our position in the country has very materially changed, and a force of 62,000 European soldiers represents a power far in excess of that which it represented in 1857. In those days the British troops were scattered in small forces throughout the country, and it was a matter of great difficulty, delay, and expense to concentrate even a small British force on any one spot in India. When the mutiny broke out we had hardly 400 miles of railway complete in the country, while at the present moment we have 8312 miles of railway open.[1]

"All our great cantonments, all our fortresses and arsenals, save one, are now connected with each other, and with the seaboard, by railway. The strength of our European troops for action at any point, within or without the borders of British India, has thus been enormously increased. For example, whereas

[1] In 1902 nearly 28,000 miles of railway were open or under construction.

in 1857 a regiment took three or four months to march from the seaboard to Lahore, it can now move from Calcutta to Lahore in a week. Reinforcements from England, which then occupied three months on a voyage round the Cape, now land in Bombay within thirty days of leaving England. Again, the power of British troops has been indefinitely increased by their armament with breech-loading rifles, and by the substitution of rifled field-pieces of higher power for the smooth-bore six-pounder, nine-pounder, and mountain guns of the mutiny era. In any contest within the borders, or on the frontiers of India, these improved armaments would tell heavily; for the troops of Afghánistan, Burma, Nepál, Gwalior, Hyderabad, and the Cis-Sutlej States, are for the most part still armed with smooth-bore muzzle-loading weapons."

Before the mutinies of 1857, the infantry of the Bengal army was, as I have already said, mainly recruited from the Brahmans and Rájputs of Oudh and the North-Western Provinces. Although men of fine physique, they were not remarkable for fighting efficiency, and the former reputation of the Native army of Bengal was certainly exaggerated. Most of its triumphs were mainly due to the British troops who were associated with it. The ruinous consequences of drawing the larger proportion of our soldiers from a single class, under the influence of the same feelings and interests, and holding more than any other people in India the strictest prejudices of caste, were shown by the events of 1857. The old system was abandoned, and I quote from the Report of the Indian Army Commission a description of that which took its place :—

"The systems of recruiting for the several armies are diverse. Regiments of the Madras and Bombay armies draw their recruits from many tribes and castes over the several recruiting grounds of those presidencies, and the Bombay regiments have an admixture of Sikhs and Hindustanis from Northern India in their ranks. These armies are thus composed of what are called 'mixed recruits'—that is to say, of corps in which men of different races, several religions, and many provinces are thrown together into the same company or troop. In the Bengal and Punjab armies the majority of corps are what are called 'class-company regiments'—that is to say, the regiments draw recruits from three or more different races and recruiting grounds, but the men of each class or race are kept apart in separate companies. Thus, an infantry regiment may have two companies of Sikhs, two companies of Hindustani Brahmans and Rájputs, two companies of Punjabi Mohammedans, one company of Trans-Indus Patháns, and one company of Dogras from the Kángra or Jamu hills: such a regiment would be a class-company regiment; the native officers of each company would ordinarily belong to the race, tribe, or sect from which the company was recruited. In the Northern army are a limited number of 'class regiments,' which are composed of men belonging to one caste or tribe. Such, for instance, are the Gurkha corps, recruited entirely from the hardy short-statured highlanders of the Nepál hills, the Pioneer regiments, which consist exclusively of men of the Muzbi tribe, who in the early days of Sikh rule were despised outcasts, whose noblest calling was thieving, but who are now among the flower of the Northern army."

During the last few years further changes have been made with the object of securing greater military efficiency, and important reforms have been carried out in the Bengal, Madras, and Bombay armies.

The system of "class regiments" has been extended to the infantry of the Bengal army, and each battalion of this force is now composed of men of one race—Brahmans, Jats, or Rájputs, as the case may be.

In the infantry of the Bombay army Sikhs are no longer recruited. They are now grouped in battalions by themselves, or in class-company regiments serving in the Punjab, or in Burma. Nearly all cavalry regiments, however, except in Madras, include a considerable proportion of these admirable soldiers in their ranks.

In Madras the changes have been many. The annexation of Burma, which rendered necessary the maintenance of a garrison in that country, has been one of the chief causes, and several battalions for which men of Madras were formerly recruited in class-company regiments now enlist Punjabis, Gurkhas, and other men of Northern India. The experiment is also being made of forming Moplahs and men of Coorg into class regiments, and it is hoped that these and other tribes will furnish useful contingents to the army.

The Native army is recruited by voluntary enlistment. The infantry are clothed, armed, and equipped by the State, but the men provide their own food, and, with some assistance, they themselves, according to the old custom of the country, build the lines in which they live. On foreign service beyond sea, or in campaigns beyond the frontiers of India, they receive rations from the Commissariat. Except in the Madras command, where the Native cavalry are in these respects on the same footing as the infantry, this branch of the service is organised on what is called the Silladár system. The men provide their own uniform, their arms, excepting breech-loading carbines, their equipment, and their horses; they feed themselves and their horses, build their own lines, and provide their own camp equipage and carriage on the line of march. Their pay is fixed at a rate which enables them to meet all these charges.

Considering the great variety of the sources from which the Native army is recruited, there is much variety in its military qualities, and all recent measures have been designed with the object of enabling the Government of India to place rapidly in the field the largest possible number of troops composed of the best fighting material. It would be difficult to find in any country finer soldiers than Sikhs, Patháns, and Gurkhas, and in case of necessity there would be no difficulty in making at short notice a large addition to their numbers. There can be no doubt that a large portion of our Native army is now equal to the troops of any European State, and is fit to take its place anywhere in the field by the side of British soldiers.

The most efficient section of the Native army is undoubtedly that of the North, stationed in the Punjab and on the north-western frontier, and consisting entirely of men belonging to the most vigorous and martial races of India. Among its other excellent elements it comprises several battalions of Gurkhas, soldiers whose fighting qualities can hardly be surpassed. The Punjab Frontier Force, a most efficient body, formed until some years ago a virtually distinct army under the Government of the Punjab, and although it has since been brought, like the rest of the army, under the orders of the Commander-in-Chief, it retains its separate organisation.

Although the old name of the "Bengal Army" has been partially retained, it had, as already noticed, long become somewhat of a misnomer, for there was not a single native of Bengal in its ranks, and only a small part of it was ever stationed in Bengal. In Bengal Proper there are a few thousand men at places on the railway connecting Calcutta with Northern India, and near the frontier of Nepal and other Hill States, and there are usually four or five thousand men in Calcutta and its neighbourhood. In the rest of the Lieutenant-Governorship of Bengal, with its population of more than 78,000,000, there are hardly any troops. Sir William Hunter was well within the mark when he said that, in that province, "probably 40,000,000 of people go through life without once seeing the gleam of a bayonet or the face of a soldier."

The "Officers of the Indian Army," known until the 1st January 1903 under the designation of the "Indian Staff Corps," supply the British officers of the Native army. A Staff Corps for each of the three armies of Bengal, Madras, and Bombay was established in 1861, when the Native army was reorganised. The officers of the Corps were, in the first instance, transferred from the East India Company's Army, and subsequently they were drawn from British regiments of the line or artillery. In 1891 the three Staff Corps were amalgamated into a single body, and the Officers of the Indian Army, as they are now called, are about 2700 in number. They are mainly recruited by the appointment of candidates from the Royal Military College at Sandhurst, but some are accepted from the British army serving in India. After the probation of a year's duty with a British regiment in India, and another year's duty with a Native regiment, and after passing examinations in the Native languages and in professional subjects, an officer is finally approved for service, and he is then eligible for staff employment or command in any part of India. In respect of regimental appointments, an officer ordinarily remains with the territorial branch of the army to which he was first posted, but he may be transferred by exchange to a regiment belonging to another command. The Officers of the Indian Army are employed not only in the Native army and in military appointments on the staff, but also in a large number of civil posts. They hold the majority of appointments in the political, or, as we should call it in England, the diplomatic department, and many administrative and judicial offices in non-regulation provinces.

Before 1857 duties were often performed by the Native army which were really duties of police, and the great reduction, amounting to more than 90,000 men, made in the numbers of the army after the suppression of the mutinies, was followed by a complete reorganisation of the police throughout India. The number of men available for military duty was, therefore, not diminished to the extent that the figures seem to show. Exclusive of the village police, of whom there are some 700,000, the regular police force in India consists of about 170,000 officers and men, of whom more than half have firearms, and are more or less drilled. There is no part of British India in which the people habitually carry arms, or commonly possess them, and the occasions are rare—not, on an average, more than two or three in each year—on which, usually in consequence of religious disputes between Hindus and Mohammedans, or between other sects, it is necessary to call out troops to assist the civil power in maintaining order. Considering that the population of British India exceeds that of the five Great Powers of Europe together, this furnishes an illustration of the quiet character of the people.

In 1885 the altered position of Russia on the frontiers of Afghánistán, and the apprehension of war, rendered it necessary to reconsider the whole question of our military position. The result was a determination to increase both the European and Native army. The British force received an addition, in cavalry, artillery, and infantry, of about 11,000 officers and men, while the number of the Native troops was increased by 19,000. Five new battalions of Gurkhas were added to the infantry. Altogether the army in

India was increased by about 30,000 men. In 1900 the total strength was nearly 223,000 officers and men of all arms, of whom rather more than 76,000 were British. This is exclusive of the active Reserve, consisting of men who have served with the colours in the Native infantry from five to twelve years. There are now about 20,000 men in the Reserve, but it may ultimately attain much larger proportions.

Apart from the addition to its numbers, the efficiency of the British troops in India has been greatly increased by other causes. Among all the changes that have occurred since the transfer of the Government to the Crown, there is not one over which we have better reason to rejoice than the improvement in the health of our soldiers. The Royal Commission which inquired in 1859 into the sanitary condition of the army reported that the average death-rate among the British troops in India, for the forty years ending with 1856, had been 69 per thousand. This was six times as high as the rate among Englishmen of the same ages at home. The Commission expressed the hope that the rate might be reduced by measures of sanitary improvement to 20 per thousand, or even lower. This hope has been more than fulfilled. In the ten years ending with 1879 the death-rate was 19 per thousand, and during recent years the average has been less than 16 per thousand.[1] No efforts have been spared to improve in every way the position of the British soldiers in India. They now live in barracks which, in comfort and in all sanitary conditions, excepting those conditions of climate over which we have no control, probably surpass any that

[1] It must be admitted that this comparison is not altogether accurate, because the figures given by the Royal Commission included all the deaths that had occurred in the numerous campaigns of the previous forty years. Making, however, allowance for this, the rate of mortality was extremely high.

can be found in any other country. Every regiment, battery, and depot has its regimental institute, a sort of soldiers' club, with refreshment department, library, reading and recreation rooms, a temperance association room, and a theatre. The issue of spirits has been diminished, and is discouraged, while every encouragement is given to useful employment and occupation for the men. Cantonments for 25 per cent of the whole force have been provided at stations in the Himálaya or other mountains. The education of soldiers' children is provided for partly in regimental schools and partly in the Lawrence Asylums in the hills, excellent institutions, originally founded by the liberality of Sir Henry Lawrence, and now largely assisted by the Government.

Other measures have greatly added to our military strength in India. All points on the north-western frontier at which attack seems possible are now guarded by strongly-fortified positions, and connected with the railway system of India; the principal ports have been fortified and armed with modern guns, and the defence of the harbours is secured by a flotilla of turret-ships, torpedo gunboats, and torpedo boats. The Native army and Volunteers have been, or are about to be, armed with the latest pattern rifle, and the establishment of a cordite factory will render the army self-supporting, to a great extent, in regard to its ammunition in case of necessity. Another very important measure has been the formation of Volunteer corps. There are already in India 31,000 Volunteers, nearly all British, of whom 30,000 are effective and well armed. The defensive value of this force can hardly be over-stated. If it had existed in 1857, many of the catastrophes of that time would undoubtedly have been prevented.

Supreme authority over the army in India is

vested by law[1] in the Governor-General in Council. The Military Member of Council has charge of the Military Department, which corresponds to the War Office in England. Subject to the administrative control of the Governor-General in Council, the chief executive officer of the army is the Commander-in-Chief in India. Until 1893 he held special command of the troops in the Bengal Presidency, and he exercised a general control over the armies of Madras and Bombay, each of which had its local Commander-in-Chief. The Governments of those Presidencies possessed, until the same time, certain administrative powers.

Although the ultimate military authority rested with the Governor-General in Council and Commander-in-Chief in India, this system of divided control led to much inconvenience, especially in time of war, and it became clear that it must be altered, and that the armies of Madras and Bombay must no longer remain in the exceptional position of being partially subject to the control of the Provincial Governments and the local Commanders-in-Chief. The necessary change could not be made without the authority of Parliament, and it was not until the close of 1893 that this was obtained. The delay did not prevent the completion of many other reforms in military administration, and before 1893 all the Army Departments, except the Medical, had been brought directly under the orders of the Supreme Government.

The Act of 1893 abolished the offices of the Provincial Commanders-in-Chief; it provided that the powers which had been exercised by them should be transferred to such officer as the Commander-in-Chief in India, with the approval of the Governor-General in Council, might

[1] 3 and 4 Will. IV. c. 85.

appoint; that the powers of the Commander-in-Chief in India should extend to the whole of India; that all the powers of military control which had been vested in the Governments of Madras and Bombay should cease, and be exercised by the Governor-General in Council; and that the officers commanding the troops in those Presidencies should no longer be members of the Provincial Councils.

The result of these changes, which came into effect in April 1895, was as follows:—

Four great commands were constituted, each under a Lieutenant-General, the whole being under the direct command of the Commander-in-Chief in India. The Punjab Command includes the Punjab and North-West Frontier Province, with the Punjab Frontier Force, which retains its organisation as a separate body. The Bengal Command includes the territories under the Civil Governments of Bengal, Assam, and the United Provinces of Agra and Oudh. The Madras Command, until the beginning of 1903, included not only the whole of the Madras Presidency, and other territories formerly garrisoned by the Madras Army, but the Province of Burma. This now forms a separate command. The Bombay Command includes the Bombay Presidency, Baluchistán, and parts of Rájputána and Central India.

I have not yet referred to the armies of the Native States. They look formidable on paper, numbering, according to some estimates, 85,000 men, but a small portion only of these so-called armies has any military organisation. They consist for the most part of men who can hardly be called soldiers. The majority of them are maintained for purposes of display, without the least idea that they can ever be used for fighting. The so-called army includes multitudes of the armed retainers of the chiefs and nobles, and nearly the whole of the men whom we should class as police.

Among all the armies of the Native States, that of Gwalior is the most completely organised. It consists of about 11,000 men, of whom about 6000 are cavalry, all fairly drilled and disciplined, with several fully-equipped batteries of artillery. A very small part of the Gwalior troops consists of men recruited in that country. The great majority of them come from our territories, and chiefly from the classes which before the mutinies of 1857 supplied the bulk of our Bengal army. The Government of Sindhia is, as I shall show, that of a foreign Maráthá dynasty; the people are unwarlike and disinclined for military service. The strength of the forces which may be maintained is regulated by treaty with the British Government.

The largest of the armies of the Native States is that of the Nizam of Haiderabad, also a foreigner in the country belonging to him. It is so heterogeneous a body that it is difficult to state its numbers, but that part of it which may with some show of reason be called an army has been estimated at about 45,000 men. A portion of it has been reorganised and improved. Many of these troops are foreign mercenaries from distant parts of India, and many are Patháns from our northern frontier. While they perform no useful service to the Nizam, it has been necessary to watch and overawe them, and the necessity has been imposed on us of always keeping a large force of British and Native troops at Haiderabad. A Native force, called the Haiderabad Contingent, consisting formerly of more than 7000 men of all arms, under the command of British officers, but recently reorganised and reduced in numbers, has also been maintained by our Government at Haiderabad. The charges for the Contingent have been met from the revenues of the Berár districts, which were assigned to us for the purpose in 1853 by treaty with the Nizam, and which, as I explain elsewhere, are now virtually British territory.[1]

The troops of the Rájputána States are, on paper, numerous, but the figures have no military significance. The men are not, for the most part, soldiers in the service of the State, but the members of a military class. There is no doubt of the loyalty of the Rájput chiefs or of their followers.

The troops of the Sikh States deserve mention. "They are" (in the words of the Indian Army Commission) "of good material; they are well officered, and have on occasions done excellent service for the British Crown. They are devoted to their chiefs, who are conspicuously loyal, and bound to the British Government by mutual goodwill and good offices, which have extended over many years."

The troops of the Native States possess, as a rule, no arms of precision, no breech-loading rifles, no rifled ordnance, and very little organised artillery. They are, for the most part, as Sir Lepel Griffin says, "an undrilled, wretchedly armed rabble, and two or three of our regiments, with a battery of horse artillery, would disperse 50,000 of them." They are not armies in the ordinary sense of the term.

One important addition has to be made to the foregoing observations. During the Viceroyalty of Lord Dufferin arrangements were made with several of the Native States, possessing specially good fighting material, for maintaining a number of selected troops in such a condition of efficiency in arms, equipment, drill, and

[1] Chapter XXIV.

organisation, as shall make them fit to take the field side by side with British soldiers. Other States have engaged to furnish transport corps, which have already been most useful in time of war. The total number of these special contingents is now about 17,500 men. Both officers and men are, for the most part, Natives of the States to which they belong, but British officers are appointed to inspect them, and to advise in regard to their training and equipment. The Kashmir Imperial Service troops saw active service in the operations for the reduction of the mountain principalities of Hunza and Nagar, and behaved with conspicuous gallantry. Since then in the Tirah and other campaigns on the North-Western Frontier, and more recently in China, contingents from other States have proved themselves a valuable, keen, and loyal addition to our regular troops.

CHAPTER XXIV

THE NATIVE STATES

Area, population, and revenue of Native States—Meaning of the term Native States—Prevalent mistakes—Native States not nationalities —Different classes of Native States—Mohammedan and Marátha States—Their foreign character—Ancient dynasties preserved by the British—The Governments of Native States—The personal despots—The tribal chiefs—The supremacy of the British Government—Our relations with Native States—The doctrine of lapse—Right of adoption—Assumption by Queen Victoria of title of "Empress of India"—The Coronation Durbar of January 1903—The character of Native rulers—Frequent necessity for British intervention—The annexation of Oudh—Condition of Oudh before annexation—Deposition of the Gaikwar—The States of Central India—Desire of the British Government to maintain the Native States—Their misrule their sole danger—The conditions essential to their preservation—The restoration of Mysore to Native rule—Improvements in the administration of Native States—Colleges for the education of Native chiefs—The Imperial Cadet Corps.

THE Native States of India cover an area of 679,000 square miles, and contain a population of 62,500,000. Their total revenues are estimated at about £15,000,000. Counting them all, there are more than 600 of them, but the great majority are so insignificant in extent, and their rulers have so little authority, that they do not deserve the name of States. The largest, that of the Nizam of Haiderabad, has an area of 83,000 square miles, and a population of more than 11,000,000; Gwalior, 25,000 square miles, and a population of 3,000,000;

Mysore, 29,000 square miles, and 5,500,000. Several others have between 1,000,000 and 3,000,000 people.[1]

Excepting the Himálayan State of Nepál, which since 1815 has been enabled by its geographical position to maintain a constant attitude of complete but friendly isolation, no Native State within the limits of India has any real independence; but, subject to this general fact, their rulers have every degree of power and importance, from the petty chief with little or no political authority, to princes with large revenues and considerable armies, with whose internal administration, under ordinary circumstances, we hardly interfere.

I am obliged to use the term "Native State," but this expression only signifies a State not directly administered by Englishmen. The rulers of some of the principal Native States of India are almost as much foreigners to the people that they govern as we are ourselves. The term "Native States" is apt to convey the idea that they are Indian nationalities existing in

[1] The following list shows the area, population, and approximate revenue of the principal Native States:—

	Square miles.	Population.	Approximate revenue.	Religion of ruler.
Haiderabad. (The Nizam)	82,700	11,141,000	£3,300,000	Mohammedan
Bhopál	6,990	666,000	270,000	,,
Baháwalpur . . .	17,300	720,000	137,000	,,
Gwalior. (Sindhia) . .	25,000	3,000,000	1,092,000	Hindu
Indore. (Holkar) . .	8,400	851,000	570,000	,,
Baroda. (Gaikwár) . .	8,100	1,950,000	1,130,000	,,
Mysore	29,400	5,539,000	1,250,000	,,
Travancore . . .	7,100	2,950,000	663,000	,,
Jaipur	15,500	2,700,000	455,000	,,
Jodhpur	35,000	2,000,000	343,000	,,
Udaipur	12,700	1,000,000	247,000	,,
Bikanir	23,300	584,000	143,000	,,
Rewah	12,600	1,320,000	107,000	,,
Kutch	7,600	450,000	131,000	,,
Patiála	5,400	1,597,000	411,000	Sikh
Kashmir	80,900	2,906,000	460,000	Hindu

the midst of our great foreign dominion. This, indeed, is the popular English belief. It is assumed that in our conquest of India we imposed our rule on peoples who had previously been governed by princes of their own race, that we took the place of ancient native dynasties which we destroyed, and that, having kept for ourselves the more valuable provinces, we have, for one reason or another, allowed some portions of India to retain their Native governments. No suppositions could be more contrary to fact. When, after the death of Aurangzíb in 1707, the Moghal empire was breaking up, a scramble ensued for the fragments, and this lasted through the greater part of the eighteenth, and the earlier part of the nineteenth century. The chief competitors during the struggle were the Maráthas, the Mohammedan powers of Southern India, and the English. The larger share of the gain fell to the English, but the other competitors had no better titles than our own. All alike were foreigners in the countries for which they were contending.

Those who desire to learn the truth on this subject should read Sir Alfred Lyall's *Asiatic Studies*, to which I have often referred, and Professor Seeley's *Expansion of England.*

"One of the popular notions in England and Europe (I am quoting from Sir Alfred Lyall) regarding the establishment of the English empire in India, is that our conquests absorbed nationalities, displaced long-seated dynasties, and levelled ancient nobilities. These are some of the self-accusations by which the average home-keeping Englishman justifies to himself the indulgence of sitting down and casting dust on his head whenever he looks back upon the exploits of his countrymen in India —an attitude which is observed by foreigners with suspicion or impatience according to their insight into English character. Yet it would be easy to prove that one important reason why the

English so rapidly conquered India was this, that the countries which fell into our hands had no nationalities, no long-seated ruling dynasties or ancient aristocracies, that they had, in fact, no solid or permanent organisation of the kind, but were, politically, treasure trove, at the disposal of the first who, having found, could keep. The best proof that in these countries the English destroyed no organised political institutions is the historical fact that in the countries which they annexed none such had been left for them to destroy. On the other hand, where indigenous political institutions of long standing still exist, it is the English who have saved them from destruction."[1]

The principal Native States of India may be roughly divided into two classes. The most important of the first class are the Mohammedan State of Haiderabad and the Marátha States of Gwalior, Indore, and Baroda. They survived the struggles of the close of the eighteenth and the beginning of the nineteenth century, and their chiefs are in all cases foreigners to the people under their rule. None of these States are much older than our own dominion; the principal officials are usually as foreign as the chiefs; the armed force mainly consists of foreign mercenaries; and there is little more sympathy between the people and their rulers than that which exists in British territories. I have repeatedly pointed out how misleading are such terms as "Natives of India," "People of India," and other general expressions; and this warning is especially necessary in regard to the "Native States." It can never be assumed that because the chief of a Native State is a so-called "Native of India" he has rights essentially differing in kind from our own. If a question arises whether our own administration or that of a Native ruler is to be preferred, Englishmen usually suppose that the choice must lie between giving to the people the foreign

[1] *Asiatic Studies*, p. 181.

government of the English or the national government of their own countrymen. For instance, there was much discussion some time ago whether we ought to restore to the Nizam the districts of Berár which had been assigned to us, and which have been for many years under British administration. Few had any suspicion of the fact that the Mohammedan Government of Haiderabad would be almost as foreign as our own to the people of Berár, who are Hindus having nothing in common with their former rulers.

The Nizam holds the first place among the Native princes of India. The founder of the ruling family was one of Aurangzíb's viceroys; in 1724 he was virtually independent. Nearly the whole population is Hindu; but although at the present time (1903) a Hindu is the Chief Minister of the State, Hindus have usually had little or no share in the administration: everything has been in the hands of Mohammedan foreigners. The army chiefly consists of foreign mercenaries. The Haiderabad State is the chief surviving relic of Mohammedan supremacy in India. With the not very important exceptions of Bhopál and Baháwalpur, the latter of which States had, however, a more autonomous and legitimate origin, the other States under Mohammedan rulers, about twenty in number, are politically insignificant. The population of the so-called Mohammedan States is altogether about 14,000,000, but of this number at least 12,000,000 are Hindus. Even in Haiderabad, where the Mohammedans have been in power for centuries, they form less than a tenth part of the population. A very small proportion of the 62,500,000 Mohammedans of India live under rulers of their own faith; by far the greater number of them are our own subjects.

The principal remnants of the Marátha power are the three States of Gwalior, Indore, and Baroda, and of these Gwalior, under the rule of Sindhia, is the most important. They all came into existence about the middle of the eighteenth century. Their chiefs are entirely foreign to the people. In the words of Sir Lepel Griffin, they are "the representatives of the predatory hordes which, until crushed by British arms, turned the fertile plains of Central India into a wilderness. These Marátha dynasties have nothing in common with the people they govern. Their race is different and their language is not understood." The population of the three Marátha States is nearly 6,000,000; but, except the rulers and their followers, there are no Maráthas.

Among the more important of the Native States of which I have been speaking, there is not one the Government of which can be said to have a more legitimate or national origin than that of the British Government itself in its Indian dominions.

I come now to the second of the classes into which the Native States of India may be divided. Judged by their area and population and political importance, these States are inferior to those of the former class, but they are more numerous and far more interesting. They are the only parts of India where ancient political institutions and ancient dynasties still survive, and their preservation is entirely due to the British Government. The principal States of this class are those of Rájputána; and there are many others in Central India, in Bundelkhand, Baghelkhand, and in the Bombay Presidency. In his *Asiatic Studies*, Sir Alfred Lyall has described the States of Rájputána, the most interesting of the whole. They were saved by the British Government from destruction by the Maráthas. They are twenty in number, with an area of some 150,000 square miles and a population of more than 12,000,000. The constitution of these States is very different from that of the Mohammedan and Marátha States. In the latter, the ruler formerly exercised absolute personal power. In consequence of his responsibilities to the British Government, it can no longer be said that this is true. For instance (I am quoting from Sir Alfred Lyall), Sindhia, the head of the Marátha State of Gwalior, "is the representative of the single family of a successful captain of armies who annexed in the last century all the territory he could lay hands on, and whose son finally encamped so long in one place that his camp grew into his capital some sixty years ago. . . . He is a despot of the ordinary Asiatic species, ruling absolutely the lands which his ancestor seized by the power of a mercenary army."[1]

In States like those of Rájputána, on the other hand, where ancient institutions have been preserved, the constitution of the governing authority is very different. The chief is the hereditary head of a military clan the members of which have been for centuries lords of the soil. He and the minor chiefs and nobles are supposed to be descended from a common ancestor; he is *primus inter pares*, and while all the branches of the original stock are ready to join their chief in time of danger, his actual power over them is, under ordinary circumstances, very greatly limited.

Owing to the custom of adoption, through which no Hindu family need become extinct from failure of heirs, some of the ruling families of Rájputána go back to an unknown antiquity. In the States of Udaipur, Jodhpur, and Jaipur, there seems no reason to doubt that the

[1] *Asiatic Studies*, p. 196.

families to which the present chiefs belong have ruled in the same territories for more than a thousand years. In States of this kind there is often a strong feeling of attachment on the part of the people towards their chief.

There are other States of a different character which have nothing in common with those which I have last mentioned, except that they owe their present existence to the British Government. The largest of these is the Frontier State of Kashmir, with an area of 81,000 square miles, and a population of 2,900,000. It was given by Lord Hardinge to Ghulab Singh in 1846, after the first Sikh war. The treaty under which the grant was made declares the supremacy of the British Government, and a nominal tribute is paid every year by the Máharája.

Mysore, in Southern India, has an area of 29,000 square miles and a population of 5,500,000. Its Hindu rájas contrived to maintain more or less independence until the middle of the eighteenth century, when Hyder Ali took possession of their country. It remained in his hands and in those of his successor, Tippoo Sultan, until the capture of Seringapatam by the English in 1799. Mysore was then restored by Lord Wellesley to the old Hindu dynasty. In consequence of gross oppression and misgovernment, it became necessary in 1830 to place British officers in charge of the administration. The Rája died in 1867, leaving an adopted son, and the British Government announced its intention of restoring the government to the heir when he reached his majority. This promise was carried out in 1881 in a manner which I shall presently notice.

The ancient Hindu State of Travancore, at the southern extremity of India, was rescued from Tippoo by the British, and still remains in the possession of its rájas.

The principal Native States of the Punjab also owe their continued existence to English protection. Without it they would have been utterly swept away by Ranjit Singh. There are altogether thirty-six of these States, with a population of more than 4,000,000.

The supreme authority of the British Government has become a fact which no Native State in India thinks for a moment of disputing. These States are often called "feudatory," but there is no analogy between their relations with the British Government and the incidents of ancient feudal tenure. The expression has come into use, as Sir Charles Aitchison says, "merely from want of a better or more convenient term to denote the subordination of territorial sovereignties to a common superior, combined with the obligation to discharge certain duties and render certain services to that superior."

In the case of the more important States, our supremacy was long ago recognised, more or less completely, by treaty; in the case of the smaller States, whether expressed and formally recorded or not, it has become one of the obvious conditions of their existence. Some of the States, so far as their internal administration is concerned, are substantially independent, unless their government becomes so scandalously bad and oppressive that intervention is forced upon us; in other States the authority of the chiefs is more strictly limited; in many of the smaller States it hardly exists in any independent form. But whether the State be great or small, there are certain rights which the paramount power always asserts. No Native State can have any political communication with any other Native State, or with any Foreign Power, without the consent of the British Government; no Native State can maintain more troops or military establishments than are required for purposes of internal administration, for the support of the reasonable dignity of the chief, or except in accordance with its recognised obligations towards the British Government; there is no Native State in which civil war would be permitted, or in which, in case of gross and systematic injustice and tyranny, the British Government would not interfere for the protection of the people. This last right is the necessary consequence of our absolute power, and it has been repeatedly exercised. There is no Native chief who might not be tried and punished for a crime of special atrocity by a tribunal constituted by the British Government. It will be understood from all this that rules of international law which govern the relations between independent States cannot apply to the relations between the British Government and the Native States of India.

There is no dynasty in India which would not, without the custom of adoption, long ago have become extinct. It may also be said that it is the rule, as much as the exception, that a Native prince has no direct heirs. I need not dwell on the significance of this fact.

Whether an adopted son had the same right as a natural heir to succeed to the government of a State without the sanction of the paramount power was a question in regard to which there had been no uniform custom or practice before the time of Lord Dalhousie. He laid down the broad principle that while we were "bound in duty as well as in policy to act on every such occasion with the purest integrity and in the most scrupulous observance of good faith," it was right that "on all occasions where heirs natural shall fail, the territory should be made to lapse, and adoption should not be permitted, excepting in those cases in which some strong political reason may render it expedient to depart from this general rule." He recorded his "strong and deliberate opinion that, in the exercise of a wise and sound policy, the British Government is bound not to put aside or to neglect such rightful opportunities of acquiring territory or revenue as may from time to time present themselves." These views were not based on any lust of dominion, but on the sincere belief that it was our obvious duty to extend to the people of all parts of India, when it became possible to do so, the benefits of our Government. This "doctrine of lapse" was carried into practical effect by Lord Dalhousie in several cases. The most important was that of Nágpur, a State with an area of 80,000 square miles and several millions of people. The Rája had died without an heir, and the State was declared to have lapsed to the British Government. If the policy of Lord Dalhousie had continued to be followed, the extinction of nearly all the Native States of India would have been a question of time only, but it was completely abandoned by his successor.[1]

The mutinies of 1857 showed conclusively that the Native States are a source to us, not of weakness, but of strength. In the words of Lord Canning—"These patches of Native Government served as a breakwater to the storm which would otherwise have swept over us in one great wave." With hardly an exception, they remained faithful in circumstances of the severest trial and difficulty. Before Lord Canning left India a *sanad* was issued to each of the principal Hindu chiefs, assuring

[1] It has been pointed out to me that this "doctrine of lapse" was declared by Lord Dalhousie to be inapplicable to "Hindu sovereignties which are not tributary, and which are not and have never been subject to a Paramount Power." It does not appear to me that these exceptions to Lord Dalhousie's general rule had much practical significance.

him, in the name of the Queen, that, on failure of natural heirs, the British Government would recognise any adoption of a successor made by himself or by any future chief of the State, in accordance with Hindu law or the customs of his race. The Mohammedan chiefs received assurances that every form of succession allowed by Mohammedan law to be legitimate would be recognised by our Government. From the principle thus laid down there has been no departure. In default of regular adoption, the British Government exercises the undisputed right of selecting the successor whom it may think most fit. In case of a minority, it invariably asserts a right of interference, limited only by its own sense of what is proper.

The supremacy of the British Government over all the Native States in India was declared in 1877, in a more emphatic form than it had received before, by the assumption by Queen Victoria of the title of Kaisar-i-Hind, Empress of India.

When, in 1876, Mr. Disraeli proposed that the Queen should assume this new title, there were no limits to the scorn with which the suggestion was received by his opponents, and it may be doubted whether he found much real sympathy from a majority of those who felt bound to support him. But he possessed that gift without which, as he said to me himself, no statesman can be truly great—the gift of imagination. "Touch and satisfy," he said in the House of Commons, "the imagination of nations, for that is an element which no Government can despise. This will be an act which will add splendour to the Throne of the Queen, and will add security to her Empire." His conviction of the power which imagination exercises on the minds of men, and especially of Orientals, was fully shared by Lord

Lytton, who was then Viceroy, and its truth has, in this case, received ample proof.

No such gathering of chiefs and princes had been seen in India, in historical times, as that of January 1877 at Delhi, when, with a pomp such as the East alone can show, all the great chiefs of the Native States of India came to make the formal acknowledgment of their dependence on the British Empress. The 1st of January 1903 saw repeated at Delhi, on a far grander scale and with far greater splendour than that of 1877, the assemblage of ruling chiefs and nobles from all the States and Provinces of India, representatives, some of them, of countries as far apart as Iceland from Constantinople, summoned by Lord Curzon to celebrate the Coronation of Edward the Seventh as King and Emperor. No spectacle so magnificent can have been seen in Europe since the Triumphs of Ancient Rome, and it may be doubted whether, when Aurelian passed through the city with Zenobia and the spoils of Palmyra, and "the arms and ensigns of conquered nations," Rome itself witnessed a more splendid pageant than when the British Viceroy entered Delhi with the brother of the Emperor, or when he afterwards received in solemn Durbar the homage of the princes of India. The time has passed in which it was necessary to defend the policy of the measure which proclaimed the paramount sovereignty of the British Crown. No Indian statesman doubts its wisdom or the profound practical importance of its political results. It has given to the British power a position different from that which it held before; it has swept away old jealousies that were not extinct, and has made more loyal the ruler of every Native State in India. Not many years ago it would have been difficult to believe that we should see in London great Rájput princes who, to prove their loyalty, had thrown aside the prejudices of caste and immemorial custom, and that Sindhia, the descendant of Marátha chiefs, who had fought with us for supremacy in India, and was now ruling one of its most important States, would be proud to ride as Aide-de-camp at the Coronation of the King and Emperor. The Emperor of India has become to its chiefs and people a great and real personality, in place of "the impersonal power of an administrative abstraction."[1]

There has been, but only in recent years, a marked and satisfactory improvement in the administration of the Native States. To this I shall refer again, but as lately as 1883, Sir Lepel Griffin, than whom no one could at that time speak with greater personal knowledge, declared that, although there were many honourable exceptions, the Native States of India were for the most part "a wilderness of oppression and misrule." This conclusion was that of all those most competent to judge, and it was certainly my own.

I think it useful to refer to the former condition of some of these States, because it cannot be doubted that if the vigilance of the British Government were relaxed, that condition would often become no better than it was not long ago. It is to our intervention before misrule became altogether insufferable that many of these States owe their continued existence. Without going back to more distant times, when all conditions were different, if we examine the history of the principal Native States during the greater part of the latter half of the last century, we can hardly find a single case in which the record was one of uninterrupted tranquillity and fairly good administra-

[1] *History of Lord Lytton's Indian Administration*, by Lady Betty Balfour.

tion. From time to time there was a just and benevolent chief, but sooner or later came almost always the same story; our interference for the protection of the people against their ruler became inevitable. Even within the last few years it has sometimes become necessary for the British Government to assume the administration of the State, and on several occasions the chief has been deposed because he was guilty of atrocious crimes.

I will give some instances in which interference has been inevitable, and as the first of them I will take the annexation of Oudh. Although this is now an old story, for the Native Government ceased to exist in 1856, it is still an instructive example of what has happened in a time not very distant, and I wish to refer to it for another reason. We still sometimes hear the annexation of Oudh quoted as one of the iniquitous proceedings of the British Government, and as an illustration of its lust of dominion.

General Sleeman, the representative of our Government in Oudh, gave from personal observation a description of the country at that time, and its accuracy has never been called in question. I will give some account, often in his own words, of his report.

Oudh is naturally one of the richest countries in India, as large as Holland and Belgium together, with a population at the present time of nearly 13,000,000. Government in Oudh, deserving the name, there was none. The King did not pretend to concern himself with any public business. His ambition was limited to that of being reputed the best drum-beater, dancer, and poet of the day. Sometimes he might be seen going in procession through the streets of Lucknow, beating the drum tied round his neck. Singers, fiddlers, poets, eunuchs, and women were his only associates. The Prime Minister, "a consummate knave," after keeping an enormous share for himself and his creatures, distributed the revenues and patronage of the country. The fiddlers controlled the administration of civil justice; that of criminal justice was made over to the eunuchs; each of the King's favourites had authority over some court or office through which he might make a fortune for himself. The minister kept the land revenue, and "employed none but knaves of the very worst kind in all branches of the administration." Every office was sold; commands in the army were put up to auction every season, or oftener, and the purchase money was divided among the minister, the singers, the fiddlers, and the eunuchs. The principal singer had two regiments at his disposal. The minister was as inaccessible as the King himself. Petitions and reports were usually made over by him, if he gave any orders at all, to the commander-in-chief, who was an infant, to the King's chamberlain, or footman, or coachman, chief fiddler, eunuch, barber, or any person uppermost in his thoughts at the time. Courts of justice were unknown, except as affording means of extortion to the judges. The charge of the so-called police throughout the country was sold to the highest bidders. There was only one road that deserved the name in Oudh, made for the benefit of English travellers from Lucknow to Cawnpore, a distance of about forty miles.

The atrocities that went on throughout the country would pass belief, if the evidence of the truth were less complete. I will give a few illustrations, taken from General Sleeman's narrative.

The districts of Bahraich and Gonda have an area of more than 5000 square miles, and they now contain more than 2,000,000 inhabitants. Shortly before General Sleeman's visit, a man called Raghubar Singh was their local Governor, with large bodies of the King's troops and of his own armed retainers at his disposal. In two years his extortions and crimes had reached such a point, that these districts, which had once been in a flourishing condition, and noted for their fertility, had become for the most part uncultivated. The English officer deputed by the Resident to inquire into the facts reported that "villages completely deserted in the midst of lands devoid of all tillage everywhere meet the eye; and from Fyzabad to Bahraich he passed through these districts, a distance of eighty miles, over plains which had been fertile and well cultivated till Raghubar Singh got charge, but now lay entirely waste, a scene for two years of great misery, ending in desolation."

The Rája of Bondi was one of the principal landholders in this part of Oudh; his estates contained some three hundred villages. He objected to the extortionate demands of Raghubar Singh, and this was the consequence. Parties of soldiers were sent out to plunder and seize all the respectable residents they could find. They sacked the town of Bondi, pulled down the houses of the Rája, and those of his relations and dependants; and, after looting all the towns and villages in the neighbourhood, they brought in 1000 captives of both sexes and all ages, who were subjected to every sort of outrage until they paid the ransom demanded. The Rája escaped, but his agents and tenants were horribly tortured. Soon afterwards, detachments of soldiers were again sent out to plunder; 1500 men and 500 women and children were brought in as prisoners, with 80,000 animals. All were driven off pell-mell through the rain for three days. The women were driven on by the troops with the butt-ends of their muskets; many of the children were trodden to death. The prisoners were tied up and flogged and tortured, red-hot ramrods thrust into their flesh, their tongues pulled out with hot pincers. Many perished from torture and starvation. The women and children were all stripped of their clothing. For two months these atrocities continued. Similar horrors went on in other parts of Bahraich, and not very many years ago the English officer in charge of that district reported that its population would at that time have undoubtedly been much larger but for the former atrocities of Raghubar Singh. General Sleeman tells us that no single person concerned in these crimes was ever punished.

There were then in Oudh 250 forts in the possession of the great landholders, with 100,000 men, maintained to fight among themselves, or against the Government. General Sleeman's two volumes are filled with descriptions of the enormities that were going on, almost under his own eyes, of open war, of villages attacked and plundered, of horrible murders and outrages. "Every day," he writes, "I have scores of petitions delivered to me by persons who have been plundered of all they possessed, had their dearest relations murdered or tortured to death, and their habitations burnt to the ground by gangs of ruffians, under landlords of high birth and pretensions, whom they had never wronged or offended. In these attacks neither age, nor sex, nor condition are spared."

In General Sleeman's narrative I have found hardly anything to relieve the uniformity of his terrible story except this:—

"In the most crowded streets of Lucknow, Europeans are received with deference, courtesy, and kindness. The people of the country respect the British Government, its officers, and Europeans generally. Though the Resident has not been able to secure any very substantial or permanent reform in the administration, still he has often interposed with effect, in individual cases, to relieve suffering and secure redress for grievous wrongs. The people of the country see that he never interposes except for such purposes, and their only regret is that he interposes so seldom, and that his efforts when he does so should be so often frustrated or disregarded. In the remotest village or jungle in Oudh, as in the most crowded streets of the capital, a European gentleman is sure to be treated with affectionate respect, and the humblest European is as sure to receive protection and kindness, unless he forfeits all claim to it by his misconduct."

For many years one Governor-General after another had gone on protesting against the atrocities of which some illustrations have been given. At last came "the great Proconsul" Dalhousie. He knew that since the British Government, without moving a soldier or spending a rupee, had absolute power to put an immediate end to these abominations, it was on the British Government that the responsibility really rested for suffering them to continue. There was only one complete remedy, and Lord Dalhousie applied it by declaring the whole of Oudh to be British territory. I find one defect only in his most wise and righteous action; he was too merciful to the miserable King and to the demons who had been destroying one of the most populous and fertile countries of India. There could be no greater contrast than that presented by Oudh under Native and under British Government: it is now as peaceful as any part of England; life and property are safe, and justice is honestly administered.

For atrocities committed on a vast scale the case of Oudh stands alone, but I will give a few illustrations of the condition into which some of the Native States have fallen in much later times, and which have rendered the interference of our Government inevitable.

Baroda is the principal Native State of Western India. It covers 8100 square miles, and has a population of nearly 2,000,000. Its ruler, the Gaikwár, claims precedence over all the Native chiefs of India. In 1863 Malhár Ráo was imprisoned on a charge of having attempted the life of the Gaikwár, his brother; at the end of 1870, on his brother's death, he was released, and he assumed the government of the State. Before long his proceedings had become so scandalous that the British Government was compelled to make a formal inquiry into his administration. It was shown that general discontent prevailed through his dominions; in one district there was open rebellion; public offices were sold to the highest bidder; payment of extortionate demands of revenue was compelled by torture; respectable women were seized in open day in the streets of Baroda by the Gaikwár's servants, and taken to the palace to be converted into household slaves or worse; the condition of the agricultural classes was desperate; and the whole administration was infamous. The Prime Minister was forcibly poisoned in prison, and it was hardly possible to doubt that this was done under the direct orders of the Gaikwár. It was proved that, for an act by which he had been personally offended, the Gaikwár had caused one of his servants, without any trial, to be tortured to death.

In 1874 he was informed by the Government of India, Lord Northbrook being Viceroy at the time, that, if immediate and satisfactory reforms were not carried out in the administration of the State, his deposition would follow. He showed no inclination to alter his conduct. Soon afterwards an attempt was made to poison the British Resident at his court, and there was every reason to believe that the Gaikwár had personally instigated the crime. A commission, of which the Chief Justice of Bengal was president, and of which the rulers of two of the principal Native States were members, was appointed for his trial. The Native chiefs pronounced that the charges were not proved, but the Chief Justice and the English members found that he was guilty, and there was not the least doubt that they were right. As the judgment was not unanimous, the Gaikwár escaped the extreme penalty that he deserved, and which, if he had been formally convicted, he would probably have suffered. He was deposed, and a member of another branch of the Gaikwár's house was selected by the British Government as his successor. When the rule of Malhár Ráo ended, it was found that out of an expenditure in his last year of £1,700,000, which was greatly in excess of the revenue, he had squandered £700,000 in gifts to favourites and on his personal pleasures, and £200 remained in the public treasury.

The two important Marátha States of Central India, Gwalior and Indore, ruled respectively by Sindhia and Holkar, have together an area of more than 33,000 square miles, and a population of nearly 4,000,000. I make the following quotations from an official report for 1885 by Sir Lepel Griffin, Agent to the Governor-General in Central India :—

"The largest states in this agency, Gwalior and Indore, are those in which the rulers spend the least on administration, and most neglect all those requirements which we specially associate with progress and civilisation. . . . Those districts that are under the direct control of Sindhia's officials give little cause for trouble or complaint to the Government, although the administration is lax and apathetic. Those, however, which are given in jagír to his great courtiers are constant sources of anxiety. Neglected by the grantees, who reside at the capital, they are made over to rack-renting agents, who support their authority by Afghán and Mekráni mercenaries, who are the scourge of the country-side. Damodar Panth, the agent of one of the principal nobles of the Máharája, has long been notorious for his open encouragement and support of crime in his master's jagír. Having sufficient proof of his complicity in numerous cases of dacoity and robbery, I have, with the full consent of the Máharája, caused his arrest, and he is now being tried on these serious charges, while the bands of dacoits, which had been allowed with impunity to plunder that part of Málwa, are being broken up. . . . During 1883-84 the oppression exercised in Indore city called for the severest condemnation on the part of the Government of India, and the senior Prince Shivaji Ráo Holkar was specially censured and removed from all concern with public business. I have had during the past year to remonstrate with the Durbár on many occasions and in strong terms against action which appeared to me to have been taken against individuals unjustly, and in defiance of the commonest principles of justice and equity. . . . The judicial administration of Indore must be held to be deteriorating and not improving. The reforms instituted by Sir Mádhava Ráo are being gradually abandoned from motives of false economy. . . . If I am unable to say much that is good of the two great Mahratta States included in Central India, this is no matter for surprise. In the Rájput States which abound in Central India, and which are rather oligarchical than autocratic, there is on the part of the chiefs a far more kindly and unselfish attitude towards the brotherhood and the people generally than in a Mahratta State, the despotic egoism of which is fatal to all progress and civilisation. The ruler considers the soil of the State as his own; the people are his slaves; the entire revenue is his private pocket-money, to hoard, lavish, or waste, without any right of remonstrance or complaint on the part of his subjects. The disease of such governments is chronic and intolerable. It is impossible that they can be other than evil, and it is a false and foolish policy to use towards them the language of false compliment, and to pretend that they are other than irretrievably bad, until a higher civilisation and the example of the British Government shall have demonstrated that the rights of princes have no existence apart from the rights of the people."

In another paper, also referring to the States of Central India, Sir Lepel Griffin wrote as follows:—

"The peasants are little better than serfs. The importation of foreign slaves is prevented by the vigilance of the British authorities alone. Torture is a recognised part of judicial and police procedure. . . . Only a few months ago I was compelled to refuse to return the visit of a ruling chief who was openly accused of squeezing the juice of chillies into the eyes of recusant witnesses. He was an old gentleman of the most soft and courteous manners, and the idea that chillies could be objected to as a means of judicial investigation did not appear to have occurred to him. . . . Administration of justice has virtually no existence; a bribe procures the acquittal, or escape, or release of a criminal. Every offence can usually be compounded for money. Numerous boundary disputes between Native States come before me, and the consideration which governs every case is that both States have, as a matter of course, supported a wilfully exaggerated claim by perjured witnesses and forged documents. One of the first chiefs in India punishes and ruins the headman or cultivator of a village who may give truthful evidence contrary to any boundary claim the State has chosen unjustly to advance. . . . The actual demand of the Government per head of the population is double, treble, or quadruple what it is in British India."

Speaking of Kashmir with personal knowledge, Sir Lepel Griffin said in 1883 that "nothing escapes taxation, and bare life is all that the State leaves to the cultivator, whose position is harder and as hopeless as that of a slave." The shameful maladministration of this State was too long tolerated, but at last, in 1889, the patience of the British Government was exhausted. The Máharája was for a time deprived of all authority, and although he was subsequently allowed to resume his position as head of the State, it was under new conditions, the administration being carried on by a

Council of State, acting under the advice of the British Resident.

In 1884 the condition of Bhopál, a State with nearly 1,000,000 inhabitants, became such that it was necessary for the Government of India to remove the husband of the reigning princess from power, and to appoint an English minister to carry on the administration. The land revenue had been arbitrarily raised from £170,000 to £410,000; the payment of more than £1,000,000 was demanded in a lump sum from the people; justice became a mere engine of corruption and oppression; districts were ruined and depopulated; the police were no better than dacoits who shared their plunder with men in high places. Although, through the efforts of the English minister, all this was reformed, we were told that many years must elapse before the people of Bhopál could recover from the ruin which they suffered.[1]

[1] In 1894 a valuable work, *Our Indian Protectorate*, was published by Sir Charles Tupper of the Indian Civil Service. It gives a very clear account of the relations between the British Government and its Indian Feudatories. Sir Charles Tupper, while he fully acknowledges that many Native States are well administered, gives some terrible illustrations "to show that the battle with cruelty, superstition, callous indifference to the security of the weaker and poorer classes, avarice, corruption, disorder in all public affairs, and open brigandage is by no means over even at the present day." I will quote one passage only from Sir Charles Tupper's work. "We are not far yet from the confusions of the last century, and deep in existing societies lie predatory instincts which, in the absence of strong control, might soon fill whole provinces with pillage and alarm. In a State where there was a good deal of corruption, and the torture of prisoners was not unknown, a colony settled not long ago, consisting of the descendants of Thugs. In 1888 there were in three villages 800 of these people all told. They had no occupation except theft, robbery, and the disposal of stolen goods. . . . In a circle of three States not less than 400 miles from the villages of these Thugs, a formidable band of robbers was lately making depredations. In the four years ending February 1889, twenty-two villages had been plundered by daring gangs, forty-seven murders committed, fifty-one persons wounded, and about two hundred hostages carried off, of whom many were ransomed at enormous gains to the brigands. In another State, in 1885 and 1886, seven or eight bands of dacoits, each fifty to one

In 1887 the Chief of a small Native State was removed from power in circumstances too abominable to be described.

In 1895, in consequence of the conduct and intemperance of the Chief of Bhartpur, a State well known in the history of the beginning of the last century by its successful resistance to a British army, the Government of India was compelled to interfere for the protection of the people, and the Chief, although not formally deposed, was deprived of his powers of administration. In 1900 he shot and killed one of his personal servants who had offended him; all his rights were then declared by the Government of India to be forfeited; he was placed permanently in confinement; his infant son was selected as his successor, and during the minority the administration of the State is to remain under British supervision.

In 1901 the uncle of the Chief of the Panna State died in circumstances which showed that he had been deliberately poisoned, and the reasons for supposing that the Chief himself had instigated the crime were so strong that the Government of India ordered his suspension from power, and assumed the administration of the State until all the facts had been ascertained by a Commission specially appointed. The guilt of the Chief was clearly proved; in April 1902 he was deposed, deprived of all his rights and honours, and placed in permanent confinement; and his principal agent in the actual commission of the crime was sentenced to death. The Governor-General in Council reserved to himself the right of selecting a successor as ruler of the State.

hundred strong, mostly carrying firearms, had reduced a tract of country some 120 miles long to a state of terror; in the villages all valuables were hidden, and if the dacoits failed to discover the property they expected, the greatest barbarities were practised."

Enough has been said to show the condition of many of the Native States of India not long ago, and to illustrate the fact that even now the cases are not rare in which the interference of our Government becomes unavoidable. Happily, matters are now far better than they were, and States, the condition of which formerly deserved the strongest condemnation, are now fairly well administered. The improvement has been especially marked under the vigorous rule of Lord Curzon. The British Government now fully recognises the responsibilities which rest upon it as the paramount power in India. Its supervision is exercised in a far more reasonable manner than was formerly the case. It can no longer be said, as Sir Henry Lawrence said many years ago, that if ever there was a device for ensuring maladministration, it was that of a Native ruler backed up by British bayonets, and directed by a British Resident. Owing to the continued efforts of our Government in encouraging and providing means for their better education, many of the Native chiefs have become more enlightened and more alive to their duties towards their people. The example of the increasing prosperity and wealth of the people living under our Government has had powerful effects. The improved means of communication, and especially the extension of railways, have brought about great changes throughout India, and the people themselves in the Native States are no longer as helpless and silent as they once were; they are becoming alive to the fact that in the last resort they can appeal to the British Government for protection against oppression.

There are not many positions in which a man has larger powers for good than that of the enlightened ruler of a Native State. He is protected by the British

Government from all anxiety outside his own territory. He requires no armed force except for the maintenance of order among his own people. He has at his disposal, in many cases, very considerable resources. His State shares, as a rule, without any charges being imposed on it, the benefits derived from the railways and other public works constructed by our Government. He has no difficulties such as those that beset on all sides our own administration. Wise and upright chiefs, followed by worthy successors, might bring their States into a condition of almost utopian prosperity. But, if the opportunities are great, so have been the temptations which lead to failure and dishonour, and unrestricted personal power is inevitably doomed in India to the same ultimate fate which has attended it elsewhere.

The British Government has for many years past ceased to desire further extensions of territory in India, and it is difficult to imagine circumstances under which the annexation of a Native State would now be considered expedient. The complete recognition of the right of adoption and the experience of the last quarter of a century have in this respect removed from the minds of the Native Princes all suspicion of the policy of our Government. There is only one apparent cause by which the political existence of any of these States could now be imperilled. We are far from desiring that their government should necessarily be like ours, but as our own administration improves, and everything in India becomes increasingly open to public criticism and inquiry, the more impossible will it be for us to tolerate gross oppression and misgovernment.

The problems to be solved are often difficult, especially in those States, the most interesting in India, and the most worthy of preservation, where old political institutions still survive. Where the ruler is a petty despot, with few or no checks on his arbitrary power, the principles on which we ought to act are easier to define. No real progress in such States is possible while their governments remain purely personal, based upon nothing more permanent than the will of the Chief, whose character and capacity are accidents, and while the authority of the paramount power is exercised on no fixed system, but spasmodically, by special acts of intervention as necessity arises.

The first serious attempt to give a clear definition of the principles on which the relations of the Imperial Government towards the Native States of India ought to be conducted was made by Lord Lytton when he was Viceroy. In 1830 the administration of Mysore had fallen into a miserable condition. Offices were sold to the highest bidder; the people were oppressed and impoverished, and at last broke into revolt. Lord William Bentinck, who was then Governor-General, ordered, as the only sufficient remedy, the transfer of the entire administration into the hands of British officers. Mysore was fortunate in finding in Sir Mark Cubbon an admirable Governor. "The history of the province under his rule (I quote from an official report) is the history of a people made happy by release from serfdom, and of a ruined state restored to financial prosperity."

In 1868 the deposed Rája died, and the British Government resolved that when his adopted son, who was then only six years old, attained his majority, the Government of the State should be entrusted to him.

In 1879 it became necessary to settle the manner in which this resolution should be carried out; it was clear that more than 5,000,000 people, who had been under

British rule for fifty years, could not be made over like sheep, and the conditions under which the transfer of the Government was to take place were embodied in a formal instrument. Among the principal of these were the following :—

1st. A clear distinction must be drawn and permanently maintained between the private fortune of the Chief and the public revenues of the State ; a civil list of fixed amount must be assigned to the Chief, and the rest of the revenues must remain available for public purposes only, through appropriation by constituted authorities.

2nd. There must be permanent security for the observance of established laws, rights, and usages, and the laws must only be altered by suitable legislative machinery.

3rd. Provision must be made for the judicial independence of the civil and criminal courts, and justice must be dispensed by regularly constituted tribunals.

4th. The assessment and collection of the revenues must be made under fixed rules ; all rights in the land must be defined and maintained, and no fresh taxation imposed except in accordance with law.

Under the principles thus laid down, and which have been acted upon ever since, the administration was made over, in 1881, to the Native Chief. His civil list was fixed at £130,000 a year, and he cannot appropriate more than that sum for his personal expenditure. The revenue of the State is now about £1,250,000. The administration is carried on by the Máharája with the assistance of a Council, the members of which are Natives of the country. When the Government was transferred it was provided that all laws then in force should be maintained until altered by competent authority; new laws can only be made under a regular system of procedure, and they require the sanction of the Governor-General in Council.

The objects with which this system was initiated were summed up as follows by the Government of Lord Lytton:—

"The experiment of placing the Máharája of Mysore at the head of a constitutional government—that is, a government conducted upon fixed and fundamental principles—makes a new departure in the policy of the Imperial Government towards the Native States of India. To determine the proper method of dealing with these States, and of discharging the responsibilities which they entail upon the paramount power, has always been, and still is, a problem of great difficulty; for the improvement of their condition, and their gradual assimilation to the general system and standard of the Imperial Government, is almost essential to their preservation. . . . The Supreme Government has been obliged of late years to interpose frequently in the affairs of Native States. The incapacity or grave misconduct of a ruler has produced complications which have demanded immediate and stringent remedies, or the interval of a long minority has made it necessary to superintend more closely a State's management. . . . The policy now framed proceeds upon the broad principle that in order to guard against chronic misrule in a Native State, and to obviate the necessity for frequent and arbitrary interposition by the Supreme Government to remedy the consequences of such misrule, it is expedient to avail ourselves of every opportunity of placing some reasonable limitations upon the personal power of the ruler, or of the minister to whom the administration may be entrusted. The limitations thus imposed must be brought on public record, in order to place them beyond question or controversy, and in certain cases the general power of supervision to be exercised by the Supreme Government may need to be strengthened and extended. These principles may form the groundwork of a settled policy which will guide the Government of India in the general discharge of its responsibilities towards Feudatory States. A new and valuable precedent will have been established, and this, with the experience which will have been gained in Mysore, may enable us in future to deal systematically with similar questions of reorganisation or reform. The contrast presented by the steady growth of orderly civilisation in British India, and the increased publicity that is now given to the internal condition of our Feudatory States, are likely to render more and more imperative the duty of interference in restraint of serious mismanagement. We may thus hope gradually to raise the general standard of administration in Native States, and to make some progress toward the important political object of consolidating their institutions upon an improved and stable foundation."[1]

The system thus introduced into Mysore has worked efficiently and well. While it has placed reasonable checks on the arbitrary power of the ruler, his proper authority has been maintained, the administration has been in Native hands, and there has been no necessity for that frequent interference by the British authorities which in some other States has often been unavoidable, but which is nevertheless incompatible with good government.

The Máharája died in 1894, leaving as his heir an infant son, and it became necessary for the Viceroy to appoint a regent during the minority of the young Chief. The choice fell upon his mother, and its wisdom was shown by the intelligence and dignity which, throughout the minority, she showed in the management of the affairs of the State. Her son received an excellent English education, and careful training to prepare him for the proper performance of his future duties, and, in 1902, he was formally installed by the Viceroy as Máharája.

The wisdom of the principles laid down for the Government of Mysore has been amply proved by experience, and although they have not been applied in other cases in precisely the same form, they are in

[1] Despatch from Government of India to Secretary of State, 22nd May 1879. Parliamentary Return, Mysore, 1881.

practical accordance with those on which the Government of India now regulates its proceedings towards the Native States when necessity or fitting opportunities occur. Such opportunities have not been unfrequent. There have often been long minorities during which the administration of the State has been reorganised and reformed, and when the time has come for placing the young Chief at the head of his Government, this has been done under suitable conditions which he is bound to observe, and which cannot be altered without the consent of the paramount power. An illustration is seen in the important Marátha State of Gwalior, the gross misgovernment of which not many years ago has been already described. During a long minority the State was brought into a condition of greatly increased prosperity and wealth, and when the minority ended the Chief was able to take his place at the head of a well-organised administration as an educated, intelligent, and enlightened man, alive to the duties which he owed to his people. I have already noticed his presence in London at the Coronation of the King. He gave another example of his loyalty by fitting out at his own expense a hospital ship for the service of the troops in China, and by himself accompanying the expedition.

In January 1903, Holkar, the ruler of Indore, after attending, in token of his loyalty to the British Crown, the great Durbar at Delhi, abdicated his chiefship in favour of his son, a boy twelve years old. During his minority every care will be given to his education and training, and the administration of the State will be reformed and carried on by a Council of Native Ministers, with the help, when it is required, of the British Resident. Thus we may reasonably hope that in both of the Maráitha States of Central India, Gwalior and Indore, the foundations of good government have been laid.

Kashmir offers another example of the results obtained by the wise intervention of the British Government. Speaking of this State with personal knowledge, Sir Lepel Griffin wrote, in 1883, that "nothing escapes taxation, and bare life is all that the State leaves to the cultivator, whose position is harder and as hopeless as that of a slave." The shameful maladministration of this beautiful country was too long tolerated, but at last, in 1889, the patience of the British Government was exhausted. The Máharája was for a time deprived of all authority, and when, after some years had elapsed, and the administration had been completely reformed, he was allowed to resume his position as head of the State, it was under new conditions. The government is successfully carried on with a Council, acting with the advice, when necessary, of a British Resident, in a manner very similar to that established in Mysore. It has become virtually a Constitutional Government, and the gross oppression from which the people long suffered has ceased.[1]

Among the more important Native States Haiderabad, the largest of them all, is probably that in which, although here also there has been improvement, the administration still remains the most unsatisfactory. There is no part of India in which the people have less sympathy with their rulers, men, as I have already

[1] A complete and most interesting account of Kashmir will be found in Sir Walter Lawrence's work, *The Valley of Kashmir*. He was employed there for several years; a settlement of the Land Revenue and Survey was carried out under his orders, and it is to him that no small part of the honour is due for the immense improvements that have been effected in the administration of the State.

shown, of other countries and of another faith. Frequent interference by the British Government has been necessary; the misfortune has been that it was not, in past times, more complete and efficacious. Excepting sometimes for a short period, no Government in India has been worse than that of the Nizam. Latterly, the wise influence of the Viceroy, Lord Curzon, has brought about valuable reforms, and the Nizam has entrusted to a British Officer the supervision of the finances of the State, which had fallen into a state of the utmost confusion. Not the least useful part of Lord Curzon's work in Haiderabad has been the final settlement of the long-standing difficulties connected with our administration of Berár. This province, with an area of nearly 18,000 square miles, and a population, in 1903, of 2,754,000, had long been under the dominion of the Nizam, and in 1853 it was assigned to the British Government, with the object of providing from its revenues the charges for the so-called Haiderabad Contingent, a force of more than 7000 men under the command of British officers, which was maintained permanently at the capital of the State. The terms of the treaty under which Berár was assigned to us became, in process of time, a constant cause of dissatisfaction and complaint on the part of the Nizam's Government. The revenues of Berár under British administration largely increased. The Nizam was entitled under the treaty to whatever surplus revenues remained after all necessary charges had been met, but the amount of those charges was left to the discretion of the British Government, whose views regarding administrative requirements and the necessity for material improvements differed greatly from those of the Government of the Nizam. Frequent attempts were made to obtain the abrogation of the treaty and the restoration of the province, and, sometimes by means which commend themselves not only to Oriental chiefs but to those who profit by them, and of which I will say nothing, it was not difficult to find in England loud advocates of the claims of the Nizam. Nor were honourable advocates wanting, influenced by sentiment, or ignorance, or by the not uncommon assumption of Englishmen that our treatment of India constantly involves some gross injustice to the people of the country. To restore to a Mohammedan Government, one of the most corrupt and oppressive in India, and one almost as foreign to the people of the country as our own, a great Hindu population, which for a long period had been prospering under British rule, would have been a disgrace and a crime.[1] All controversies on this subject were settled in 1902 by Lord Curzon on terms which, while they protected the people of Berár, gave liberal recognition to the claims of the Nizam. A fixed annual payment is made by the British Government to the Government of the Nizam; his nominal rights of sovereignty are maintained; and Berár has become, for all practical purposes, a British province.

I must not close this chapter without referring to the measures that have been taken for enabling the chiefs of Native States to obtain an education that will make them more competent to discharge the duties that fall upon them.

When the Indian Universities were first established, Lord Canning expressed the hope that the time was near when the nobility and upper classes of India would

[1] Almost the whole population of Berár is Hindu. Out of a total of 2,754,000, in 1901, there were only 212,000 Mohammedans.

think that they had not had the dues of their rank unless they passed through the course of a University. This expectation has not been fulfilled. The upper classes, even where no religious objections have existed, have for the most part kept themselves aloof. India being a country where the influence of birth and position is great, this has been unfortunate, but it is not surprising. The princes and chiefs and great landholders of India have seldom been educated. To be absolutely illiterate involves, even at the present time, no discredit; sometimes, indeed—but it may be hoped that this is ceasing to be true—it is held to be honourable, because to be anything else would be a violation of immemorial custom. Native chiefs and nobles had, with rare exceptions, no disposition to send their sons to our colleges, not only because they cared little for education, but because they were afraid of loss of social dignity, or contamination of caste.

To meet these difficulties an excellent beginning was made when Lord Mayo was Viceroy, by the establishment of special colleges. The Mayo College at Ajmir was founded by Lord Mayo for the education of the sons and relatives of the chiefs, nobles, and principal families of Rájputána. Many of them sent their sons to the college. It was liberally endowed by the chiefs, and received a grant-in-aid from our Government, and boarding-houses for their cadets were erected by all the principal States. Similar colleges were afterwards established at Indore, Lahore, and Rajkot. English and Oriental languages, mathematics, history, and geography are among the studies. "It is not desired," the Education Commission wrote, "to make these young chiefs great scholars, but to encourage in them a healthy tone and manly habits."

The Viceroy, Lord Curzon, has spared no efforts to increase the efficiency of these colleges, and in 1902 he took another step of great interest by the formation of an Imperial Cadet Corps, which is ordinarily to be recruited from the Chiefs' Colleges. The Corps, in the words of the rules framed by the Viceroy, "has been organised with the main object of providing a military training for selected members of the aristocracy of India, and of giving them such a general education that whilst, in course of time, they may be able to take their places in the Imperial Army as British officers, they may never lose their character and bearing as Indian gentlemen. With this object in view, the Cadets will be expected to acquire during their training a good knowledge of the English language, and at the same time to maintain an enthusiasm for their own history and traditions. The Cadets will be treated in every way as soldiers, and will be required to behave as such. Discipline will be strict. The moral side of their character will be closely watched; any tendency to immoral or unmanly practices will be sternly suppressed, and as the education is to be essentially military, every endeavour will be made to keep the Cadets in good physical condition. The Corps will remain under the direct surveillance of His Excellency the Viceroy, who takes a deep personal interest in its welfare, and will himself inspect it periodically. The Cadets will be in attendance on His Excellency on occasions of State. . . . The course of instruction will last for between two and three years. During the first year the Cadets will be taught drill, riding, and military exercises out of doors, whilst in-door instruction will be given in English and such elementary mathematics, etc., as are required for a study of military science. . . . At the close of the period of training, there will be an examination in order to assist the Government of India in the bestowal of such Commissions on Lieutenants in the Imperial Army as it may be decided from time to time to confer."

"Great interest," the Government of India stated, "was displayed in the scheme by the princely and aristocratic families for whose scions it was intended to provide an opening, and numerous applications for admission were received." The number of young men, selected with rare exceptions from those between the ages of seventeen and twenty, and receiving education at the Chiefs' Colleges, was limited at the outset to about twenty. Four of the ruling chiefs have already been included in it. The Honorary Commandant of the Corps is the well-known Chief, Máharája Dhiraj Sir Pertab Singh; there is a British Commandant, and British and Native Adjutants. The Imperial Cadet Corps was in attendance on the Viceroy at the great Coronation Durbar of January 1903, and gained much admiration for its manly and distinguished bearing.

If future Viceroys continue to give their personal care to the development of the scheme which Lord Curzon has thus initiated, we may reasonably hope that it will lead to results of no small importance in the Native States of India.

Some account has already been given of the Armies of these States, and of the arrangements under which some of them furnish contingents for Imperial Service.[1]

[1] Chapter XXIII.

CHAPTER XXV

CONCLUSION

Cruel customs—Neglect of social questions—Reasons for avoiding their discussion—The employment of Natives in the public service—Political hypocrisy—The duty of maintaining our dominion—Offices to be retained by Englishmen—Natives of India often as much foreigners as Englishmen in provinces other than their own—Sir Syad Ahmad Khán on Mohammedans and Hindus—The results of British Government—The popularity of our Government—Lord Lawrence's opinion—Reasons why our Government cannot be popular—The dangers to which our dominion is exposed—The principles on which our Government must be conducted.

THERE is no province in India without customs which we think must be repugnant to all civilised men, but which are almost universally respected because they are believed to have been divinely ordained, or which have come down from a remote antiquity. There is hardly a province in which horrid and cruel practices would not instantly spring into vigorous life if our watchfulness were relaxed. The prohibition of the burning of widows was, and is still, disapproved by all but a small minority of Hindus. I doubt whether the majority even of the more highly educated classes approve it. I gave in a previous chapter an account of the wholesale murder of female children, which, in parts of India, has gone on for centuries, a custom against which the Hindu, however enlightened, hardly ever raises his voice, and which, with all our efforts, we have not yet succeeded in eradicating. But for us, even in the provinces where education has made its greatest progress, Káli would still claim her human victims. Not many years ago, in a time of drought, near a railway station twenty-five miles from Calcutta, a human head was found before her idol, decked with flowers; and in another temple in Bengal a boy was savagely murdered and offered to the goddess. While a former edition of this book was passing through the press, a ghastly story came from the Central Provinces of the sacrifice of a young man to the local gods, in obedience to a widely prevalent belief and ancient practice that this is a sure means of obtaining a plentiful harvest. Horrors such as these receive no general condemnation in India, nor does the determination of our Government that they shall be suppressed often gain for us any practical signs of approval or sympathy even from the educated classes. Interference with ancient custom is usually an abomination to a Hindu, whether it be his own custom or not.

There are in India many questions of another order which are still more difficult to solve, because we cannot deal with them by the strong hand of the law. I will mention one only as an illustration, the custom of child marriage. As its not unfrequent consequence multitudes of girls are given over to outrage, or, if they belong to the higher classes of Hindus, doomed to lives of miserable and degraded widowhood. Some of the most holy Brahmans of Bengal made, not long ago, a living by being husbands. A child of five or six was given as perhaps the fortieth or fiftieth wife of some old man; sometimes two sisters were given to the same man, and sometimes to one who had not long to live.[1] Though it might be certain that the girl must soon be a widow, this was considered preferable to allowing her to remain unmarried. Every one has heard of the wretched fate which widowhood in India often involves, at least among the upper classes, with whom the practice of re-marriage does not prevail.

Nothing could be more valuable than to receive the advice and help of highly-educated Natives of India on such subjects as these, and to know that they were striving, by the example of their own lives, to teach their less instructed countrymen to abandon these abominations. No greater encouragement could be given to those who desire to see educated Natives admitted to a larger share in the administration than the certainty that they were anxious to help us towards ampler knowledge of the wants and feelings of the people, and to make us better able to deal with problems that now seem too hard to solve.

Unhappily, in regard to these great social questions the Government seldom receives such advice or assistance. There are admirable exceptions, and some leaders of Native opinion are generally found to support the Government when it insists on carrying out a reform which it has initiated, but it would not be easy to give instances in which an influential Native of the country has himself taken the lead in proposing a measure of social improvement.

It is easy to understand why these questions are

[1] Mr. O'Donnell, in his Report on the Census of Bengal, 1891, states that this abominable practice, known as Kulinism, now exists only to a very limited extent, and that it is strongly condemned by public opinion. An interesting description of the former and present marriage customs of the Kulins, and of other classes of Brahmans will be found in Mr. Risley's *Tribes and Castes of Bengal*.

avoided. Some of these Native gentlemen are silent because they dare not, by speaking of them, bring themselves into collision with the cherished beliefs and prejudices of their countrymen; others are silent because in regard to these matters they are at heart as intensely conservative as the mass of the population, and have little desire for changes in social and religious usages which have come down from a venerable antiquity. It is, on the other hand, safe to indulge in the political commonplaces which they have learned in our schools and colleges. They obtain in this way the applause of Englishmen who know nothing of India and of the difficulties with which the true friends of Indian progress have to deal, who see nothing good in any political institutions except those of their own particular type, and assume that certain abstract principles are applicable to all sorts and conditions of men.[1]

I said in a previous chapter that I should return to the subject of the admission of Natives of India to the more important public offices. I showed that the number of Englishmen employed in the Civil Service

[1] I make the following quotation from the Report of Mr. Baines on the Census of 1891:—"A serious development of the Brahmanic system is indicated by some of the superintendents in their census reports, and that is the strong tendency, in the present day of peace and plenty, to manifest their prosperity, firstly, by prohibiting the marriage of widows, and then by insisting upon carrying out strictly the Brahmanic injunction, and save themselves from the place to which the law-maker consigns them, by getting all their girls married before they have reached womanhood. Many cases have occurred within recent years to show that any movement among the literate classes in the direction of the abrogation of these two precepts is but mouth deep, whilst their heart is with the observance of them to the utmost. *Longum iter per præcepta; breve et efficace per exempla*, but when opportunities occur for carrying into practice amongst themselves or their families some of the reforms they have been so strenuously endeavouring to impose upon others, it is remarkable to note what an amount of filial piety and of deference to the feelings of those to whom their respect is due comes into play, to prevent them from becoming martyrs to their principles."

is extraordinarily small, that the greater part of the civil administration is already in Native hands, and that the Native Civil Service performs its duties, as a whole, with high efficiency.[1]

Subject to certain conditions, the true principle on which we ought to treat this question of the employment of Natives in posts of importance was laid down in the Act of Parliament passed in 1870 to which I have already referred. That principle is that almost all offices in India shall be open to Natives, but to those only "of proved merit and ability."

In the case of Englishmen, whether in India or at home, it has been found that, considering the dangers and abuses which attend the distribution of valuable patronage, the first appointments to offices in the higher branches of the public service may with advantage ordinarily be filled by those who, in competitive examinations in their early youth, are successful in satisfying certain literary and other tests. Although this system has, on the whole, worked well with Englishmen, it is open even with them to objections and drawbacks, and to think of applying it to the Natives of India is nothing less than absurd. Not the least important part of the competitive examination of the young Englishman was passed for him by his forefathers, who, as we have a right to assume, have transmitted to him not only their physical courage, but the powers of independent judgment, the decision of character, the habits of thought, and generally those qualities that are necessary for the government of men, and which have given us our empire. The stock-in-trade with which Englishmen start in life is not that of Bengális; but I must not say this of Englishmen only, for it is also, in a great measure, true

[1] Chapter VI.

of the more vigorous races of India, although their time has not come for competitive examinations.

Few would go farther than I would go in opening the public service in India to Natives "of proved merit and ability," but it is well to avoid "political hypocrisy." "Is there," Lord Salisbury asked, "any man who will have the hardihood to tell me that it is within the range of possibility that a man in India should be appointed Lieutenant-Governor of a province, or Chief Commissioner, or Commander-in-Chief of the Army, or Viceroy, without any regard whatever to his race?" Some will answer even this question in the affirmative. There will always be people ready to accept with composure any political folly, provided that it involves some triumph of sentiment over sense, and some appearance of national humiliation. When we say that we cannot always ignore differences of race, this is only another way of saying that the English in India are a handful of foreigners responsible for the government of nearly 300 millions of people. I have said that we are foreigners in India in a different sense from that in which we are foreigners in Paris, and that the people of one Indian province are often almost as much foreigners to the people of another province as we are ourselves; still, we are foreigners, and although I suppose that no foreign government was ever accepted with less repugnance than that with which the British Government is accepted in India, the fact remains that there never was a country, and never will be, in which the government of foreigners is really popular. It would be the beginning of the end of our empire if we were to forget this elementary fact, and were to entrust the greater executive powers to the hands of Natives, on the assumption that they will always be faithful and strong supporters of our government. In this there is nothing offensive or disparaging to the Natives of India. It simply means that we are foreigners, and that, not only in our own interests, but because it is our highest duty towards India itself, we intend to maintain our dominion. We cannot foresee the time in which the cessation of our rule would not be the signal for universal anarchy and ruin, and it is clear that the only hope for India is the long continuance of the benevolent but strong government of Englishmen. Let us give to the Natives the largest possible share in the administration. In some branches of the service there is almost no limit to the share of public employment which they may properly receive. This is especially true of the Bench, for the performance of the judicial duties of which Natives have shown themselves eminently qualified, and in which the higher offices are equal in importance and dignity and emolument to almost any of the great offices of the State. Even on the Bench, however, there are important administrative duties for which some degree of English supervision is necessary, nor would it be politically wise to place this great department of the Government altogether in Native hands. Prejudices of race may be regretted, but they cannot be ignored, and it would be a dangerous experiment to give to Native judges an unlimited power of control over English magistrates. For my own part, subject to some restrictions, there are few judicial offices in India that I would not throw open to Natives of their own provinces. But let there be no hypocrisy about our intention to keep in the hands of our own people those executive posts—and there are not very many of them—on which, and on our political and military power, our actual hold of the country depends. Our Governors of provinces, the chief officers of our army, our District officers and their principal executive subordinates must be Englishmen under all circumstances that we can now foresee, and in all departments of essential importance there must be selected Englishmen to maintain a standard of high efficiency.

It is not only in regard to the employment in India of our own countrymen that we ought never to forget differences of race. It is quite as essential to remember them in connection with the employment of Natives. I have often insisted on the fact that, strictly speaking, there is really no such country as India.[1] I must repeat that such terms as "People of India" and "Natives of India" are meaningless in the sense in which they are frequently used. The term "Natives of India" applied generally to Brahmans from Bengal, Parsis from Bombay, Sikhs from Lahore, Gurkhas from Nepal, and to Gonds from the Central Provinces, has no more meaning than the term "Natives of Europe" applied generally to Englishmen, Poles, Spaniards, and Turks. As I have said before, no countries and no peoples in Europe differ from each other so profoundly as countries and peoples differ in India. No good administration or permanent political security is possible unless facts of this kind are remembered. It ought never to be forgotten that it can never be assumed that because a man is a "Native of India" he has any natural claim, different in kind from that of an Englishman, to be employed in the public service in every part of India. Often, indeed, you may go much further. I used no terms of exaggeration when I said that a Native of Calcutta is more of a foreigner to the hardy races on the frontiers of Northern India

[1] See Chapter I.

than an Englishman. To suppose that the manlier races of India could ever be governed through the feebler foreigners of another Indian country, however intellectually acute those foreigners may be—that Sikhs and Patháns, for instance, should submit to be ruled by Bengális—is to suppose an absurdity. To ignore this order of facts is made especially dangerous by the position which the Mohammedans hold in India. The Mohammedan of Northern India often remembers with pride that his ancestors belonged to the ruling race, and he accepts with natural regret, but with no humiliation, the government of Englishmen. Although he may not love them, he admits that they must be respected. But the thought of being governed by a Hindu foreigner from Bengal fills him with indignation and contempt.

I have already referred to the proposal that competitive examinations for the Covenanted Civil Service should be held in India as well as in England. It cannot too often be repeated that the adoption of such a plan could in no way tend to make our government more popular or to render it, in public estimation, less than at present a government of foreigners. It would transfer a certain number of important offices now held by Englishmen to men drawn from a very small class of Hindus who have alone received the sort of education which would enable them to pass the necessary examinations, who, although we choose to call them "Natives of India," would be to at least 200 millions of the Indian populations almost as much foreigners as we are ourselves. One of the inevitable consequences would be the anger and discontent of the more intelligent of our Mohammedan subjects.

I remember a conversation which I once had with one of the most eminent members of the noble families of Oudh, the well-known Maharája Mán Singh, a man of rare sagacity, whose intellect, position, wealth, and influence made him the most important personage in his province. Referring to this subject of holding competitive examinations for the Civil Service in India, "I am afraid," I said, "that for a long time to come there would be no candidates from this part of India; it is only in Bengal that young men could be found who would have any chance of success in such an examination as that required. The result would be that you would some day have a Bengáli as your chief District officer." I shall not forget the scorn with which he drew himself up and replied to me, "And does any one think that we, the men of this country, would stand that? Do you suppose that you could govern us with Bengális? Never!"

This book was almost ready for the press [1] when the reports reached England of some remarkable speeches made by Sir Syad Ahmad Khán at two great meetings of Mohammedans in Northern India. I referred in a previous chapter to Sir Syad Ahmad Khán, and to the work to which his life was devoted.[2] I mention these speeches because they illustrate the practical importance of the fact on which I have repeatedly insisted, with which I began this book, and with which I wish to end it, that the most essential of all things to be learnt about India is that it is a continent filled with the most diverse elements, that it is the strong hand of England alone which maintains peace among them, and that, if our vigilance were relaxed, anarchy and bloodshed would spread themselves over the land. No Englishman could speak with higher authority than Sir Syad Ahmad Khán, and there was no one, Englishman or Native,

[1] First Edition, 1888. [2] Chapter XVI.

more worthy of respect for his wisdom and of admiration for his character. It was his special aim in these speeches to protest on behalf of his Mohammedan fellow-countrymen against the assumption that they could be treated as belonging to the same nation as the Hindus of Bengal, and to express his contempt for the political nostrums which it is often proposed to apply throughout India. If these were adopted, the result, he said, would be that "there would be no part of the country in which we should see at the tables of justice and authority any faces except those of Bengális. I am delighted to see the Bengális making progress, but what would be the result on the public administration? Do you think that the Rájput and the fiery Pathán would remain in peace under Bengális?"

". . . Suppose that all the English were to leave India, who would be rulers of India? Is it possible that under those circumstances Mohammedans and Hindus could sit on the same throne and remain equal in power? Most certainly not. It is necessary that one of them should conquer the other and thrust it down. You must remember that although the number of Mohammedans is less than that of the Hindus, and although they contain far fewer people who have received a high English education, yet they must not be thought insignificant or weak. Probably they would be by themselves enough to maintain their own position. But suppose they were not. Then our Musalman brothers, the Patháns, would come out as a swarm of locusts from their mountain valleys—like a swarm of locusts would they come—and make rivers of blood to flow from their frontier on the north to the extreme end of Bengal. This thing—who after the departure of the English would be conquerors—would rest on the will of God. But until one nation had conquered the other and made it obedient, peace could not reign in the land. This conclusion is based on proofs so absolute that no one can deny it. . . . Be not unjust to the British Government, to whom God has given the rule of India. And look honestly, and see what is necessary for it to do to maintain its empire and its hold on the country. You can appreciate these matters; but they cannot who have never held a country in their hands nor won a victory. O my brother Musalmans! I again remind you that you have ruled nations, and have for centuries held different countries in your grasp. For seven hundred years in India you have had Imperial sway. You know what it is to rule. Be not unjust to that nation which is ruling over you. And think also on this, how upright is her rule. Of such benevolence as the English Government shows to the foreign nations under her there is no example in the history of the world."

These are illustrations of the opinions of a man more universally honoured by those who deserve honour in India, than perhaps any other man that could be named, and who was entitled to speak on behalf of all that is best and enlightened among Indian Mohammedans. Nor must it be supposed that these views were prompted by prejudices of race or religion. No man could have shown more conspicuously than Sir Syad Ahmad Khán his absolute freedom from such influences, or have given by the conduct of his life stronger practical proof of his respect and regard for his Hindu fellow-subjects. He merely stated what he and his Mohammedan brothers know to be the truth.

"It is better," says a famous writer, "to follow the real truth of things than an imaginary view of them." If intelligent men in England would make themselves acquainted with "the real truth of things," they would understand how purely imaginary is that "Indian nation" and that "People of India" of which we hear so much.

I must now bring this work to a close. I have endeavoured to give some general idea of what India is and of the results which she has obtained from the establishment of our power. No reasonable man can doubt the answer that we must give to the question whether the 300,000,000 of people inhabiting the numerous countries of India have benefited by our government.

The first great and obvious fact, overshadowing all other facts in significance, is this, that in place of a condition of society given up, as it was immediately before our time, to anarchy and to the liability to every conceivable form of violence and oppression, we have now absolute peace. Let not this unspeakable blessing of the Pax Britannica be forgotten. There are not many European countries where protection to life and property is so complete. Excepting England and her colonies, and the United States of America, there is hardly a country in the world where there is so little needless interference on the part of the Government with personal liberty, or such freedom in the public expression of opinion in matters of politics and religion. Except when not unfrequently the fanaticism and intolerance of rival sects of Mohammedans and Hindus burst into violent conflict, and show what would instantly follow if the strong hand of our Government were withdrawn, unbroken tranquillity prevails. Justice is administered under laws of unequalled excellence and simplicity. There is hardly any country possessing a civilised administration where the public burdens are so light. Mr. J. S. Mill declared his belief that the British Government in India was "not only one of the purest in intention, but one of the most beneficent in act, ever known among mankind." I do not doubt that this is still truer now.

Whether all this makes our Government really popular is another question.

When Lord Lawrence was Viceroy, in 1867, many of the most experienced officers in India were invited to give their opinion whether our Government was more generally popular than that in the Native States. As might have been anticipated, nearly all the answers were affirmative, but I shall only refer to that of Lord Lawrence himself. His conclusion was given in these words: "The masses of the people are incontestably more prosperous, and—*sua si bona nôrint*—far more happy in British territory than they are under Native rulers." No Englishman knew India better than Lord Lawrence. That the people had been made more prosperous by our administration was, in his opinion, beyond controversy, but when it came to the question of their happiness and of our popularity, well—at any rate they *ought* to be more happy. The proviso is significant, *sua si bona nôrint*.

The truth is that, in a country in the condition of India, the more actively enlightened our Government becomes, the less likely it is to be popular. Our Government is highly respected; the confidence of the people in our justice is unlimited. That accomplished traveller, Baron von Hübner, says in his excellent book, *Through the British Empire*, that if proof were needed to show how deeply rooted among the people is this trust in English justice, he would quote the indisputable fact that throughout India the Native prefers, in civil and still more in criminal cases, to go before an English judge. "I think," he says, "it would be impossible to render a more flattering testimony to British rule." The duty was once imposed upon me of transferring a number of villages which had long been included in a British district to one of the best governed of the Native States. I shall not forget the loud and universal protests of the people against the cruel injustice with which they considered they were being treated. Every one who has had experience of similar cases tells the same story.

The sympathies between the people and their English rulers can hardly be anything but imperfect. The system of caste and the differences in all our habits make social intimacy difficult. Instances of insolence and brutality on the part of Englishmen undoubtedly occur, but the assertion that they are very frequent is false. At the same time it is true that the ordinary Englishman is too rough and vigorous and straightforward to be a very agreeable person to the majority of the Natives of India. These, however, are not reasons which seriously affect the popularity of our Government. Because, according to the only standards that we can accept, it is good it can hardly be popular.

I never heard of a great measure of improvement that was popular in India, even among the classes that have received the largest share of education. No one who has lived, as I have done for the better part of my life, among the people can have towards them feelings other than those of sympathy and affection and respect. They have qualities which deserve all admiration, but they are intensely conservative and intensely ignorant, wedded, to an extent difficult for Europeans to understand, to every ancient custom, and between their customs and religion no line of distinction can be drawn. We often deceive ourselves in regard to the changes that are taking place. We believe that our Western knowledge, our railways, and our telegraphs must be breaking up the whole fabric of Hinduism, but these things, as I have said before, have touched only the merest fringe of the ideas and beliefs of the population of India. The vast masses of the people remain in a different world from ours. They dislike everything new, they dislike almost everything that we look upon as progress, and they live, for the most part, in blind ignorance of the aims and ideas of their rulers.

Among all the dangers to which our Indian dominion is exposed, the ignorance of the people is the greatest. The task of removing or at least of diminishing this ignorance is the highest of our duties, but its accomplishment can only come in a distant future, for we have to deal not with a single country and a single people, but with a multitude of countries that we choose to include under the general name of India, and with a multitude of different peoples, constituting, perhaps, in numbers, one-fifth part of the population of the world. So long as this ignorance continues, no one can say what belief or suspicion or unreasoning panic may not spread like wildfire through the country, or what may be its consequences. No one now doubts that the mutiny of the Bengal army, whatever it may subsequently have become, had its real origin in a panic of this kind, in the general and honest belief of the soldiers that our Government intended to destroy their caste, which involved everything that was most valuable to them in this world and in the next. It is hardly less true now than it was in 1857 that we are liable at all times to such dangers as this. Nothing is too foolish or too extravagant for general acceptance. This ought never to be forgotten. Ominous signs from time to time appear which ought to remind us how easily in India a terrible conflagration may be lighted up. There is no limit to the liability of such a population to be influenced by the assurances or suggestions of religious fanatics and political agitators, or to be disturbed by interference with its prejudices and beliefs.

It would thus be an error to suppose that the British Government is administered in a manner that altogether commends itself to the majority of the Indian population. This we cannot help. Considerations of political prudence compel us to tolerate much that we should wish to alter, and to abstain from much that we might desire to see accomplished, but, subject to this most essential condition, our duty is plain. It is to govern India with unflinching determination on the principles which our superior knowledge tells us are right, although they may be unpopular. I will quote Sir James Stephen's summary of the principles which we enforce, and with it I may fitly close this book :—

"The English in India are the representatives of a belligerent civilisation. The phrase is epigrammatic, but it is strictly true. The English in India are the representatives of peace compelled by force. The Mohammedans would like to tyrannise over Hindus in particular, and in general to propose to every one the alternative between the Koran, the tribute, and the sword. The Hindus would like to rule—over Hindus at least—according to the principles of the Brahmanical religion. They would like to be able to condemn to social infamy every one who, being born a Hindu, did not observe their rites. They would like to see suttee practised, to prevent the re-marriage of widows who were not burnt, to do away with the laws which prevent a change of religion from producing civil disabilities, to prevent a low-caste man from trying or even testifying against a Brahman; and Mohammedans, and Hindus, and Sikhs would all alike wish to settle their old accounts and see who is master. The belligerent civilisation of which I spoke consists in the suppression by force of all these pretensions, and in compelling by force all sorts and conditions of men in British India to tolerate each other. Should the British Government abdicate its functions, it would soon turn order into chaos. No country in the world is more orderly, more quiet, or more peaceful than British India as it is; but if the vigour of the Government should ever be relaxed, if it should lose its essential unity of purpose, and fall into hands either weak or unfaithful, chaos would come again like a flood."

INDEX

THE END